TRAUMA AND BEYOND

TRAUMA AND BEYOND

THE MYSTERY OF TRANSFORMATION

URSULA WIRTZ

SPRING JOURNAL
BOOKS

PUBLICATIONS IN JUNGIAN PSYCHOLOGY
www.springjournalandbooks.com

Published by:
Spring Journal, Inc.
New Orleans, Louisiana, USA
Website: www.springjournalandbooks.com

Cover image:
Abstract Head: Mysterium.
Alexei Jawlensky, 1925.
Oil on cardboard (16.7 in by 12.8 in).
Private collection.

Editorial and production assistance:
Drummond Books, drummondbooks@gmail.com
Cover design, typography, and layout:
Northern Graphic Design & Publishing
info@ncarto.com

Text printed on acid-free paper

Library of Congress Cataloging-in-Publication Data Pending

DEDICATION

This book is dedicated with gratitude to the memory
of my compassionate Zen master,
Silvia Ostertag, Rin'un Roshi,
Sanbô Kyôdan School.

Without her encouragement and her faith in me,
I could not have written
this book.

CONTENTS

EDITORS' FOREWORD

The Zürich Lecture Series in Analytical Psychology was established in 2009 by the International School of Analytical Psychology Zürich (ISAPZURICH) and Spring Journal Books for the purpose of presenting, annually, a significant new work by a selected Jungian psychoanalyst or scholar who has previously offered innovative contributions to the field of analytical psychology by either:

- bringing analytical psychology into meaningful dialogue with other scientific, artistic, or academic disciplines;
- showing how analytical psychology can lead to a better understanding of contemporary global concerns relating to the environment, politics, religion; or
- expanding the concepts of analytical psychology as they are applied clinically.

For the Series, the selected scholar delivers lectures over a two-day period in Zürich based on a new book-length work, which is then published by Spring Journal Books. We are delighted to publish *Trauma and Beyond* by Ursula Wirtz as the fourth volume in the Zürich Lecture Series.

—Murray Stein and Nancy Cater, Series Editors
Zürich Lecture Series in Analytical Psychology

ACKNOWLEDGMENTS

This book would not have been possible without the generous funding of the Susan Bach Foundation (Zürich) and a grant from the Oswald Family Foundation (USA). I wish to express my deepest gratitude for their support.

In preparing the manuscript for this book, I had the great good fortune to have found Ann Lammers, who patiently translated major portions of it from German into English. I admire her courage in embarking on this venture without any prior acquaintance with me, and I am deeply grateful to her for her work.

I am grateful to my colleague Annemarie Moser, my first reader, for her encouragement and supportive criticism. I want to thank my colleagues Mary Tomlinson and Andrew Fellows and my friends Ruth and Jeannette, who helped polish the language of those sections of the manuscript that I wrote myself in English.

Special thanks go to my friend Annemarie Angst, for her never-ending, compassionate, and caring assistance on many levels, tending my garden, preparing dinner, and in particular helping me to improve my inferior sensation function by assisting me in the time-consuming hunt for original sources and accurate references.

I am indebted to Alain Dussert, Director of Library Services at Pacifica Graduate Institute, for providing me, as an ISAP faculty member, with access to the institute's many well-researched and inspiring dissertations.

Most of all I would like to thank my patients, from whom I was privileged to learn about light in darkness and hope in despair. They gave me permission to share with my readers their experiences, dreams, paintings, and symbolic representations.

The remarkable editing of Michael Mendis and his crucially important suggestions clarified my thinking and writing and resulted in a smoother and more coherent text. Although it took a long time to get the manuscript into its final shape after I finished writing it, the challenge of overcoming the many obstacles I faced ultimately proved to be meaningful and in resonance with the manuscript's contents.

Last but not least, I want to thank my beloved of thirty-three years, Jürg Zöbeli, a Freudian psychoanalyst, for his loving presence in my life, his patience with my long periods of incubation, and his readiness to discuss the ideas germinating in me whenever I resurfaced from my descent. I am grateful for the gift of walking together with him as kindred souls in the spirit of Zen.

PERMISSIONS

SOURCES AND ABBREVIATIONS

For frequently cited sources, the following abbreviations have been used:

CW: Jung, C. G. *The Collected Works of C. G. Jung*. Edited and translated by Gerhard Adler and R. F. C. Hull. 20 vols. Princeton, NJ: Princeton University Press, 1954–1979. Given with volume number and paragraph number (§).

ESV: Biblical quotations are taken from the English Standard Version unless indicated otherwise.

MDR: Jung, C. G. *Memories, Dreams, Reflections*. Edited by Aniela Jaffé. Translated by Richard and Clara Winston. London: Vintage Books, 1989.

RB: Jung, C. G. *The Red Book: Liber Novus*. Edited by Sonu Shamdasani. Translated by Mark Kyburz, John Peck, and Sonu Shamdasani. New York: W. W. Norton, 2009.

INTRODUCTION

Who would have thought of this! The darkness brings
forth light,
The something comes from naught, death does
engender life.
    —Angelus Silesius, *The Cherubinic Wanderer*

When Nancy Cater and Murray Stein first entrusted me with the challenge of being fourth on the list of authors and lecturers for the Zürich Lecture Series in Analytical Psychology (ZLS)—note the number *four!*—my initial reaction was to refuse. I turned to the *I Ching* for advice, and the answer I received was so paradoxical that I needed the silence of a Zen *sesshin* to come to a decision. Ultimately, I surrendered and accepted the challenge but not without trepidation at the *nigredo* that I would undoubtedly have to face, delving deep into narratives of stagnation, alienation, and hopelessness. For it was clear to me that my creative process in writing this book would mirror the traumatic theme with which I was dealing.

Writing this book has not been a linear or Apollonian process. The dark, archetypal powers of Dionysian dismemberment have activated my complex relation to the topic of trauma and hovered over certain phases of this work. In the discourse of quantum physics, there is no such thing as a detached observer; rather, as the observer, I form a unity with the thing I observe. My way of understanding and practicing trauma therapy is therefore shaped in important ways by the subjective factor, by how I became the person I am. So I see it as my duty to sketch out my personal, historical, and cultural background and the interdisciplinary networks that influence my trauma perspective.

The archetypal motif of dying and becoming has been constellated for me since birth. I have come to understand, on a very deep level, my calling to heal the wounds of my lineage, my genealogical inheritance, of which I only later became aware. My own personal myth has shaped the lenses through which I see and understand trauma. I was born into the house of Hades: my aging father had died a few weeks before I was born, and my mother had not yet overcome her grief for their baby boy, who had died shortly before I was conceived. My soul carried the imprint of death from my very beginnings in the dark womb of my mother. I believe that already in the weeks prior to my birth an unconscious matrix was constellated that initiated me into the mystery of dying and becoming. Reflecting on issues of transgenerational transmission and the flow or blockage of psychic energy I became aware that in writing this book I was also tending to the unfinished business of my ancestors and their unprocessed traumas.

I was born in 1946 in the Ruhr District of postwar Germany, the land of victimizers and victims. My earliest political memories are associated with the war narratives of my mother, my grandmother, and my aunt, with their horrifying reports of carpet bombings, burning houses, and people nearly trampled to death during the panic outside the bunker. They told stories of the collective furies of *Kristallnacht* ("The Night of Broken Glass") in November 1938 and of fear, hunger, and deprivation. My playgrounds were landscapes of rubble. On my way to school, I would pass houses leveled by bombs and the bunker, a grey concrete hulk that gave rise to wild fantasies.

War and peace are the themes that gave direction to my life and inspired me to commit myself to solidarity with people who have experienced war, injustice, and sexual violence. I have engaged socially, politically, and therapeutically for justice and empowerment, reconciliation and forgiveness; I have ridden through the war-devastated cities of the former Yugoslavia in a tank and have worked there as a supervisor for therapists treating female survivors of mass rapes. I also did supervision in Switzerland at the Red Cross walk-in clinic for victims of war and torture. In my private practice in Zürich, I saw many Jewish patients, and for ten years I was a supervisor at a Jewish psychosocial agency.

My further education has been in integrative gestalt therapy, and in initiation therapy as developed by meditation teacher and therapist Karlfried Graf Dürckheim at his Centre for Existential and Psychological Formation and Encounter in Todtmoos-Rütte, in the Black Forest of Germany. I have also studied EMDR (eye movement desensitization and reprocessing) and acquainted myself with energy therapy. All of these combine with my clinical experience to create a perspective on trauma that is at the same time social-political-cultural, interpersonal, intrapsychic, archetypal, symbolic, and spiritual.

As a Jungian, I have had the opportunity to offer training in societies that have been subjected to collective trauma. My activity as a board member for a Swiss foundation devoted to therapy for war trauma made it possible for me to engage internationally in the work of peace and reconciliation.

Although I have never been the victim of human-generated violence, I did undergo a limit-experience in the deserts of Rajasthan, which taught me in the most intimate way possible about liminality, imminent death, and the relativity of space and time. I am an experienced rider and passionate about riding in the desert, but once when I was traveling on camelback, my young camel panicked, which led to a serious fall. I suffered crushing injuries to my upper abdomen and back, and it was unclear for three days whether I would bleed to death internally from a possibly ruptured liver. After the accident, for five days and five nights I was carried through the desert by camel, lying on a wooden pallet, since my spinal injuries and fractured sternum prevented me from sitting up. I experienced moments of being both in time and out of time, suspended in that liminal space of stillness between life and death. It was a truly numinous experience: excruciating pain, waiting in the silence of the desert, listening at night to the music of the stars, blinded during the day by the glare of the sun. The desert silence spoke to me and awakened my imagination. This liminal state forever transformed my relation to life and death and to the paradox of loss and gain.

Two other dimensions that I bring to my understanding of trauma are my study of philosophy, which acquainted me with the worlds of truth and meaning, and my meditation practice in the Zen tradition. Thus, I have tried to bring together in this book clinical knowledge about trauma and the wisdom of the philosophical and spiritual traditions.

This book, then, is the fruit of my contemplative "self-incubating state of meditation."[1] It is the harvest of thirty years as an analyst, during which I have wandered with anguished souls, neither alive nor dead, and exiled bodies appearing like shades, through the wastelands and plains of oblivion. I have often experienced my journeying with survivors of trauma through those imaginal realms of the netherworld as a true "journey to hell," encountering states of mind that border on madness.[2]

When I later conceived of my title for this book—*Trauma and Beyond*—I thought of our craving as human beings for a "beyond," the psychic energy of yearning, intrinsic to humans, that carries us from womb to tomb. I had been fascinated by the linguistic musings of Josephine Evetts-Secker—the third lecturer/author in the ZLS— on the language of the soul, remembering how she had been haunted by the archaic paradigm of *whence* and *whither*, the archaic *yonder*, and the distant *beyond*. Her inspiring work resonated with me, as I wrote about the descent into the depths to retrieve the lost and dismembered fragments of the soul, to re-member life *before* the trauma, to integrate life *after* the trauma, and to hope for a life *beyond* trauma.

Jung is reported to have said that the Red Book "told of the battle between the world of reality and the world of the spirit."[3] In his *Protocols*, he compares the *Seven Sermons to the Dead* and the unfinished Red Book to the sort of house we encounter in dreams. He notes that his patients, and he himself, usually felt that the dream house was in need of another room or that it contained rooms that were not there in the real world. He goes on to say that when people dream of houses, after awakening they have the feeling that they ought "to solve the question of this house, to do something with it."[4] Along these lines, I approach the metaphorical house of the Red Book in search of a remedy for individual and collective traumatic suffering, "dreaming the house onward," so to speak.

The Red Book is an unfinished house. It ends abruptly, leaving the reader hanging in the air, perhaps just the way it was meant to be.[5] I feel especially drawn by this unfinished house, for I believe it needs an additional room that will reconcile the spirit of the depths with the clinical demands of the spirit of the times. On the last page of the Red Book, only one word appears: *Möglichkeit* (possibility). No period, no comma, only this: *Möglichkeit.* The page is exactly like all the other pages except that but for this lone word it is blank.[6]

In this book I explore the relationship between possibility (the open-ended finale of the Red Book) and reality, pondering the wisdom of living systems and the dynamics of order and disorder. Because trauma disrupts the psyche's intrinsic movement toward change and metamorphosis, I draw on chaos theory, the self-organizing features of complex adaptive systems, and quantum physics, all of which shed light on the processes of emergence and change.

This book, then, is about dying and becoming, about the potential for transforming trauma. I have tried to understand the transformative power of suffering, how inner deadness can change into something meaningful and alive. With John P. Wilson, a researcher in the area of psychotraumatology, I believe that trauma possesses the potential for "transcendent experience."[7] Devastating as it is, I am convinced that trauma can give rise to personal growth; it can serve as an opening to transcendence and to the expansion of consciousness. Pursuing this conviction, in the chapters that follow, I look at trauma broadly through three separate but interrelated lenses: the spiritual, the mythological, and the clinical.

I begin with the spiritual lens, exploring posttraumatic growth and seeking deeper insights into the spiritual dimension of trauma as existence in extremis, a meaning disorder that may push one into an awareness of one's own nothingness. I invoke the tormented language of the poetry of the Shoah (Holocaust) to shed light on the processes of wounding and awakening, passing away and returning into being.

Moving on to the mythological lens, I present trauma as a descent, viewing Kali's rage as the fire of transformation, Medusa's petrifying gaze as an archetypal image for trauma's power to immobilize, and Ariadne's yearning for death as the trauma victim's descent into the oblivion of psychic numbing.

Finally, taking up the clinical lens, I explore echoes in contemporary trauma therapy of the Red Book, Jung's journey from spiritual emergency to spiritual emergence after he had "reached a dead end."[8] Circumambulating existential complementarities, I investigate trauma's paradoxes and draw attention to the relational field as the crucible of transformation. Clinical vignettes illustrate the operation of the transcendent function as it works to bring about transformation. The dialectical relationship between victim and victimizer leads to an exploration of the central role that sacrifice plays in transcending trauma, a motif that can be traced in myths and fairy tales.

The experiential modes of being and doing, of loving presence and critical reflection, the two wings of Buddhist psychology, provide valuable insights into working with traumatized individuals and their tortuous emotional and cognitive states. I have found the correspondences between the contemplative traditions and contemporary neuroscientific research to be very fruitful in gaining a better understanding of the interface between science and spirituality, and how these two epistemologies come together in trauma therapy.[9] Knowledge about the relational brain and awareness that the brain takes shape according to what the mind focuses on are particularly helpful to the trauma therapist, for mental exercises have a profound impact on brain physiology and enable the practitioner to control his or her internal states.

* * *

On November 13, 1960, the year before his death, Jung wrote: "I have failed in my foremost task, to open people's eyes to the fact, that man has a soul and there is a buried treasure in the field and that our religion and philosophy are in a lamentable state."[10] This book is about the search for soul after soul murder, a search for this buried treasure. The state of the soul, which Jung so ruefully lamented in his day, is even more lamentable today, for the soul has become increasingly lost in modern discourse, and the materialistic rejection of and disdain for the spiritual has led to a soulless psychology. Working with trauma, however, requires a soulful approach, a holistic worldview that unites emotions and thoughts, psyche and matter, body and soul.

It is my hope that the tapestry of this book, woven out of strands drawn from the spiritual, archetypal, and clinical realms, will present a clearer, more multidimensional image of the complexities and hidden depths of trauma.

NOTES

[1] C. G. Jung, *Psychology and Alchemy*, vol. 12, *The Collected Works of C. G. Jung*, ed. and trans. Gerhard Adler and R. F. C. Hull (Princeton, NJ: Princeton University Press, 1953, 1968), § 441. References to *The Collected Works of C. G. Jung* are hereafter abbreviated CW, giving the volume number and paragraph number.

[2] Jung, *CW* 12, § 441.

[3] Cary Baynes, quoted in C. G. Jung, *The Red Book: Liber Novus*, ed. Sonu Shamdasani, trans. Mark Kyburz, John Peck, and Sonu Shamdasani (New York: W. W. Norton, 2009), p. 213. *The Red Book* is hereafter abbreviated *RB*.

[4] Deirdre Bair, *Jung: A Biography* (Boston: Little, Brown, 2003), p. 297.

[5] Jung, *RB*, p. 325.

[6] In the epilogue, Jung says that when he received the text of the alchemical tract, *The Secret of the Golden Flower*, from Richard Wilhelm, the essential contents of the Red Book "found their way into actuality," and after that he could work on it no more. Jung, *RB*, p. 360.

[7] John P. Wilson, "Trauma Archetypes and Trauma Complexes," in *The Posttraumatic Self: Restoring Meaning and Wholeness to Personality*, ed. John P. Wilson (London: Routledge, 2006), p. 188 (and throughout the book).

[8] C. G. Jung, *Memories, Dreams, Reflections*, ed. Aniela Jaffé, trans. Richard and Clara Winston (London: Vintage Books, 1989), p. 171. *Memories, Dreams, Reflections* is hereafter abbreviated *MDR*.

[9] See Rick Hanson with Richard Mendius, *Buddha's Brain: The Practical Neuroscience of Happiness, Love, and Wisdom* (Oakland, CA: New Harbinger Publications, 2009).

[10] C. G. Jung, letter to Eugene Rolfe, November 13, 1960, quoted in Sonu Shamdasani, *Jung and the Making of Modern Psychology: The Dream of a Science* (Cambridge, UK: Cambridge University Press, 2003), p. 351.

PART I

THE SPIRITUAL LENS: DYING AND BECOMING

When I first encountered the etched and enameled four-sided mask, *All My Faces*, by the German artist Hede von Nagel, who grew up in Nazi Germany, my first thought was that I had witnessed the unveiling of the many faces of trauma. The shiny, gold-plated "Nice Guy" face (figure I.1), inscribed with superficial clichés and small-talk lines and the artificial smile contrasting with the penetrating, staring eyes, reminded me of patients defensively hiding their inner core, sacrificing their true self in order to survive. As I read the inscriptions on the "How They See Me" face (figure I.3), with their haunting messages, surrounding the mirror fragments, the trauma gradually unfolded and revealed the "Depressed Face" (figure I.2) with the words *Love* and *Death* inscribed on the eyelids. The poignant, meticulously etched sentences covering the face sounded like the lamentations of trauma survivors I had so often heard:

> I am so sick and tired of life—I survived. They threw bombs at me—I survived. They tried to starve me—I survived. They tried to put me down—I survived. They made me obedient and submissive—I survived. They made me forget who I am—

I survived. They made me feel guilty all the time—I survived. . . .
They did not teach me how to live and love—I survived. I hate
them because they helped me survive. I hate myself—why did
I survive? Will I survive? I would like to kill myself—kill them.

The fourth side of the helmet, "The Real Me" (figure I.4), is a hinged
panel that can be opened to reveal the artist's true face. When it is
closed, one can read what she is yearning for: "serenity, courage,

Figure I.1. *All My Faces*: Nice
Guy Face

Figure I.2. *All My Faces*:
Depressed Face

Figure I.3. *All My Faces*:
How They See Me

Figure I.4. *All My Faces*: The
Real Me

honesty," and above all: "I want to be the woman I really am." I include these photographs of this fine, award-winning work to amplify the many faces of trauma.[1]

NOTES

[1] My thanks to Hede von Nagel for permission to print these photographs. *All My Faces* won the Award of Excellence for Enamels at Artist-Craftsmen of New York, Lever House, New York, September 19 to October 3, 1971.

CHAPTER ONE

UNVEILING THE
FACE OF TRAUMA

I n exploring the many faces of trauma and the divergent claims
that have been made with regard to it, what comes to mind is the
old Sufi parable of the blind men and the elephant, in which five
blind men encounter an elephant and examine it by feeling its body
parts. Each likens the elephant to an object that is familiar to him,
based on the body part he touches, and each is convinced that he knows
what an elephant is, yet none of them has any idea what the elephant
looks like as a whole.

Trauma has similarly been conceptualized in multifarious ways.
Mardi Horowitz holds that traumatic life events have the traumatic
effect that they do because they cannot be assimilated into the victim's
inner schemata of self in relation to the world.[1] According to Ronnie
Janoff-Bulman, traumatic events destroy the victim's fundamental
assumptions about the safety of the world, undermine the positive value
of the self, and cause a disturbance of affectivity, a state Thomas Ogden
calls "formless dread."[2] Henry Krystal asserts that trauma produces a
regression in affect, a deficit in the capacity for symbolic representation,
and fantasy formation.[3] D. W. Winnicott emphasizes the necessity of
a good "holding environment" to deal with the disintegration anxiety

caused by traumatic events with their menacing threat of nonexistence.[4]
Heinz Kohut's self-psychology model speaks of the dissolution of a
coherent self under the influence of trauma.[5] In analytical psychology,
Donald Kalsched shows how trauma ruptures the transitional
processes of human relatedness that constitute meaning.[6] As Robert
Jay Lifton sees it, trauma victims suffer from impaired human
relationships, from what he calls "the broken connection," which
results in a state of being outside of culture, "our means of symbolizing
death and continuity."[7] Lifton believes that trauma disrupts the
capacity to develop images and symbolic forms that provide a sense
of continuity. He claims that these symbols must be transformed and
reanimated in order to find new meaning.

The common thread in these various views is that the ego's central
role as a planning, controlling authority is powerfully exploded by
trauma. Traumatic experiences may thus lead to a radical breaking in
and breaking apart of existing ego structures, resulting in a
disintegration of the previous psychic structure. The psychological
concept of self-regulation and control and the consciousness of being
an autonomous, intentional human agent no longer hold. Being
helpless, handed over, determined by outside forces, these are the
coordinates of traumatic experience. In a traumatic event, ego
boundaries are overrun, and one learns that the everyday ego is utterly
insubstantial. As a result, the ego undergoes a monstrous relativization,
being degraded to meaninglessness and threatened with fragmentation
and destruction. The ego, which once guaranteed one's identity, seems
to have no use any more. One is overcome by a sense of extreme
vulnerability. For the annihilation of the ego is a form of dying.

This "passing away" of the ego also appears in mystical writings,
in which it characterizes transpersonal states of awareness. Thus, the
loss of boundaries and the sense of emptiness caused by trauma can
be experienced as a liberation from attachments, in which
enmeshment in the material world loses its importance. The
immaterial may take on an overpowering numinosity, giving rise to
developments previously unthinkable. Boundary experiences in the face
of impending death can give rise to states of transparency. Jung attested
to this following his near-fatal illness, in a letter he wrote to Dr. Kristine
Mann while recovering:

> The only difficulty is to get rid of the body, to get quite naked
> and void of the world and the ego-will. When you can give
> up the crazy will to live and when you seemingly fall into a
> bottomless mist, then the truly *real* life begins with everything
> which you were meant to be and never reached. It is something
> ineffably grand.[8]

Confronted by the outer limits of life, one loses the familiar sense of
being physically in the world. Then consciousness of another reality
seems to shine forth. This beyond cannot be put into words, but it
can be felt to be meaningful, to surpass the ego.

Traumatic experiences activate archaic levels of the psyche and
constellate an archetypal landscape highly charged with affect. Often
the experience of archetypal suffering inspires the use of religious and
mythological language as a means of expressing the inexpressible. We
refer to trauma as an experience of "hell," of "God in exile." We describe
it as a terrifying encounter with the dark side of God; we imagine a
"*Deus absconditus*," whose absence makes us perceive "heaven as an
abyss" and inflicts on us the archetypal experience of being cast out
and forsaken, like the biblical Job.[9] The yawning abyss is an often-used
metaphor for the aftermath of a trauma experience, the "black hole,"
the "void," the experience of "anti-creation," the severing of the thread
of life, the creating of an "irreparable tear between self and reality," a
deep rift in the psyche.[10]

Trauma can be seen as a meaning disorder in which the vessel is
broken and the ego-Self axis is disrupted. But it can also be a potential
catalyst for a new orientation in life. In her seminal work on trauma,
writing about how repeated trauma forms and deforms the personality,
Judith Herman emphasizes that trauma can force "the development of
extraordinary capacities, both creative and destructive."[11] When
trauma strikes, our perception of the world and ourselves undergoes
a radical reorganization. The English word *catastrophe* is derived
from a Greek word that originally signified a turning point, and it
is precisely at such turning points that an *enantiodromia* can occur.[12]
In dynamic systems theory, such turning points are known as phase
transitions, which occur when a given variable reaches a certain critical
threshold. This concept is explored by Jungian analyst George Hogenson
in terms of "symbolic density."[13]

My experience with survivors of trauma has given me some understanding of the paradox of "dying and becoming" ("*Stirb und werde*"), which gives soul to every living thing and binds together the cycle of coming into being and departing from it; it is the rhythm of loss and gain, darkness and light, of getting stuck and transcending to a different plane of consciousness. The poles of death and life belong together as a paradoxical unity; as Jung said, "waxing and waning make one curve."[14] This principle of an eternal movement between polar opposites is part of the Jungian understanding of the psyche's self-regulation. In trauma therapy, I have come to experience this dynamic principle that nothing stays the way it is—this "grim law of enantiodromia"—as a comfort.[15] If I see, with Heraclitus, that the deepest reality is to be found in constant flux, then I know that even the greatest despair and the deepest suffering are subject to this dynamic and can turn around. My work is rooted in the paradoxical wisdom of enantiodromia, that whatever exists will be destroyed and replaced by something new, that becoming and dying are two aspects of the same process.

In the spiritual borderland of traumatic loss of meaning, in the black hole of despair and hopelessness, human beings no longer feel in relationship with the totality of being, but alone, having fallen out of all familiar, meaning-creating connections. The frightening, unfamiliar, numinous dimension into which their experience has thrown them produces a far-reaching estrangement from ego and the world. Traumatized individuals have become lost to themselves and to their environment, helplessly at the mercy of a silent cosmos.

Trauma therapy is a path on which there are multiple points of access to bring home the estranged parts, to move from fragmentation to integration, on three levels: the intrapsychic level, where broken-off aspects of one's person can be pulled together into a whole; the interpersonal level, in which contact is once again resumed with the Thou of the other person; and the transpersonal level, where one can flow back into the stream of life.

I have encountered people on the margin who have borne witness to the human capacity to transcend one's limitations. Some are people of faith who, finding themselves in situations of greatest distress and danger, have nevertheless not lost their awareness of an ultimate spiritual security. Dietrich Bonhoeffer, before he was hanged on April 9, 1945, in a concentration camp, was able to say to Payne Best, with his execution in mind, "This is the end, for me the beginning of life."[16] From prison he wrote powerful poems about resistance and surrender, among them the wonderfully comforting message to his family, later set to music:

> With every power for good to stay and guide me,
> comforted and inspired beyond all fear,
> I'll live these days with you in thought beside me,
> and pass, with you, into the coming year.[17]

The archetype of the wounded healer, who heals through his or her own wounds and personal acquaintance with liminality, always comes to life for me when I meet victims of torture in recovery centers, working with therapeutic teams who themselves have survived torture and persecution. The healers, themselves traumatized men and women, have made spiritual care-giving their life's work. They live in consciousness of a calling, a mission in the best sense of the word, to assist others in becoming human again, and in so doing, they become a bit more human themselves.

Spiritual people feel they have a task to accomplish in this life. Their starting point is the conviction that something is meant to come into the world through them. In this regard, Judith Herman, in her foundational book on understanding traumatic disorders, declares: "While there is no way to compensate for an atrocity, there is a way to transcend it, by making it a gift to others. The trauma is redeemed only when it becomes the source of a survivor mission."[18] Trauma healers make it their mission to reform structural relationships by removing abuse and violence and to work actively for a more humane society.

Trauma and the Soul

Trauma victims often experience their trauma as a loss of soul and even conceive of it as the soul being murdered, as spiritual stagnation and death. Thus, the search for soul, the restoration of what has been lost, and the reintegrating of split-off parts lie at the core of trauma therapy.

Soul is an ambiguous concept; its profundity cannot be captured by formal definitions.[19] I think of soul as that eternal part of a living being that constitutes our sense of identity and infuses our life with meaning. In his early writings, Jung made a distinction, though not consistently, between psyche and soul, a distinction that understood soul as "a clearly demarcated functional complex that can best be described as a 'personality.'"[20] In later years, he asserted that "the soul possesses by nature a religious function" and that just as the eye permits us to see light, so it is the soul that makes it possible for us to perceive God.[21]

I resonate most with the evocative power of the term *soul* that Diane Cousineau Brutsche captures in her article "Lady Soul."[22] She sees soul as the feminine aspect of the self and speaks of "a feminine archetypal image as the foundation of our human notion of soul."[23] Interpreting the tapestry *The Lady and the Unicorn* at the Cluny Museum in Paris, she identifies the lady as Lady Sophia, or Lady Soul. Thus, soul murder, in my understanding, is connected with the destruction of this archetypal foundation in the feminine, that is, in matter, and with the severing of our connection to the beyond, the transcendent realm of the self.

The Numinosity of Trauma

There is a numinous quality to the soul. As noted earlier, in Jung's understanding, the soul possesses by nature a "religious function." However, though the soul is spiritual by nature, it nevertheless resides in the body, and embodiment is therefore crucial to its functioning. Traumatic experiences have a dramatic impact on both body and soul, and there can be no healing of soul without tending to the physical body. Damage done to the body affects the state of one's being in the world and might even prevent the Self, in the Jungian sense, from being embodied.

Jung's *Liber Novus*, now published as *The Red Book*, is a reflection on the nature of the soul.[24] It advises us to nourish the soul and nurture it back into life. For Jung, the concept of the soul helps us turn to our inner world and internal processes.[25] In the Red Book he calls out: "My soul, where are you? Do you hear me?" and he laments that he previously experienced his soul as, in his words, "a dead system that I had contrived, assembled from so-called experiences and judgments."[26]

Jung wondered which "Beyond" sheltered his soul while he was suffering from spiritual alienation. With unflinching honesty born of self-reflection, Jung set out in the Red Book to recover his soul and wake up to the awareness of his own fragmentation and egoic strivings. He consciously decided to surrender and let himself "drop," thus loosening his identification with his ego, and to enter into the frightening realm of the collective unconscious. Yielding without question to what is beyond the ego meant that he had to trust completely in the wisdom of the unconscious on his lonely sacrificial journey into the depths. This is a gift or grace that the majority of my patients do not have. The Red Book is a powerful record of the felt presence of the objective psyche by way of an altered state of consciousness. It is important to note that it is this depotentiation of the ego—the shedding of the persona possession, *not* the annihilation of the ego—that facilitates spiritual growth and expands consciousness. Traumatic experiences may actually precipitate such a development if the ego complex is strong enough to contain the psychic energy welling up from the unconscious. Often, however, structural deficiencies and a disrupted ego-Self axis necessitate great caution and gentle ego-strengthening in working to help the patient cope with the traumatic wounding of his or her sense of identity.

In therapy, the task can be to call back soul by way of offering the sanctuary of the safe analytic relationship. Just as a garden needs tending, so we need to tend our soul in order for healing meaning to unfold. This is a challenging task for traumatized individuals, who experience their inner landscape not as a blooming garden but as a desert where nothing grows.

As depicted in the Red Book, Jung's initiation included his meeting the Spirit of the Depths, which ultimately led to a deepened understanding "of the things of the soul."[27] This concept of "dropping" into the depths provides a path toward emotional transformation.

The experiences Jung describes in the Red Book are initiatory experiences with a numinous quality. I suggest that there is a similar numinous core to trauma: the experience of being totally overpowered, an emergency state that can become the catalyst for a quest for meaning, the hidden light in the heart of darkness. Just as Jung gave "careful and scrupulous observation" to his numinous experiences and recorded them in the Red Book, analysts need to listen carefully and compassionately to the voices of anguished souls, taking an observing stance and always keeping in mind that trauma survivors are more than the sum of their wounds.[28] Like Jung, I see traumatic experiences not only as events that penetrate the psychic skin but also as a descent into "the dark night of the soul."

Whether in analyzing the myths of Dionysus, Chiron, Osiris, or Hephaestus or in describing the alchemical process, analytical psychology has always stressed both the numinosity of destructive forces and their transformational aspect. Without suppressing the cruel reality of death, it consistently views death in its unifying, symbolic aspect. The referential character of death, as pointing toward transcendence, is thus brought into our field of vision.

In order to understand traumatic irruptions into life, it is helpful to deepen our understanding of numinosity. An event that is experienced as traumatic, powerful, and dangerous has a numinous character; it reveals the dark face of the *numinosum*, a term Jung borrowed from Rudolf Otto.[29] Jung describes the numinous as "a dynamic agency or effect, not caused by an arbitrary act of the will. On the contrary, it seizes and controls the human subject, who is always rather its victim than its creator."[30] The gripping quality of numinosity characterizes traumatic experiences and nightmares and testifies to something beyond the ego.

Encountering the numinous can cause horror, fear, and disturbance, but it can also induce an extraordinary state of astonishment and fascination. Otto referred to this as *mysterium tremendum et fascinans*. The archetypal meeting with an all-powerful Other, whether in a dream, an active imagination, or a state of stilled consciousness, may be experienced meaningfully as a contact, a calling, or a state of being observed which grips and transforms. Thus, there is healing potential in the numinous.[31] This kind of highly affective experience is often reported in situations of painful extremity originating in the archetypal level of the psyche.

Just as for Jung even diseases can take on a numinous character, so the trauma archetype also has a numinous quality.[32] When speaking about the numinosity of what overwhelms us, Jung says that God meets us in both good and evil. He wrote that "God . . . is the name by which I designate all things which cross my willful path violently and recklessly, all things which upset my subjective views, plans, and intentions, and change the course of my life for better or worse."[33] This theme is also taken up by a Jungian colleague, Greg Mogenson, in his book, *A Most Accursed Religion*. He writes:

> My point is simply that trauma is inherently religious. The soul's functioning can be as held in thrall by the monolithic perspectives of the spirit that would save it as by the monolithic brutalities of matter that afflict it. [34]

Murder, mass rapes, war, torture, terrorism, and natural catastrophes overwhelm the soul and overrun the defensive boundaries that normally protect us. In these extreme states, trauma is experienced as surpassing all that is humanly imaginable, and thus it is perceived by the soul as numinous.

Soul Murder

For over a century, the destruction of the integrity of the soul through archetypal suffering has been given the name *soul murder*. The term refers to any crime, any destructive attack on human dignity and identity, that serves to annihilate that which makes us human. I used this term in my first book on trauma, *Seelenmord: Inzest und Therapie* [*Soul Murder: Incest and Therapy*].[35] There I described how incest survivors refer to their experiences in terms of soul murder: "The night my father first raped me, it felt like he murdered my soul." Exploring the symptoms and sequelae of this violation, placing incest in the context of myths and fairy tales, I attempted to break the conspiracy of silence that pervaded the field of Freudian and Jungian analysis. Because similar terminology was being used for victims of the Nazi terror and for survivors of sexual exploitation, I compared societal repression regarding the Holocaust with the collective taboo regarding sexual abuse.

William G. Niederland introduced the term *survivor syndrome* into psychiatric literature with his book *Folgen der Verfolgung: Das Überlebenden-Syndrom Seelenmord* [*Consequences of Pursuit: The Survivor Syndrome Soul Murder*].[36] He asserted that victims of violence who are not killed physically are nevertheless subjected to the crime of soul murder; they walk as though dead in the midst of life. The confrontation with the possibility of imminent death, with arbitrariness and senselessness, leads to paralysis, apathy, depression, profound guilt, and shame. The feeling of being outside of culture and different from all others has a long-term impact, not only for the survivors but also for the next generation. Working in my practice with the second generation of the Shoah, I was constantly confronted with transgenerational trauma, that is, with the transmitted legacy of spiritual alienation, loss of meaning, loss of hope.

Trauma can be understood as an overwhelming encounter with the dark, terrifying God-image, the silent God. The God of trauma is a sinister God, unjust, terrible, a god who brings chaos and destruction. Jung repeatedly emphasized that this dark God wants to take form in the dark human being: "But God . . . wants to become man, and for that purpose he has chosen the creaturely man filled with darkness . . . to become the vessel for the continuing incarnation."[37] For traumatized people, God seems to be in exile. The divine Self retreats, leaving them in the archetypal situation of abandonment. To them, God is dead or unavailable. All illusions about the ego and the world are dissolved into nothingness. Here the cocoon of our normal thought and perception patterns is broken open. This breaking open of frozen structures and expectations can become an opening to another realm of consciousness, surpassing our ordinary reality.

In the traumatic event, all our God-images can shatter. Then we no longer have anything we can hold on to. I remember how deeply struck I was on reading the words of Elie Wiesel on the wall of the United States Holocaust Memorial Museum in Washington, DC:

> Never shall I forget those flames, which consumed my faith forever. Never shall I forget that nocturnal silence which deprived me, for all eternity, of the desire to live. Never shall I forget those moments, which murdered my God and my soul and turned my dreams to dust. Never shall I forget these things, even if I am condemned to live as long as God Himself. Never.[38]

In my practice I have often encountered this loss of faith, this experience of being thrown into a silent cosmos without any perceivable divine presence.

In "Answer to Job," Jung spoke of the necessity of "submitting," of surrendering to the archetypal violence of God and his injustice. Whenever the self is traumatized, we are dealing with spiritual questions;

for the Self, in Jung's sense, is the *"imago Dei,"* rooted in the transpersonal, paradoxical God.

In Kalsched's understanding, traumatic experiences expose us to the diabolical side of the Self, which does not permit life to reassert itself after trauma.[39] He speaks of an internalized, traumatogenic, inner-psychic factor, which hinders life and leads to a kind of antilife power. On the one hand, this power guarantees survival; on the other, it prevents life from having any further creative thrust.

Human-generated trauma manifests a principle of destruction that annihilates values, destroys the future possibilities of life, and undermines one's trust in the world and in oneself. Anything that splits or destroys meaning can be accounted as evil. The question arises as to whether there are governing powers, even in the darkness of evil, that are able, finally, to restore healing and meaning.

My patients often ask the pressing question: Is there a release from evil, or is evil an a priori, a matter of destiny, a fateful existential reality? In this regard, Jung writes:

> I saw that my soul had fallen into the power of abysmal evil. The power of evil is unquestionable, and we rightfully fear it. Here no prayers, no pious words, no magical sayings help. Once raw power comes after you, there is no help. Once evil seizes you without pity, no father, no mother, no right, no wall and tower, no armor and protective power come to your aid. You fall powerless and forlorn into the hand of the superior power of evil.[40]

To be sure, evil as such, as an entity that embodies evil, such as the devil, has largely disappeared from Western consciousness; it is no longer a metaphysical construct, but there is still evil in and around us in that which we do and that which we allow. Nevertheless, the metaphors of the devil and hell repeatedly show up in survivors' narratives of their homecoming from the wastelands of war and other traumatic experiences. I see before me the broken survivors of the Russian campaign, the armless and legless, those with heads scarred by bullet wounds, and I hear the gloomy background melody of their mute despair. Soldiers with posttraumatic stress disorder (PTSD) are not war heroes. Neither are child soldiers, conditioned to kill without reflection. I remember the statements of young soldiers, survivors of war in the former Yugoslavia: "My life was hell." And I think of the disturbing book by Eugen Drewermann, *Heimkehrer aus der Hölle: Märchen von Kriegsverletzungen und ihrer Heilung* [*Survivors of Hell: Fairy Tales of War Wounds and Their Healing*], which uses the style of the Grimms' fairy tales to describe how soldiers are dressed and drilled by war, how they—in the language of fairy tales—turn into beasts, make pacts with the devil, and cease to exist as human beings.[41] In the fairy tale, the devil commissions the discharged soldier, when asked where he comes from, to answer: "From hell." Human-generated trauma deforms a person's inner being to the point where it is unrecognizable. It is the business of hell (and torture) to destroy the human soul, to bring about the spiritual crippling of what is most essentially human.

In my work I have learned much about this "hell," about mass murder, inhumanity, slaughter, and torture, about revenge and cruelty, but also about the miracle of reconciliation, about wisdom and the art of surviving beyond rage, hatred, and ruthlessness. Dante is always before me in these hours; so are the copperplate etchings of Gustave Doré, which impressed me even as a child, and paintings by Hieronymus Bosch and Goya. In my encounters with people severely traumatized by war and torture, the gates to the underworld seem to be opened. Archetypal elements from the books of the dead and journeys to the other side from diverse cultures have cleared the way for me to approach the cold, dead depths of the underworld. I have searched for a compass to orient myself in these landscapes of death, to keep from getting lost in these regions of hell, with their hellish emotions. Psychiatric terminology speaks of affective disorders and the frozen defenses of the ego. How different, and how much more moving, is Dante's description of souls frozen in perpetual ice, crouching silently in a corner in imponderable coldness, their gaze averted, never giving an answer.

Trauma therapy has shown that as a rule the encounter with evil may elicit one of four typical responses: fight, flight, freezing, or fragmentation. One may flee from evil, evade it, avoid it, split it off, or fight it actively. It is the context and dimensions of evil that determine the human response to it. There is a kind of evil from which one should protect oneself by fleeing. In her works on evil in fairy tales, von Franz points out that not all evil contains creative, transformative potential. She warns of being contaminated by evil. Archetypal evil has the power to make us fall into a complex-ridden state of possession, in which the ego's strength is overcome. She warns that many dark powers must be kept at a distance, and sometimes the only appropriate response is flight.

For the philosopher Hannah Arendt, radical evil destroys the roots of humanity in that it negates the human person as such.[42] She speaks of "radical evil" as that which ought not to have happened, as something with which one cannot be reconciled. Perhaps radical evil represents the structural principle of evil, the irrational desire for evil for its own sake, a truth that according to Arendt is absolutely indescribable and leads to speechless horror and incomprehension that drives us nearly mad. This radical, archetypal evil can be neither healed nor integrated nor humanized. The more archetypal an evil act is, the more impersonal and incomprehensible, and the more dangerous, it is. It can only be warded off and avoided. Gazing into the face of such absolute evil brings about annihilation.

Coming to terms with the reality of *malum morale*, as Leibniz called human-generated evil, is an excruciating necessity for survivors of torture and violence. With my patients, both men and women, I have learned to differentiate between the spirits, discerning which traumatic experiences can be integrated and which can only be sealed away. My Jungian colleague Andreas Schweizer maintains that hidden behind archetypal evil is the *Deus nudus,* the naked God. We cannot bear the gaze of this God but must turn away to the *Deus humanus,* to "that God revealed in our deepest humanity."[43] In the Red Book, Jung too writes that the *Deus absconditus*, the God of darkness and disorientation, uses human beings for self-actualization. Jung's teleological view of evil poses a serious challenge in the context of trauma, for he sees it as being necessary—just as necessary as good—for wholeness and as having its own meaning and purpose.[44]

When one's own evil is split off, the results are destructive for the other onto whom evil is projected. We see this painfully demonstrated in the connection between self-hatred and xenophobia and its traumatizing consequences for the social collective. The stamping out of evil as a moral imperative often gets instrumentalized in politics: I think of President George W. Bush's statements about the "Axis of Evil" and the "War on Terror." These characterizations opened up the possibility of responding to the threat posed by weapons of mass destruction by victimizing civilians in the name of preventing the spread of evil.

Translated into psychoanalytic terms, one might say that we need a mature form of identification with the aggressor, recognizing our own aggressive and sadistic impulses, in order to integrate our shadow side more fully. It is essential to be reconciled with oneself to prevent evil's reenactment. We must achieve a state of agreement with ourselves, as Hannah Arendt writes, since we can never leave ourselves behind. Life condemns us to living intimately with our inner enemy, from whom we can never be freed.[45]

Loss of Soul and "Broken Courage"

The demonic forces of evil have many faces. Here, I draw upon the experience of the survivors of the brutal Khmer Rouge genocide in Cambodia to understand the complexity of traumatic suffering, including the prevalence of a cultural trauma complex. It is therapeutically important to uncover the metaphorical ways in which a culture manifests trauma in the aftermath of affliction. When I walked over the Cambodian "killing fields" and thought of the nearly two million people who were killed, tortured, or starved to death, I wondered how the collective soul of the culture could cope with such overwhelming annihilation of spirit and how or even whether the Cambodian people would be able rebuild their cultural identity. I learned about the Cambodians' struggle to come to terms with the horrors of the past and about the affect-laden images and energies that form the trauma-based cultural syndrome specific to Cambodia.

Chhim Sotheara, a Cambodian psychiatrist and executive director of the Transcultural Psychosocial Organization (TPO) Cambodia in Phnom Penh, generously shared with me his papers on *baksbat* (broken courage).[46] From his work, I learned about another face of soul murder, or loss of soul, in the wake of mass atrocities. *Baksbat* is a cultural syndrome of distress that is susceptible to intergenerational transmission. It is distinct from PTSD and is grounded in the spiritual beliefs of the Cambodian culture. Survivors of atrocities in Cambodia use metaphorical language to communicate what is essentially inexpressible in ordinary language. Out of fear lest their identity be revealed and in order to avoid traumatic memories, they say that they "planted the kapok tree," using the mute tree as a metaphor for seeing nothing, hearing nothing, and speaking nothing.

Many survivors in Cambodia become extremely passive, resolving to refrain from doing anything and just wishing it would all go away. The vegetative symptoms manifest in specific forms and imagery connected to memory: people pierce their ears or mark a stone in remembrance of their traumatic experience. They develop a tendency toward submissiveness, lose their courage and hope, dare not make decisions, become incapable of confrontation, are fearful of helping others, cannot rely on themselves, and become extremely mistrustful of others as well as of the spirit domain. Chhim's research highlights these differentiated tendencies, and I find them to be particularly important, because without an appropriate understanding of indigenous concepts such as *baksbat*, clinicians might not understand how trauma manifests in the metaphysical realm of souls and spirits. And as is true with all cultural complexes, the clinician needs to approach this syndrome without pathologizing the individual patient, who swims in an all-encompassing sea of cultural complexes.

Chhim, himself a Cambodian national, lived through the genocide of the Pol Pot regime and has treated survivors of the Khmer Rouge for more than a decade. He characterizes this syndrome as a permanent "breaking of the body or spirit" or, in the words of the Supreme Patriarch and author of the first Khmer dictionary, the "psychological break down [*sic*] of courage."[47] Chhim prefers to refer to it as "broken courage." I was particularly interested to learn that traditional healers, when they want to describe the excessive fear associated with *baksbat*, talk about loss of soul. This soul loss takes various forms. Chhim notes that according to Khmer belief, there exist nineteen small souls and one large soul, the "crystal soul," in the human body. Severe trauma can cause the loss of all nineteen small souls; they jump out of the body or they flee to the tips of the hairs on the body. In clinical terms, the loss of the crystal soul resembles complete dissociation, psychosis, or seeming death. Traditional healers, shamans throughout history and in all world cultures, know methods that can be used to call back the soul into the body if it is not too late and the soul has not been out of the body for too long. In various regions of Cambodia, ceremonies are held to call the soul back, sometimes involving singing. The healing practice calls to the soul, tells the soul not to let the evil spirit cheat the soul, and tries to convince the soul to "remember, gain insight, and return."[48]

I often think about the shamanic aspect of therapeutic work, when the purpose of that work is to summon the soul back into life. Shamanic healers believe that they must become one with the person in need of healing. They stand in for the patient, taking the illness upon themselves. In a similar vein, Jung writes that the analyst "quite literally 'takes over' the sufferings of the patient and shares them with him."[49]

The Cambodian conception of loss of soul puts me in mind of Jung calling out to his lost soul in the Red Book: "My soul, where are you? Do you hear me?"[50] In his twentieth-century Swiss Protestant psyche, his soul was personified as female, and in particular, as the biblical Salome. He found that he had to interact with and confront Salome in order to find himself again, to emerge from the trauma. This is the opposite of planting the mute kapok tree. I think a collaboration between the Jungian archetypal view of cultural complexes and a culture-specific perspective on the indigenous symptomatic features of experienced trauma might be of great help in understanding and healing the horrific wounds of any traumatized society.

NOTES

[1] Mardi Jon Horowitz, *Stress Response Syndromes* (New York: Jason Aronson, 1976).

[2] Ronnie Janoff-Bulman, *Shattered Assumptions: Towards a New Psychology of Trauma* (New York: Free Press, 1992); Thomas H. Ogden, *The Primitive Edge of Experience* (Lanham, MD: Rowman and Littlefield Publishers, 2004), p. 39.

[3] Henry Krystal, *Integration and Self-Healing: Affect, Trauma, Alexithymia* (Hillsdale, NJ: Analytic Press, 1988).

[4] D. W. Winnicott, *The Maturational Process and the Facilitating Environment* (New York: International Universities Press, 1965).

[5] Heinz Kohut, *The Restoration of the Self* (New York: International Universities Press, 1977).

[6] Donald Kalsched, *The Inner World of Trauma: Archetypal Defenses of the Personal Spirit* (London: Routledge, 1996).

[7] Robert Jay Lifton, *The Broken Connection: On Death and the Continuity of Life* (New York: Simon and Schuster, 1979); *The Life of the Self: Toward a New Psychology* (New York: Simon and Schuster, 1976), p. 7.

[8] C. G. Jung, letter to Dr. Kristine Mann, February 1, 1945, in *C. G. Jung Letters, Vol. 1: 1906–1950*, trans. R. F. C. Hull (London: Routledge and Kegan Paul, 1976), p. 357.

[9] John Felstiner, *Paul Celan: Poet, Survivor, Jew* (New Haven, CT: Yale University Press, 1995), p. 166.

[10] David Becker, quoted in Anne E. Cudd, *Analyzing Oppression* (New York: Oxford University Press, 2006), p. 248, note 6.

[11] Judith L. Herman, *Trauma and Recovery: The Aftermath of Violence—From Domestic Abuse to Political Terror* (New York: Basic Books, 1992), p. 96.

[12] Jung borrowed the Greek term *entiodromia* (literally "a reversal of direction") from Heraclitus to denote the principle of perpetual change.

[13] George B. Hogenson, "The Self, the Symbolic and Synchronicity: Virtual Realities and the Emergence of the Psyche," *Journal of Analytical Psychology* 50, no. 3 (2005): 271–284.

[14] Jung, *CW* 8, § 800.

[15] Jung, *CW* 7, § 112.

[16] Eberhard Bethge, *Dietrich Bonhoeffer: A Biography*, rev. ed., ed. Victoria Barnett, trans. Eric Mosbacher et al. (Minneapolis, MN: Fortress Press, 2000), p. 1022.

[17] Eric Metaxas, *Bonhoeffer: Pastor, Martyr, Prophet, Spy* (Nashville, TN.: Thomas Nelson, Inc., 2010), p. 497. The first two lines of the refrain in the German version of the song are: "Von guten Mächten wunderbar geborgen, erwarten wir getrost was kommen mag."

[18] Herman, *Trauma and Recovery*, p. 207.

[19] Donald E. Kalsched, *Trauma and the Soul: A Psycho-Spiritual Approach to Human Development and Its Interruption* (London: Routledge, 2013).

[20] Jung, *CW* 6, § 797.

[21] Jung, *CW* 12, § 14.

²² Diane Cousineau Brutsche, "Lady Soul," *Spring*, 82 (2009): 101–113.

²³ *Ibid.*, p. 104.

²⁴ The Red Book was begun in 1915 as *Liber Novus*.

²⁵ Jung, *CW* 6, § 877.

²⁶ Jung, *RB*, p. 232 and note 39.

²⁷ Jung, *RB*, p. 207.

²⁸ Jung, *CW* 11, § 6.

²⁹ Rudolf Otto, *The Idea of the Holy* (Oxford: Oxford University Press, 1970).

³⁰ Jung, *CW* 11, § 6.

³¹ Lionel Corbett, *The Religious Function of the Psyche* (London: Routledge, 1996).

³² C. G. Jung, *Letters, Vol. 1: 1906–1950*, trans. R. F. C. Hull (London: Routledge and Kegan Paul, 1973), p. 377.

³³ C. G. Jung, letter to M. Leonard, December 5, 1959, in *Letters, Vol. 2: 1951–1961*, trans. R. F. C. Hull (London: Routledge and Kegan Paul, 1976), p. 525.

³⁴ Greg Mogenson, *A Most Accursed Religion: When a Trauma Becomes God* (Putnam, CT: Spring Publications, 2005), p. 16.

³⁵ Ursula Wirtz, *Seelenmord: Inzest und Therapie* (Stuttgart: Kreuz Verlag, 1989).

³⁶ William G. Niederland, *Folgen der Verfolgung: Das Überlebenden-Syndrom Seelenmord* (Frankfurt: Suhrkamp Verlag, 1980).

³⁷ Jung, *CW* 11, § 746.

³⁸ Elie Wiesel, *Night* (New York: Bantam Books, 1982), p. 32.

³⁹ Kalsched, *The Inner World of Trauma*.

⁴⁰ Jung, *RB*, p. 289.

⁴¹ Eugen Drewermann, *Heimkehrer aus der Hölle: Märchen von Kriegsverletzungen und ihrer Heilung* (Ostfildern: Patmos Verlag, 2010).

⁴² Hannah Arendt, *Men in Dark Times* (New York: Harcourt, Brace and World, 1968); *On Violence* (New York: Harcourt, Brace and World, 1970).

⁴³ Andreas Schweizer, *Der erschreckende Gott: Tiefenpsychologische Wege zu einem ganzheitlichen Gottesbild* (Munich: Kösel Verlag, 2000), p. 218.

⁴⁴ For an in-depth discussion of Jung's debate with Victor White on the problem of evil, see Ann Conrad Lammers, *In God's Shadow: The Collaboration of Victor White and C. G. Jung* (Mahwah, NJ: Paulist Press, 1994).

⁴⁵ Hannah Arendt, *Über das Böse: Eine Vorlesung zu Fragen der Ethik*, trans. Ursula Ludz (Munich: Piper Verlag, 2006).

⁴⁶ Sotheara Chhim, "*Baksbat* (Broken Courage): A Trauma-Based Cultural Syndrome in Cambodia," *Medical Anthropology* 32, no. 2 (2013): 160–173; "Baksbat (Broken Courage): The Development and Validation of the Inventory to Measure Baksbat, a Cambodian Trauma-Based Cultural Syndrome of Distress," *Culture, Medicine, and Psychiatry* 36, no. 4 (2012): 640–659.

⁴⁷ Quoted in Chhim, "Baksbat (Broken Courage): The Development and Validation," p. 644. Chhim explains that the word *bak* means "break (or broken)" and the word *sbat* means "body" or "form," thus *baksbat* means "broken body" or "broken form."

⁴⁸ Chhim, "*Baksbat* (Broken Courage): A Trauma-Based Cultural Syndrome," p. 167.

⁴⁹ Jung, *CW* 16, § 358.

⁵⁰ Jung, *RB*, p. 232.

CHAPTER TWO

TRAUMA AS A
SPIRITUAL EXPERIENCE

I n my opinion, we cannot reflect adequately on trauma and the
treatment of liminal states without a deep understanding of
formative spiritual experiences, since the spiritual dimension is
always constellated in this work. Trauma therapy has an intrinsically
spiritual core. It fosters the embodiment of something essential, the
reconnection of the ego with the numinous core of being and a
transformation of consciousness that results in a reintegration of the
personality on a new level. In trauma therapy, the clinical and the
spiritual approaches should be wed. I wish to show that whenever
something totally overpowering and beyond our daily reality is
experienced, some serious emergency or traumatic shock, the
traumatized person turns to mythological or biblical language to
frame the experience in an archetypal system of meaning. Jung
always pointed out that in moments of panic or highly charged
emotional states, when one feels defeated, religious imagery and
symbols emerge, a result, Jung might say, of the soul's "religious
function." He wrote: "The God-image is not something invented; it is
an experience that comes upon man spontaneously."[1]

I think the turning to the spiritual, to the sense of meaningfulness that transcends the ego, provides humans with what is most needed in the pit of utter despair. Trauma results in an existential confrontation with the realization that one's inner structure has been shattered and a painful awareness of one's vulnerability. This anguish challenges us as we work through such nightmarish experiences while holding on to the belief that the best of ourselves lies in our worst suffering and that light is born out of darkness. The pressing questions are: How do I recover my lost soul? How do I overcome my alienation from myself? How do I foster the transformation of my consciousness?

Following the postmodern tradition, my starting point is an undogmatic spirituality, as convincingly presented by Harald Walach, based on his research in scientific methodology and the history of science.[2] By "undogmatic spirituality" I mean a spirituality freed from traditional institutional contexts and based on the experiential core common to all religions. Spirituality signifies a connection to and a relationship with an embracing, infinite value, the Ultimate, the transcendent dimension, as well as to and with fellow human beings and creation as a whole.

The Spiritual Dimension

Spirituality can be described only approximately, as a transreligious dimension of human existence, a life orientation with respect to something transcendent—the All, the One, or the Ultimate—which may be experienced but not rationally grasped. This Oneness is variously named in different cultures and consciousness traditions as the divine or the Buddha-nature, as atman or Tao. An experience of the All transforms the one who undergoes it. It seems to be connected with a sense of fulfillment in life characterized by serenity, wisdom, mercy, and peace and with a life the goal of which is to realize the values of the beautiful, the good, and the true.

Derived from the Latin *spiritus*—meaning air, wind, breath, soul, spirit, mind, inspiration, courage—the verb *spiro* encompasses in its horizon of meanings both "breathe, live" and "be fulfilled, be ensouled." This semantic field is of special significance for the treatment of trauma, since healing in this realm has to do with retrieving the lost soul, filling the deathly stillness with life, propelling back into meaning that which has suffered a crisis and loss of meaning, and feeling the breath of life return. *Spiritus*, as living breath, points to an inner, invisible principle of life, known in Sanskrit as *prana*, in Greek as *pneuma*, and in Hebrew as *ruach*.[3]

Traumatized people I have worked with appear to know something about the transpersonal, spiritual dimensions of human existence, although, as Kalsched has pointed out, the relationship to the numinous can also be in the service of a defense, a spiritual bypass, in which the energies of the numinous world substitute "for the self-esteem that should come from embodied gratifications in the human world."[4]

Trauma survivors often undergo intense subjective experiences of dismemberment, disintegration, and, consequently, altered states of consciousness after an encounter with the numinous mythopoetic structure of the unconscious. Traumatic shock may cause a spiritual crisis, given that in situations of existential extremity and suffering one comes face-to-face with nothingness. Crisis may nevertheless turn into opportunity. In a traumatic experience the construct of subjectivity dissolves, leading to a severe lesion of the ego. Such experiences of annihilation tend to break down one's customary interpretation of the world. The shattering of the usual defense mechanisms and the old value system creates a void, an empty space, an opening in which something new may emerge.

According to Jung, from humanity's earliest days the spiritual dimension and the quest for meaning have formed an essential part of our nature. They are an a priori, a fundamental requirement, and they bind us together with becoming and passing away, enabling us to face life and death, for transformation and destruction are aspects of the same dynamic life process. For me, then, spirituality is a fundamental way of being in the world, a framework through which we try to live, both in our inner consciousness and in our outer behavior, in a close relationship with ourselves, our physical and social environment, and the Infinite. As Jung wrote,

> The decisive question for man is: Is he related to something infinite or not? That is the telling question of his life. . . . In the final analysis, we count for something only because of the essential we embody, and if we do not embody that, life is wasted.[5]

Becoming a whole human being, finding and responsibly fulfilling one's proper place in the greater whole—that is the goal of individuation. The conception of daily life as spiritual exercise is common to all traditional paths of wisdom.[6] Spirituality also has to do with the art of letting oneself be and with the capacity of human nature to grow beyond itself, to strive for self-transcendence. To proceed with attention to one's consciousness involves taking responsibility for oneself and for all creation, acknowledging the familial connection of all that exists, in full consciousness that we are all bound together as parts of a greater whole.

The undogmatic understanding of the spiritual is foreshadowed in Jung's Red Book, in his seemingly heretical "mystical" sayings, which run counter to the anthropomorphic God-images of most religious traditions. His call for the birth of God in the human soul has its ancestry in the thought of Meister Eckhart, with whose writings Jung was closely acquainted. His heterodox conception of God testifies to his experiential knowledge of the unity of all that is. He believed that the divine and the human are functions of each other. Precisely because he incorporated this undogmatic spirituality, Jung was later accused of being unscientific. He was criticized for being unempirical, a mystic whose psychology was actually metaphysics. But today, when one considers the worldwide resonance of the Red Book, it is obvious that this mystical aspect fascinates people and, on a deeper level, apparently nourishes them as well. Perhaps our historical period needs more of Meister Eckhart.

Thanks to nuclear and chemical weapons, we now have the godlike capacity to reign over death, the power to "empty out the apocalyptic vials of wrath" and threaten the very survival of our species.[7] For this reason, there is a pressing need for a change in our ethical consciousness and a return to a mystical understanding of God and humankind. Jung insisted that we acknowledge not only that we depend on God, but that God depends on us. What is required, then, is for us to dissolve our projections onto God and to open ourselves to the experience of an unfathomable being, to whom we are connected and who is embodied in us. Jung wrote: "The naïve assumption that the creator of the world is a conscious being must be regarded as a disastrous prejudice, which later gave rise to the most incredible dislocations of logic."[8]

If I grasp that spirituality is the experience of the reconnection of the ego with the greater whole, a reality working throughout my life and touching me in the deepest core of my being, then I am able to adopt a very specific mode of presence in my therapeutic attitude. In this mode, I am in contact with the secrets of life and death, and with the "religious" dimension of the soul. For Jung, religion is "a careful consideration and observation of certain dynamic factors that are conceived as 'powers': spirits, daemons, gods, laws, ideas, ideals."[9] Religion, in Jung's usage, is not a confession of faith, but a form of consciousness based in the experience of the numinous. There is a spiritual libido driving us to become what, in our innermost being, we are ordained to be.

Human beings have, in Karlfried Graf Dürckheim's view, a "dual origin": we participate in the earthly order and in the heavenly order, and we must fulfill our duties to be justified in both these realms.[10] We belong both to the time- and space-limited world and to the unconditioned reality beyond time and space. Stretched between these contradictions, which comprise our wholeness, we have integration as our life assignment and our responsibility.

Spiritual Transformation through Trauma

As human beings with a dual origin, we are partly physical and partly transcendent, and it is our task to work on a reliable bond between the ego and the Self. For Jung, the Self opens a "window on eternity."[11] The transcendent function is a powerful capacity, residing deep within us, to transcend the physical and spiritual givens of life, however torturous they may be. Jung first encountered this function during his great crisis. He took the experiences described in his Red Book so seriously that they fundamentally transformed his life and thought. In my view, these contacts with Being, in which transcendence broke into human consciousness, served as the starting point for Jung's new understanding both of himself and of the world and provided the foundation of his analytical psychology.

I think that the human race has only just become mature enough to admit that inner experience is a legitimate scientific mode for the exploration of reality. Today, the branch of psychology devoted to consciousness is studying the spiritual core dimensions and what they mean for the development of personality. Movements abound that give central importance to the value of inner experience and promote the practice of awareness and presence. In the German-speaking world, those who research trends are using complexity and social process theories to show that the culture of "I" belongs to the old paradigm and that current approaches offer a better orientation to the complex structures of our ever-more-rapidly changing society. Megatrends are the driving power of change that transform from within all aspects of our everyday life, that is, our social, economic, and ecological systems.

The futurist Matthias Horx has studied these structural changes in human organizational systems and demonstrated that the society of fun and excitement has long since been replaced by a *society of meaning.*[12] Scholar of religion Paul Zulehner discerns an "addiction to spirituality" and a "God-hunger after God-fasting," which he says is a reaction to the top-headedness and one-sidedness of our dominant consciousness.[13] Researchers speak of the current respiritualization as a megatrend following the too-long era in which individuals were estranged from the invisible dimension, which has no name and yet influences reality, as Paracelsus declared, and in which the isolated ego experienced transcendental homelessness and loss of orientation.[14] We no longer know what we want, and according to Viktor Frankl, "in contrast to man in former times, he is no longer told by traditions and values what he should do."[15] It is understandable—in an era when the individual lacks both home and homeland and we struggle to come to terms with individualization and globalization—that we are once again in search of a *spiritus* that can integrate knowledge and recognition into our feeling and manifest itself in the way we live, love, and work. The observable boom in spirituality is more than a passing fad; it points to a deep-rooted process of social transformation not unrelated to the amount of violence and destructiveness that currently prevails in our societies.

Conferences and publications in growing numbers focus on the integration of spirituality into the discourse of the medical-psychological sciences. Science seems, hesitantly, to be discovering spirituality. In both scientific investigation and spiritual practice I see a common thread: the desire for knowledge, the need to grasp reality as it is and venture into new areas of truth and essence. In this process, the question can become very personal for scientists: To what extent have scientists become personally involved in the development and transformation of consciousness? For the degree to which an issue can be plumbed depends on the nature of the investigator's personal experience with it.

Jung believed that "man's worst sin is unconsciousness," for in unconsciousness the human being fails in his or her spiritual duty of self-knowledge.[16] We are summoned to realize the potential of our true selves. Self-actualization means the realization of our being. We have a moral duty to be faithful to our essence and acknowledge our personal life pattern. In the Red Book, Jung's soul admonishes him: "You have been too unconscious for a long time. Now you must go to a higher level of consciousness."[17] The same thought appears in the spiritual traditions, namely, that the highest human achievement is to come to oneself and wake up. Jung, along with Erich Neumann, contributed decisively to the psychology of consciousness, providing experiential access to the transcendent dimension and to the understanding of wholeness, unity, final cause, and ultimate reality. For Jung, "to kindle a light in the darkness of mere being" by creating consciousness is "the sole purpose of human existence."[18]

Consciousness is a process, an interplay of the patterns through which we perceive reality. As Michael von Brück puts it, "consciousness arises ever anew, according to the patterns inherent within it; it is capable of learning and is constantly engaged in change."[19] Psychological maturation after severe traumatization can be seen as the evolution and unfolding of consciousness. Traumatic states are boundary experiences which have the power to destroy us but are also capable of producing a radical transformation of consciousness, an encounter with what lies on the other side of the boundary.

The concept of individuation, whose conceptual underpinnings are foreshadowed in the Red Book, encompasses all the elements that Harald Walach calls the "building blocks of a spiritual image of the world and the human being."[20] These elements represent a sort of bridge between science and spirituality. In them are found the foundational experiences of oneness and connectedness common to all spiritual traditions: awareness of the relativity of the ego and time, the complementarity of phenomenal and absolute reality, and the transcending of body-soul dualism. Modern science has begun to explore these elements, and today efforts are being made to integrate discoveries from the realm of spiritual experience into science and into the practice of analysis. As an analyst, one is required to look beyond the garden fence of one's familiar truths and become acquainted with the discoveries of neighboring disciplines, so as to open the way for reciprocal, fruitful dialogue instead of hostile projections.

In the archetypes of the collective unconscious can be encountered the fundamental inner experience of interconnection, the "relationship of all that is," which is the common core of all spiritual traditions. The psychological maturation process mediates the relativity of the individual ego complex and the experience of that which transcends the ego, the experience of the Self. Spiritual practice no longer strives to perceive the ego as the navel of the world and the center of being but to transcend it and relativize its absolute demands. During trauma, this transnarcissistic experience happens in a completely involuntary manner, not step-by-step as when one is on the path of spiritual practice. The ego becomes unhinged, and everything one formerly believed in—all one's convictions about oneself, the world, and God—are shattered.

The relativity of the ego is an idea that I have encountered in the collected wisdom of the most diverse cultures. The primal questions of humanity concerning destruction and re-creation, dismemberment and restoration, have found their symbolic form there. In myths, fairy tales, and the testimony of survivors, as well as in literature and poetry, I have sought the wisdom passed down through human history concerning the dignity of the human being, including the meaning and orientation mediated through rituals and symbols.

My philosophical background has helped me when exposed to inhumanity and cruelty beyond words. Socratic and Stoic paradoxes have taught me about the violent movements of the soul and how to deal with them. I rely on Seneca's writings on anger, on consolation, and on tranquility of mind when facing the abyss of trauma in survivors who are trying to remain lucid and cultivate hope in the midst of atrocities and assaults on human dignity. In 1971, integrative gestalt therapist Hilarion Petzold introduced the term *clinical philosophy* into the psychotherapeutic field as an enrichment of our practice.[21] I believe I have gained much from embracing the notion of clinical philosophy.

In the initiation rites of the most diverse cultures I have found the theme of "death as a friend" used as a sacred key to the deeper mysteries of life. In a similar way, the spiritual traditions often describe death as a threshold experience, a form of transition into life. Death and resurrection are viewed as complementary in Christianity. The schools of meditative practice speak of death as being the death of the ego and as a precondition for becoming conscious of another reality. The philosopher Martin Heidegger characterized *Dasein* as "being toward death" (*Sein zum Tode*), meaning that our being in the world is conditioned by the boundary of death.[22] Thus, living is a learning to die, a rehearsal for death, a conscious confrontation with the fear of dying while one is still alive.

Our unconscious and the language of dreams, formed as they are in primary and secondary processes, point to the relativity of space and time. The complementarity of phenomenal reality and a deeper, absolute reality, the synthesis of body and soul, were recognized early on by Jung in his experiences of synchronicity, in which material reality is meaningfully related to psychic reality and apparent coincidences are endowed with a deeper meaning. In the analytic interpretation of psychological developmental processes, matter, energy, and spirit are revealed as manifestations of a single fundamental substance.

The relativity of time is a familiar concept in meditative and spiritual practices. It can also be encountered, paradoxically, during states of overwhelming emotional and physical pain, in which time seems to stand still. Meister Eckhart speaks in mystical terms of the collapsing of past, present, and future into a timeless present, the *nunc stans*.[23] In trauma, we find a similar dissolution of time that parallels the *nunc stans* of the mystics, a painful eternal now, in which the future does not exist and the past is lost. Contemporary findings in neurobiology indicate that through the altered neuronal processes that accompany shock, our experience of time can undergo fundamental changes. Time becomes nonlinear, and death becomes part of the present moment.

My study of mysticism helped me to understand trauma, for in it I found striking parallels to the traumatic experience. Both conditions involve a crisis of meaning and extreme states of fear, suffering, ego loss, emptiness, and the void, which dissolve the distinction between subject and object. The "mystical psychology" of Teresa of Ávila describes the way mystics experience self-realization and how "to rise above the mud of our personalized misery."[24] John of the Cross, imprisoned and vegetating for months at a time under inhuman conditions in the darkness of a cell, knew about the traumatic experience of being separated from man and God. Called back from the "dark night of the soul," he writes about the human capacity for transformation.[25]

It seems as though, in descending into one's own abyss, it becomes possible to gain access to the essential, to another kind of seeing and knowing. I am reminded of the exhortation of Angelus Silesius: "Man, become essential" (*"Mensch, werde wesentlich"*).[26] Becoming essential means awakening to the truth of one's own essence and the essence of the world and then living out of this truth. It is a deeply spiritual concern, the goal of individuation. The mystic Johannes Tauler describes crisis as a place in which one has a consciousness-altering encounter with God, as an opportunity for deeper self-knowledge and discovery of the path into one's inner core.[27]

One may draw parallels between the three-stage mystical path—purification (*via purgativa*), insight (*via illuminativa*), and union (*via unitiva*)—and the various stages in trauma therapy. In dealing with trauma, too, we are involved in a process of purification from blockages, a process of working through and integration, and a process of re-membering, imagining, ordering, and revaluing, which leads to the creation of meaning and a consciousness of solidarity and new relationships in the social network. Following the deconstruction and fragmentation of a traumatic experience, trauma therapy attempts to envision and reconstruct a new life pattern, one in which the victim's consciousness of his or her identity and his or her trust in other people and the world as a whole can be created afresh and the plurality of the everyday world can be experienced as an overarching unity.

My own spiritual practice has sharpened my perception and awareness of the transformational potential in situations of psychic extremity. It has taught me to watch carefully for patterns of meaning that my traumatized patients create in their attempt to understand and regulate their suffering. Trauma research has shown that what is primarily responsible for the consequences of trauma, and hence determines the treatment process, is not the traumatic event as such, but rather the meaning that the victim ascribes to it in the context of his or her entire life. Thus, when trauma breaks into the reality of a person's life, I have learned to pay close attention to the ways it is symbolized, to the basic patterns of how that person attempts to work through the suffering. I must attend to the attitude the patient takes toward the unavoidable and the unchangeable and to his or her verbal images of pain, fear, and hope. I must understand the context and the meaning that the traumatic event has for this individual at this moment, in order to grasp more deeply his or her way of seeing and being. Only when I am able to see into this person's mental framework, into his or her patterns of perceiving reality, can I begin to reframe, that is, to open up spaces for exploration, to shift perspectives, to try out other ways of seeing, and to recontextualize, so that the trauma does not lead to fixation and petrifaction. In this regard, Jung said, "My aim is to bring about a psychic state in which my patient begins to experiment with his own nature—a state of fluidity, change and growth, where nothing is eternally fixed and hopelessly petrified."[28]

In the case of severely traumatized individuals, this is an extraordinarily difficult task, since they are marked by rigidity and multiple blockages. However, it is only by adapting to adverse life circumstances that we can take evolutionary steps and develop the flexibility and capacity to create new ways of thinking and behaving. A traumatized person must see himself or herself as able to self-transform. The traumatized individual is transformed by the shattering event, but at the same time must produce a transformation of his or her own, because he or she cannot go on as before. Trauma survivors must recreate themselves through the interpretation and reinterpretation of things beyond their grasp. Only in this way can the subject reconstitute itself as "identity in change." Reality emerges in the play of possibilities. Identity is an elastic concept which owes much of its elasticity to the fluid character of the psyche. It can be understood only as a process, as in Goethe's theory of morphology and metamorphosis.

People in extreme situations are challenged by fate to accept their suffering, even when its meaning cannot be discerned. Destruction, death, and the ineluctable pain of loss can have the effect of an initiation. Catastrophic crises can turn into new opportunities for life when one faces the associated suffering squarely and strives to accept it. Often this has the feel of a leap into the abyss. Zen masters teach that it is not enough to accept the unavoidable; one must enter fully into this inevitability. Only then will the abyss become fertile ground. At the point of deepest darkness, when one experiences total rupture, there may be a breakthrough to the light.

Dürckheim, who based his initiation therapy on a foundation of analytical psychology but also incorporated aspects of Zen Buddhism, believed that only through extreme suffering and exposure to annihilation can that which is indestructible in us arise within. He referred to the "opening of the eye of being" ("*Öffnung des Wesensauges*"), the permeability and transparence to transcendence and the wheel of transformation.[29] He was trying to understand what psychotherapy can offer someone in an extreme situation—a painter who suffers loss of vision, a violinist who loses an arm, a dancer struck down by multiple sclerosis. For Dürckheim, these cases are test situations that can be turned into opportunities for healing on the inner path.

Initiation therapy identifies three fundamental experiences in human life: the fear of annihilation, the despair of meaninglessness, and the wretchedness of isolation. As human beings we seek certainty, meaning, and love. The violation of these primal needs through traumatic events leads us to an abyss of despair and helplessness; yet this feeling of total loss, this nakedness, can be turned around into a sense of something that surpasses us and transcends our understanding. A reversal can occur whereby this energetic, polarized field of meaning and meaninglessness is transformed into an experience of the Absolute, in which even symbolic death is no longer encountered as an ultimate barrier but as a new beginning. In analytical psychology, the transcendent function facilitates such a rebirth and brings us to another level of being.

This rebirth is experienced as a total reversal of all that is familiar, as the leap of consciousness to a completely new level. It is like the death of the old and an awakening of the new. In every death is contained a kernel of life, since every life already conceals death within it. This spiritual awakening into another dimension of reality, this broadening into the transpersonal realm, can fundamentally transform all the functions of consciousness, perception, thinking, feeling, and intentionality. It can set in motion a process of development and maturation, which grows out of the transformative power of suffering. In his biography, Nelson Mandela reflects on the connection between wounding and growth:

> The policy of apartheid created a deep and lasting wound in my country and my people. . . . But the decades of oppression and brutality had another, unintended effect, and that was that it produced . . . men of such extraordinary courage, wisdom, and generosity that their like may never be known again. Perhaps it requires such depth of oppression to create such heights of character.[30]

For me, Nelson Mandela is a moving example of how the confrontation with evil can make one capable of taking the risk of loving, of how suffering and pain can open the heart, and of how the acceptance of powerlessness and of one's vulnerability can lead one to an active humanity. Through transformative energy, out of the unbearable tension of opposites, a new attitude becomes possible, rendering the whole person more transparent to the revelation of transcendence in immanence.

In encounters with destructive life events we are challenged to get to the deepest place in oneself, compelled to take seriously the Delphic injunction, "Know thyself." To obey this command, we need to engage in a process of *ruminatio*, a wrestling with meaning and with the secrets of life and death. The suffering of traumatized individuals resembles a *via negativa*, that is, the descent into a darkness of spirit, in which one no longer has access to one's body. Under conditions of extreme pain, one plunges into a bottomless pit of nothingness. One experiences cosmic despair, for there is nothing left to lose because all has been lost. However, having accompanied my patients down this path, I am continually amazed to see how such a *via negativa* can be turned into a *via transformativa*.

When we confront death during a liminal experience, our relationship to space and time is altered. We become acutely aware of our finitude and the extent of our limitations, and our normal decision-making faculties shut down. When pain takes possession of us, so that inner and outer are no longer distinguishable, our perception of self and body becomes radically altered. The boundary between ego and non-ego dissolves. Extreme pain becomes symbolic of death. Thus, after experiencing unbearable pain, we might say, "I died a thousand deaths." In the boundary experience of undergoing pain during torture, speech is reduced to nonverbal sounds, to whimpers and groans. We are thrown back to a preverbal stage when we had no words to express ourselves.

Unconscious personality formation and spiritual experiences are two processes that involve mystery and the ineffable. These life processes can be accessed only by subjective experience, not by the objective observations of science. The failure of language is especially apparent when we are dealing with intimations of timelessness. We may attempt to convey this experience with words such as "It seemed to last an eternity." Being at a loss for words, being unable to express ourselves, we undergo a complete breakdown in relational structures and we experience increasing social isolation. To this is often added the enormous guilt of feeling our inner world emptied, of having failed to defend our personhood, and despair over losing both ourselves and the world. This state of vulnerability can, nevertheless, render us open to new possibilities. One of my tortured patients, who sensitized me in a special way to this condition of archaic dependence and agony, developed an extreme sort of psychic permeability, which enabled him to open up and perceive the subtle energy field of his environment.

The Unity of the Material and the Spiritual

The division between material and spiritual reality, the split between body and soul, is not found in spiritual traditions that teach the unity of being. A similar oneness appears in the world of quantum physics. As physicist and Right Livelihood Award–winner Hans-Peter Dürr explains it, "matter is not composed of matter, but reality is merely potentiality. The world has not an ontic structure, . . . but rather a holistic, process-type structure, based on fundamental immaterial relations."[31] He says, "The concept that matter is the primary aspect, and relationships between it, connectedness or shape . . . is secondary, is no longer valid. Modern physics reverses this ranking: form before substance, relationality before materiality."[32] The world is represented as a unity, as the One that cannot be divided, whose wholeness can be described only in images and similes.

Here we encounter the complementary pattern of thought, the logic of both-and, which goes beyond our traditional, dualistic splitting into either-or. Early on in his career, Jung exposed this duality of spirit and matter as a thought pattern to be overcome, and he referred in a preliminary way to nonduality. In the Red Book he developed a vision of the *unus mundus*, parallel to his concept of unitary reality, which took visible form in his mandalas. Perhaps one could say that the Red Book reveals the psyche's tendency to move beyond dualism; betrayal, disorientation, and despair can push beyond dual consciousness to an affirmation of life as it really is.

Physics' new conception of matter, neurobiology's advances in understanding consciousness, the exploration of complex adaptive systems, and the concept of emergence have all been invaluable for trauma therapy. Together, they intimate that our perceiving, thinking, relative ego is both a part of the whole and also the whole, without a clear, dualistic separation between the two, as Jung demonstrated in the Red Book. Analytical psychology is in harmony with the bootstrap theory, which maintains that everything is bound to everything else. If we want to avoid collective suicide, we need to be conscious that, together with the inanimate world and the rest of animate nature, we form a whole that is more than the sum of its parts.

With Jung, I am convinced that the "catastrophe of the modern" stems from one-sidedness, that is, from the dominance of particularity over wholeness and of rationality over intuition. In the dichotomy between knowledge and wisdom, *logos* and *eros*, the rational pole is overvalued. Our task, individually and collectively, is to develop a higher level of consciousness in which knowledge gives way to wisdom. I have sometimes encountered this more visionary perspective in the posttraumatic Self.

In my work I often experience the perspective of quantum philosophy as a comfort, because it emphasizes the reciprocity that binds together all that is—emerging and passing away, form and emptiness. Quantum physics has made discoveries that enable us to understand the complementary analytical network of relationships as a quantum field. As expressions of a deeper level of reciprocal connection and interdependence, these invisible, nonspatial, atemporal quantum fields constellate effects that arise exclusively from physical potentialities and probabilities, just as manifestations of archetypes in the analytical situation represent psychic probabilities. Synchronistic phenomena in trauma therapy, *kairos* experiences, aha moments, and shared somatic phenomena point to the underlying field of interdependencies extending beyond face-to-face encounters in space and time.

According to the holistic paradigms of modern physics as I understand them, reality is potentiality, flux, ongoing metamorphosis, a relational structure always open to change and transformation.[33] Trauma therapy is conducted in this sort of framework: opening horizons, creating a new identity from the combination of possibilities, always with the awareness of the potential for destructiveness, but also for dignity. I consider it a truly analytic stance to see in traumatic experiences the potential for an awakening to the reality of all that is just as it is. Despite the criticisms leveled at the ideal of wholeness, the principle of wholeness and acceptance of "suchness" are justified as guiding fictions on our path. Jung writes:

> But the right way to wholeness is made up, unfortunately, of fateful detours and wrong turnings. It is a *longissima via*, not straight but snakelike, a path that unites the opposites in the manner of the guiding caduceus, a path whose labyrinthine twists and turns are not lacking in terrors.[34]

Realistically this wholeness, as the basic principle of the universe, can never be experienced through our dualistic consciousness, but we have the fiction of wholeness to guide us.

Although wholeness is rationally inconceivable, Jung and the spiritual traditions treat it as an empirically knowable reality. They teach us that the Buddha-nature belongs to our original being, that we enter the world whole; therapeutic art is a kind of midwifery that helps to birth what is already present, wanting to come into the world. I share Jung's belief in the Aristotelian concept of an organizing entelechy, the inherent potential within the acorn to become an oak, the a priori existence of potential wholeness.

The idea that we are aware of the truth at a deep level and need only to be reminded of it, that every act of learning is really a bringing to consciousness, is fundamental to the Socratic tradition. Socrates held that we have at our command an empirical knowledge, even if it is not always immediately accessible to us, and when we are led to this knowledge, we realize that we knew it all along. Likewise, I understand my work in the field of trauma to be that of accompanying people to the place where they once again recall what they originally knew.

The Healing Power of Spiritual Values

The spiritual values of hope, trust, love, and compassion guide my therapeutic work with traumatized individuals. Jungian psychology for me is a psychology of hope, an ensouled psychology. "Hope dies last," says the proverb, indicating how deeply anchored in human beings is the hope of changing unbearable circumstances and transcending set limits. Nelson Mandela writes that throughout his years in prison, he never abandoned hope. The glimmer of humanity that sometimes shone in the eyes of his guards, even for a second, was enough to inspire him to go on living, reminding him that love is more natural to the human heart than hate, and that "Man's goodness is a flame that can be hidden but never extinguished."[35]

Human beings in extremely painful situations vacillate between hope and despair. Whoever harbors hope maintains a state of openness and resists being locked into the role of victim. Kant's question, "For what may we hope?" is especially pertinent in the context of trauma. Hope is a powerful motivating factor, moving us to reconstruct ourselves and the world in our imagination, in our behavior, and in our dreams. Traumatized individuals often hope to find a path back into life and to bind their fragmented selves into a meaningful whole, so that a modicum of order might be re-created out of their chaos. As a therapist, I am as familiar with hope as I am with doubt and insecurity. I am accustomed to tolerating uncertainty and bearing with the temporary blackness of the *nigredo*.

Analytical psychology's radical turn toward the inner life, the task of connecting with the numinous core of being and the archetype of meaning, requires a spiritual attitude, which is also manifested in openness to the penetration of the divine into the human sphere: *Vocatus atque non vocatus deus aderit*.[36] The myth created by Jung concerns the dialectical relationship between the human and the divine. Thus, it is ultimately a spiritual myth, which does not seek God outside the soul. Jung observes: "It was only quite late that we realized (or rather, are beginning to realize) that God is reality itself and therefore—last but not least—man. This realization is a millennial process."[37] I have often reflected on the ways in which this revolutionary insight into the intrapsychic origins of religious experience can be fruitfully applied to spiritual crises in trauma work.

The mystical core of Jung's psychology is apparent not just from his references to the works of Meister Eckhart and Jakob Böhme; he is thoroughly convinced that all mystical experiences have archetypal roots and that the goal of all spiritual striving is the relationship with the "eternal ground," where modern man "stands before the Nothing out of which All may grow."[38] Trauma can lead to a spiritual centering, a painful differentiation of the soul, which involves the expansion of the field of consciousness for the purpose of becoming the human being one is meant to be. Engaging in a search for wholeness amid the brokenness of a traumatic experience involves developing the capacity to live and to die. In this process, one gains self-knowledge and insight into the human spirit, into the essence and paradoxes of reality. In the last analysis, these spiritual insights facilitate not only individual survival but also our collective survival as a planet.

Taking as its point of departure the unity of the Self, Jungian psychology directs our attention beyond the dualistic worldview. It embraces interdependence and adopts a systemic perspective and is thus in a position to overcome the positivist paradigm and heal the split between matter and spirit, between humanity and God. As Dourley observes, "Jung, citing Archimedes, who discovered the laws of buoyancy, would strongly suggest God and humanity are in the same bathtub. A move by either affects the other."[39]

In Jung's valuing of *eros*, the relational function, I see a deeply spiritual component, which provides a role for the heart in therapy. When working with traumatized women, I have observed that the betrayal of Eros and his broken wings are continually present. What is needed, then, is a return of the divine feminine to heal the wounds of estrangement from self. Once again it is a question of bringing the fragments together and binding them into a whole. Trauma therapy challenges us in our full humanity; as the alchemical dictum says: *Ars requirit totum hominem* [art requires the whole person]. It is shaped by trust in the indwelling healer, faith in the soul's entelechy and self-regulation. Energies of spiritual transformation are activated through an alert attention to the telos of dreams when deciphering the imagistic speech of the soul. Faith in the process is needed to bear the tension of being stretched between the opposites, as well as a belief in the sacredness of the therapeutic encounter, the subtle energy field of the relationship. The delusion of being able to manage everything has to be let go and patience, the ability to wait and to yield, cultivated. As little as I can force the river's flow, so little can I hasten the psychic river of my patients.

In my practice, I often use parables from the Zen tradition to illustrate a theme, clarify a paradox, or bring in a meta-perspective. I find Buddhist insights very helpful. Psychoanalysts Gerald Weischede and Ralf Zwiebel speak of the balance we must cultivate in our work between knowing and not knowing, participatory observation and association and focusing, silence and speech, waiting and intervention.[40] I also cherish the Zen paradox of the "artless art" described in Eugen Herrigel's *Zen in the Art of Archery*, that is, the art of aiming at the target without thinking, of releasing the bow without intention.[41] Another paradox that I find useful is "Be spontaneous."[42] It resembles the paradox of "wanting not to want," or what Arnold Beisser calls "the paradoxical theory of change," which underlies all gestalt therapy, namely, that "change occurs when one becomes what he is, not when he tries to become what he is not."[43]

This mode of consciousness arises from an attitude which tries to let go of concepts, expectations, and judgments and to be as open and alert as possible and experience the moment directly, in other words, to be totally present. In the analytical psychology tradition, Lionel Corbett takes a similar position. He writes:

> This kind of work can never predict outcome, nor can it ever superimpose any kind of preexisting theoretical template such as a cognitive paradigm. Unless the therapist is open to the polymorphic appearances of the archetype, we do violence to the individual's soul. Notions of "management" or "treatment plans" are meaningless in this area, and tend to repeat the traumas of childhood.[44]

In this quasi-meditative state, everyday consciousness, with its focus on action and intervention, takes a backseat. Jung taught young therapists a similar lesson: "Learn the best, know the best—then, when you come to your patients, forget everything."[45]

Our challenge in trauma therapy, then, is to learn many things but throw them away at the appropriate time. We have to deal with the paradox of being goal-oriented in an unintentional way, of being suspended between the "beginner's mind" and the "expert's mind."[46]

NOTES

[1] Jung, *CW* 9ii, § 303.

[2] Harald Walach, *Spiritualität: Warum wir die Aufklärung weiterführen müssen* (Klein Jasedow: Drachen Verlag, 2011). See also Ken Wilber, *Integral Spirituality: A Startling New Role for Religion in the Modern and Postmodern World* (Boston: Integral Books, 2006), and Renaud van Quekelberghe, *Grundzüge der spirituellen Psychotherapie* (Eschborn: Verlag Dietmar Klotz, 2007).

[3] Van Quekelberghe, *Grundzüge*, p. 32.

[4] Donald Kalsched, *The Inner World of Trauma: Archetypal Defenses of the Personal Spirit* (London: Routledge, 1996), p. 143.

[5] Jung, *MDR*, p. 325.

[6] This conception is shared by Karlfried Graf Dürckheim, *The Way of Transformation: Daily Life as Spiritual Practice*, trans. P. L. Travers and Ruth Lewinnek, adapted by Ravi Ravindra and Priscilla Murray (Sandpoint, ID: Morning Light Press, 2007).

[7] Jung, *CW* 11, § 747.

[8] Jung, *CW* 11, § 600, note 13.

[9] Jung, *CW* 11, § 8.

[10] Karlfried Graf Dürckheim, *Our Two-fold Origin: As Promise, Experience and Mission*, trans. George Unwin (London: George Allen and Unwin, 1983).

[11] Jung's mandala *Window on Eternity* was drawn in 1927 from his own dream image.

[12] Matthias Horx, *Das Megatrend Prinzip: Wie die Welt von Morgen entsteht* (Munich: Deutsche Verlags-Anstalt, 2011).

[13] Paul M. Zulehner, *Christenmut: Geistliche Übungen* (Munich: Gütersloher Verlagshaus, 2010), p. 69.

[14] Paracelsus, *Selected Writings*, ed. Jolande Jacobi, trans. Norbert Guterman (Princeton, NJ: Princeton University Press, 1951).

[15] Viktor E. Frankl, *Man's Search for Ultimate Meaning* (Cambridge, MA: Perseus Publishing, 2000), p. 94.

[16] Jung, *CW* 9i, § 455.

[17] Jung, *RB*, p. 211.

[18] Jung, *MDR*, p. 326.

[19] Michael von Brück, "Spiritualität: personale oder transpersonale Entwicklung?" *Existenzanalyse* 28, no. 2 (2011): 8 [my translation].

[20] Harald Walach, "Bausteine für ein spiritulles Welt- und Menschenbild," *Transpersonale Psychologie und Psychotherapie* 7, no. 2 (2001): p. 63 [my translation].

[21] Hilarion G. Petzold, "Philosophie Clinique, Thérapeutique philosophique, Philopraxie," inaugural lecture on the appointment to professor of pastoral psychology at the St. Denis Institute, Paris, 1971.

[22] Martin Heidegger, *Being and Time*, trans. John Macquarrie and Edward Robinson (New York: Harper and Row, 1962), p. 247.

[23] Meister Eckhart, "Sermon 2," *The Complete Mystical Works of Meister Eckhart*, trans. M. O'Connell Walshe (New York: Crossroads Publishing, 2009).

[24] Teresa of Ávila, *The Interior Castle,* trans. Mirabai Starr (New York: Riverhead Books, 2003), p. 47.

[25] John of the Cross, *Dark Night of the Soul*, trans. Mirabai Starr (New York: Riverhead Books, 2002).

[26] Angelus Silesius, *The Wanderer: Epigrams of a European Mystic*, trans. Werner Pelz (Sheffield, UK: Cairns Publications, 2001).

[27] Johannes Tauler, *Sermons*, trans. Maria Shrady (Mahwah, NJ: Paulist Press, 1985).

[28] Jung, *CW* 16, § 99.

[29] Karlfried Graf Dürckheim, *Meditieren—wozu und wie: Die Wende zum Initiatischen* (Rütte: Johanna Nordländer Verlag, 2009), p. 98. See also Karlfried Graf Dürckheim, *The Way of Transformation*.

[30] Nelson Mandela, *Long Walk to Freedom: The Autobiography of Nelson Mandela* (Boston: Little Brown, 1994), p. 622.

[31] Hans-Peter Dürr, "The Living and the Nonliving: The Physical Basis of Life," *Electromagnetic Biology and Medicine* 24 (2005): 183. The Right Livelihood Award is often referred to as the Alternative Nobel Prize.

[32] Hans-Peter Dürr, "Inanimate and Animate Matter: Orderings of Immaterial Connectedness—The Physical Basis of Life," in *What Is Life?—Scientific Approaches and Philosophical Positions*, eds. Hans-Peter Dürr, Fritz-Albert Popp, and Wolfram Schommers (Hackensack, NJ: World Scientific Publishing, 2002), p. 153.

[33] Walach, *Spiritualität*. See also van Quekelberghe, *Grundzüge*; and Brewster Y. Beach, "God as Trauma" (talk given at the Fall Conference of Journey into Wholeness, Kanuga Conference Center, Henderson, NC, October 2002), accessed August 14, 2013, http://www.cgjungpage.org/index.php?option=com_content&task=view&id=602&Itemid=40.

[34] Jung, *CW* 12, § 6.

[35] Mandela, *Long Walk to Freedom,* p. 622.

[36] Jung carved this Latin inscription above the door of his house in Küsnacht, Switzerland. In English the inscription reads: *Called or not called, God will be there.*

[37] Jung, *CW* 11, § 631.

[38] Jung, *CW* 10, § 150.

[39] John P. Dourley, *On Behalf of the Mystical Fool: Jung on the Religious Situation* (Hove, UK: Routledge, 2010), p. 13.

[40] Gerald Weischede and Ralf Zwiebel, *Neurose und Erleuchtung: Anfängergeist in Zen und Psychoanalyse—Ein Dialog* (Stuttgart: Klett-Cotta Verlag, 2009).

[41] Eugen Herrigel, *Zen in the Art of Archery,* trans. R. F. C. Hull (New York: Vintage Books, 1999).

[42] Paul Watzlawick, *The Language of Change: Elements of Therapeutic Communication* (New York: W. W. Norton, 1993), p. 100.

[43] Arnold Beisser, "The Paradoxical Theory of Change," in *Gestalt Therapy Now: Theories, Techniques, Applications,* ed. Joen Fagan and Irma Lee Shepherd (New York: Harper and Row, 1971), p. 77.

[44] Lionel Corbett, *The Religious Function of the Psyche* (London: Routledge, 1996), p. 61.

[45] C. G. Jung, *C. G. Jung im Gespräch: Interviews, Reden, Begegnungen* (Einsiedeln: Daimon Verlag, 1986), p. 221.

[46] Shunryu Suzuki, *Zen Mind, Beginner's Mind* (Boston: Shambhala Publications, 2006).

CHAPTER THREE

TRAUMA AS A
CRISIS OF MEANING

Extreme trauma shatters our sense of identity and undermines any beliefs we may have about the meaning of our place in the cosmos. According to Jung, "meaninglessness inhibits fullness of life," whereas "meaning makes a great many things endurable—perhaps everything."[1] The analytic understanding of psychoneurosis is that it involves the suffering of a soul bereft of meaning.[2] Jung claimed that about a third of his patients suffered not from a clinically identifiable neurosis but from a lack or loss of meaning in their lives. Trauma therapy needs to address this existential issue. For as human beings we are, in Maurice Merleau-Ponty's words, "condemned to meaning."[3] Trauma therapy must take seriously the necessity of helping the traumatized individual to find a meaning that will enable him or her to go on living. Jung's comment at the end of his life states it well:

> The world into which we are born is brutal and cruel, and at the same time of divine beauty. Which element we think outweighs the other, whether meaninglessness or meaning, is a matter of temperament. . . . Probably, as in all metaphysical

questions, both are true: life is—or has—meaning and meaninglessness. I cherish the anxious hope that meaning will preponderate and win the battle.[4]

Between Meaning and Meaninglessness

When the universe of meaning is broken apart by trauma, the trustworthiness of the self and the world is damaged or destroyed. This experience forces us to acknowledge the illusory character of our assumptions about self, the world, and our God-image; it empowers us to know reality for what it is, and thus to free ourselves from anthropomorphic images of the divine. Every search for meaning, every moment of despair over meaninglessness, affects our spiritual understanding of the world and ourselves.

When the trauma of violence overruns the ego's defenses, we experience a deadening of the senses and a consequent inability to perceive any kind of meaning in our existence. For meaning is perceived through our body; it is mediated by our senses. Torture, genocide, and mass rape force us to form a trauma paradigm that is no longer centered on drives and conflicts but on the existential loss of meaning and value. Therapy must include processes that help trauma victims relocate themselves in the midst of the complexity, confusion, and absurdity of their traumatic experiences and transcend their temporary incapacity for apprehending meaning.

As a general matter, the world is becoming increasingly more complex and less transparent at an accelerating pace. As we seek to come to grips with a rapidly changing world, we need to orient ourselves within its complex, nonlinear systemic interconnections and to identify basic patterns that will enable us to keep up with the flow of life. We must also develop a tolerance for uncertainty such that we do not become overwhelmed by anxiety when confronted with not knowing.

Together with Jürg Zöbeli, I have occupied myself intensely with the question of meaning in psychotherapy. Our book, *Hunger nach Sinn* [*Craving for Meaning*], attempts to explore boundary experiences in depth, using the search for meaning and the dialectic between finding and creating meaning as guiding motifs.[5] The connotations of the German word *Sinn* (meaning) suggest a dynamic process in which meaning is perceived through the senses (*Sinnen*) on an ongoing basis.

Meaning is thus associated with striving; it provides orientation and affects our self-understanding as applied to our life as a whole. For this reason, our lives cannot have just one meaning, forever set in stone. Rather, meaning is always "on the way," a phenomenon that makes for a highly diverse range of meaning possibilities over a lifetime. Just as the soul is *naturaliter religiosa*, so, I believe, the yearning for meaning is inherent in human nature, an a priori. It is an existential matter, a creative striving to achieve wholeness.

Insofar as meaning involves transcendence, it constitutes an inscrutable secret, which can only be adumbrated using symbols, paradoxes, myth, and art. This raises the question of what the ultimate ground of being is. As Lao-tzu taught, true meaning (*Sinn*) cannot be thought (*ersinnt*), otherwise it would not be true meaning. Dürckheim writes of an encounter he had in Tokyo with a Japanese practitioner of Zen Buddhism. After the latter had stared for a long time, with evident fascination, at a painting of a Bohemian landscape by Caspar David Friedrich, which hung over Dürckheim's desk, he asked the surprising question: "Was he *through*?" Dürckheim asked what he meant by "through" and received a three-part question in response: "Was he still afraid of death? Did he see the meaning even in meaninglessness? Was he standing in the sign of universal love?"[6] The questions of the Japanese Zen Buddhist regarding a painting that for him apparently was of great transparency and gripping power of expression suggests an attitude on his part that we would connect with wisdom, with the ability to bear the paradoxes of life, to overcome the fear of death, and to meet the meaninglessness of life with love.

Blows of fate and the encounter with death summon up a struggle with the secret of suffering and its conquest. In this context, questions arise about identity. Trauma survivors ask: Who am I, when I am nothing any more? What is my purpose? What wants to be brought into the world through me, now that I have experienced trauma and, miraculously, survived? They are challenged, inescapably, to understand "the meaning of the numina that cross our path."[7]

For those of us in the practice of healing-oriented psychotherapy, these shattering, disruptive afflictions demand that we wrestle for meaning in non-meaning, and yet the boundaries of our own self-understanding are challenged and our hapless efforts at a metaphysical interpretation of suffering come to naught. We must, then, be able to

endure it when our personal belief in transformative healing crashes
into the gates of the underworld, coming up against boundaries that
defy crossing. The fruitlessness of such questioning is conveyed elegantly
in folk sayings. I remember seeing the following inscription on the wall
of a house in the Junkergasse in Bern, Switzerland:

> Life combines the sound of bells
> For baptisms, weddings, funerals.
> You ask: Whence, whither, why?
> There's no reply.[8]

"Baptisms, weddings, funerals" point to milestones on the path of life,
situations of joy or grief that compel us to look back and look ahead.
They have a place of honor in every culture and are celebrated with
rites of passage. These are nodal points of transformation—miniature
versions of the passing away of the old and the coming into existence
of the new, expressing the theme of "dying and becoming," letting
go and beginning afresh; they signify the dialectical process of life,
growth, and death.

Crises are unavoidable accompaniments to the processes of life and
of individual and collective evolution. They enable us to unfold and
develop our inherent potential. For example, in the third hexagram
of the *I Ching* [*The Book of Changes*], "Difficulty at the Beginning,"
this principle is represented by the image of a blade of grass, which
pushes up with effort through the hard earth, overcoming obstacles
to reach the sunlight.[9] This Chinese pictogram symbolizes the
difficult climb to a higher stage of development, the evolutionary process
as driven by adversity. Growth and maturation are always associated
with growing pains.

I have met many traumatized individuals whose sustaining values
and unconscious foundational convictions were destroyed in powerful
ways. They had lost their conviction that the world is basically good,
meaningful, and predictable and that they themselves are valuable
and worthy of love. For such individuals, the overriding questions
are: What possibilities for meaning still exist for me? How can I
commit again to life, after being rejected from life and degraded to
nothing? Trauma therapy involves a recommitment to life, a probe
into the darkness, lighting a "futile" flame, trying once again if

possible to open a connection to the original ground of being. When traumatic eruptions carry us away from the course of our life and we cannot locate ourselves as we used to, then, as we try to find a new orientation to the essential, a sense of life's deeper dimensions may appear, that even in the most destabilizing crisis, creative forces are still active in the unconscious.

In wartime Bosnia, I talked with leg-amputated soldiers in a hospital in Sarajevo and met with children and teachers in schoolhouses perforated by grenades. I also spent supervision hours with therapists in Zenica who were working with mass-raped women. Those experiences taught me a lot about the capacity for self-transcending growth in times of extremity. They showed me especially the human capacity to stand up to the circumstances of war through self-distancing and humor. Telling jokes in times of war and oppression relativizes the nightmare that has been experienced. This practice gives substance to the idea that "humor carries a breath of transcendence," as my Zen teacher would say. Albert Camus was right when he wrote, at the end of his novel *The Plague*, "what we learn in time of pestilence [is] that there are more things to admire in men than to despise."[10]

When entering the catacombs of death and the dungeons of speechlessness, I need to maintain confidence that, even in the darkest shadow of abysmally deep despair, there is the possibility that light can shine out. So I maintain a respectful relationship to the dialectic of being and becoming. It is necessary to accept what cannot be changed, taking it as it is, while plumbing it for its transformative possibilities. In therapeutic work, I regard spirituality as a gold mine. A respectful spiritual attitude helps the helpless to hold on. We do not have to be stripped of our understanding by looking inhumanity in the eye; we do not have to become inhuman ourselves or be terrified to death by the madness of trauma.

Spiritual approaches are relevant not only in trauma therapy and consciousness research, but also in the context of Martin Seligman's positive psychology, in the concept of *salutogenesis* (a term coined by Aaron Antonovsky to designate the creation of health and well-being), in resource research, in attachment theory, and in stress-reduction research. Empirical inquiries by psychotherapists that bring spiritual perspectives into the therapeutic process have made it clear that connection to a larger, more embracing whole, looking beyond existential limitations, can provide inner comfort and support and increase the capacity for "containment."[11]

Betwixt and Between: Trauma and Liminality

Trauma locates the individual in the realm of liminality. The Latin word *limen* signifies a boundary, a threshold, a frontier, or an entrance. The threshold between two different modes of existence can be a highly transformative space. Threshold situations challenge the individual to reestablish his or her identity, since familiar truths no longer apply. Here, where the old order has collapsed and the experience bears the stamp of real or symbolic death, one must make the crossing into a new space, where new structures and meaning must be invented.

Based on Mircea Eliade's distinction between the sacred and the profane, anthropologist Victor Turner developed the notion of "liminal space" as a boundary, a space of transformation, whose atmosphere is characterized by ambiguity and ambivalence.[12] It is a paradoxical space, sometimes experienced as a void pregnant with meaning, sometimes as an unbearable state of suspension. The ancient Greeks associated this ambiguous space with the shape-shifting Hermes, god of boundaries, invisibility, crossings, and transitions, the soul's guide to the underworld, familiar with the realms of both light and shadow. The symbolism of the boundary (simultaneously rigid and permeable) is central to understanding liminal states. On one hand, boundaries are an ordering principle of reality: they provide protection, create identity, and guarantee security. On the other hand, they have a destructive aspect: when violated, they can lead to fragmentation, collapse, rupture, psychosis, and borderline conditions.

As a boundary, liminal space is a zone of transition, in which one has the experience of being outside of physical space and chronological time. Liminal space is located at the boundary between order and chaos, where one is in a state of extreme openness and vulnerability. Liminality is thus intimately associated with the archetypal realm, where a confrontation with the collective unconscious and its ineffable nature is experienced as a *mysterium tremendum* or as a life-sustaining encounter that helps us overcome even the most traumatic disruptions. It is an alluring state, highly charged with transformational opportunities and energy for re-creation and re-configuration.

The ability to enter into this unpredictable, mysterious no-man's-land is often brought to the surface by trauma, near-death experiences, or creative illnesses. Near-death experiences and extreme traumatizations lead to experiences in which the "skin-encapsulated ego" is dissolved: survivors leave their bodies, and an observing ego—as in meditative and spiritual trance states—becomes a kind of witness. Perhaps this is the key to understanding the dissociative effects that can result from traumatic experiences. Traumatized individuals often move back and forth across the boundary between the physical, material world and the immaterial world of consciousness. Through this experience of boundary crossing, they may experience themselves as undergoing a transformation, having been compelled to enter the underworld and submit to its power, without any assurance that they will be able to climb out of it again into the world of everyday reality.

Turner describes the liminal state as a state at the margin, "betwixt and between," in which one is bereft of familiar structures. Similarly, people who are displaced or tortured undergo an initiation into the unknown; deprived of status, property, and a homeland, they feel invisible and are often removed from any human support system whatsoever. They are cast into a state of disorientation and ambiguity, a state often riddled with paradoxes, as Turner pointed out, where space and time no longer mean anything. Liminality is full of agony, desperation, and confusion. As an analyst, I have to endure with my patients the rigors of this transitional space, this in-between realm, where one no longer is what one used to be and not yet what one might become.

I conceive of traumatic states as sojourns in liminality, on the threshold between the real and the unreal, between the land of the living and the netherworld, between the material and the spiritual. Some of my traumatized patients feel like wayfarers, moving through different realms, wandering about in a twilight zone, feeling strangely familiar with the underworld into which they were thrust by trauma and yet also belonging to the reality of the upper world. The sojourn in liminality can prepare the way for synchronistic and paranormal experiences in the psychoid realm of the psyche. Sometimes the psychic wounds become a gateway to an expanded form of consciousness that connects us with our primordial roots. Jerome Bernstein, in his book

Living in the Borderland, writes about nonpathological borderland experiences of heightened sensitivity and apperception of nonrational reality.[13] He claims that individuals who have a deep understanding of archetypal dynamics and an intimate familiarity with the collective unconscious are often considered mad. Because of our cultural biases, we dismiss their visions and experiences as psychopathology. They themselves, however, experience their borderland reality as sacred.

In this state, traumatized patients may appear as though their soul has fled their body. But according to the ancient wisdom of various traditions, the soul cannot return to the spirit world if the physical body is not actually dead; consequently, the soul of a trauma victim is trapped in a sort of limbo, betwixt and between. Retrieving the soul from this limbo becomes the task of the shaman—or the analyst. In analysis, we work on making the body a safe place again so that the soul can return without danger.

Trauma victims hesitate to step over the threshold without a reliable compass of values to help them navigate the uncharted territory that awaits them. Pain and sorrow prevail, as does an overwhelming desire to die. Yet there is also a faint hope for a life not yet lived, a tentative envisioning of a new path. Often, I observe an oscillation between falling apart and gathering the pieces together again, between fragmentation and individuation, and a desperate attempt to bring the pieces "home" and regain a sense of meaning. In these liminal states, something cracks open and archetypal energy floods the empty space, often with an intensely numinous power, since the ego has been annulled by the trauma.

Poets Paul Celan and Nelly Sachs

Jewish lyric poet Paul Celan lived a life of deadly contradictions, and this experience brought forth poetry that speaks of the mystery of life and death. Coming out of traumatic persecution and broken relationships, seared by pain and melancholy, living in darkness, always close to death, this poet of trauma created possibilities of existence through his writing.

Like many of his fellow Jewish poets, Celan suffered the trauma of exile. He was born in 1920 in the city of Czernowitz in the Bukowina region (present-day Ukraine). Under occupation, first by the Soviet Union (1940) and then by Romanian and German troops (1941), he was banished to the city's ghetto. He was deeply shaken by the deportation and murder of his parents. In 1948, after forced hard labor in Romanian work camps, he went into exile in Paris. A part of his soul remained forever exiled, split off from the rest of his personality. He mourned endlessly for his losses: loss of family and friends, loss of home and safety. Above all he mourned the loss of what it means to be human, the loss of innocence.

In Celan I see a wayfarer between two worlds, forever a stranger in both. He is a pilgrim of transitional space, moving between life and death, past and future, marked by hope as the one possible answer to the *conditio inhumana*. His poems bear witness to the transformative power of the zone between life and death, but also to its destructive aspects. His life was often lived under pressure of pursuit, going from one place to another. His poetic art was a journey through liminal spaces, crossing thresholds and moving beyond the conventional boundaries of language, as he sought healing from his deep encounter with the suffering of fallen humanity.

To me the concept of liminality seems especially relevant for poets of trauma. Since Celan's poems move in liminal space and time, his metaphorical language is the creative language of the wayfarer, forever stepping over thresholds. He evokes our imaginative powers, which enable us to follow him into new modes of thought and being. The metaphors of his verse conjure that imaginal realm that Henry Corbin called *mundus imaginalis*: a world of noetic value that permits all universes to exist in a symbolic relationship with one another.[14]

Celan always felt himself to be an outsider, a stranger dwelling on the margins, in a "betwixt-and-between" state. This state of groundlessness found striking expression in his comment (made in his acceptance speech in Darmstadt on receiving the Georg Büchner Prize in 1960) in regard to Büchner's fictional character, Lenz, who complained of being bothered by the fact that he could not walk on his head. Celan's comment was: "A man who walks on his head . . . sees the sky below, as an abyss [*Abgrund*]."[15] Just before making this comment, he spoke of locating "the strangeness, the place where the person [Lenz] was able to set himself free as an—estranged— I."[16] He went on to suggest that "the strange, the abyss *and* Medusa's head . . . all seem to lie in the same direction," and that "along with the I, estranged and freed *here, in this manner*, some other thing is also set free."[17] However, the freeing aspect of this liminal abyss has its opposite pole: collapse, rupture, destruction, and death. The polarity of this archetype is painfully evident when we work with addicts, the psychotic, or those suffering from a borderline disorder. Paul Celan's traumatic end, suicide by drowning in the Seine, a no-man's-land of the Styx, is also a witness to the dangerous aspect of the estrangement that comes from being led by Hermes through the land of betwixt and between.

When I read Gabriel Marcel's *Tragic Wisdom and Beyond*, which describes the radical insecurity enveloping humanity today, the triumph of evil, death, and despair, I thought of Celan as a *homo viator*, a man of tragic wisdom, "making his way along that very narrow path which runs along a high and dangerous mountain ridge."[18] This path also reminds me of the prologue to Liber Primus of Jung's Red Book, entitled: "Der Weg des Kommenden" ("The Way of What Is to Come"). The Red Book is the testimony of a *homo viator*, or "wayfaring man," a person wandering through different realities, going to great lengths to waken the dead, just as Celan did.[19] I understand the Red Book as an account of a pilgrimage, a transformational journey of reconnection with the soul, meeting with the Spirit of the Depths in liminal space. I believe that writing the Red Book was Jung's survival strategy, a process of making meaning, in the same way that poetry was for Paul Celan and for fellow poet Nelly Sachs. The act of writing saved each of them from suffocating in the boundless abyss, although it did not ultimately save Celan's life.

Nelly Sachs is another poet who endured boundary conditions in the life of the soul and yet believed in growth and maturation. In a letter to Celan, she wrote:

> There is and was in me, and it's there with every breath I draw, the belief in transcendence through suffusion with pain, in the inspiritment of dust, as a vocation to which we are called. I believe in an invisible universe in which we mark out our dark accomplishment. I feel the energy of the light that makes the stone break into music, and I suffer from the arrow-tip of longing that pierces us to death from the very beginning and pushes us to go searching beyond, where the wash of uncertainty begins.[20]

I see in Nelly Sachs the archetypal traces of Hecate, a goddess of dual nature like Hermes.[21] Hecate is responsible for illness, madness, and nightmares but is also the protector of the threshold; she guards the entrance to Hades, gives humans the gift of visions, and serves as midwife for new life. She was described in Orphic hymns as the "Three-Faced One" who binds together and makes whole that which is fragmented. Hecate presides over life and death, and as a death goddess, she is also a soul guide who initiates humans into the realm of the transpersonal and the transcendent. This resonates with the poetry of Nelly Sachs.

As Sachs grew older, she suffered increasingly from paranoid anxieties and had to be committed repeatedly to a psychiatric clinic for treatment of her delusions of persecution. Perhaps we could say that she had frequent visits from Hecate in her liminal aspect. She repeatedly lost the balance between maintaining ego boundaries and opening herself trustingly to the world and would thus fall into an anxious, paranoid, depressed withdrawal. Sachs surrendered herself to these states of being suspended in liminal space, and yet she did not give up hope or faith and kept on writing, even in the darkest times. I am reminded of the book of Job:

> For there is hope for a tree,
>> if it be cut down, that it will sprout again,
>> and that its shoots will not cease. (Job 14:7)

As the experiences of Jung, Celan, and Sachs demonstrate, liminality is pregnant with potentiality, for this zone between life and death holds the mystery of growth. In it, the petrified soul can de-petrify, and one can begin to explore who one is, was, and will be. Liminal experiences can precipitate a development of consciousness, in which the relativity of the small ego becomes apparent and the door to another dimension is thrown open.

The Emergence of Meaning Following Trauma

When a person's fundamental strengths and basic assumptions are shaken to the core, the capacity for emotional regulation is called into play. Then, to integrate the seismic event into the fabric of life, an intensive working-through is needed, a *ruminatio*, which includes a reappraisal of the situation, an act of cognitive-emotional adaptation, and the assignment of meaning to the event. This complete reorganization of the individual's conceptual system is comparable to a paradigm shift or to a pattern of rupture and repair. One must allow the enormity of this rupture in the ethical system to become conscious in order to understand what requires healing.

Torture and concentration camps lead us to the very edge of the world, where the human being "stands before the Nothing out of which all may grow."[22] I have often asked myself how human consciousness makes sense of this experience of the void, and how I as an analyst can respond to the agony of meaninglessness. The alchemical images of *nigredo* and *mortificatio* aid me in understanding the descent into darkness of unmeaning. Thomas Moore writes:

> This mortification, the feeling of being overwhelmed and torn apart, prepares you for new ideas and a fresh start. You can't be renewed unless past behavior and thinking are shredded and packed away. But this can't happen without torment.[23]

The alchemical stage of *nigredo* (blackness) involves the death of the old in preparation for the birth of the new. This state of blackness is marked by dismemberment, *mortificatio*, the death and annihilation of the ego, and *putrefactio* (rotting). In the trauma context, these phenomena take the form of psychic fragmentation, dissociation, depression, a blocked libido, and "disunion with oneself."[24] Jung understood this *nigredo* as an "affliction of the soul."[25] Something is being killed and dissolved in order that it might be reborn in a new form, in order that new meaning might emerge. In my practice, I encounter this *nigredo* as the "complete stagnation of psychic life," as total confusion, imbalance, and wretchedness.[26]

From the disorientation that accompanies the loss of meaning and value and from the confrontation with darkness and evil, a new conscious stance emerges, a changed attitude, the *albedo*. In this stage, the soul is challenged to transform itself, to bring about an *enantiodromia*. In analysis, when situations arise involving loss of hope, lack of orientation, and crisis of meaning, those are exactly the times when paradigm shifts can occur. In the next phase, the *rubedo*, when possibility becomes reality and takes on form, the integration of the trauma becomes the focus. The broken bridge from ego to Self can now be repaired, and a transpersonal experience of soul recovery occurs, in which all the opposites are united.

In the *nigredo, mortificatio,* and *putrefactio* of the concentration camps, ethics was turned on its head: what used to be good was now bad; conscience was undermined and the image of humanity perverted. In the words of Primo Levi: "It is man who kills, man who creates or suffers injustice; it is no longer man who, having lost all restraint, shares his bed with a corpse."[27] A poem by the Peruvian poet Juan Gonzalo Rose neatly expresses this reversal of values, this upending of the ethical order:

> The Question (La Pregunta)
>
> My mother told me:
> if you stone the white fledglings,
> God will punish you;
> if you hit your friend,
> the boy with the donkey face,
> God will punish you.
>
> It was God's sign
> of the two sticks;
> and the commandments of God
> fitted into my hands
> like ten more fingers.
>
> Today they tell me:
> If you do not love war,
> if you do not kill a dove a day,
> God will punish you;
> if you do not strike the black,
> if you do not hate the Amerindian,
> God will punish you;
> if you give the poor ideas
> instead of a kiss,
> if you talk to them of justice
> instead of charity,
> God will punish you,
> God will punish you.
>
> Mama, is that really
> Our God?[28]

In the concentration camps, selected inmates were stamped as destined for the crematoria. Nevertheless, even in such hopeless circumstances, which seemed to negate the possibility of finding meaning, many of them were ready to look for it. Primo Levi was convinced that the belief that life has meaning is rooted in every fiber of our being, as an inextinguishable part of human nature. But under conditions of severe trauma, he felt, life derived its meaning not from anything grand or metaphysical but simply from feeling the warmth of the sun and seeing the sky once again, from being alive for one more spring. In extreme adversity, meaning can be found in sharing one's last piece of bread, in hearing the first blackbird sing, in feeling the spring air after the rattling cold of winter.

Holocaust survivor Victor Frankl bore witness to the transformative power that a meaning-oriented philosophy had in his life during the three years he spent in various concentration camps.[29] He used the term *logotherapy* to designate his meaning-centered method of doing therapy, a method based on the concept of "the will to meaning," by which he meant the primal human drive to find meaning, to make the incomprehensible comprehensible and restore coherence. His message was: "Say yes to life in spite of everything." He believed that meaning could be found even in suffering and that the central human values consist in a freely chosen attitude toward what cannot be changed. He wrote: "When a man finds that it is his destiny to suffer, he will have to accept his suffering as his task; . . . his unique opportunity lies in the way in which he bears his burden."[30]

Not all Holocaust survivors share this meaning-centered perspective, however. Elie Wiesel has asserted that no answer can be given to the "why" of Auschwitz. He wrote: "Auschwitz signifies . . . the defeat of the intellect that wants to find a Meaning—with a capital M—in history."[31] In a similar vein, Theodor Adorno declared:

> It is . . . impossible, I would say, to insist after Auschwitz on the presence of a positive meaning or purpose in being. . . . To assert that existence or being has a positive meaning constituted within itself and orientated towards the divine principle . . . would be . . . a pure mockery in face of the victims and the infinitude of their torment.[32]

And yet, although Wiesel says one must learn to be silent about Auschwitz, because it eludes all attempts to put it into words, he writes again and again about his experiences in concentration camps. I see in this narrative compulsion an effort to find forms of symbolization that can serve as a mode of healing and working through. Along similar lines, Primo Levi described his drive to write as a search for a narrative identity in the belief that he could heal himself through storytelling. When writing, he felt at peace, as if he was a person again.[33]

Only when we are able to understand life and develop a healing fiction can we endure life's tribulations. Traumatic experiences hold up a mirror before us, showing us the reality of human existence and its potential for good and evil. From this often arises a new orientation to meaning and values despite all the tragedy. In an afterword to his book about his Holocaust experiences, *The Reawakening*, Primo Levi wrote: "if I had not lived the Auschwitz experience, I probably would never have written anything," and further on: "in its totality, this past has made me richer and surer."[34]

Through my experience with people who have consciously chosen to bear witness to what was and what can be, I have learned that what is important is not to remain stuck in the past but to pay attention to the power of human creativity and with this in mind to work with others to make the world a better place. A deepening of spiritual insights, a valuing of life, and a caring for creation—these are part of what is involved in the emergence of meaning after serious trauma.

NOTES

[1] Jung, *MDR*, p. 340.

[2] Jung, *CW* 11, § 497.

[3] Maurice Merleau-Ponty, *Phenomenology of Perception*, trans. Colin Smith (London: Routledge Classics, [1958] 2002), p. xxii.

[4] Jung, *MDR*, pp. 358–359.

[5] Ursula Wirtz and Jürg Zöbeli, *Hunger nach Sinn: Menschen in Grenzsituationen—Grenzen der Psychotherapie* (Stuttgart: Kreuz Verlag, 1995).

[6] Karlfried Graf Dürckheim, *Vom doppelten Ursprung des Menschen* (Freiburg: Herder, 1973), p. 87 [my translation].

[7] Jung, *CW* 11, § 746.

[8] "Aus Tauf- Hochzeits- und Grabgeläut / Mischt sich der Klang des Lebens. / Woher, wohin, wozu? / Du fragst vergebens" [my translation].

⁹ *I Ching*, or *The Book of Changes*, trans. Richard Wilhelm, rendered into English by Cary F. Baynes (Princeton, NJ: Princeton University Press, 1950/1967/1977), p. 16.

¹⁰ Albert Camus, *The Plague*, trans. Stuart Gilbert (New York: Vintage Books, [1975] 1991), p. 308.

¹¹ Liane Iris Hoffmann, "Spiritualität und Religiosität in der psychotherapeutischen Praxis. Eine bundesweite Befragung von psychologischen Psychotherapeuten" (PhD diss., The Carl von Ossietzky University of Oldenburg, Oldenburg, Germany, 2009), accessed August 15, 2013, http://oops.uni-oldenburg.de/909/1/hofspi09.pdf. See also: Ulrike Hundt, *Spirituelle Wirkprinzipien in der Psychotherapie: Eine qualitative Studie zur Arbeitsweise ganzheitlicher Psychotherapeuten* (Münster: LIT Verlag, 2007).

¹² Victor Turner, *The Ritual Process: Structure and Anti-Structure* (Chicago: Aldine Publishing, 1969); *Dramas, Fields, and Metaphors: Symbolic Action in Human Society* (Ithaca, NY: Cornell University, 1974).

¹³ Jerome Bernstein, *Living in the Borderland: The Evolution of Consciousness and the Challenge of Healing Trauma* (London: Routledge, 2005).

¹⁴ Henry Corbin, "*Mundus Imaginalis*, or, the Imaginary and the Imaginal," trans. Ruth Horine, in *Working with Images: The Theoretical Base of Archetypal Psychology*, ed. Benjamin Sells (Woodstock, CT: Spring Publications, 2000), pp. 71–89.

¹⁵ Paul Celan, *Collected Prose*, trans. Rosemarie Waldrop (New York: Routledge, 2003), p. 46.

¹⁶ *Ibid.*

¹⁷ *Ibid.*, p. 47 (italics in original).

¹⁸ Gabriel Marcel, *Tragic Wisdom and Beyond*, trans. Stephen Jolin and Peter McCormick (Evanston, IL: Northwestern University Press, 1973), p. 143.

¹⁹ Lance S. Owens, "Jung and *Aion*: Time, Vision, and a Wayfaring Man," *Psychological Perspectives* 54, no. 3 (2011): 253–289.

²⁰ Paul Celan and Nelly Sachs, *Correspondence*, ed. Barbara Wiedemann, trans. Christopher Clark (Riverdale-on-Hudson, NY: Sheep Meadow Press, 1995), pp. 5–6.

²¹ See the excellent essay by Velimir B. Popovič, "Hekate, or, On Being Trivial in Psychotherapy," in *Archetypal Psychologies: Reflections*

in Honor of James Hillman, ed. Stanton Marlan (New Orleans: Spring Journal Books, 2008), pp. 369–395.

[22] Jung, *CW* 10, § 150.

[23] Thomas Moore, *Dark Nights of the Soul: A Guide to Finding Your Way through Life's Ordeals* (New York: Gotham Books, 2004), p. 77.

[24] Jung, *CW* 8, § 61.

[25] Jung, *CW* 14 §§ 351, 493.

[26] Jung, *CW* 16, § 469; Jung, *CW* 14, § 306.

[27] Primo Levi, *Survival in Auschwitz: The Nazi Assault on Humanity*, trans. Stuart Woolf (New York: Simon and Schuster, 1986), p. 171.

[28] Quoted in Gustavo Gutiérrez, *On Job: God-Talk and the Suffering of the Innocent*, trans. Matthew J. O'Connell (Maryknoll, NY: Orbis Books, 1987), p. vii.

[29] Viktor E. Frankl, *Man's Search for Meaning: An Introduction to Logotherapy*, trans. Ilse Lasch (New York: Pocket Books, 1984).

[30] *Ibid.*, p. 99.

[31] Elie Wiesel, *Legends of Our Time* (New York: Schocken Books, 1968), p. 183.

[32] Theodor W. Adorno, *Metaphysics: Concepts and Problems*, trans. Edmund Jephcott (Stanford, CA: Stanford University Press, 2001), pp. 101–102.

[33] Primo Levi, *The Periodic Table*, trans. Raymond Rosenthal (New York: Schocken Books, 1984), p. 151.

[34] Primo Levi, *The Reawakening*, trans. Stuart Woolf (New York: Simon and Schuster, 1965), p. 230.

CHAPTER FOUR

THE TRANSFORMATIVE POWER OF SUFFERING

T he current scientific interest in positive psychotraumatology
is by no means intended to diminish the importance of trauma
or to minimize the suffering that accompanies its painful
reality. Nor does it seek to cast doubt on trauma's potential to cause
severe disruptions in the individual's sense of identity. Rather, it
provides a theoretical framework by which we might gain a better
understanding of the processes of traumatization, despair, and growth
and a more holistic perspective on traumatic experiences. Its scope
encompasses the paradoxical nature of human life in its entirety,
especially the paradox that gain may even occur through loss. People
affected by trauma-generated suffering are forced into the extremes of
polarized thinking and initiated into a state of unresolved paradox as
new ways of being are revealed from the realm of wisdom. In states of
traumatic distress, the persona is stripped away like a husk, or, in the
language of the spiritual traditions, a shedding of self, not gradual but
sudden, takes place, leading to a transformed engagement with life.
The suffering associated with extreme trauma thrusts the individual
abruptly into an awareness of life's transience and dissolves the rigid
boundaries between self and other. This can lead either to a dangerous

psychotic breakdown or conversely to a deeper consciousness of the interconnectedness of all things.

The Paradigm of Posttraumatic Growth

Pioneering research spearheaded by Tedeschi and Calhoun has uncovered processes of radical transformation following traumatic disturbances.[1] These findings represent a positive turn in hitherto deficit-oriented trauma research. They support a new trauma paradigm, known as "posttraumatic growth" (PTG), a concept entailing more than just coping, resilience, and hardiness. In this paradigm, transforming suffering is a profoundly subjective task: it challenges the innermost core of the sufferer's humanity.

In the recent research into posttraumatic growth, I see a reversion to the archetypal functions of trauma, namely, both destruction and also transformation and renewal. In this tradition, various terms have been applied to psychic states with the potential for growth that may arise in diverse contexts. Dabrowski calls such states *positive disintegration*, signifying symptoms of an expanding consciousness.[2] Ellenberger designates them as a *creative illness*, and Eliade speaks of them as an *illness of shamanic initiation*.[3] They have also been called *metanoia* (change of mind), a Greek term appropriated by Jung and R. D. Laing to denote a process of productive self-healing and an attempt at self-repair, even in psychotic episodes. Transformational crises that lead to a new orientation and to greater stability have also been described as "super-healing" (*PlusHeilung*).[4] These varying conceptions make it clear that we are dealing with an archetypal idea, namely, that we can grow through our encounters with resistance and limitations. Like trees growing around obstacles, we can circumvent or surmount the psychic barriers posed by traumatic events, thanks to our archetypal survival skills.

Transformational changes after trauma and the experience of stress-related growth to a level beyond former functioning have been described in recent years in the context of bereavement, cancer, rape, childhood abuse, and war traumas. It must be remembered, however, that what fosters growth is not the traumatic experience as such, but the struggle with it. As described by Tedeschi and Calhoun in their model for personal growth resulting from trauma, the process of coping with the event is the actual catalyst for personal growth.[5]

Posttraumatic growth or posttraumatic maturation can best be observed in three dimensions: (1) self-image and self-perception, (2) relationship with others, and (3) the philosophical framework and spiritual convictions that govern the trauma victim's life. Questionnaires—for example, the Posttraumatic Growth Inventory— have been designed at institutions researching severely traumatized individuals specifically to measure empirically five aspects of personal maturation after traumatic experiences:

1. relating to others: a sense of increased compassion, closeness, and understanding of others;
2. new possibilities: the development of new interests and a perception of new opportunities that were not available prior to the traumatic event;
3. personal strength: feeling more vulnerable, yet stronger for having encountered the traumatic event, and a sense of increased self-efficacy or self-reliance;
4. spiritual change: increased understanding of spiritual matters and/or stronger religious beliefs following the traumatic event; and
5. appreciation of life: a greater appreciation of one's life and a new sense of priorities about what is important.[6]

In the war-wasted former Yugoslavia, I admired especially the Bosnians' sense of humor, which they used effectively to ridicule the madness of the war and what it did to the survivors. In such humor one sees the capacity for distancing oneself and for discovering new creative possibilities for dealing with the absurdities of traumatic events. It reminds me of a remark that Etty Hillesum made in her diary following a description of the hellish "wailing and howling" all around her in one of the Nazi concentration camps she was in. She wrote: "And yet now and then that bright and bubbling good humor of mine rises to the surface again, it never really leaves me."[7] In my view, the contrasting negative focus of traditional trauma research is a cul-de-sac, the one-sidedness of which is an inadequate response to the complexity of psychic processes, which eliminates the role of philosophical and spiritual traditions in coming to terms with the existential questions of suffering and evil. I therefore consider the new paradigm to be a welcome compensation, despite the highly disunited focus of the empirical research.

As early as 1992, Ronnie Janoff-Bulman described the "shattered assumptions" of victims of trauma, at the same time drawing attention to the beneficial changes they experienced.[8] By becoming conscious of their vulnerabilities, they expanded their personal competencies. Many survivors developed greater self-confidence as a consequence of tapping into the strength of their will to survive and by making a more realistic assessment of the relative safety and danger of the world. Through their creative encounters with adverse life circumstances, many increased in maturity.

And yet, critical voices warn of the illusory, defensive character of the concept of posttraumatic growth (PTG). In a provocative essay, David Becker cautions against putting one's faith in what he views as the one-sided, naïve, linear "growth" perspective.[9] He speaks sarcastically of "growth prophets and resource fanatics" and their failure to recognize suffering and the enormity of destruction. He goes so far as to identify their so-called wise thoughts as agents of symbolic violence, ideological tools for reinforcing the dominant structures through a "conspiracy of silence."[10] In the concept of PTG he sees only a countertransference reaction in the face of unbearably intense suffering, whose purpose is to help victims to endure their impotence and helplessness.

I do not share this extreme view but see the process of critical consciousness building as entirely consistent with posttraumatic growth processes and the salutogenic perspective. Integrative gestalt therapist Hilarion Petzold, in his writings on potential-oriented thinking, uses a humanistic-melioristic approach to integrate sociopolitical and economic dimensions, connecting positive psychology with a critical, interdisciplinary, political-psychological perspective.[11] I do not, however, share his highly critical stance regarding the inclusion of the spiritual dimension in the clinical context, which he justifies on the grounds that to do so would be to abandon the scientific tradition in which clinical psychotherapy is rooted.

Various researchers have emphasized the "dark side" of overcoming trauma: denial, avoidance, wishful thinking, and distortion of meaning.[12] In their article "The Janus Face of Self-Perceived Growth," Andreas Maercker and Tanja Zoellner lay out the possibilities and limitations of Tedeschi and Calhoun's model of PTG.[13] I like their differentiated treatment, which does not fundamentally question the value of this concept but expands it. They draw attention to its constructive, self-transcending, self-transforming side, as well as its deceptive, illusory side. They do not deny that existential confrontations with painful events can open up access to forms of knowledge and judgment that have the character of wisdom.

In the long years of my practice, I have viewed protective illusions as a coping strategy, but I have also been privileged to witness growth following traumatic experiences, leading to wisdom and greater maturity. For some victims, then, trauma has positive long-term consequences, including greater psychic strength. Such individuals work through their difficult destinies in admirable ways, becoming kinder and more human rather than bitter and also more engaged in future-directed social activity, in which values such as solidarity and compassion occupy a central place.

My Chilean patient Jorge, with whom I worked for several years, was such a person, one who strongly affirmed life after many wretched years of incarceration and torture. He had been affiliated with the socialist youth political organization, which endorsed a "new Chile," had done volunteer work in poor neighborhoods, and had printed flyers in his small print shop (offset printing was his business) and distributed them. He was arrested three days after Pinochet's accession to power. So began a nightmare of inhumanity and torture that continued for many years. A dangerous and adventuresome escape eventually brought him to Switzerland. He was then haunted not only by the physical violence but also by the terror of insecurity, a sort of existential nausea, that tainted his days and nights, darkened his dreams, and clouded his relationships. Between sobs he recalled: "They want to obliterate your personality, till nothing is left of you but a cringing worm that they force to eat shit."

When Jorge first became my patient, he suffered from the now well-documented long-term aftereffects of torture. The terror was still stored in his body and poisoned his mind. What moved me so much in my work with Jorge, who allowed me to glimpse these "spaces of death," was his unshakable faith and his determination to live, free of hatred. Jorge agreed, after due consideration and careful preparation, to appear in Hans Haldimann's Swiss documentary film *Weiterleben* [*Survival*], in order to break the silence, disclose the truth, and testify to the value of being a survivor. In the film, he stands in front of that former house of horrors and deep, dark suffering, now converted into a museum, and declares: "I have survived; I have outlived the outrage; I'm standing on solid ground again. In spite of all that happened, my spirit is unbroken!" This was his victory.

Three other torture survivors appear in the documentary. One is a Congolese woman who was beaten unconscious for days on end and whose husband was murdered. And yet she was able to say: "I have become a strong woman; one must forgive—or one can't move on." Another, a Kurdish man, whose experience was similar to Jorge's, said: "If I can manage to live beyond the torture, the torture has lost, not I." He writes poetry, manages a small restaurant, and keeps moving forward in life. These are all moving testimonies to the dignity of the human soul, though not without suffering and deep psychic and physical wounds.

In my experience, spiritual answers often emerge in response to highly emotive crisis situations. When we are overpowered, unconscious strengths may also emerge, saving us and giving us an answer. Jung liked to quote Friedrich Hölderlin:

> Near is God
> And hard to apprehend.
> But where danger is, there
> Arises salvation also.[14]

Here is expressed a wisdom that could be the fruit of traumatic experiences. Wisdom means freedom from illusions of invulnerability, the relativization of the small ego in the face of boundary experiences, and the quantum leap to that which transcends the ego. It has to do with consciousness of one's limitations, competence in dealing with complexity and uncertainty, and a capacity to give meaningful shape to one's life through reflection, with calmness, humility, and self-knowledge. To live wisely means to live with ambiguity, to tolerate contradictions, to be able to doubt, to know and not know, and to practice tolerance.

In the contemplative spiritual traditions, the concept of wisdom is connected with a deep knowledge of and insight into the essence of reality. It is related to the capacity to free oneself from illusions and to transcend the rigid boundaries between self and other, between subject and object. Self-knowledge and self-transcendence support the consciousness of the interconnection between self, other, and creation as a whole. These are the signs of spiritual growth that can be observed when a person's attitude to suffering undergoes a radical transformation and when consciousness of a greater reality expands the personality beyond its former limits. The core experience is of continuous transformation, of the fluidity in one's relations with the world, of the recognition that nothing remains the same; even I myself, in my own identity and my understanding of the world, am subject to this transformation, as traumatic experiences reveal in a terrifying way.

Wisdom involves one's dealings with the everyday but also with ultimate things, with questions about the meaning and the absurdity of human existence and the meaning and purpose of evil. Dostoyevsky, Dante, Nelly Sachs, Rose Ausländer, Else Lasker-Schüler, Etty Hillesum, and Imre Kertész, to name but a few, are witnesses in this tradition, setting forth the dynamic of transformation and its link with existential suffering. Suffering is valued in various spiritual traditions for its ability to forge a path to being and truth, examples of which are found in the suffering of the mystic John of the Cross and his "dark night of the soul" and the lamentations of the biblical Job, who declared:

> I will speak in the anguish of my spirit;
> I will complain in the bitterness of my soul. (Job 7:11)

In the Buddhist tradition, spiritual change is a central element of awakening, a change that involves insight and the overcoming of suffering and frustration, *dukkha*, in the process of becoming conscious of one's true nature. Here, too, the enormity of suffering is not denied, but one tries not to identify with it. Nonattachment is the key concept, derived from spiritual practice.

Hinduism sees suffering as belonging indissolubly to life. In the symbolic world of this belief system, Shiva embodies the destructive as well as the creative aspect of divine activity, and the continual destruction and renewal of the world is one of the paradoxes of life. Thinking about Shiva's dance, about the dynamics of maintenance and destruction, the verses from Ecclesiastes echo in my mind:

> For everything there is a season, and a time for every
>   matter under heaven:
> a time to be born, and a time to die;
> a time to plant, and a time to pluck up what is planted;
> a time to kill, and a time to heal;
> a time to break down, and a time to build up;
> a time to weep, and a time to laugh;
> a time to mourn, and a time to dance;
> a time to cast away stones, and a time to gather
>   stones together;
> a time to embrace, and a time to refrain from embracing;
> a time to seek, and a time to lose;
> a time to keep, and a time to cast away;
> a time to tear, and a time to sew;
> a time to keep silence, and a time to speak;
> a time to love, and a time to hate;
> a time for war, and a time for peace. (Ecclesiastes 3:1–8)

For me, this text incorporates the rhythmic dance of life, just as Shiva represents the Hindu concept of cyclical time. These amplifications help me when I am working with traumatized people, for they contain the wisdom of becoming and passing away. Even the most painful losses and wounds have their time; we are stretched on the wheel of these contradictions and compelled to live both sides of the polarities to the fullest. There can be no escaping, no evading this fateful, perpetual dance of life. We are called upon to embrace, in its entirety, whatever befalls us.

Such scriptural texts encourage us to let the whole of life into our field of vision. When we are feeling fragmented they can help us awaken to a new consciousness of the meaning of life and death, so that we are more willing to set out on the dark path that leads through shadow realms. The dialectic of the text encourages complementary thinking and an openness to new experiences, even those that are sinister, dangerous and difficult to grasp in our either-or thinking. In these verses is mediated a kind of knowledge that not only helps with survival but also frees us from any entangling identification with only one part of existence. Wisdom is needed to recognize that even apparently negative, destructive evil has its time and purpose.

Wounding and Awakening

The poetry of darkness and interiority resonates deeply with traumatic affliction. Such poems are attempts by those who feel overwhelmed to transcend their experiences of pain and horror through the use of creativity. The tragic destinies of Paul Celan, Primo Levi, Bruno Bettelheim, and Jean Améry bear witness to the cruel paradox of acquiring wisdom through wounding.

In his writings Améry unsparingly revealed the deadly movement from existence to nonexistence, the ultimate succumbing to the forces of darkness, because "[n]othing has healed."[15] Identity remains destroyed; trust in the world is still lost; soul, mind, and consciousness are still annihilated. The motif of the wound and its poetics has undergone a particular concentration in the context of the Shoah. In poetry about the dying and the dead, the never-healing wound of the *Muselman* is evoked, the wound of the shadowy, wavering near-corpse of a human, who lacks space for consciousness. Paul Celan's lyrics circle again and again around the wounds and scars associated with the stigmata and the Passion of Christ. According to ancient traditions, scars were marks of ownership on the bodies of slaves, criminals, and animals, made by branding. Traumatized people feel similarly branded by their scars. The Auschwitz number tattooed on the left arm brings to mind the visibility and invisibility of outer and inner wounds.

The plunge by wounded and broken spirits into hopelessness, into the abyss of perdition, reminds me of hell; it evokes images and mythic stories of torture and endless suffering, of the land of death from which no one ever returns alive. Dostoyevsky's insight into hell as the suffering of no longer being able to love reverberates in my heart and mind when inquiring into the existential conundrum of the mystery of trauma and the question of what can move the traumatized psyche toward the other shore. Hell is an intrapsychic reality for individuals who suffer from persecution, torture, terrorism, and abuse, a somber state, alienated from oneself, fellow humans, and nature, an experience of loss of soul, of living in a psychic desert.

For the ancient Egyptians, the Land of the Dead lay in the West, from which there was no way back. It was a place of annihilation, without escape.[16] For the Greeks, whether it was Tartarus or Hades, from such underworld regions no one could be rescued. In the Hebrew tradition, in the book of Job we read:

> he who goes down to Sheol does not come up;
> he returns no more to his house,
>   nor does his place know him any more. (Job 7:9–10)

Améry writes bitterly of this loss of home, especially the home of personality, of feeling at home in one's own body: "Whoever has succumbed to torture can no longer feel at home in the world."[17]

The unhealing wound, the wound of exile, of being a stranger, both inwardly and outwardly homeless, confronts us with the question of whether healing or rescue is possible after traumatic injuries. "Will you save me?" whispers the sobbing boy, who suffers from a mortal wound, in Kafka's short story, "A Country Doctor."[18] The patients in my practice, both men and women, ask, "Will I ever be healed from this excruciating wound?" Rescue and salvation and the yearning for healing and liberation from constriction are associated with the spiritual dimension. The German edition of Judith Herman's book on trauma is titled *Die Narben der Gewalt: Traumatische Erfahrungen verstehen und überwinden* [*The Scars of Violence: Understanding and Overcoming Traumatic Experiences*]. This title suggests that today's wounds may become tomorrow's scars, leaving marks that sink into the body (as if inscribed by Kafka's penal colony apparatus) and into the pain memory; yet these wounds can also be transcended, as trauma survivors testify.[19] I recall the statement of a concentration camp survivor:

> Life is like a pearl necklace with pearls of many different colors. The Shoah [the Holocaust] is like a large black pearl in this necklace. It changed my life. But there are several dozen other pearls in the same necklace. And I have experienced so many beautiful and interesting things in my life. My life was so full and rich.[20]

Along with shattering testimonies to human criminality, there are many testimonies to the transformative power of wounds and suffering, of growth through affliction, touching on the numinous aspect of spiritual life. I have learned to understand the complementarity of wounding and spiritual transformation as a paradox, a mystery that cannot be adequately encompassed in the concept of salutogenesis. I often think that the processes of transformation point to a reality that is ultimately ungraspable (*unverfügbar*), leaving me in a perpetual state of not knowing. Here the field of psychotraumatology runs up against a limit, for its methods cannot grasp that emptiness is pregnant with fullness and that the darkness of the void may give birth to a healing light. I consider it especially important to transcend the dichotomy of the pathogenic versus the salutogenic model, wound versus growth, deficit orientation versus resource orientation.[21] This dualistic way of thinking cannot do justice to the complexity of the ways human beings react to severely traumatizing life events.

Trauma research has attempted to develop theories and concepts that can systematize the full range of human reactions to trauma. We try to grasp reality through an accumulation of knowledge, but a life lived under traumatic conditions cannot be summed up or organized in a theoretical system. The work of Tedeschi and Calhoun mentioned at the beginning of this chapter are initial efforts to show that benefit can be derived from severe losses, and van der Kolk and his colleagues also attempt in their work to demonstrate the variety of ways traumatized people adapt and achieve mastery.[22] Yet the spiritual transformation process that sometimes comes through extreme suffering is not adequately illuminated.

In the borderlands of the soul, faced with the realization that human beings have survived broken worlds without becoming broken and empty themselves, we must go beyond grasping at understanding; rather, we must allow ourselves to be grasped. Our available trauma concepts fall too short. They do not help us understand how, in the darkness of inhumanity, some people retain the capacity for goodness without becoming bestial or brutal themselves. Why and how a person can endure the hell of being flung out beyond the borders of the world without his or her humanity being annihilated by this seismic event is perhaps finally unknowable. Carl Friedrich von Weizsäcker said, in connection with the exorbitant demands on logic made by quantum physics, that scientists yearn to return to causal determinism, but this wish is a manifestation of unfinished grief work. Traumatized individuals must accomplish a similar grief work, accepting the fact that there may be no answer to the question "Why?" if they hope not to remain stuck in rumination.

In *Survival in Auschwitz*, Primo Levi describes his arrival at the camp, tortured by terrible thirst. Outside the window, within arm's reach, he saw a beautiful icicle. He grabbed it eagerly and broke it off, to quench his thirst. At once a hefty guard came and snatched the icicle from him. "Why?" asked Levi. "There is no why here," his tormentor replied.[23] Likewise, in hell there is no why.

Nietzsche's dictum, "God is dead," and Jung's comment that there are no longer any gods whom we can invoke to help us express a bitterly learned truth for many traumatized people. Hans Jonas spoke about the concept of God after Auschwitz, asserting that "'Auschwitz' calls . . . the whole traditional concept of God into question."[24] Gratuitous suffering on a massive scale has made it impossible to believe in a God who is simultaneously almighty, all wise, and all good. Eugen Drewermann demonstrates the incompatibility of these three concepts, arguing that one of the three must be abandoned if the other two are to be maintained. Either God is almighty and all wise but lacks the goodness to create a world free of evil, or he is all good and almighty but lacks the wisdom to establish goodness in the world, or he lacks the power to realize his goodness and wisdom in the world.[25]

Gratuitous, unmerited suffering unsettles us and initiates the process of coming to consciousness, for in pain we become aware of ourselves in a new way. Suffering can be a school of life; it forces us to the limits of what we can bear. In pain and suffering, the ego's structures are broken. When we experience ourselves as nothing but an open wound, when pain threatens to kill off reason, we are inwardly broken open to such an extent that something entirely new and unexpected can force its way into this gaping rift from the beyond, even in the horrors of the Shoah. Etty Hillesum testified to this experience in this passage in one of her letters:

> New thoughts will have to radiate outward from the camps themselves, new insights, spreading lucidity, will have to cross the barbed wire enclosing us and join with the insights that people outside will have to earn just as bloodily, in circumstances that are slowly becoming almost as difficult.[26]

In her memoir of the Holocaust, Ruth Klüger shows that concentration camps were certainly not schools for humaneness and tolerance; nevertheless, in them one can learn something about people and what they can become when exposed to the greatest extremity.[27] As the fruit of these experiences, she believes it is possible to harvest philosophical insights into human nature and the essence of the soul. Survival alone does not count, but the how of survival. Often, how one really is may not be revealed until one's attitude becomes clear in how one dies.

Having death consciously before our eyes can also prepare us spiritually to perceive life, to the last breath, as a precious thing. On the threshold of death we might become more permeable to the transpersonal as it operates in life. Sometimes, light falls upon life only when death is near and works its transformative alchemy. With patients in liminal situations, I have often observed archetypal experiences and archetypal dream symbols bring about a change in their attitude to life. In the place where we feel crucified, we may encounter a transcendent dimension, enabling us to die into a new way of living as the prayer often attributed to St. Francis of Assisi expresses, "It is in dying that we are born to eternal life." At the age of eighty-five, Jung wrote to a Mother Prioress: "I try to accept life *and* death. . . . In ultimate situations of life and death complete understanding and insight are of paramount importance, as it is indispensable for our decision to go or to stay and let go or let stay."[28]

Wound or Wisdom: Paul Celan and Nelly Sachs

Was wär es, Mutter: Wachstum oder Wunde—versänk ich mit im
Schneewehn der Ukraine?
[Which would come, Mother: wakening or wound—if I too sank
in snows of the Ukraine?][29]

These are the words of Paul Celan to his mother, killed in Ukraine with a shot to the neck. *Wachstum* (literally, "growth") *oder Wunde?* Wakening or wound? In the context of trauma, this either-or question is an impossible one. In trauma we have only the paradox of wounding *and* wakening—wakening despite the wound, wakening through the wound. Like Celan, Jung was in touch with the spirits of those who died before their time. He wrote that they "will live, for the sake of our present incompleteness, in dark hordes in the rafters of our houses and besiege our ears with urgent laments, until we grant them redemption."[30]

Perhaps, like Celan and Jung, all of us have unfinished business with our dead loved ones, but few people ever succeed in transforming a tragic fate into the dignity of a human task. In this transformation, the poets of trauma have a convincing record of success. Jung, too, committed himself entirely to what wanted to be born, redeemed, and realized in the depths of his soul. He circumambulated the ineffable, as did Celan, trying to grasp what cannot be grasped but only felt as the Beyond. I see the religious function of the soul working in both these men in a marvelous way. Jung writes: "This life is the way, the long sought-after way to the unfathomable, which we call divine."[31]

Celan's poetic question, "Wakening or wound?" corresponds to Jung's question in the Red Book: "Is chaos also a foundation?"[32] But these questions also evoke psychotraumatology's research regarding suffering and transformation and the transcending of trauma. "Trauma and Growth" has become the thematic center of gravity for the *Zeitschrift für Psychotraumatologie, Psychotherapiewissenschaft und Psychologische Medizin* [*Journal of Psychotraumatology, Research in Psychotherapy, and Psychological Medicine*].[33] In scholarly literature we encounter the semantic field of "growth" (Celan's original German word, *Wachstum*) in terms of spiritual growth, transcendent growth, transformational growth, adversarial and stress-related growth, transformational coping, thriving, perceived benefits, learned lessons, and positive psychological changes. Contemporary research is concerned with these questions: Does traumatic wounding possess transformational potential? Is self-reported growth actually real? Can there be any kind of maturation or deepened appreciation of life after traumatic wounding and the experiencing of atrocities? Is unimaginable suffering a gateway to spiritual development? Or are these pseudo-maturations merely forms of defensive self-delusion, arising under the pressure of the tyranny of positive thinking? Are we seeing anything beyond coping or meaning-based, proactive, life-management skills? How do traumatized people become agents of transformation and change? Is there redemption in the transcendent realm of the Beyond?

When I try to probe the possibility that growth may follow shattering traumatic events, I have in mind something beyond adaptive strategies for the purposes of survival or the perception of enhanced well-being. I am thinking of resilience as an energy that draws on spiritual sources of strength. Resilience is generally understood as the ability to withstand and react constructively to trauma. It has to do with the way an individual perceives, appraises, approaches, and tackles severe stresses and challenges. In considering posttraumatic growth, I have in mind a state of heightened awareness, mindfulness, and openhearted acceptance. I am thinking of an ability to experience life as it is, to surrender to the numinosity of suffering, to draw on the sacred resources of the Self, and of a sense of purpose beyond mere survival, a deepened sense of connectedness.

I view the processes of maturation and healing in terms of how the relationship between ego and Self is developed through traumatic experiences. Deep suffering is often an encounter with the dark side of the divine, and it inspires a longing for sanctuary in a chaotic world. Consider poems such as Celan's "Death Fugue," which has been called the "*Guernica* of European postwar literature," or his cycle of 1963, "Die Niemandsrose" ("No One's Rose"), the first poem of which reads:

> There Was Earth Inside Them
>
> There was earth inside them, and
> they dug.
> They dug and dug, and so
> their day went past, their night. And they did not praise God,
> who, so they heard, wanted all this,
> who, so they heard, witnessed all this.
>
> They dug and heard nothing more;
> they did not grow wise, invented no song,
> devised for themselves no sort of language.
> They dug.
>
> There came a stillness then, came also storm,
> all of the oceans came.
> I dig, you dig, and it digs too, the worm,
> and the singing there says: They dig.
>
> O one, o none, o no one, o you:
> Where did it go then, making for nowhere?
> O you dig and I dig, and I dig through to you,
> and the ring on our finger awakens.[34]

Drawn from Celan's real-life experiences in the Romanian labor camps, in which he shoveled earth day after day, the seemingly meaningless digging in the poem evokes a dynamic that I recognize from my work with severely traumatized people: ruminating, being sunk into themselves, engaged in endlessly repetitive inward digging, burrowing, searching for a possible trace of meaning, trying to dig themselves out of desperation, out of the land of death, the no-man's-land. But this digging is also a search for fragmented, lost memories, a digging against forgetting, a digging into the depths, an effort to make a trench into one's innermost being. It is an endless ruminating in the vicious circle of "Why? Why me?" The senses, with which we make sense of things, seem almost to die away in this process of rhythmic digging. Those who are so fixated on the repetition of digging are no longer in contact with themselves or the world. They cannot see or hear, and in the end they no longer have hope or believe in anything.

Reading Celan's poem, I am reminded of Jewish clients who told me about the phenomenon of the *Muselman* in the concentration camps. A *Muselman* was one who had been selected for death because he or she had already lost the will to live and moved about staggering listlessly like a living corpse. I remember, with a paralyzing sense of constriction, one Jewish patient of mine who displayed the *Muselman* symptoms in one of her sessions with me. Draped in a gray cloth, she slowly paced the room without a sound. The *Muselmänner* at Auschwitz, as described by Primo Levi, had no story to tell. They were "no-men who march and labor in silence, the divine spark dead within them, already too empty to really suffer. One hesitates to call them living: one hesitates to call their death death."[35]

Celan's diggers evoke this image of someone who has gazed into the face of Medusa. For traumatized diggers, God is in exile. How often I have seen people protesting against a God who could know and will all this, a sadistic, unreliable, abandoning God. For Primo Levi it was quite clear: Auschwitz exists, so there is no God. Condemned by fate to continue living without their original hold on faith, survivors describe the feeling of being dead inside a living body. They experience the withdrawal of the divine Self, the archetypal situation of abysmal abandonment: no protective being offers firm ground any more, and the living connection to the soul's creative power withers away. Celan depicts the loss of emotional and creative power, a state in which no song can be invented, no language devised, no symbolic distance from the event established. Nothing is transcended in this eternal digging, but when the soul grows quiet, it is overwhelmed by an affective storm.

But then, there emerge in Celan's poem an I, a You, and a We. An opening happens; something new becomes visible and audible in the excavated inner space. The sudden turn toward "singing" provides a numinous clue, leading to an appeal, an evocation of absence, a lament, directed at an unidentified, enduring You. In this dialogical orientation toward a possible You, I see a process of overcoming the solitude of digging. Language throws a bridge over the gulf of muteness, though still without a clear destination. On the occasion of being awarded the Bremen Literature Prize in 1958, Celan explained that he had written poems "so as to speak, to orient myself, to find out where I was and where I was meant to go, to sketch out reality for myself."[36]

This attempt at orientation, at bringing together an identity that joins the "before" and the "after" of trauma, at sketching out a new reality, is also part of trauma therapy. People always try to symbolize their life experiences, to connect them with an ordered system of meaning, in order to create a sense of continuity. My patients also try to express the inexpressible, to summon the lost, to create something new. Language and speech are a central theme in trauma therapy. We know that Broca's area, in the left hemisphere of the brain, the area responsible for putting personal experiences into speech, is turned off during traumatic shock. This also explains the speechless terror of trauma victims, which manifests first of all in physical reactions and which cannot be expressed in language. In Celan's case, however, language did not abandon him. Words remained his faithful companions to the end. He wrote:

> Reachable, near and not lost, there remained in the midst of the losses this one thing: language. It, the language, remained, not lost, yes in spite of everything. But it had to pass through its own answerlessness, pass through frightful muting, pass through the thousand darknesses of deathbringing speech. It passed through and gave back no words for that which happened; yet it passed through this happening. Passed through and could come to light again, 'enriched' by all this.[37]

In the creative power of Celan's language, in his stepping out of silence to give expression to suffering, I see a path to the transcending of trauma. In this he resembles Emmanuel Levinas, Rose Ausländer, and Nelly Sachs, writers who also felt an obligation to bear witness to the unspeakable darkness of destruction that they had experienced. Hungarian novelist Imre Kertész believed it was "one's religious duty" to understand the world "totally independently of the crippling religions of crippling churches," a religious duty not only to try to understand evil, but also to perceive the existence of the good, and to tell the stories that resist being told.[38] Nelly Sachs knew the saving function of the word. She wrote to Celan that her poems were "just ways of rescuing breath from suffocation."[39] Both poets transformed traumatic memories and built bridges from then to now in an attempt to transcend their wounds.

Celan's poetry is a bridge over the abyss of trauma made entirely out of words. His poems testify to an enduring trust in something indestructible, even when this trust is missing from the man himself and his life. The last lines of "There Was Earth inside Them" ("O you dig and I dig, and I dig through to you, / and the ring on our finger awakens") bear witness to the mystery of meeting and connecting and the potential for their realization. Relationships, symbolized by the ring, have the power to set us free from interminable digging and to open us up to shining hope, to an experience of the Self. In this poem Celan offers himself and his readers hope, such as is sought by those who work through their trauma in therapy. Elsewhere, he wrote: "A poem, as a manifestation of language and thus essentially dialogue, can be a message in a bottle, sent out in the—not always greatly hopeful—belief that somewhere and sometime it could wash up on land, on heartland perhaps."[40]

I read Celan's poems as sketches for existence, containing room for possibility without offering answers to Whence? Whither? Why? His poems, written in his mother tongue, which is also the murder tongue, are sketches of truth, paradoxical, multifaceted, difficult to decipher. Yet they always seek to plumb the mystery of the encounter between ego and reality, and they point to a telos. As he wrote, "With every poem, for the length of the poem, we stand in mystery. Out of this sojourn comes the 'Dark.'"[41] In his speech on receiving the Georg Büchner Prize, Celan stressed that the poem stands "in the mystery of encounter."[42] For long stretches, in trauma therapy, I also experience myself as standing in mystery, moving about in the dark, often in the inconceivable, trying to open myself, gropingly, to the mystery of the other.

Celan's verse is like a finger pointing to the essential reality springing from the encounter with numinosity. He bears witness that beyond the experience of being hurled outward into nothingness, into no-man's-land, songs can still be sung. His poems contain intimations of hope, like the tentative movements of survivors seeking a credible present and future. Apparently, he did not share Adorno's view that "to write poetry after Auschwitz is barbaric."[43] In fact, it would appear that for Celan, Auschwitz made writing poetry all the more necessary.

In his Büchner Prize acceptance speech, Celan spoke of the necessity of the "you," in statements that remind me very much of Buber and Levinas: "The poem intends another, needs this other, needs an opposite. It goes toward it, bespeaks it. For the poem, everything and everybody is a figure of this other toward which it is heading."[44] Just as the poet needs the reader, so the traumatized person needs a you who hears and sees him or her and works against his or her tendency to fall silent. In the duality of the therapeutic encounter, the therapist's images and associations bring an empathic, cocreated response into the relationship that helps the sufferer to bear the pain and to feel his or her own existence more securely.

I read Celan's poems as a stupendous attempt to help humanity affirm itself, over and beyond traumatic encounters with barbarity; to wrestle through to a "heartland" where wisdom prevails rather than hatred, and trust rather than estrangement from self. They are not exaggerated, exalted hymns to transcendence but the desperate struggles of memory, repetition, and working through—the magical Freudian formula for psychotherapy—suffering in the depths and bearing witness to an unshakeable confidence in what human beings are capable of. From his work speaks the voice of humanism and an ethics that will not be silenced by the confrontation with evil.

In trauma, as a result of inner and outer threats, the boundaries of the self are pushed farther and farther inward, resulting in a defensive attitude of caution and distrust. Traumatic experiences often lead to the destruction of sustaining object relations in the inner world, relations through which the self-image is maintained. This relational breakdown causes far-reaching changes in psychic structure, having to do with differentiating, shutting out, and cutting off. Based on his work with torture victims in Chile, David Becker has described how severely traumatized people attempt to produce a new balance between the inner and the outer world and reorient themselves to a world that has apparently become utterly destructive to them.[45] He calls this a "balance of destruction." To give up this defensive reaction, to turn toward the world once again with trust, requires great inner effort and a large helping of *Deo concedente*.

Many trauma poets suffered from a loss of boundary between inner and outer, from the collapse of inner psychic structures, from feelings of deep vulnerability and the fear of annihilation. Paul Celan and Nelly Sachs were repeatedly tormented by traumatic storms, but both relied on the saving, soul-restoring power of the word. Thus, faced with the bitterness of the "incurable wound of life," both struggled to endure in the face of despair, "to help bring stars to birth."[46] Celan's and Sachs's work must be read as poetry against hopelessness, expressing a "nevertheless" in a no-man's-land of breakages and breakthroughs.

To me, Celan's poems bespeak an enduring trust in something indestructible, an undying hope, even when trust was broken in his personal life. In his lonely death in the Seine he lost his life, but he triumphed in his poetry. I understand his life in terms of sequential traumas: the ghetto and deportation, the murder of his parents, the survivor guilt of having left them alone, the horrors in the Romanian labor camps, the anti-Semitic hostilities in Paris, and the death of his son immediately after birth. And overshadowing all this, the unjustified accusations of plagiarism by Claire Goll intensified his feeling of living "under dark skies." In his correspondence with his publisher Rudolf Hirsch, Celan himself used the concept of trauma and spoke of stigmatization.[47]

> Unlike Rilke, who wrote in his requiem for Wolf Graf von Kalckreuth, "Wer spricht von Siegen? *Überstehn ist alles*" ("Who speaks of victories? *Survival is everything*"), Celan was not content with mere survival.[48] He considered such a thing to be indecent, insisting that one has to write for one's life in order to survive. By persisting in writing, he grew and was broken. Struck and destroyed in the core of his existence, unredeemed and suffering deeply from the disruption of everything meaningful, he

nevertheless wrote himself into a lost, broken wholeness. His verse is rich in paradoxes, and there, too, I see the aspect of wisdom shining forth, rooted in experiential knowledge and in a search for the truth of life. The wisdom that I see in Celan's and Sachs's texts is, to quote Gabriel Marcel, a "tragic wisdom."[49] It is the wisdom of Nietzsche, who ended in insanity, and of Sachs, who was locked up in psychiatric clinics for months at a time. It is a wisdom born from the immanence of death in life, from an awareness of the fundamental insecurity enveloping us all. These verses, from Celan's poem "Psalm," are a moving example.

> Psalm
>
> No one kneads us again out of earth and clay,
> no one incants our dust.
> No one.
>
> Blessed art thou, No One.
> In thy sight would
> we bloom.
> In thy
> spite.
>
> A Nothing
> we were, are now, and ever
> shall be, blooming:
> the Nothing-, the
> No-One's-Rose.
>
> With
> our pistil soul-bright,
> our stamen heaven-waste,
> our corona red
> from the purpleword we sang
> over, O over
> the thorn.[50]

Similarly, I read Nelly Sachs's poems as signs of hope and peace, as wisdom runes of reconciliation, written in the "dwelling places of death," to quote the title of one of her volumes. Her poems are like prayers of the soul, written against the cycle of violence, and for love's manner of being. The traumatic events that brought her to the verge of the abyss, to the brink of darkness and death, she identified as her

teachers. "If I could not have written, I would not have survived. Death
was my teacher. How could I have occupied myself with anything else?
My metaphors are my wounds."[51] The following poem by Sachs,
"Chorus of the Rescued," expresses something deeply moving. It
contains an important lesson I learned from her, which has influenced
my attitude to severely traumatized individuals.

Chorus of the Rescued

We, the rescued,
From whose hollow bones death had begun to
whittle his flutes,
And on whose sinews he had already stroked
    his bow—
Our bodies continue to lament
With their mutilated music.
We, the rescued,
The nooses wound for our necks still dangle
before us in the blue air—
Hourglasses still fill with our dripping blood.
We, the rescued,
The worms of fear still feed on us.
Our constellation is buried in dust.
We, the rescued,
Beg you:
Show us your sun, but gradually.
Lead us from star to star, step by step.
Be gentle when you teach us to live again.
Lest the song of a bird,
Or a pail being filled at the well,
Let our badly sealed pain burst forth again
and carry us away—
We beg you:
Do not show us an angry dog, not yet—
It could be, it could be
That we will dissolve into dust—
Dissolve into dust before your eyes.
For what binds our fabric together?
We whose breath vacated us,
Whose soul fled to Him out of that midnight

> Long before our bodies were rescued
> Into the ark of the moment.
> We, the rescued,
> We press your hand
> We look into your eye—
> But all that binds us together now is leave-taking.
> The leave-taking in the dust
> Binds us together with you.[52]

In every line of this psalm-like lament one can feel what is past actualizing itself in the present and how much time is needed for the process of integration, for extreme traumas bring about a chaotic reaction that cannot be grasped by consciousness. Thus, every orientation or adaptation is rendered inconceivable, and the affected person is thrown into total confusion, disorientation, and estrangement. A naïve belief in posttraumatic growth shatters in the face of writing such as this. Yet the longing for life remains alive and is realized in its own time. In my work, I listen for the rhythm of timing and pacing indicated by my patients. The Red Book teaches me to trust the psychic process, to perceive the soul's time, and to accompany incubation processes as patiently and carefully as if I were attending a pregnancy, until the time comes for new life to be born.

I have personally met many individuals who embody the mystery of surviving with dignity, who bear witness in a simple, human way to the dignity of the human soul and the transformation of suffering into a wise way of being. As real as the destructive power of trauma is, equally real is the capacity of the human spirit to bring forth meaning in meaninglessness and to make this world a better and wiser place.

I remember my late Polish Jewish friend, Halina, an art historian from Cambridge, Massachusetts. One summer, when she was in Germany doing research on Alexander von Humboldt, she was invited to a party with a group of German men. They were sitting on a terrace, enjoying delicious food and plentiful wine, when some of the men were moved to intone a popular patriotic folksong: "This is my native land, here I'm at home." Hearing this, Halina calmly interrupted them, saying: "I know that tune, but the words I learned are different." And slowly rolling up her sleeve to expose the Auschwitz number tattooed on her left forearm, she sang, in her beautiful bell-like voice, the chilling lyrics of the Auschwitz version:

Where the Vistula and the Sola rivers flow
Mid swamps, guardhouses, and barbed wire, down below
Lies the camp called Auschwitz, that accursed nest,
Hated by the prisoner like the evil pest.

Dead silence ensued. And yet Halina was a person without bitterness
or hate, capable of embracing Germans, including me, with openness
and kindness, free of any resentment. She trusted the good, the beautiful,
and the true in life. She was able to speak about the nightmare of being
in the camp, even about the agonizing moment when, working in an
office there, she came across the record of the murder of her father, in
the very camp where she and her mother were still living.

I was deeply impressed by this amazing woman, full of optimism
and a wonderful sense of humor, a person of great integrity and goodness
of heart. Her spirit was not broken, though she was confined in the
Krakow ghetto when she was fifteen and later interned in several
concentration camps, including Auschwitz, and witnessed unbelievable
cruelty and evil. In spite of all her experiences of degradation and
dehumanization, she preserved a love for life, for people and animals
and plants, which touched me deeply and taught me about
transcending trauma, about reconciliation, forgiveness, and the moral
obligation not to forget.

Together, we celebrated the publication of her book *And Yet, I Am
Here!*, a record of resilience and growth in the wake of the Holocaust.[53]

NOTES

[1] Richard G. Tedeschi, Crystal L. Park, and Lawrence G. Calhoun,
eds., *Posttraumatic Growth: Positive Changes in the Aftermath of Crisis*
(Mahwah, NJ: Lawrence Erlbaum Associates, 1998); Richard G.
Tedeschi and Lawrence G. Calhoun, "Posttraumatic Growth:
Conceptual Foundations and Empirical Evidence," *Psychological Inquiry*
15, no. 1 (2004): 1–18; Lawrence G. Calhoun and Richard G.
Tedeschi, eds., *Handbook of Posttraumatic Growth: Research and Practice*
(Mahwah, NJ: Lawrence Erlbaum Associates, 2006).

[2] Kazimierz Dabrowski, *Positive Disintegration* (Boston: Little,
Brown, 1964).

³ Henri F. Ellenberger, *The Discovery of the Unconscious: The History and Evolution of Dynamic Psychiatry* (New York: Basic Books, 1970); Mircea Eliade, *Shamanism: Archaic Techniques of Ecstasy*, trans. Willard R. Trask (Princeton, NJ: Princeton University Press, 1972).

⁴ Hartmut Kraft, *PlusHeilung: Die Chancen der großen Krisen* (Stuttgart: Kreuz Verlag, 2008).

⁵ Richard G. Tedeschi and Lawrence G. Calhoun, *Trauma and Transformation: Growing in the Aftermath of Suffering* (London: Sage Publications, 1995).

⁶ Richard G. Tedeschi and Lawrence G. Calhoun, "The Posttraumatic Growth Inventory: Measuring the Positive Legacy of Trauma," *Journal of Traumatic Stress* 9, no. 3 (1996): 455–471.

⁷ Etty Hillesum, *Etty: The Letters and Diaries of Etty Hillesum, 1941–1943*, ed. Klass A. D. Smelik, trans. Arnold J. Pomerans (Grand Rapids, MI: William B. Eerdmans, 2002), p. 495.

⁸ Ronnie Janoff-Bulman, *Shattered Assumptions: Towards a New Psychology of Trauma* (New York: Free Press, 1992).

⁹ David Becker, "Extremes Leid und die Perspektive posttraumatischen Wachstums: Realitätsverleugnung, naives Wunschdenken oder doch ein Stück wissenschaftlicher Erkenntnis?" *Zeitschrift für Psychotraumatologie Psychotherapiewissenschaft, Psychologische Medizin* 7, no. 1 (2009): 21–33.

¹⁰ Yael Danieli, "Psychotherapist's Participation in the Conspiracy of Silence about the Holocaust," *Psychoanalytic Psychology* 1, no. 1 (1984): 23–42.

¹¹ Hilarion Petzold, Ilse Orth, and Johanna Sieper, "Psychotherapie und 'spirituelle Interventionen?'—Differenzielle Antworten aus integrativer Sicht für eine moderne psychotherapeutische Praxeologie auf 'zivilgesellschaftlichem' und 'emergent-materialistisch-monistischem' Boden," *Integrative Therapie* 1 (2009): 87–122.

¹² Chris R. Brewin, "Psychological Defenses and the Distortion of Meaning," in *The Transformation of Meaning in Psychological Therapies: Integrating Theory and Practice*, ed. Mick Power and Chris R. Brewin (New York: John Wiley and Sons, 1997), pp. 107–123.

¹³ Andreas Maercker and Tanja Zoellner, "The Janus Face of Self-Perceived Growth: Toward a Two-Component Model of Post-Traumatic Growth," *Psychological Inquiry* 15, no. 1 (2004): 41–48.

[14] Jung, *CW* 5, § 630.

[15] Jean Améry, *At the Mind's Limits: Contemplations by a Survivor on Auschwitz and Its Realities*, trans. Sidney Rosenfeld and Stella P. Rosenfeld (Bloomington, IN: Indiana University Press, 1980), p. xi.

[16] Hermann Kees, *Totenglauben und Jenseitsvorstellungen der alten Ägypter* (Berlin: Akademie-Verlag, 1956); Erik Hornung, *Ägyptische Unterweltsbücher* (Zürich: Artemis-Verlag, 1972).

[17] Améry, *At the Mind's Limits*, p. 40.

[18] Franz Kafka, *The Penguin Complete Short Stories of Franz Kafka*, ed. Nahum N. Glatzer (London: Allen Lane, 1983), p. 224.

[19] *Ibid.*, pp. 140ff.

[20] Veronika Chanoch, quoted in Revital Ludewig-Kedmi, *Opfer und Täter zugleich? Moraldilemmata jüdischer Funktionshäftlinge in der Shoah* (Gießen: Psychosozial-Verlag, 2001), pp. 271–272; my translation.

[21] Aaron Antonovsky, *Unraveling the Mystery of Health: How People Manage Stress and Stay Well* (San Francisco: Jossey-Bass Publishers, 1987).

[22] Bessel A. van der Kolk, Alexander C. McFarlane, and Lars Weisaeth, eds., *Traumatic Stress: The Effects of Overwhelming Experience on Mind, Body, and Society* (New York: Guilford Press, 1996).

[23] Primo Levi, *Survival in Auschwitz: The Nazi Assault on Humanity*, trans. Stuart Woolf (New York: Simon and Schuster, 1986), p. 29.

[24] In his acceptance speech upon receiving the Leopold Lucas Prize for 1984 at Tübingen University; for an English translation of his original speech in German, see Hans Jonas, "The Concept of God after Auschwitz: A Jewish Voice," *The Journal of Religion* 67, no. 1 (1987): 1–13; quote on p. 3.

[25] Eugen Drewermann, *Wenn die Sterne Götter wären: Moderne Kosmologie und Glaube* (Freiburg: Herder Verlag, 2004).

[26] Hillesum, *Etty: The Letters and Diaries*, pp. 586–587.

[27] Ruth Klüger, *Still Alive: A Holocaust Girlhood Remembered* (New York: Feminist Press, 2001).

[28] C. G. Jung, letter to the Mother Prioress of a Contemplative Order, dated March 26, 1960, in *C. G. Jung Letters, Vol. 2: 1951–1961,* trans. R. F. C. Hull (Princeton, NJ: Princeton University Press, 1972), p. 547.

[29] Paul Celan, *Die Gedichte: Kommentierte Gesamtausgabe*, ed. Barbara Wiedemann (Frankfurt: Suhrkamp Verlag, 2003), p. 399;

English translation: *Selected Poems and Prose of Paul Celan*, trans. John Felstiner (New York: W. W. Norton, 2001), p. 9.

[30] Jung, *RB*, p. 297.

[31] Jung, *RB*, p. 232.

[32] Jung, *RB*, p. 298.

[33] Pia Andreatta and Dietmar Kratzer, eds., *Zeitschrift für Psychotraumatologie, Psychotherapiewissenschaft und Psychologische Medizin*, Themenschwerpunkt: Trauma und Wachstum 7, no. 1 (2009).

[34] John Felstiner, *Paul Celan: Poet, Survivor, Jew* (New Haven, CT: Yale University Press, 1995), p. 26; Celan, *Selected Poems and Prose*, p. 135.

[35] Levi, *Survival in Auschwitz*, p. 90.

[36] Celan, *Selected Poems and Prose*, p. 396.

[37] *Ibid.*, p. 395.

[38] Imre Kertész, *Kaddish for an Unborn Child*, trans. Tim Wilkinson (New York: Vintage Books, 2004), p. 66.

[39] Paul Celan and Nelly Sachs, *Correspondence*, ed. Barbara Wiedemann, trans. Christopher Clark (Riverdale-on-Hudson, NY: Sheep Meadow Press, 1995), p. 4.

[40] Celan, *Selected Poems and Prose*, pp. 395–396.

[41] "Mit jedem Gedicht stehen wir 'gedichtlang' im Geheimnis. Von diesem Aufenthalt kommt das 'Dunkel.'" Paul Celan, *Der Meridian*, ed. B. Böschenstein and H. Schmull (Frankfurt: Suhrkamp Verlag, 1999), p. 90.

[42] Paul Celan, *Collected Prose*, trans. Rosemarie Waldrop (New York: Routledge, 2003), p. 49.

[43] Theodor W. Adorno, *Prisms*, trans. Samuel and Shierry Weber (Cambridge, MA: MIT Press, 1983), p. 34.

[44] Celan, *Collected Prose*, p. 49.

[45] David Becker, *Ohne Haß keine Versöhnung: Das Trauma der Verfolgten* (Freiburg: Kore Verlag, 1992).

[46] Celan and Sachs, *Correspondence*, p. 73.

[47] Paul Celan and Rudolf Hirsch, *Briefwechsel*, ed. Joachim Seng (Frankfurt: Suhrkamp Verlag, 2004), pp. 85–86.

[48] Rainer Maria Rilke, "Requiem für Wolf Graf von Kalckreuth," in *Die Gedichte* (Frankfurt: Insel Verlag, 2006), p. 413.

[49] He wrote: "For man today, it seems that wisdom can only be tragic wisdom." Gabriel Marcel, *Tragic Wisdom and Beyond*, trans.

Stephen Jolin and Peter McCormick (Chicago: Northwestern University Press, 1973), p. 201.

[50] Celan, *Selected Poems and Prose*, p. 157.

[51] Nelly Sachs, letter to Gisela Bezzel-Dischner dated July 12, 1966, in Inka Bach and Helmut Galle, "Nelly Sachs: In den Wohnungen des Todes und Sternenverdunkelung," in *Deutsche Psalmendichtung vom 16. bis zum 20. Jahrhundert* (Berlin: Walter de Gruyter, 1989), pp. 360–377; my translation.

[52] Nelly Sachs, *O The Chimneys: Selected Poems, Including "Eli," a Verse Play*, trans. Michael Hamburger, Christopher Holme, Ruth and Matthew Mead, and Michael Roloff (New York: Farrar, Strauss, and Giroux, 1967), pp. 25–27.

[53] Halina Nelken, *And Yet, I Am Here!* (Amherst, MA: University of Massachusetts Press, 1999).

CHAPTER FIVE

BEYOND EMBITTERMENT

Das eben ist der Fluch der bösen Tat,
Daß sie, fortzeugend, immer Böses muß gebären.
[This is the curse of every evil deed,
That, propagating still, it brings forth evil.]
　　　　　—Schiller, *Die Piccolomini*, act 5, scene 1;
　　　　　translation by Samuel T. Coleridge

Reconciliation and Forgiveness

One of the key questions for traumatized people, arising repeatedly and demanding an answer, is whether it is possible to be reconciled with what has been done to them. After a "breach of civilization" like the Holocaust, is forgiveness really possible? After expulsion, persecution, and destruction of identity, is it even possible to think about reconciliation and forgiveness, let alone put them into action? Does forgiveness make transformation possible and with it restore the capacity to go on living? For those who survive individual and collective experiences of violence and inhumanity, the pressing question must be faced again and again: How do I deal with states of possession by the archetype of revenge, hatred, and retaliation?

When we think about forgiveness, we tend to think also of confession of guilt, repentance and the payment of a penalty, restitution, and punishment. Can forgiveness be a power—a gift, even—freely given to one who has not asked for it, who regrets nothing, and who makes no promise of improvement or rehabilitation? Jacques Derrida poses these questions in the context of postmodernism and comes to the conclusion that forgiveness actually goes beyond the boundaries of the possible.[1] To forgive is to do the impossible, to excuse the unforgivable and reconcile with the irreconcilable.

Working in crisis-ravaged regions and within the framework of war trauma, I have often been forced to confront the difficult relationship between trauma and the processes of reconciliation. Examples of these processes include the Gacaca courts in Rwanda, the Truth and Reconciliation Commission in South Africa, and the projects taking place in KwaZulu-Natal to develop rituals for purification and reconciliation. Sezam, a local organization in Bosnia, makes efforts to support teachers of all ethnicities in the painful and difficult process of reconciliation and peacemaking. Challenging work is also being done in Cambodia in transitional justice. Such collective processes of reconciliation are a work of humanization within a society. As a working-through of conflict after trauma, these processes are part of the basic elements of a peaceful society. Only by working through conflicts and coming to terms with their consequences can they be transformed, both intrapsychically and interpersonally.

My experience with projects in the former Yugoslavia and Gaza has made me aware how enormously difficult it is to work toward peaceful coexistence, but it has also convinced me that the collective work of reconciliation is absolutely indispensable, because hatred is ubiquitous. Global conflicts between Christians and Muslims, anti-Semitism and racial hatred, the genocide in Rwanda and Armenia, the years of apartheid in South Africa, the wars in Chechnya and the Congo, and the mass murders of the First and Second World Wars all bear witness to the degree to which hate, revenge, and retaliation have shaped our collective history and continue to shape it, being passed on from generation to generation. If they are not worked through, they are reenacted and the cycle of violence is perpetuated.

It is important to understand reconciliation not just as a psychosocial virtue for the purpose of collectively mastering the traumatic past and promoting peaceable conditions for the future but also as an avenue to broaden the perspective we need to take in dealing with religious, philosophical, and psychotherapeutic issues at the individual level. For too long, forgiveness has been regarded as an exclusively spiritual phenomenon, with the result that its psychic dimension (the promotion of emotional freedom) has been neglected.[2] However, since the mid-1980s, "forgiveness research" as a task for the field of psychology has received increasing attention, particularly in the United States.[3]

One way of framing forgiveness psychologically is as abandoning our right to resent those who hurt us unjustly and treating them with compassion, generosity, and love.[4] While the issue of whether forgiveness and reconciliation promote posttraumatic healing is still controversial, it is clear that the work of remembering is a prerequisite for working through traumatic injustice, whether in the life of the individual or in societies torn by violence. Only through remembering can people reconcile with each other and live with each other in a dialogical and peaceful way. On the individual level, the moral reconstruction of a society and the emergence of a new order correspond to the building up of psychic structures and the emergence of a new identity.

Reconciliation and forgiveness represent a lived attitude, a conscious commitment to nonviolence. The renunciation of violence is based on the spiritual insight that everything is interconnected. Healing from trauma requires awareness of the split that has occurred and an acknowledgment of the hostile parts of ourselves, coupled with an adequate mourning for their loss. The emotion of grief can disentangle us from the defensive use of feelings such as resentment and the desire for revenge, which arise ultimately from a failure to grieve properly. As long as we remain stuck in defense strategies, we deny reality. Mourning can cause these defenses to dissolve and open the way for healing and reconciliation.

From his work with torture victims in Chile, David Becker has concluded that in the treatment of severely traumatized people, the acknowledgment of aggressive impulses, such as hatred and rage, actually encourages healing and facilitates forgiveness and reconciliation.[5] This paradoxical conclusion can be understood by differentiating between destructive and constructive anger. Destructive anger locks the trauma victim into endless rumination and makes him or her vulnerable to possession by archetypal images of violent revenge, whereas constructive anger may be a catalyst for the motivation to change unbearable conditions. Constructive anger helps the victim face conflict with courage instead of avoiding it, and this opens the way for fruitful mourning. Trauma not only diminishes the capacity to live; it also subverts the capacity for healthy aggression.

Integrating the Shadow

The concepts of constructive anger and healthy aggression can be understood in terms of the Jungian concept of shadow integration. Integrating the shadow carries the potential for healing, for it brings about an inner reconciliation as a precursor to the outer reconciliation. From the neuropsychologist Rick Hanson, I heard a didactic tale about a Native American elder, a grandmother, who was asked why she was so happy, so wise, so loved and respected. Her response was: "It's because I know there are two wolves in my heart, a wolf of love and a wolf of hate. And I know that everything depends on which one I feed each day." We must become well acquainted with both wolves and recognize our own aggressive and sadistic impulses. We must become reconciled to the wolf of hate within before we can be reconciled to the wolves of hate in the outer world. Only the acknowledgment of our own feelings of hate can prevent the reenactment of hatred. It is the only way we can avoid projecting the split-off, unacceptable, repressed aspects of ourselves onto others.

In therapy, it is often difficult to help the patient become conscious of the binding power of hatred and repression. Hatred clings. It causes us to fixate on the negative; it casts a dark shadow on our perceptions, thoughts, and feelings. Once it is integrated into consciousness, we are freed from old burdens, our dignity is restored, and we are presented with a new beginning for the next stage in life.

Reconciliation with the estranged parts of ourselves throws us back upon ourselves; it takes us inward until we reach our own deepest center. From that place, where we are at peace with ourselves, we can start out on the path that leads toward others.

In letting go of fixations and negative patterns of thought and behavior, the trauma survivor enters a creative process of confronting his or her self-alienating complexes. In the Buddhist tradition, attachment and greed are counted as the cause of suffering. Free spaces open up when we can see through our attachments and overcome them, when we can let ourselves be and accept the process of becoming. Trauma survivors often feel the need to surrender to the paradox of the human condition. However, such a surrender can take place only through an act of free will. It cannot be forced from the outside, by therapy, religion, or politics. I regard it as extremely important that victims of violence not be forced into forgiveness, neither to release their abusers from responsibility nor to achieve wholeness themselves. For this reason, I regard it as therapeutic folly to hold up reconciliation and forgiveness as expectations for the patient, as if they were indispensable for healing. The patient must come to them of his or her own accord in his or her own time.

Coming into Being and Passing Away: Etty Hillesum

Etty Hillesum, a gifted young Dutch-Jewish intellectual, full of joie de vivre and visions for the future, was murdered in the Auschwitz-Birkenau concentration camp at the age of twenty-nine. She left behind letters and diaries, which are of great psychological and spiritual importance and have been translated into many languages. Her life witnesses to an impressive individuation process of psychic maturation and spiritual development under the most traumatizing conditions. Speaking from a completely personal perspective, I believe she has something essential to say about spiritual rootedness in the face of the abyss. She believed that what she could do for others was to "keep turning them back towards themselves, catch and stop them in their flight from themselves, and then take them by the hand and lead them back to their own sources."[6] Her efforts were intended to fight against dehumanization and the loss of dignity through love rather than hate.[7] In her diary on June 20, 1942, she wrote:

> True peace will come only when every individual finds peace
> within himself; when we have all vanquished and transformed
> our hatred for our fellow human beings of whatever race—even
> into love one day. . . . It is . . . the only solution.[8]

In her letters and diaries I find an extraordinary model of how to
deal with suffering when faced with the threat of destruction and
annihilation, and how to take a stance toward that which I am powerless
to change. She too was an exiled soul, with a "nomadic consciousness,"
and the deep-rooted conviction that trauma and growth together form
a single meaning.[9] I include a discussion of her letters and journals
because her short, tragic life demonstrates an impressive individuation
process of posttraumatic maturation and spiritual anchoring. In her
diary entry for July 6, 1942, she wrote:

> There are moments when I can see right through life and the
> human heart, when I understand more and more and become
> calmer and calmer and am filled with a faith in God that has
> grown so quickly inside me that it frightened me at first but has
> now become inseparable from me.[10]

I have tried to grasp how a young woman riding the death train to the
gas chambers of Auschwitz on September 7, 1943, was able to write
this final postcard and throw it from the carriage: "We left the camp
singing."[11] She lived the last twelve weeks of her life at Auschwitz; her
death was registered in November 1943.

Her diaries are a continuous internal dialogue with God, but her
image of God is very individualistic and undogmatic. She had grown
up without any kind of religious commitment. God was for her a
metaphor for humanity's greatest inner adventure, the human desire
to connect with what is deepest inside us. From her diaries it is also
evident that she felt particularly touched by Jung's view that God is
an image that the limited human mind creates in order to express an
unfathomable and ineffable experience. She wrote in her diary: "that
part of myself; that deepest and richest part in which I repose, is what
I call God."[12] In her unorthodox understanding of God, I see the
spiritual legacy of Jung and Rilke, as in this passage:

> But one thing is becoming increasingly clear to me: that You
> cannot help us, that we must help You to help ourselves. And

that is all we can manage these days and also all that really matters: that we safeguard that little piece of You, God, in ourselves. And perhaps in others as well. Alas, there doesn't seem to be much You Yourself can do about our circumstances, about our lives. Neither do I hold You responsible. You cannot help us, but we must help You and defend Your dwelling place inside us to the last.[13]

Encouraged strongly by her psychotherapist, she read Jung intensively. She was fascinated by the meaning he gave to the unconscious and by his emphasis on intuition and imagination. She yearned to explore her "soul-landscape," as she called her inner world. Her individuation process started with an unflinching self-analysis, which she had begun in the context of therapy with the Jungian psycho-chirologist Julius Spier. She discovered in herself a profound contemplative facility. She was supported in developing this by Spier, who had studied with Jung in Zürich and later practiced in Berlin and then sought refuge in Amsterdam. She embarked on a quest for knowledge of the soul by practicing a kind of listening within. For this special kind of listening, she used the untranslatable German word *hineinhorchen*:

Even if one's body aches, the spirit can continue to do its work, can it not? It can love and *hineinhorchen*—"hearken unto"— I so wish I could find a Dutch equivalent for that German word. Truly, my life is one long hearkening unto myself and unto others, unto God. And if I say that I hearken, it is really God who hearkens inside me. The most essential and the deepest in me hearkening unto the most essential and deepest in the other. God to God.[14]

What I do is *hineinhorchen* (to hearken to) . . . Hearkening to myself, to others, to the world. I listen very intently, with my whole being, and try to fathom the meaning of things.[15]

It was also Spier, her therapist, mentor, friend, and lover, who encouraged her to keep a diary, and thus writing became for Etty a form of survival in the Shoah. From him she learned the paradox of healing, namely, that it comes from suffering and embracing that suffering. She had no illusions; she was fully aware that the Nazis wanted nothing short of annihilation for the Jews. Yet she tried to integrate this knowledge into an attitude of all-embracing acceptance and to stay firm in her faith in the indestructible part of her soul so as to suffer with dignity.

Her early diary entries reveal a restless spirit, a troubled soul, inwardly torn, suffering from psychosomatic problems. They portray a young woman with relationship conflicts searching for her feminine identity, in despair, repeatedly falling into the "pit of uncertainty," afraid of going mad like other members of her family.[16] Her study of law had shown her the one-sidedness and limitations of purely rational thinking. She longed to make a connection between head and heart, to find another attitude to life, which would provide a way out of her sense of estrangement and meaninglessness. She told herself: "You shouldn't live on your brains alone, but on deeper, more abiding sources."[17]

But the reflections in her diary point far beyond her personal problems to a quest for spiritual development, for firm ground in the abyss of the Westerbork concentration camp, a Dutch transit camp, the last station before final deportation to Auschwitz. Her letters from Westerbork describe the camp as "hell"; but she always also indicated that words and images were insufficient to evoke the true horror of the place.[18] In her diary she commented wryly: "Dante's *Inferno* is comic opera by comparison."[19]

Deep insights into her own nature and the nature of humanity in general; an analysis of the spirit of the times; descriptions of the transit camp as an anteroom to hell; philosophical observations about the relation between ego and Self, between human and God; reflections on meaning and values, on the art of living and dying, and on the nature of healing in traumatizing conditions that defy healing—all these make Etty's letters and diaries a vivid documentation of humanity in the midst of inhuman circumstances. Her thoughts about individual and collective suffering, about the problem of evil and the shadow, about love and hate, about chaos and cosmos—these are all thoroughly Jungian in nature, bearing a spiritual stance in the face of traumatic conditions. She was familiar with the paradoxes of human existence, had an eye for beauty in the midst of horror, and wrote about visions of defeat and new beginnings. Her indomitable spirit shines through in the following passage from her diary:

> I had visions then of ruined cities. I saw old cities vanish and
> new cities arise, and I thought to myself: even if the whole of
> this world is bombed to bits, we shall build a new world, and
> that one too will pass, and still life will be beautiful, always
> beautiful. It was just a vision. Cities tumbling into the abyss
> and new ones rising up, and so on through the ages, and life,
> which is so beautiful.[20]

I have always read her letters and diaries as a conversation
between ego and Self, a dialogue between her and that transcendent
Other, whom she called God, and who manifested himself to her
as an inner presence. Her yearning for the absolute expresses a new
spirituality, addressed not to an Almighty God, but rather to a God
whom we must help every day to be born in us. For this reason,
many scholars think of her as an "atypical" modern-day mystic.[21]
She is regarded as being of the caliber of Simone Weil and Dietrich
Bonhoeffer and as "a signal representative" of the "death-cell
philosophy" of the twentieth century.[22]

I find her writings extremely moving, for they witness to her ability
to face traumatic situations with neither bitterness and hatred nor
defeatism. From Westerbork she wrote: "It has been brought home
forcibly to me here how every atom of hatred added to the world makes
it an even more inhospitable place."[23] In the camp, where people were
stripped of their positions, their possessions, and their dignity, what
finally counted, she observed, was a person's ultimate values and
whether these could stand up to the challenge. In her writings she
advocated that one must concentrate on the essentials, cultivating
compassion and love for the entire human race. In the crowded barracks
crammed with the hunted and persecuted, she did not lose her love of
life. For her, even this was part of a "great, meaningful whole."[24] Her
love for the whole of humankind shows a humanity that could not be
extinguished. It witnesses to her never-ending search for meaning in a
seemingly meaningless world. She wrote:

> More arrests, more terror, concentration camps, the arbitrary
> dragging off of fathers, sisters, brothers. We seek the meaning
> of life, wondering whether any meaning can be left. But that
> is something each one of us must settle with himself and with
> God. And perhaps life has its own meaning, even if it takes a
> lifetime to find it.[25]

When reading her diaries, I am often reminded of the Red Book. Both Jung and Etty began with an inner and outer situation of chaos; both saved themselves through writing. Through their inner struggle, each of them established a stance, a method for dealing with overwhelming experiences. Many of Jung's themes in the Red Book are found also in Etty Hillesum's writings. In her dialogue with her soul, she describes visions and dark, threatening inner images. She writes of the importance of inner sight, turning to one's innermost being, struggling for the birth of a new image of God in one's own soul. She also describes her confrontation with the shadow side of human existence:

> The rottenness of others is in us, too. . . . I no longer believe that we can change anything in the world until we have first changed ourselves. And that seems to be the only lesson to be learned from this war. That we must look into ourselves and nowhere else.[26]

She was fully aware that any possible change in the world of the collective must begin with a transformation in the world of individual, subjective consciousness. If one desires to "repair the world," as the Jewish phrase *tikkun olam* might be translated, one must begin by working on oneself.[27]

Etty emphasized endurance, the balancing of opposites, and the value of paradox, especially the paradoxical relationship between head and heart. Selections from her diary were initially published in the original Dutch under the title *Het denkende hart van de barak* (*The Thinking Heart of the Barracks*), a title drawn from the prayer she prayed as she lay awake at night while the other girls and women in the camp slept: "Let me be the thinking heart of these barracks."[28] She called her head the "workshop" in which everything must be "thought through" and clarified and her heart "the fiery furnace in which everything must be felt and suffered intensely."[29] The complementarity of thinking and feeling, cognition and affect, head and heart, was an important element in her effort to grapple with the incomprehensible. To think with the heart is a feminine modality, a way to overcome dualities. This mode of existence knows that spirit and matter are complementary, and it regards coming into being and passing away as aspects of a single wholeness. So Etty wrote:

> I am not alone in my tiredness or sickness or fears, but at one with millions of others from many centuries, and it is all part of life, and yet life is beautiful and meaningful too. It is meaningful even in its meaninglessness, provided one makes room in one's life for everything, and accepts life as one indivisible whole, for then one becomes whole in oneself.[30]

Her experience of the great "Thou," the ultimate ground, the precious otherness in her psyche, recalls Jung's experience of the Self. The psychology of the East, too, whose Taoist principle of *wu wei* was so important to Jung, can be discovered in her texts. She had this insight:

> This is something people refuse to admit to themselves: at a given point you can no longer *do*, but can only *be* and accept. And although that is something I learned a long time ago, I also know that one can only accept for oneself and not for others. . . . I know we can't do anything about it. I have never been able to "do" anything; I can only let things take their course and, if need be, suffer.[31]

Her texts also contain many Buddhist thoughts, which circle around themes of emptiness and fullness, presence and nothingness. She suggested that by becoming completely empty we make space for the experience of fullness, the experience of a profound presence that occurs in the stillness, the silence. In her notes she explores the paradox that when we admit death into our life, our life is enlarged and enriched. Etty practiced breathing and yoga exercises to find her spiritual balance.[32] These strategies for bodily and spiritual mastery have become firmly established in the work of trauma therapy.

Etty's accounts of life in the camps are rich in life-affirming symbols, even in the midst of all the dying and passing away. They testify to the many transformations she underwent. I do not believe that these were rationalizations or trauma compensation and adaptation. Rather, I see in her notes the lived, experienced paradox of the unity of beauty and terror.

Etty made an intensive study of Rilke's letters and copied his writings into her diary. She called him her greatest teacher and inspiration, a person with values and a conscience, someone who helped her to master life. His limitless affirmation of life in both its terror and splendor and his passion for wholeness had a comforting and supportive influence on her, for Rilke, in giving his exultant yes to life, did not shut out pain, loneliness, and death. He wrote that the most dreadful terror of life must be embraced, even if one is destroyed by it.[33]

Etty Hillesum faced the traumatic circumstances and extreme suffering of detainees in the concentration camps with tremendous patience, attention, courage, and empathy. She never lost faith in the meaningfulness of life, even when she heard on the radio in 1942 that 700,000 Jews had been slaughtered in Germany and the occupied territories in the previous year alone. She reflected:

> And yet I don't think life is meaningless. . . . I have already died a thousand deaths in a thousand concentration camps. I know about everything and am no longer appalled by the latest reports. In one way or another I know it all. And yet I find life beautiful and meaningful.[34]

Etty's first-person accounts constitute for me a valuable gateway to the intertwined realities of immanence and transcendence in borderlands of trauma.

NOTES

[1] Jacques Derrida, "On Forgiveness," in *On Cosmopolitanism and Forgiveness*, trans. Mark Dooley and Michael Hughes (London: Routledge), pp. 27–60.

[2] See David Viscott, *Emotionally Free: Letting Go of the Past to Live in the Moment* (New York: McGraw-Hill, 1992).

[3] American Psychological Association, *Forgiveness: A Sampling of Research Results* (Washington, DC: Office of International Affairs, 2006); a PDF version can be downloaded at http://www.apa.org/international/resources/forgiveness.pdf. And see, for example, Michael E. McCullough, Kenneth I. Pargament, and Carl E. Thoresen, eds., *Forgiveness: Theory, Research, and Practice* (New York: Guilford Press, 2000); Donna S. Davenport, "The Functions of Anger and Forgiveness: Guidelines for Psychotherapy with Victims," *Psychotherapy* 28, no. 1 (1991): 140–144; and Everett L. Worthington Jr., ed., *Handbook of Forgiveness* (Hove, UK: Routledge, 2005).

[4] Robert D. Enright, Suzanne Freedman, and Julio Rique, "The Psychology of Interpersonal Forgiveness," in *Exploring Forgiveness*, ed. Robert D. Enright and Joanna North (Madison, WI: University of Wisconsin Press, 1998), pp. 46–47.

[5] David Becker, *Ohne Haß keine Versöhnung: Das Trauma der Verfolgten* (Freiburg: Kore Verlag, 1992).

[6] Etty Hillesum, *Etty: The Letters and Diaries of Etty Hillesum, 1941–1943*, ed. Klass A. D. Smelik, trans. Arnold J. Pomerans (Grand Rapids, MI: William B. Eerdmans, 2002), p. 399.

[7] On Etty Hillesum's spiritual stance, see also Rachel Feldhay Brenner, *Writing as Resistance: Four Women Confronting the Holocaust* (University Park, PA: Pennsylvania State University Press, 1997).

[8] Hillesum, *Etty: The Letters and Diaries*, p. 435.

[9] Meins G. S. Coetsier, *Etty Hillesum and the Flow of Presence: A Voegelinian Analysis* (Columbia, MO: University of Missouri Press, 2008), p. 5.

[10] Hillesum, *Etty: The Letters and Diaries*, p. 481.

[11] Etty Hillesum, letter to Christine van Nooten dated September 7, 1943; *ibid.*, p. 659.

[12] *Ibid.*, p. 519.

[13] *Ibid.*, pp. 488–489.

[14] *Ibid.*, p. 519.

[15] *Ibid.*, pp. 90–91.

[16] *Ibid.*, p. 14. For a detailed biography, see Patrick Woodhouse, *Etty Hillesum: A Life Transformed* (London: Continuum, 2009).

[17] Hillesum, *Etty: The Letters and Diaries*, p. 126.

[18] For example, in her letter to Christine van Nooten dated June 21, 1943; *ibid.*, p. 604.

[19] *Ibid.*, p. 494.

[20] *Ibid.*, p. 308.

[21] Francesca Brezzi, "Etty Hillesum, an 'Atypical' Mystic," in *Spirituality in the Writings of Etty Hillesum: Proceedings of the Etty Hillesum Conference at Ghent University, November 2008*, ed. Klaas A. D. Smelik, Ria van den Brandt, and Meins G. S. Coetsier (Leiden: Brill, 2011), pp. 173–190.

[22] Archbishop of Canterbury Rowan Williams, "Foreword," in *Etty Hillesum: A Life Transformed*, by Patrick Woodhouse (London: Continuum, 2009), p. x.

23 Hillesum, *Etty: The Letters and Diaries,* p. 590.

24 *Ibid.,* p. 527.

25 *Ibid.,* p. 62.

26 *Ibid.,* p. 245.

27 Frits Grimmelikhuizen, "The Road of Etty Hillesum to Nothingness," in *Spirituality in the Writings of Etty Hillesum: Proceedings of the Etty Hillesum Conference at Ghent University, November 2008,* ed. Klaas A. D. Smelik, Ria van den Brandt, and Meins G. S. Coetsier (Leiden: Brill, 2011), p. 434.

28 Edward van Voolen, "Foreword," in *Etty: The Letters and Diaries of Etty Hillesum, 1941–1943,* ed. Klass A. D. Smelik, trans. Arnold J. Pomerans (Grand Rapids, MI: William B. Eerdmans, 2002), p. vii; Hillesum, *Etty: The Letters and Diaries,* p. 543; see also p. 515.

29 Hillesum, *Etty: The Letters and Diaries,* p. 87.

30 *Ibid.,* p. 466.

31 *Ibid.,* p. 628.

32 *Ibid.,* pp. 6, 9, 35, 37, 394.

33 Rainer Maria Rilke, *Die Briefe an Gräfin Sizzo: 1921–1926,* ed. Ingeborg Schnack (Frankfurt: Insel Verlag, 1985).

34 Hillesum, *Etty: The Letters and Diaries,* p. 456.

CHAPTER SIX

TRAUMA THROUGH THE MYTHOLOGICAL LENS

Trauma as Descent

When viewed through a mythological lens, trauma is perceived as a descent of the soul, a dropping or falling down. It is sometimes experienced as a sudden violent attack in which one is pulled down or an agonizing loss of soul too overwhelming for consciousness to contain. Often, it is experienced as a descent to the deepest, darkest region of one's being where one is forced to reevaluate one's core assumptions about life and death. It calls for an enlargement of consciousness, which is a potentially transformative psychological and spiritual experience, although it comes at a high price. As Jung wrote to Victor White, "I wanted the proof of a living Spirit and I got it. Don't ask me at what price."[1]

When I am working, I often think of Virgil's motto, *"Labor omnia vincit improbus"* ("Hard labor overcomes everything").[2] It takes enormous strength, effort, and perseverance to accompany the psychically dead on their journey back into life. The joint descent into the underworld is—as Virgil says—*insanus labor*, a "labor of madness," which requires "spirit" and a "robust temperament," and the involvement of our whole being.[3] Sometimes one does not succeed, though one has toiled hard over long stretches in the wasteland of the soul. This reminds me of Homer's depictions of Hades, in which trees bear fruit but drop them before their time. Nothing ripens; the fruit withers half-grown. In a similar way, therapeutic efforts can remain fruitless if the undertow back toward the world of darkness is too strong.

Sometimes, however, as we return from this underworld, a radical shift in perspective on life takes place. Jungian analyst Betty De Shong Meador writes about the treasures from the underworld that might be brought back after an initiation into darkness.[4] She provides a moving description of the wounds to the feminine self that come with living in a patriarchal culture, and she emphasizes the necessity for women to re-root themselves in their own feminine ground. This is a particularly pressing and painful task for women who have been sexually abused and deprived of their instinctive rootedness. Retrieving what is inherent in them and reuniting with what was lost or stolen requires going down into the darkness. These women return from their descent with a different way of perceiving the world, a seeing "with the eye of death," and with a knowledge of the deeper mysteries of life. The myth of Inanna, with its central symbolism of dismemberment, echoes in my work with traumatized women and their process of dismembering, fragmenting, and reassembling the pieces.[5]

Within the spiritual traditions, St. John of the Cross's "dark night of the soul" testifies to a similar journey into the depths of darkness in search of its hidden luminosity. Working with survivors who have experienced major existential catastrophes, I know that the idea of transformation, of finding the treasure hidden in a field, is not a romantic, esoteric notion drawn from alchemy or invented in the ivory tower of archetypal psychology but part of the archetype of death and rebirth inherent in our human condition. Jungian analyst James Hollis reminds us that the "swamplands" of the souls, those dismal places of loss, betrayal, and despair, can provide life with a heightened awareness of meaning and purpose. He cites the aphorism: "Religion is for those who are afraid of going to Hell; spirituality is for those who have been there."[6] Traumatized people have been there, and this book is about what I have learned from those who have come back.

There is a special archetypal landscape constellated between my patients and me when working with torture, persecution, and extreme sexual violence and abuse. I can think of no better image to amplify this state than the image of hell, the mythological place of hopelessness, torture, and suffering without end. In the narratives of my patients I have often encountered this place, which seems completely without escape or return, a darkness that overcomes the soul reminiscent of the underworld: Tartarus, Hades.

Florian Langegger, who worked at the Zürichberg Klinik, a former Jungian research center in Zürich, wrote an outstanding book on madness and chronic mental illness, *Doktor, Tod und Teufel* [*Doctor, Death, and the Devil*].[7] In it he compares madness to death and psychiatry to hell, and he draws out the relationship between the world of the chronically mentally ill and the underworld. When we met at the clinic on the occasion of a lecture I gave on the practice of psychotherapy with torture victims, we agreed that in underworld mythologies one finds the profoundest expressions of the spiritual illness that is sometimes involved in our work. But one does not need to be a Jungian to perceive these connections. Thomas Szasz, for example, criticizes the "myth of mental illness" in his writings and portrays psychiatry as a special form of religious mythology.[8]

Langegger's confrontation with the shadow aspects of psychiatry reveal realities very similar to the ones I encounter in my work with trauma patients. Many of the "healing" procedures employed by traditional psychiatry appear, from a current perspective, to resemble torture. A striking comparison can be drawn between the intrapsychic states of resistance and hopelessness associated with traumatic suffering and the ways societies react to the psychically disturbed in their midst, as well as the feelings of hopelessness and resignation on the part of medical professionals facing incurable mental illness.

The interwovenness of life and death can be seen in the state of living death, in a form of soul loss within a living body. My patients often describe themselves as dead and invoke, metaphorically, the realm of the underworld. If I want to approach such spiritual wastelands with empathy, I have to inform myself about their true nature. My supervisor, psychiatrist Gaetano Benedetti, from whom I have learned a great deal about creativity, empathy, and compassion in psychotherapy, often discussed psychotic patients in terms of the unlived life, alienation from self and the world, inner death, and regions of the soul in which personhood is annihilated. His deeply human attitude toward these states of suffering has been an important model for me. In the experience of reading Dante, too, I find a supervisory quality; for he reminds me of the importance of having a Virgil, a seasoned guide to help me avoid the dangers as I progress through the circles of hell.

Mythology provides images and patterns for conceptualizing this passage down under and its transformative potential. I think of Homer's *Odyssey*, particularly Canto 11, in which Odysseus arrives at the deep waters of the river Oceanus, the sad place of sorrows, where he meets the poor wretches, the dead, deprived of their bodies.[9] They are shades, ghosts, shadows enshrouded in darkness. Odysseus turns pale with fear at the sight of such horrors. He seeks out Teiresias, the wise blind priest and prophet, to ask him about his future. It seems that in this dark, sad fringe of Hades wisdom is alive; it has something to offer as a gift to enlarge consciousness. In mythological imagery, this dawning of a new consciousness is often depicted as conquering death and reclaiming life, as a journey of transformation and renewal. In the *Odyssey*, Odysseus encounters the abyss of suffering. He sees the dreadful fate of Tantalus, tortured by thirst but forever unable to quench it. He sees Sisyphus and his seemingly meaningless engagement with the pitiless rock of his punishment, which rolls down the hill immediately after he has pushed it up to the top—again, and again, and again. This imagery from the deeper layers of the unconscious psyche calls out for attention and raises questions of values and meaning.

Listening to traumatized people trying to articulate their experience, I encounter the same images that literature and art employ to evoke this gloomy place of torment: the abyss, the dark pit, blackness blacker than black. Mythological imagery depicts a spiritual condition of estrangement from the source, an isolation from community with the living, a condition of being outside of society. This descent to the lower regions, the underworld, the abode of the dead, Sheol, Hades, or Tartarus, is often experienced as a journey with no hope of ever returning, a fear of getting lost in the darkness of psychosis, enslaved by devils. Human imagination the world over has been fascinated with these places and many have portrayed these dark hidden lands of hellish suffering in literature and art, Dante, Virgil, Milton, Blake, Rimbaud, Sartre, Gogol, Kokoschka, Bruegel, and Goya, to name a few.

While those who are struck by trauma are forced into an involuntary descent, Jung made a conscious decision to embark on the journey, as recorded in the Red Book and described in his autobiography:

> I let myself drop. Suddenly it was as though the ground literally gave way beneath my feet and I plunged down into dark depths.

> I found myself at the edge of a cosmic abyss. It was like a voyage to the moon, or a descent into empty space.[10]

Jung's *nekyia*, the term in classical antiquity used for the journey to the underworld, turned out to be a *via regia* to the vast realms of the unconscious in search of what was lost, to reclaim it, and to become whole again.[11] Being German, I grew up with Goethe's "*stirb und werde*" (rendered in Robert Bly's translation as "to die and so to grow") as a necessity for living life fully and passionately.[12] Characters who resurface from these hellish descents described in mythology and the mystical traditions, upon their return, usually share the insights they gained about the mystery of life and death. At torture and rehabilitation centers around the world, individuals who have been to hell and back now work to bring their deepened perspective on living and dying to others.

Jungians have contributed greatly to a deeper understanding of the soul's movement down into darkness. In particular, there are various interpretations of the Demeter-Persephone myth, a myth about an involuntary descent, Persephone's abduction into Hades, the rape of Kore, and the interpretations of fairy tales.[13] The mythical abduction story is translated into today's narrative in the case of Natascha Maria Kampusch, the ten-year-old Austrian girl who was abducted and seized by Wolfgang Prikopil on her way to school, imprisoned for more than eight years in a secret soundproof cellar without windows, beaten, and sexually violated, until she was finally able to escape.[14] This is the literal enactment of a forced descent, a story of victimhood, rape, and utter powerlessness, but also a model of how to reconnect with life and overcome the trauma of stolen innocence, lost childhood, and incapacitating wounds. Natascha makes the transition from horror and helplessness to empowerment and self-assertion. Her life had the hallmarks of possession by a demonic Hades-like figure who had dragged her into the underworld. It is indeed a mystery how her ego was not totally shattered and how she was able to free herself from the dark psychic forces that continued to haunt her after her escape and the suicide of her abductor.

Underworld experiences such as rape and other violations by masculine power profoundly alter a woman's sense of identity and bodily integrity, precipitating an existential crisis and spiritual alienation. In various cultures, multifarious forms of violence against females are rampant: acid throwing, breast ironing, bride burning, honor killing, female genital mutilation, infibulation, forced abortion, forced pregnancy, forced prostitution, sex trafficking, marital rape, the murder of pregnant women, sexual slavery, and many other practices that denigrate the feminine. In 2012, Heal Africa reported that in the Democratic Republic of the Congo 2,339 female rape victims reported to clinics in the province of North Kivu in the first six months of 2012 alone.[15] Statistics from 2013 show that in India a woman gets raped every twenty minutes and child rape increased by 336 percent between 2003 and 2013.[16] Equally shocking, in a 2011 survey in the United States, nearly one in five women admitted to being sexually assaulted.[17]

In the context of violence against women, the trauma complex is an appropriation of psychic energy and a source of deep agony, which robs women of their erotic desire and distorts their relationship to sexuality and intimacy. But it is not only sexual deadness that women suffer from after being sexually abused; it is loss of the ability to be fully present and alive so as to experience relatedness and loving intimacy. My patients appear as if the libido has totally withdrawn from their lives; indeed, it has fallen into the unconscious, where it works to produce disturbing symptoms or activate the shadow. After the annihilation of everything that truly mattered to them, they are often consumed by hate—self-hate, hate for others, and hate for the world at large.

Deeply traumatized individuals are stripped of everything and feel as naked and exposed as Inanna when everything was taken away from her. Sometimes, in this rock-bottom condition of archetypal abandonment, in this abyss of rage, disillusionment, and hate, an enantiodromia, a breakthrough can occur. In my work with these wounded souls, I provide a *temenos*, a secure space where the instinctual life can be reclaimed and the split-off parts of the psyche with their blocked psychic energies can be integrated. In order to heal their disconnection from the body and creative vitality, we search in dreams and imagination for the dark, chthonic, erotic energy that was sacrificed. It is a reunification of what has been torn asunder by traumatic forces. In this process, psychic energy is transformed, and the internal structures are rebuilt and strengthened so that greater flexibility and fluidity can develop.

In working through such devastating traumatic events, I often encounter archaic rage. I am not surprised when in dreams and active imaginations the archetypal images of wrath and maddening rage emerge as images of the Medusa, Kali, and Lilith. I consider it of the utmost importance for women to confront this rage and to get in touch with the dark energies that can assist in leading them out of numbness and petrifaction. Rage can be transformative when it is not directed against the self and "acted in" through self-harming behavior such as cutting, substance abuse, overeating, or starving oneself to death. Rage is an archetypal autonomous force, buried deep in some inaccessible layer of the unconscious, which women often fear and tend to suppress because of cultural conditioning. They have to dig out all of that all-consuming rage that turned inward.

Kali's Rage: The Fire of Transformation

Particularly with women who have been sexually abused, I have found rage to be an important healing energy, a life energy that has been held captive by collective cultural norms and repressed as unfeminine. The myth of Lilith is a good example of how female self-assertiveness and the expression of female eroticism became demonized; the literature depicts Lilith as a malicious, devouring, raging, bloodsucking monster.[18] But here I will focus on Kali, a strong female symbol of empowerment and liberation in modern feminist discourse.

In some texts, Kali is described as young and beautiful, symbolic of overcoming death, symbolic of the wisdom that life and death belong together, that death inevitably befalls all humanity. Engaging in meditation with Kali, contemplating and accepting life as it is, may lead to a wise embrace of all of life's polarities. However, in other texts, she has a frightening and shocking aspect similar to that of Medusa. She is depicted on the battlefield, fighting furiously with a sword. In some of the pictures, she is black, with disheveled hair, blood dropping from her mouth, holding a sword and a severed head. In the Red Book, Jung mentions Kali, but only in her negative aspect: "Unguided by the eye of reason, unmitigated by humaneness, the fire becomes a devastating, bloodthirsty Kali."[19]

While Kali usually symbolizes death, destruction, and terror, according to her rituals, whoever confronts her boldly can integrate and assimilate her power, and thus she turns into an agent of salvation.[20] Women identify with her liminality, her subversive existence outside the order of everyday life, her consuming rage, her violent anger, her capacity to annihilate evil forces, and, more important, her ability to unite the opposites. Kali's embodied fury represents an immense vitality. She is an ambiguous figure, dark and dangerous, yet with a healing potential that is rich in wisdom. Kali's blackness represents the darkness of the underworld, but it also points to the earth, the *prima materia* of infinite potential. Women who align themselves with her darkness and mystery can tap into her wisdom and compassion, qualities that are essential for the wounded self.

Having been sexually exploited, traumatized women feel they have entered the realm of Kali, an upside-down world with strangely perverted values, where all illusions and naive assumptions about the world are shattered. This precipitates a painful awakening to how disordered and destructive the world and human beings can be. With this clarity of vision of what life is all about and the release of all feelings, especially the dark, tabooed ones of wild fury, reconciliation with the paradoxical nature of life can occur, resulting in a widening of consciousness.

Acknowledging Kali's dark power and releasing long buried rage can be as psychically healing as physically shaking off trauma.[21] Feeling and expressing the rage and chaotic despair in a contained manner can be a way of reclaiming the body, of redeeming the part of the self that got crushed in the violent experience. Cultural imprinting usually does not allow women to act out their aggressiveness and their fantasies of power. Consequently, the repressed rage is turned inward into severely self-harming behaviors that stifle and deplete their energy.[22] Clarissa Pinkola Estés writes:

> There are times when it becomes imperative to release a rage that
> shakes the skies. There is a time—even though these times are

very rare, there is definitely a time—to let loose all the firepower one has. It has to be in response to a serious offense; the offense has to be big and against the soul or spirit.[23]

The full awareness of harboring rage, blood thirst, and revenge in one's soul can lead to a different kind of compassion for the fragility and vulnerability of being human. This may precipitate a development toward understanding such existential paradoxes and becoming wiser in the long run.

In the dreams of female survivors of sexual abuse, I have often encountered reverberations of Kali, a personified wrath embodying the dark side and the interconnectedness of sexuality, destruction, and death as the repressed, neglected, or wounded aspects of the feminine. From the depths of the collective unconscious, these images emerge as representations of a collective rage and rebellion against oppression and come to the surface crying out for an integration that will transform the female's victim identity.

However, there seems to be a deeper level at which Kali resonates with the suffering of trauma victims and their hope of surviving. I was excited to find, on my journey through India, a culturally rooted understanding of trauma in relation to Kali that confirmed my view of trauma as a potential catalyst for spiritual transformation. I learned that Hindus see Kali as "the embodiment, not of rage, but of compassion."[24] Roxanne Kamayani Gupta explains that Kali refers to the ability to *be*, a force that provides the strength to exist even in the face of traumatic annihilation. The empowerment Kali offers has to do with gaining the strength necessary to surrender to what is greater than the ego, to what one feels powerless to deal with in any other form, to "transcendent inevitability."[25]

This dynamic of wisdom embodied as spiritual energy is also inherent in the *dakinis* of Tibetan Buddhism.[26] These are fearful energetic beings with liminal wisdom. At home in the ceaseless flux of the void, these "sky dancers," or "sky walkers" as they are also called, dance over the abyss in an act of purification and transformation of ignorance of dualistic thinking. Their dance represents the leap in consciousness that is expected from those who follow in their path. As guardians of the mysteries of transformation, they bring about, through their fiery dance, a true paradigm shift from a mode of cognitive thinking and reasoning to a heart-centered mode of thinking and relating that generates compassionate action. The dance transforms the energies of negative emotions and clinging and brings an awareness of the true nature of reality. Encountering the *dakini* and gaining insight into her true nature cuts through all intellectual conceptualizations and fosters joyful wisdom.

Writing from a psychoanalytic perspective, Jeffrey Kripal draws a parallel between psychoanalysis and tantric practices. Both disciplines are devoted to exploring the nature of human beings, "the powers of sexuality, the body, life, death, and religion."[27] He makes the interesting point that individuals who have suffered sexual trauma may be particularly attracted to a Kali-like figure and her transformative rituals.[28] He and Sarah Caldwell, a female scholar whom he cites, have researched in depth the mysteries surrounding Kali.[29] In an act of "reflexive transparency," both confessed their individual experience of "sexual suffering and physical violence," which motivated their decision to plunge into the "terrifying and liberating truths of the Goddess and her ritually possessed devotees."[30]

I agree with Kripal: the answer to the question as to why anyone would want to identify with and invoke Kali, who represents "aggression and ambivalence" and throws us into the "darkest secrets of the human psyche," is this: "In order to be transformed, to lose one's egoic head and its hardened categories in an exhilarating experience of freedom and depth beyond the surface consciousness we mistakenly take as all we are."[31]

The Ravished Feminine: Medusa's Petrifying Gaze

In the Jungian understanding, it is myth, not science, that offers the better interpretation of human nature and life in its depth. Myths transcend space and time and bridge consciousness and unconsciousness. Jung wrote in the prologue to his memoirs, "What we are to our inward vision, and what man appears to be *sub specie aeternitatis*, can only be expressed by way of myth."[32]

When delving into the phenomenon of the ravished feminine, the myth of Medusa provides a lens through which images may be evoked for a deeper understanding of the acute pain, the deathly horror, and the paralyzing terror that accompany trauma.[33] Medusa is an archaic, ambiguous, mythical figure whose intrigue is helpful in approaching the paradoxical nature of trauma, the theme of life and death, and the anguish of violated and betrayed women. I know of no better symbolic way to illustrate the transformative power of rage than through this myth, which depicts the numinosity of trauma as a *mysterium tremendum et fascinans*. Medusa symbolizes the dark feminine and as such bears interesting similarities to Kali.

In our contemporary world, love and violence, sexuality and power, fatal attraction and death are linked. These traumatic connections are contained in the image of Medusa. She is a victim of betrayal by Athena, whom she served in the goddess's temple as an innocent and loyal maiden. Poseidon rapes Medusa in Athena's temple, but the innocent maiden is blamed for the rape and cursed by Athena. This is a common theme in contemporary attitudes to rape as well: women are said to invite rape with seductive behavior, the way they dress, the late hour of the night at which they dare to go out alone, and so on. As with so many present-day female rape victims, Medusa is the object of projections. Athena is enraged that Medusa's beauty induces Poseidon to desecrate the sacred precincts of her *temenos*. Medusa was a beautiful maiden with golden hair, whose beauty aroused Poseidon, but Athena, her perception distorted by her own projections, curses Medusa, transforming her into a terrifying, hideous creature with a deadly gaze and poisonous snakes in place of her golden tresses.

I "met" Medusa in her native Libya at Leptus Magna, standing face-to-face with her stone medallions. Her terrifying, haunting countenance, even seen through the weather-beaten sandstone, caused my entire being to vibrate. Transformed from a beauty into a monster, she has become an archetypal image of rage, betrayal, and shame, an archetype of the madwoman.[34] Linda Leonard has explored the motif of the madwoman, noting that she represents "a real and powerful force in the psyche" that is "feared by both men and women" because it shows the "frightening face of the feminine" and thus reveals "the potential wrath and power" of sexually abused women.[35] Leonard believes that "if we are to transform this wrathful energy into a usable, creative force, we need first to examine it carefully in ourselves and others," rather than "simply dismiss[ing] it as abnormal or 'just crazy.'"[36] The overwhelming emotional outcry after trauma, the panic that results from the heightened flooding of emotions, and the uncontained aggressive energies that are released often make women feel as if they are indeed mad and outside the normal mode of functioning.

Medusa is also betrayed and victimized by Perseus, who cuts off her head in an attempt to eliminate forever her power to victimize others. With her tortured gaze and her silent scream, she turns people into stone.[37] This symbol of petrifaction, of turning everything that meets her gaze into stone, speaks to the idea that trauma precipitates an emotional paralysis. In clinical terms, petrifaction, which often manifests itself in a loss of voice, denotes a deficit in emotion processing or a loss of the meaning-making function, both of which are of paramount importance in surviving trauma.[38] The theme of being silenced, of losing one's voice, appears repeatedly in trauma therapy. This brings to mind the story of Maya Angelou, an African-American poet, who became literally mute at the age of eight when she was sexually abused by her mother's boyfriend and remained mute for five years following that incident. She has written about her experience in several autobiographies, including *I Know Why the Caged Bird Sings*.[39] Therapeutically, speaking out is essential in restoring the trauma victim's voice, self-worth, and dignity.

The many different versions of the Medusa myth present harming and healing as complementary elements. In Apollodorus's account, Asclepius (the god of medicine and healing) used the blood that flowed from Medusa's left side to put people to death and the blood from her right side to save people and even bring the dead back to life.[40] Similarly, trauma can be an agent of psychic annihilation or of psychic resurrection and growth. The paradox of destruction and creation is also symbolized in this myth in the act of cutting off Medusa's head. Out of the wound at her neck she gives birth to two sons: Pegasus, the winged horse, a symbol of creativity and vitality, and Chrysaor, the winged boar, sometimes also depicted as a giant. According to Apollodorus, both sons were conceived as a result of Poseidon's rape of Medusa.[41] This again speaks to the creative potential of trauma.

Just as there are many versions of this myth, there are also many approaches to interpreting this dreadful aspect of the feminine.[42] Placed in the context of masculine domination over the feminine, it represents the silencing of sacred feminine wisdom, represented by the Gorgon Medusa, and more broadly, the rape of the feminine in patriarchal culture. In his essay "Medusa's Head," Freud equated decapitation with castration and used the myth to amplify his notion of castration anxiety; he saw in the snaky head a symbol of the fear-inducing female genitals.[43] The myth can also be seen to represent dissociation, in the severing of the head from the body.[44] The flight out of the body is commonly observed among traumatized women (and men as well). After rape and humiliation, female trauma survivors often feel subhuman; they are "damaged goods," lacking self-worth, alienated from the world, stigmatized, and filled with self-loathing.

The Medusa myth speaks of curse and stigmatization, rape and untamed sexual passion, decapitation and creativity, destruction and creation, the lethal and the fecund. It can be interpreted from the perspective of the traditional antithesis of *logos* and *eros*, head and heart. Medusa appears as Athena's shadow; however, these two figures are connected by the underlying unity of the goddess's sacred power. It is a myth about feminine wisdom and the molestation and eclipse of this wisdom, the severing of the self from a more intuitive way of being, and fixation and petrifaction through a trauma complex. Originally, Medusa was an ancient symbol of female power and wisdom. But in Greek culture, feminine power was feared. Medusa's beheading mythologizes the killing off of the wisdom aspect of the feminine, and what remained is the one-sided representation of her destructive potential.

On a literal level, I have often seen sexually abused girls either develop into Athenas—high achievers, perfectionists, controllers, overly adapted to patriarchal values, head-oriented, highly defensive, trapped in intellectualization, afraid of intimacy, lacking a connection to their feminine roots—or take on Medusa's shadow, acting out the dark, wild madwoman, out of control, with a promiscuous, compulsive sexuality, unintegrated, and living on the margin in a twilight zone. In clinical practice, Medusa's shadow, the defensive strategy of identification with the aggressor, is also painfully present.

Thus, Medusa is an apt metaphor for trauma, too horrifying and dangerous to look directly in the eye. In working with trauma, clinicians have learned to approach the traumatic core (the face of Medusa) only with the greatest caution, circumambulating it in a tactic reminiscent of Perseus's use of his reflecting bronze shield, fearing the power of the trauma complex and its "radical evil," which might paralyze and suck even the clinician into the dark abyss.[45] The risk of "vicarious traumatization" (the developing of symptoms similar to those of trauma victims with whom one is closely associated), is well known in this emotionally demanding field.[46]

In addition to her underworldly aspects and liminal nature—part horse, part human, part bird, and part winged demon—Medusa shares with victims of sexual violence the deadening and disembodiment of instinctual energies. The reclamation of these energies becomes the therapeutic focus, as therapists seek to empower victims to become self-nurturing and to bond with their feminine self beyond the dictates of male prescriptions.

Yearning for Death: The Trauma of Betrayal

Ariadne: Is there no Beyond?
                    —Hugo von Hofmannsthal, *Ariadne auf Naxos*

While I was reflecting on the grief, distress, and inconsolability of my traumatized female patients, I happened to see two productions of Richard Strauss's opera *Ariadne auf Naxos*. According to the opera's librettist, Hofmannsthal, the story of this opera concerns the antinomy of being and becoming. I was deeply moved by the opera—both the music and the libretto—and found myself transported into a resonant reverie that evoked images of the moods and memories of my trauma patients. To me, Ariadne seems marked by the trauma of betrayal, unprotected, "exposed on the cliffs of the heart" (to borrow a line from Rilke), beyond all comfort.[47] Abandoned and betrayed by Theseus, trapped in deep despair, she yearns for release through death. The theme of the opera correlates with the central question of trauma therapy: After tragic loss and betrayal, is a living transformation ever possible?

Ariadne appears as a crushed woman, a "broken spirit," submerged in her pain: "My mind contains nothing more than shadows chasing each other out."[48] Her psychic landscape resembles the "barren island" on which she was abandoned. Her lament expresses a clinging to what is lost, an eternal state of being stuck, with no future in sight—exactly the feelings I encounter in my practice with severely traumatized women.

The opera unfolds in a mythic, timeless space; but the dramatic structure is a mirrored interweaving of past and present. It is an artistic melding of the themes of loss and new beginnings, death and becoming (*Stirb und werde*). As with trauma, we are situated in the realm of boundaries and their dissolution. The almost intolerable spiritual tensions between complementary forms of existence are embodied in the contrast between the vivacious Zerbinetta and the life-weary Ariadne. Hofmannsthal understood the mythic elements of the opera as "abbreviations for the soul's processes," archetypal relational patterns and modes of experience.

Like many who have experienced traumatic events, Ariadne lives a de-souled existence. The thread to Thou is broken. The people around her seem like shadows, without substance, unreachable. I am reminded of a female patient of mine who felt she had lost all connection to the world, to others, and even to me as her therapist. She found a way to show me how every thread to the outer world had been broken and how she had lost herself in that breaking: she drew two pictures, a self-portrait and a picture of me as her therapist, and threaded pieces of string through the pictures, binding herself to me at the hands, the heart space, and the forehead chakra. Then she cut through the strings. She brought the pictures with her to the next session, showing this broken connection. Tuning in to the theme of rupture and repair, I carefully tied the strings back together.

Ariadne wants only to forget. It is unbearable even to think about the beauty of her past with Theseus. Her desire to drink the waters of Lethe, to sink into utter oblivion, runs deep: "What a beautiful thing it was—Theseus and Ariadne, walking in the light, rejoicing in life. But what is the use of knowing that? If only I could forget! I am utterly ashamed of being so shattered!" This reminds me of a conversation I had with war-traumatized children in Sarajevo a few days after the end of the bombings. We were sitting in an ice-cold room, freezing, when an eight-year-old shared his deepest wish: "I wish a doctor would come and give me a great big shot, so I could forget everything and not know what I've seen and heard any more."

In the opera, Ariadne's yearning to find what she has lost ("yes, this I still must find: the girl that I once was") recalls the passionate quest of sexually traumatized women to reconnect with a time before the trauma, to recover their former feelings of being well and whole. I think of a young, anorexic patient who had been sexually abused by her father for years. He had let his colleagues have sex with her in lieu of payment, had got her pregnant twice, and had compelled her to have an abortion both times. Her adult life consisted of a series of sequential traumas. She yearned for death as the final release from her endless round of suffering. Whereas Ariadne, in the opera, dreaming aloud, eagerly awaits the day when she can "wrap herself in her mantle, cover her face with a veil, and lay herself down in private and be a corpse," my patient scoured the Internet for the posts of young girls who wrote wistfully about the seductive sweetness of suicide, the absolute freedom of choosing death, the ultimate act of self-determination: rescuing oneself from the spiral of violence. She explained:

> I can't bear the painful feelings and memories any more. Pain in my soul. It hurts so much. I can't go on. I'm buried. To have to function in this world is exhausting. Unable. I can't live, I mustn't live. It doesn't suit me. I haven't earned it. Life is around me, but not in me. Done for. I am a tall order, a degenerate species. I can only feel myself through pain. Can't cry. Petrified and numb. Being normal is too hard. Self-hate. Everyone looking at me, seeing I'm dirty. A filthy, useless bunch of cells. I'd like to be a neuter. Nothing in me. Hollow and empty. Death means endless spaces. Yearning for peace. End of the great meaninglessness. Yearning for death. Wanting to be gone. Away from here. Forever. Tired of life. On the Internet, on suicide pages, I feel understood. Finally, a community that connects. I meet people who are certain about death. My spirit triumphs over my hateful body. I decide. I have myself under control. Autonomy. No more being controlled from outside. The possibility of doing it gives me security. Security for self-determination. Security for action. I observe and take part. One day, a young woman has done it. She's dared to take the step. Many in the forum admire her. Suddenly there's a gap in the forum. But I am frozen. Made of stone. I'm different. I don't admire. Emptiness inside. Uncertainty. And then the pain. I can't do "it." I'm incapable even of that. Failure. I make a conscious choice to stop going to the forums. The undertow is too dangerous for

me. I know that I am not strong. I often fight with myself;
but to run away, to flee, doesn't express who I am. Sometimes
this is very hard to bear.

In the opera, Ariadne calls out to Hermes: "You will set me free,
give me to myself. This burdensome life, take it from me. I will lose
myself entirely in you." With almost the same ecstasy, this patient has
committed herself to the melody of death and given herself over to the
archetypal pull toward the land of no return.

Ariadne's yearning for the realm of death parallels the suffering of
my patient who lived for a long time in the liminal region of Hades.
Haunted by the desire for death, while living a life that is no life, has
been the often silent lament of many severely traumatized women who
have been raped and betrayed.

NOTES

[1] C. G. Jung, letter to Victor White dated January 30, 1948, *C.
G. Jung Letters, Vol. 1: 1906–1950*, trans. R. F. C. Hull (Princeton,
NJ: Princeton University Press, 1973), p. 492.

[2] Virgil, *Georgics* I, 145–146, quoted in David R. Slavitt,
"Preface to the 1990 Edition," in *Eclogues and Georgics of Virgil*,
trans. David R. Slavitt (Baltimore, MD: Johns Hopkins University
Press, 1990), p. xvii.

[3] Virgil, *Aeneid* VI, 135, 261.

[4] Betty De Shong Meador, *Uncursing the Dark: Treasures from the
Underworld* (Wilmette, IL: Chiron Publications, 1992).

[5] Sylvia Brinton Perera, *Descent to the Goddess: A Way of Initiation
for Women* (Toronto: Inner City Books, 1981).

[6] James Hollis, *Swamplands of the Soul: New Life in Dismal Places*
(Toronto: Inner City Books, 1996), p. 8.

[7] Florian Langegger, *Doktor, Tod und Teufel: Vom Wahnsinn und
von der Psychiatrie in einer vernünftigen Welt* (Frankfurt: Suhrkamp
Verlag, 1983).

[8] Thomas Szasz, *The Myth of Mental Illness: Foundations of a Theory
of Personal Conduct,* rev. ed. (New York: Harper and Row, 1974); and
*The Theology of Medicine: The Political-Philosophical Foundations of
Medical Ethics* (New York: Syracuse University Press, 1988).

[9] As the academic chair of the Jungian Odyssey, an annual off-campus retreat organized by the International School of Analytical Psychology Zürich (ISAPZürich), I am particularly fascinated with Homer's *Odyssey*.

[10] Jung, *MDR*, pp. 179, 181.

[11] See James Hillman, *The Dream and the Underworld* (New York: Harper and Row, 1979).

[12] From the poem "The Holy Longing" (1814) by Goethe, translated by Robert Bly, in *News of the Universe: Poems of Twofold Consciousness*, ed. Robert Bly (San Francisco: Sierra Club Books, 1995), p. 70.

[13] For a discussion of voluntary and involuntary descent, see Hollie Jeanne Hannan, "Initiation through Trauma: A Comparative Study of the Descents of Inanna and Persephone (Dreaming Persephone Forward)" (PhD diss., Pacifica Graduate Institute, Carpinteria, CA, 2005), ProQuest/UMI 3302061.

[14] For more information, see Natascha Kampusch's autobiography, *3,096 Days*, with Heike Gronemeier and Corinna Milborn, trans. Jill Kreuer (London: Penguin Books, 2010); see also Allan Hall and Michael Leidig, *The Girl in the Cellar: The Natascha Kampusch Story* (London: Hodder Paperbacks, 2009).

[15] Cited in "Democratic Republic of the Congo 2012 Human Rights Report," United States Department of State Country Reports on Human Rights Practices for 2012, accessed August 26, 2013, http://www.state.gov/documents/organization/204319.pdf.

[16] Spence Feingold, "One Rape Every 20 Minutes in Country," *Times of India*, August 25, 2013, accessed August 26, 2013, http://articles.timesofindia.indiatimes.com/2013-08-25/delhi/41445745_1_panel-discussion-december-16-incident-photo-exhibition. While writing this, I read that this month, February 2013, in Bhandara, India, three young girls, sisters between the ages of six and eleven, were raped, murdered, and thrown into a well. It is a shocking statistic that between 500,000 and 700,000 females are eliminated from India's population every year through female feticide and female infanticide. See Rita Banerji, "Why Kali Won't Rage: A Critique of Indian Feminism," *Gender Forum: An Internet Journal for Gender Studies* 38 (2012), par. 9, accessed August

26, 2013, http://www.genderforum.org/issues/passages-to-india/why-kali-wont-rage/page/2/.

[17] Roni Caryn Rabin, "Nearly 1 in 5 Women in U.S. Survey Say They Have Been Sexually Assaulted," *New York Times*, December 14, 2011, accessed August 26, 2013, http://www.nytimes.com/2011/12/15/health/nearly-1-in-5-women-in-us-survey-report-sexual-assault.html.

[18] Siegmund Hurwitz, *Lilith, the First Eve: Historical and Psychological Aspects of the Dark Feminine,* 2nd rev. ed., ed. Robert Hinshaw, trans. Gela Jacobson (Einsiedeln, Switzerland: Daimon Verlag, [1980] 1999).

[19] Jung, *RB*, p. 367.

[20] David R. Kinsley, *Hindu Goddesses: Visions of the Divine Feminine in the Hindu Religious Tradition* (Berkeley: University of California Press, 1988), pp. 124–125.

[21] Mary Valentis and Anne Devane, *Female Rage: Unlocking Its Secrets, Claiming Its Power* (New York: Random House, 1994).

[22] Rebecca Livingston Pottenger, "The Maiden's Missing Anger: Contemporary Women, the Archetypal Feminine, and the Unmaking of the Patriarchy" (MA thesis, Pacifica Graduate Institute, Carpinteria, CA, 2011), ProQuest/UMI 1492815.

[23] Clarissa Pinkola Estés, *Women Who Run with the Wolves: Myths and Stories of the Wild Woman Archetype* (New York: Ballantine Books, 1995), pp. 360–361.

[24] Roxanne Kamayani Gupta, "Kālī Māyī: Myth and Reality in a Banaras Ghetto," in *Encountering Kali: In the Margins, at the Center, in the West*, ed. Rachel Fell McDermott and Jeffrey J. Kripal (Berkeley: University of California Press, 2003), p. 140.

[25] *Ibid.*, p. 141.

[26] Judith Simmer-Brown, *Dakini's Warm Breath: The Feminine Principle in Tibetan Buddhism* (Boston: Shambhala Publications, 2001).

[27] Jeffrey J. Kripal, "Why the Tantrika Is a Hero: Kali in the Psychoanalytic Tradition," in *Encountering Kali: In the Margins, at the Center, in the West*, ed. Rachel Fell McDermott and Jeffrey J. Kripal (Berkeley: University of California Press, 2003), p. 197.

[28] *Ibid.*, p. 211.

[29] Sarah Caldwell, *Oh Terrifying Mother: Sexuality, Violence, and Worship of the Goddess Kali* (Oxford, UK: Oxford University Press, 1999).

[30] Kripal, "Why the Tantrika Is a Hero," pp. 211–212.

[31] *Ibid.*, p. 217.

[32] Jung, *MDR*, p. 3.

[33] See Ovid, *The Metamorphoses of Ovid*, trans. Allen Mandelbaum (San Diego, CA: Harcourt, 1993). See also Robert Graves, *The Greek Myths* (New York: George Braziller, 1959); and Apollodorus, *The Library of Greek Mythology*, trans. Robin Hard (Oxford, UK: Oxford University Press, 1997).

[34] Sandra Edelman, *Turning the Gorgon: A Meditation on Shame* (Woodstock, CT: Spring Publications, 1998).

[35] Linda Schierse Leonard, *Meeting the Madwoman: Empowering the Feminine Spirit* (New York: Bantam Books, 1993), pp. 12–13.

[36] *Ibid.*, p. 13.

[37] Cathy Ann Diorio, "The Silent Scream of Medusa: Restoring, or Re-storying, Her Voice" (PhD diss., Pacifica Graduate Institute, Carpinteria, CA, 2010), ProQuest/UMI 3447665.

[38] See Mark Montijo, "Medusa's Gaze: What the Ancient Greeks Knew about Acute Psychological Trauma" (PhD diss., Pacifica Graduate Institute, Carpinteria, CA, 2006), ProQuest/UMI 3250881, pp. 44–47.

[39] Maya Angelou, *I Know Why the Caged Bird Sings* (New York: Bantam Books, 1997). See also Linda Leonard's chapter on the "caged bird" motif; Leonard quotes from Maya Angelou's poem, "I Know Why the Caged Bird Sings"; Leonard, *Meeting the Madwoman*, p. 71.

[40] Apollodorus, *Library of Greek Mythology*, p. 119. See also Marjorie Garber and Nancy J. Vickers, eds., *The Medusa Reader* (New York: Routledge, 2003), pp. 16–19.

[41] Apollodorus, *Library of Greek Mythology*, p. 66.

[42] See Garber and Vickers, *Medusa Reader*.

[43] Sigmund Freud, "Medusa's Head," in *The Standard Edition of the Complete Psychological Works of Sigmund Freud*, ed. and trans. James Strachey, vol. 18 (London: Hogarth Press, 1964), pp. 273–274.

[44] Montijo, "Medusa's Gaze," pp. 17, 25, 98.

[45] See Montijo, "Medusa's Gaze," p. 40. Montijo notes that "it is not Medusa herself who causes the spectator to turn to stone. The victims of Medusa all *looked* at her. . . . [T]he key to human reaction to trauma [is] in the manner of perception; the way in which the image of Medusa [is] taken in" (p. 20).

[46] Laurie Anne Pearlman and Karen W. Saakvitne, *Trauma and the Therapist: Countertransference and Vicarious Traumatization in Psychotherapy with Incest Survivors* (New York: W. W. Norton, 1995). See also I. Lisa McCann and Laurie Anne Pearlman, "Vicarious Traumatization: A Framework for Understanding the Psychological Effects of Working with Victims," *Journal of Traumatic Stress* 3, no. 1 (1990): 131–149.

[47] Rainer Maria Rilke, *The Selected Poetry of Rainer Maria Rilke*, ed. and trans. Stephen Mitchell (New York: Vintage Books, 1989), p. 143.

[48] All quotations from the libretto and Hofmannsthal are my translations, taken from the program notes, *Ariadne auf Naxos*, ed. Ronny Dietrich, Opernhaus Zürich, 2012.

PART II

THE CLINICAL LENS

W hen Ruth (Rut, in German) visited me to talk about her reaction to my book *Soul Murder* and about her experiences in the world of the spirit, she presented me with a copy of her book *Trauma and Art: Sexual Abuse and Depression*, a record of her journey of recovery from the trauma of sexual abuse and her struggle for redemption with the help of therapy.[1] I have included some of the paintings from her book along with her accompanying text as homage to her and to her courageous transformation.

NOTE

[1] Rut: Gaetano Benedetti and Gottfried Waser, *Trauma und Kunst: Sexueller Missbrauch und Depression* [*Trauma and Art: Sexual Abuse and Depression*] (Basel: S. Karger Verlag, 2004).

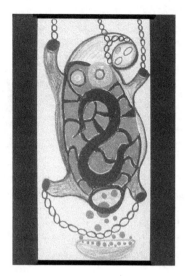

Figure II.1: After my exploitation.

Figure II.2: How I feel about my body in everyday life.

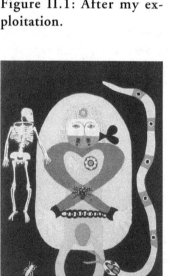

Figure II.3: Captured. There is no possibility for this child to escape from her sexual abuse.

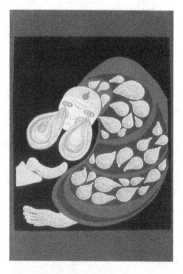

Figure II.4: Mourning. A woman of grief walks alongside each sexually abused woman.

Figure II.5: Two symbols. The stigma of abuse is painfully imprinted on my brow. The third eye, visible on my other brow, allows an expansion of my powers of perception.

Figure II.6: Vernissage. I am blossoming. I have become a flower fairy. The butterfly on my chest shows that I have made it through the dark. The poisonous snakes and evil hands are bound in chains.

CHAPTER SEVEN

RETRIEVING SOUL: ECHOES OF THE RED BOOK IN TRAUMA THERAPY

The American Jungian analyst Nancy Furlotti describes the Red Book as "medicine for our times."[1] If this is true, then my question is: How can I use the insights from the Red Book therapeutically in working through trauma without assuming that Jung's path—his abysmal "solitary way"—is the only template for patients making their way through traumatic affliction? What follows is my attempt to translate into clinical practice Jung's symbolic, philosophical, and spiritual approach to psychic suffering as described in the Red Book. I think Jung, with his extraordinary visionary capacity, anticipated, as early as 1912–1913, the major trends in contemporary trauma therapy. Current theories and techniques in clinical trauma practice echo themes found in the Red Book: soul retrieval, working the shamanistic way, undoing dissociation, ego-state therapy, focus on resources, journaling, inducing and working with fantasies, the use of metaphor and imagination, art therapy, mandala work, body-oriented approaches, and yoga.

Dissociation and Ego-State Therapy

The Red Book provides insights into fragmentation, dissociation, and the autonomous behavior of complexes. It documents the assimilation of unconscious contents into ego-consciousness, which leads to recovery from trauma and a gradual healing of dissociation. By personifying the contents of the unconscious, Jung was separating himself from them, thereby making it possible to establish a dialogue with them and thus bringing them into consciousness. Jung's nascent theory of complexes and ego-states eventually developed into the current state of the art in trauma therapy. His description in his autobiography of his conscious switching between his childhood personalities No. 1 and No. 2 is basically an intuitive conceptualizing of different ego states that he needed to integrate.[2] Likewise, the multiple archetypal figures that emerge in the Red Book, which are personifications of autonomous psychic factors, can be seen as split-off ego states. They foreshadow the psychodynamic clinical approach to trauma and dissociation known as ego-state therapy.[3]

Ego-state therapy was developed in the early 1970s by John and Helen Watkins.[4] It combines Paul Federn's concept of ego states with Jung's theory of complexes and employs hypnosis to access covert ego states that are not normally accessible to consciousness. It also uses the techniques of group and family therapy to resolve conflicts between incompatible ego states, which are conceived of collectively as a "family of self" within the individual.

The underlying theories that inform this approach are the concept of the multiplicity of personality and the dissociative spectrum. According to Federn, personality is not merely a composite of random cognitions, affects, and perceptions. Rather, these mental contents are clustered in various configurations, each around its own organizing principle, what Federn called "ego states." Ego states are formed in the course of normal development, or through introjection of significant others, or in response to trauma. All individuals contain several ego states with varying boundaries. Those who have been through traumatic experiences have deeply wounded, dysfunctional, nonadaptive ego states with rigid, impenetrable boundaries and a high degree of dissociation. The splitting off that occurs in trauma is a defense mechanism, a phenomenon that Jung was acquainted with from his early personal experiences and later incorporated into his theory of complexes.

The different ego states manifest themselves in various moods and behaviors, depending on the situation. Normally, the neural pathways in the brain enable us to switch easily between these states and adapt quickly to new or adverse circumstances. In the emotionally healthy individual, the various ego states are embedded in an overarching energy that provides the feeling of unity, coherence, and continuity necessary for a sense of self. A severe crisis can shatter this sense of unity, causing a splitting into multiple personalities or subpersonalities. This phenomenon can be seen in borderline personality disorder or, at the extreme end of the continuum, in dissociative identity disorders. The "splinter psyches" can be experienced as independent inner figures that are critical, devaluing, and mocking of the self, just like those that haunted Jung in the Red Book. The goal of ego-state therapy is to facilitate the communication to the conscious self of traumatic material that has been saved in neuronal networks and thereby to promote internal harmony and interconnectedness.

The four treatment phases of healing used today in trauma therapy parallel those used by Jung in dealing with his own troubled psychic state: (1) paying attention to safety and stabilization, (2) accessing traumatic material and resources, (3) resolving conflicts and restabilization, and (4) integration and strengthening of identity.

Stabilization is the *via regia* of trauma therapy. It is the primary way to reduce flashbacks, manage depersonalization and dissociative symptoms, scale down states of anxiety, and enable greater control and autonomy. The therapist needs to constellate an emotionally supportive field, in which emerging phenomena can be observed with great concentration and care and split-off affects can be reclaimed and reconnected with the patient's lived experience. My salutogenic, resource-oriented method is marked by the re-creation of coherence, including at the physical level. It involves a here-and-now focus and a dialogical approach. My goal is to install sensory-metaphorical elements in the inner construct, thus mobilizing the patient's creative resources.

In working on the Red Book, Jung emphasized everyday structures and attention to hourly tasks as factors essential for survival. He used stress-reduction techniques, digesting difficult material in small doses, a practice that is now part of all trauma-therapy interventions. Jung came up with these self-soothing techniques intuitively. To balance himself, he also took time off from work and practiced yoga. He freed himself from external burdens in order to recover from the psychic stress of his confrontation with violent emotions and inner images. In Toni Wolff he found an empathic, mirroring presence and a supportive, reflective companion. Her mental and spiritual support provided the framework for mentalization during his *nekyia*. And from his wife, Emma, he received the kind of everyday support that in today's trauma-therapeutic practice would be called activation of social resources.

The stages of healing in trauma therapy also echo Jung's description of the psychological processes of confession, explanation, education, and transformation. Psychoeducation is an important intervention strategy in the tasks of stabilizing patients, enabling them to bring their physiological and psychic distress under greater control, and helping them to understand more clearly the meaning of triggers and the impact of trauma on perception, memory, consciousness, motivation, affect, and body states. It is helpful to explain to patients the posttraumatic changes in ego states, to educate them about self-harming behaviors, to teach them coping skills, and to raise their awareness about the triggers for dissociation. I can clarify for them how comorbid addiction may be a dysfunctional attempt at self-healing and self-regulation. Reframing addictive behavior as an attempt at self-healing can alleviate feelings of shame and guilt. A broader understanding of the somatic expressions of chronic hyperarousal and hypervigilance as characteristic aspects of posttraumatic stress disorder is just as necessary as education about the management and mastery of rage and impulsivity and facilitation of the development of a more positive sense of self. In the trauma literature, self is understood as the central processing unit of personality, as a meaning system that organizes experience coherently, provides a sense of autonomy, vitality, and energy, and fosters adaptation and connection to others. Jung's approach to self-healing was through the use of imaginative resources, through expressing and releasing affect, and by increasing communication between his various ego states, thereby generating differentiation, confrontation, and integration. This approach has provided a useful template for today's trauma treatment.

I find the concept of ego states also helpful in the discussion of whether the Red Book is the product of a psychotic breakdown and whether the visions and images reveal a psychotic core. Although "sane or insane" seems to be the question for many readers of the Red Book, I am cautious about making statements regarding borderline conditions, as I have often seen how sense and nonsense are coupled in trauma. Jung functioned normally in his daily activities throughout the journey, and there was always an observing ego, which monitored the process. This can be seen in the insightful way in which he wrote about and illustrated his encounters with these seemingly bizarre ego states in an attempt to harness their powerful energy for healing purposes without being overwhelmed by them. Later he advised: "You must not identify with the unconscious; you must keep outside, detached, and observe objectively what happens."[5]

This misidentification and differentiation that Jung exercised upon himself required nonjudgmental observation and monitoring and distancing himself from what he was experiencing. This attitude of Jung's regarding the contents of the unconscious has become an important coping strategy in modern trauma therapy, which involves being totally present to whatever emerges, nurturing a loving presence, and gaining insight into the role of the mind in processing trauma. For Jung and the tradition of analytical psychology, careful observation and attention to all that presents itself within the psyche (*religio*) is the most appropriate means of educating and expanding consciousness.

The suspension of judgmental thinking, that is, an openness to everything that reveals itself, has a close affinity with the spiritual practice of meditation and mindfulness. By religiously observing what is happening within and without, by becoming mindful of the habitual patterns of mental activity, the rising and receding of thoughts and emotions, the therapist can develop a greater capacity for self-regulation and a reflective stance toward internal states. This capacity is essential in a therapist, because after trauma it is extremely important to process and wind down the emotions that get triggered and put the patient at risk of being flooded.

The methods that Jung intuitively applied to his own experience and recorded in the Red Book can be seen as a template for the set of attitudes to adopt in the therapeutic process, namely, nonjudgmental openness to every experience emanating from the unconscious, acceptance of the complementarity of being and doing, and appreciation of the value of reverie and presence. This set of attitudes characterizes the latest thinking in trauma therapy, where it is described as moment-by-moment, focused awareness, or *mindfulness*, a concept drawn from Buddhist practice.

Mindfulness is a way of relating, through acceptance and empathy, both to oneself in one's current state of being and those one engages with in a caring relationship. Mindfulness and presence are thus not purely phenomenological categories; they also have a spiritual reference. This becomes clear when the practice of mindfulness is compared with the Buddhist practice of pure seeing and perceiving (or "pure presence," as Richard Rohr puts it)—a kind of seeing, hearing, and perceiving that reveals to us the reality of our original nature.[6] Mindfulness can be understood as "the logic of the heart." At the same time, mindfulness involves reflection, for to be mindful is to ponder, recall, and deliberate.

In the wisdom traditions, mindfulness is known as a means for transforming experiences and behavior and ultimately as a path toward the transformation of human suffering. In the treatment of psychopathology, mindfulness has been adapted to fit psychotherapeutic concepts without necessarily hitching it to any one religious or cultural tradition.[7] In a similar vein that emphasizes the universality of the essence of mindfulness, Jon Kabat-Zinn has integrated it into the relatively new discipline of "behavioral medicine" and especially into his program of stress reduction and relaxation at the University of Massachusetts Medical Center. He writes that mindfulness

> can be learned and practiced . . . without appealing to Oriental culture or Buddhist authority to enrich it or authenticate it. Mindfulness stands on its own as a powerful vehicle for self-understanding and healing. In fact one of its major strengths is that it is not dependent on any belief system or ideology.[8]

Researching the interface between mindfulness and self-knowledge, Jungian analyst Polly Young-Eisendrath and other Zen scholars have collaborated to show that cultivation of the transcendent function can lead the therapist beyond the dichotomies of good and evil, of right and wrong, and create that

spaciousness of mind promoted by Buddhist practice.[9] It gives us
the capacity to observe accurately the powers that are in conflict
without becoming personally identified with them, the ability to
perceive what is happening on all levels, and name it. In Vipassana
meditation, naming and noting what is perceived is used to cultivate
greater awareness and insight into the fleeting nature of whatever
arises. Meditation is an invaluable tool for therapists: it develops
concentration, awareness, and insight, as well as acceptance of all
the emerging phenomena and constructs while simultaneously
reflecting on whatever is perceived. Meditation is akin to trauma
therapy in many ways: in both practices one must remain engaged
and alert for long periods of time, tolerate violent emotions without
tuning out, and carry upwelling contents with empathy but without
becoming over-identified with them. One must be a non-judgmental
witness, conscious of boundaries, and one must tolerate powerlessness
without intervening blindly. One must also remain flexible, and not
cling dogmatically to theories. Meditation helps the therapist to let
go of burdensome content, remain detached from hypothetical
interpretations, bear the patient's suffering without evading it, and
remain in resonance, a state of readiness to accept and receive.
Meditation practice refines the openness to the psychoid realm and
enhances our capacity for presence in body, mind, and soul, to
attend to the now-moment, and better serve the Self.

The practical insights of spiritual teachers who are also
psychotherapists, such as Tara Brach[10] or Jack Kornfield,[11] can be
helpful when working with traumatic states; these teachers provide
different ways of meeting who we are in our innermost core. They teach
us how to hold ourselves with compassion and an open heart, accepting
our inner states with greater tolerance and less resistance, paying
attention with loving non-judgmental care. Most of the time, trauma
patients are plagued by feelings of unworthiness, of being dirty or
flawed. They are constantly at war with themselves, raging against their
body, which they perceive as having betrayed them, despairing at their
sense of alienation from others. Cultivating a state of mindfulness helps
them to become aware of mental and physical restrictions.

Psychiatrist John Briere, a professor of psychiatry and
psychology who focuses on trauma, explains how he helps people
to break free from their perceptions and interpretations of what has

happened to them.[12] He gently introduces the possibility that what has been experienced can be viewed in a different way, that our interpretations organize how we feel about and deal with trauma. He implements mindfulness-based interventions to stimulate an awareness of the difference between thoughts and the actual state of the given post-traumatic reality. This technique is meant to help the patient gradually discern the transient nature of those troubling cognitive and emotional processes, how they arise from the past and how they are triggered in the present—and how they can be observed without identifying with them. Psychiatrist John Briere points out that mindfulness and compassion have a markedly positive effect in the treatment of trauma survivors, though there seems to be relatively little empirical research in this area reported in the trauma literature.[13]

Neuroscience has shown how meditation and mindfulness impact the brain and pave the way for transformation, decreasing stress-related cortisol and bringing awareness into the body.[14] Thus, I use mindfulness approaches with patients who have developed chronic pain and high levels of anxiety as sequelae to trauma. In mindfully discerning the difference between the primary sensory experience of pain and the cognitive processing of the somatic experience, the patient develops a subtle awareness of the impermanent, unstable nature of the sensations. This helps the patient to perceive the pain differently, and distance himself or herself from his or her experience so as to become an observer of what is happening. The ability to refrain from identifying with distressing emotions is helpful in reducing avoidant behavior: it facilitates confronting the painful emotions by reducing the fear of becoming numb or paralyzed.

In his Red Book, Jung engaged with the intrapsychic by practicing the method of inner mindfulness, which he later called active imagination. It is a method that embraces both being and doing, and offers the greatest possible openness to self-discovery, sensitive self-perception, and the precise description of experience. It requires a willingness to plunge into and actively engage with the deepest layers of the unconscious. Through active imagination, Jung translated into images the psychic contents that were oppressing him. His dialogue with these symbolic figures grounded him and widened the horizon of understanding within which he could organize his distressing emotions. He described this discovery as "coming to terms with the Other in us."[15] Moments of being are simultaneously part of active imagination. The conscious habits of censorship and judgment must be turned off. For, as Jung writes: "Consciousness is forever interfering, helping, correcting, and negating, never leaving the psychic processes to grow in peace."[16]

The notion of observing one's own soul religiously is beautifully expressed by Jung's translator Richard Hull in a letter to William McGuire, editor of Jung's *Collected Works*. Commenting on how impressed he was with the Red Book and its "real mad drawings," Hull wrote:

> ... Jung is a walking asylum in himself! The only difference between him and a regular inmate is his astounding capacity to stand off from the terrifying reality of his visions, to observe and understand what was happening, and to hammer out of his experience a system of therapy that works. ... [O]nly by his powers of observation and detachment, and his drive to understand, can it be said of him what Coleridge said in his Notebooks of a great metaphysician ...: He looked at his own Soul with Telescope / What seemed all irregular, he saw & shewed to be beautiful Constellations & he added to the Consciousness hidden worlds within worlds ....[17]

Trauma Narratives: Re-creating Identity

Jung's quest for a new myth translates into clinical language as the search for a new narrative, the creation of a new identity in the wake of the failure of formerly guiding narratives about self and the world to explain or recount accurately what happened under traumatic conditions. Empowerment after traumatic experiences involves not only confronting the shadow and abandoning old heroic modes of being, but also creating emotionally powerful narratives to deal with adversity and calling forth the wisdom of creative potential both individually and collectively. The Red Book shows the path to creating a personal myth by integrating archetypal images and symbols into the conscious ego. This creative fantasizing has a complementary effect, which balances the one-sided conscious ego.

Trauma narratives are devices for reclaiming what is lost through trauma. In them the past is reshaped into a personal myth capable of reconstituting damaged identity. "Identity" is understood as the sum total of the stories that a person tells about himself or herself and his or her life. Identity has the quality of a process, providing continuity between who the person was in the past and who he or she is now. It creates a nexus of meanings that enables a person to experience himself or herself as a coherent whole.

As a rule, the construction of identity is an active, individual process of self-construction, which unfolds in the context of a culture and a society. In telling my story, I convey a specific self-image. I tell myself who I am, was, or wish to be. This ability to tell a coherent, comprehensible life story is damaged by extreme trauma. Extreme traumas rupture the continuity of the ego; they create a massive discrepancy between the prevailing narrative and the current reality, which swiftly becomes a crisis of meaning. Articulacy falls apart as coherence is lost. The connection with other people is severed, resulting in social isolation and marginalization.

I recall a 1987 documentary film by Karl Fruchtmann, *"Ein einfacher Mensch"* (A Simple Man), in which the Jewish documentarian explored how Holocaust survivor Ya'akov Silberberg dealt with his memories of his years in Auschwitz-Birkenau.[18] There he had been forced into the *Sonderkommando* ("special unit"), his task being to handle the corpses from the gas chambers in preparation for cremation. His statements in the documentary reveal the loss of a personal narrative:

> I have no words. It is very hard to talk. It feels as if my whole life is lost in a fog. Everything has died. There is no salvation. It will never be any different, my life. It's been ruined. I am like a stone, an empty piece of nothing. I weep for the destruction of my person, my lost self. Everyone is left alone with this. No one can save himself. (My translation.)

When words are lost and a person's life story is obscured in a fog, then experiences cannot be organized into coherent lines of development, and personal identity crumbles. The eclipse of language, the death of fantasy, and the loss of the ability to symbolize lead to a collapse of identity and social estrangement, both typical sequelae of trauma. In my book *Seelenmord: Inzest und Therapie* (Soul Murder: Incest and

Therapy), I noted that child victims of sexual violence frequently describe their childhood in terms similar to those used in Silberberg's statement quoted above.[19] Both kinds of borderline-situations, different though they are, cause fractures between body, self, and the world and precipitate a desperate search to find one's voice again, to shape a new life narrative, a new myth to live by, since part of one's identity is being able to remember one's past.

As a therapist, I listen very carefully to the way life stories are constructed. From these narratives it is possible to identify the dominant archetypal pattern shaping the patient's survival strategy. We know that whenever our ego finds itself in a situation of utmost vulnerability—as in threshold situations—archetypal dynamics can break into our life and behavior with great power. The revelations Jung experienced at the time of writing the Red Book opened his inner world to such an extent that the archetypal world crowded in upon him with all its numinous force.

In such situations, the person's entire spiritual existence may be threatened. In the context of analytical psychology, Donald Kalsched has elaborated the mechanism of the archetypal "self-care system" that kicks in to stave off this threat.[20] Intrapsychic defense mechanisms are activated to avoid the terror of existentially threatening fears. This flight from awareness is the psyche's desperate attempt to save the self from destruction. Consciousness narrows to the immediate present to spare us from having to face our archaic helplessness and subjugation, our total loss of control. In this condition, the individual becomes a closed system, highly fragmented and with a radically limited capacity to act. The task of therapy, then, is to transform this rigidly closed system into an open one, capable once again of creating meaning, reconstructing the past, perceiving the present, and anticipating the future.

In dealing with narratives of violence, I have learnt to identify the relevant symbol structures and archetypal images that show up there, to discern how they organize the traumatic experience and carry and construct meaning. German analyst Christian Roesler has shown that through autobiographical narrative analysis we can learn something about healing and identity reconstruction, since in times of greatest vulnerability the psyche tends to reorient itself in terms of archetypal patterns through narratives.[21] In such narratives can be recognized the same forms found in myths, fairy tales, art, and poetry. Our challenge is to discern which archetypal patterns traumatized individuals identify with, and whether their individuation process is informed primarily by the archetype of the victim or the hero. From trauma narratives we can learn about the victim's self-attributions, the manner and form in which the trauma was overcome, and which archetype—e.g., the wounded healer, the trickster, or the hero—provided meaning and became a resource for survival. In trauma narratives I often encounter the theme of becoming an other, the archetypal theme of transformation.

Both the search for identity and the transformation of consciousness are directed at reversing the many different processes of estrangement that are set in motion by traumatic events. This goal is achieved by connecting symbolically to how one is meant to be, uncovering one's hidden truth, and remembering what has been lost to the mind through dismemberment. What matters, in my view, is the patient's need to overcome the fatal split between body and mind, between memory and emotion. Here, too, the therapeutic task is to regain control over previously unmanageable affects of the trauma complex, strengthen the unmoored, disoriented ego, and mobilize spiritual resources.[22] By releasing the repressed energy locked in the trauma complex, the trauma survivor's capacity for symbolic expression can be enhanced or restored.

In the Red Book I find the key to all trauma work: the emphasis on *integration* without getting swallowed up by or identifying with the unconscious material that is activated by the trauma. In the descent into the unconscious, one learns about integration of behavior, affect, sensation, and cognition, about integration of the shadow into the personality, and integration of the opposites of above and below, of body and soul. In "Scrutinies" (*Liber Tertius* in the Red Book), Jung engaged in a relentless self-analysis, acknowledging all his egoic shortcomings.

Accepting unacceptable traits in oneself, seeing the outer conflict as reflective of an inner opposition, is crucial in working with the dialectics of victim-perpetrator dynamics. A patient's fixation on the victim archetype holds the other primarily as a victimizer. This insistence on victimhood, which provides the survivor with a basis for identity, may feel like resistance in therapy, a stubborn refusal to try out new possibilities of thinking, feeling, perceiving. The shadow of this fixation in the role of victim appears in the patient as an embittered sense of entitlement that calls for reparation. The shadow of the victim is the perpetrator; often this victim-perpetrator dyad is re-enacted in the therapeutic setting, as any experienced trauma therapist can confirm. Through the dynamics of transference, therapists can sometimes feel like tortured victims of their perpetrator patients, who accuse them of being sadistic, and via projective identification, therapists may indeed behave like perpetrators, although consciously experiencing themselves as victims. Owning one's own shadow, and confronting evil, as Jung has shown in the Red Book, is an important step in later phases of the healing journey.

The theme of death features prominently in the Red Book, where Jung wrote: "The knowledge of death came to me that night, from the dying that engulfs the world. I saw how we live toward death ...."[23] Similarly, the encounter with death, whether literally or symbolically (as the annihilation of the ego), lies at the heart of the trauma experience. Jung wrote passionately about the need to surrender to the archetypal theme of death and renewal as "[w]axing and waning make one curve."[24] He considered this kind of surrender crucial for transformation. However, most early-traumatized individuals do not possess this heroic attitude. Very early wounding deprives them of the ego strength needed to face up to the challenge. Not all trauma survivors can bear to engage the feelings of distress that arise over the prospect that the ego might crumble and disintegrate. Some find it impossible to trust that if they yield to the seemingly unbearable agony of the *nigredo*, they will eventually undergo transformation into the light.

The Imaginal Realm

In the Red Book, the way to a higher level of consciousness is described as symbolic.[25] In trauma therapy, this symbolic dimension and the exploration of the imaginal as the *via regia* into the unconscious has been developed into techniques for working with images and visualizations to overcome the feeling of being trapped in ruminations of darkness and despair. Finding the images hidden in overwhelming emotions had, for Jung, a life-saving quality; it prevented him from being torn to pieces, as he later indicated in his autobiography.[26] In "The Symbolic Dimension in Trauma Therapy," I described how the inner images and metaphors that originate in the shared imaginal realm help to organize the patient's experience, reframe the story, and transform the often chaotic, archaic material into conceptual thinking.[27] In the therapeutic relationship, a "space for play" is needed. Patient and therapist engage in the co-creation of a shared imaginal realm, an act that facilitates the process of increasing consciousness.

The Red Book testifies to the value of active imagination, in which the focus of consciousness is lowered to subliminal levels and images are invited in without judgment. However, as helpful as visualization and active imagination can be in integrating what is split off, one has to be extremely vigilant in assessing whether the patient's ego is strong enough to process traumatic intrusions from the unconscious and to tolerate the vacuum in consciousness that Jung recommended producing through systematic exercises. Classical Jungian active imagination encourages imagining a blank screen on which something is invited to emerge. However, this approach can evoke excessive anxiety in a brittle ego. Only in later stages of the healing process can one surrender safely to the symbol-creating function of the unconscious.

Today's trauma therapy techniques draw from hypnotherapy and have been tailored to meet the specific challenges faced by dissociated trauma patients, since active imagination in its classic form is highly unstructured and can lead to affective flooding and hyperarousal. In active imagination, the ego's vigilance level is deliberately lowered in order to enter into dialogue with images rising from the unconscious. With severely traumatized individuals, however, inner images have such strength that the already-weakened ego cannot withstand their power. Thus, I believe that while Jung's insights into the efficacy and healing power of inner images and visions are the foundation of trauma therapy, the technique needs to be modified for safety.

I also use fantasies and metaphors as a matrix within which to repair the patient's damaged capacity to symbolize, but I use them in a more structured and guided form, which provides safety, integration, and stability and reconnects to the symbol systems of myths and fairy tales. Symbol making is the process of transforming concrete events and the characteristics of the outer world into an inner psychic experience. I work exclusively with adults, and therefore with traumas that occur in a developmental phase in which the capacity for symbolizing is already acquired. Very early traumatic experiences are known to inhibit the maturation of the brain, as well as the individual's development of the capacity for symbolization and of the internal system of stress regulation. In late-occurring traumas, however, the capacity for symbolization shuts down and traumatic material thus remains unsymbolized. I consider the image-making faculty of human beings as crucial for survival and the death of the symbolic function as a kind of psychic death. Thus, it is essential to restore the symbolizing capacity of trauma survivors.

Current brain research is now providing confirmation that visualization and the exercise of the imagination not only activate neuronal networks, but also build cognitive, affective, and somatic bridges, and promote the integration of operations in the left and right hemispheres.

In Germany, Psychodynamic Imaginative Trauma Therapy (PITT) has been designed especially for the treatment of trauma—for example, the methods of Luise Reddemann[28] and the imaginative techniques of Michaela Huber[29] for working with dissociative identity disorders. These approaches are concerned mainly with developing the capacity for self-soothing, self-comforting, and self-acceptance. Stabilizing and structuring interventions are given preference over conflict-centered interventions. In these approaches, images are evoked: images of a safe, sheltered inner place where one can feel protected; of a vault in which explosive traumatic material can be deposited and locked away; or of an inner garden, an inner helper, or an inner team that sits around a table and answers questions. Patients usually need the support of a therapist as they strive to draw helpful metaphors and symbols out of their prior cultural experiences. Metaphors are often far more helpful than purely abstract, rational formulations in helping survivors work through the haunting inner representations of their traumatic experiences.

In guided imagination, patients are assisted by imaginary figures, helpful animals, or the therapist at their side, who faces the horrors of the abyss with them. To control affective states of tension, the therapist often introduces images, such as that of a dimmer switch or a remote control, with which the flow of inner images can be stopped, rewound, changed from color to black and white, etc. This "screening technique" is a method of establishing some distance from the troubling, intrusive images of the traumatic event. It enables the patient to control how the images are viewed and to stop viewing them if necessary. In this respect, it resembles the desensitizing techniques of behavioral therapy. This approach is especially indicated for patients whose ego-structure is weak. A direct confrontation such as Jung dared to undertake can be retraumatizing for already severely traumatized individuals, since they are, in their weakened state, generally unable to transform the terrifying images on the imaginal plane. All their mental and sensory channels become flooded to such an extent that they become emotionally and imaginally paralyzed.

Having learned from experience to respect the power of images, trauma therapists have developed the "observer technique."[30] Drawn from meditative practices, it consciously seeks to create distance between trauma survivor and traumatic event, to establish an observing ego that functions as a witness, a "time traveler" who describes what happened "then and there." When I work with images, any element in the picture—a tree, a bird, or any other figure—can take on the role of observer and witness the traumatic event, so that the patient can avoid becoming flooded with affect. Relegating threatening contents to the framework of a picture provides some distance between patient and trauma and makes it safer to deal with intolerable affects.

Repairing the patient's damaged capacity to symbolize involves freeing the ego from archetypal possession, monitoring carefully the patient's state of emotional arousal, and providing tools for preventing emotional and imaginal overload. Just as Jung paid careful attention to whatever surfaced in his imagination, so trauma-therapeutic techniques use journaling, drawing, painting, sculpting, etc. to give voice to inner images and liberate consciousness from a one-sided left brain mode of functioning. I see Jung as a proponent of right brain dominance who realized early on the importance of intuition. This more intuitive attitude is essential when trying to assimilate highly traumatic experiences.

Tending to the images that rise from my patients' wounded sense of self, I need to enter into the deepest recesses of the secret chambers of evil. To accomplish this, I have learned from Martin Buber and

Emmanuel Levinas to respect the ultimate ineffability of the other person's experience. Yet I must keep working to discern, behind all the trauma-induced distortions and deformations, the true face and being of each of these deeply wounded souls.

Working with Mandalas

The mandalas in the Red Book are a testament to Jung's artistic and intuitive abilities. He confessed that while he was drawing them, he had no idea why he was doing so or what they meant—they were spontaneous creations. Jung later reflected that they probably served as a kind of grounding strategy for him while he was in a state of chaos. Drawing mandalas helped him to center and contain what threatened to swamp him. He referred to them as "cryptograms" of the emotional and cognitive state that he was in. He gradually came to realize what they really meant: "Formation, transformation, the eternal mind's eternal recreation."[31]

Trauma therapy makes use of mandalas in a similar manner. Traumatic affects are usually overwhelming, and "free painting," like "mess painting," can consequently threaten the ego, which is already being devoured by the violent, affect-laden, upwelling contents of the unconscious. Art therapy creates a safe container by placing the picture within a circle, which circumscribes the irrupting energy and thus enables the patient to exercise some control. The patient paints within the limits of this boundary, into the circle—or into a triptych, whose three panels depict three aspects: (1) before the trauma, in the left panel; (2) after the trauma, on the right; and (3) the core of the traumatic experience, in the middle.

I am very impressed with the project "Soñando Alto" (Dreaming Big), sponsored by the Combos Educational Corporation in Medellín, Colombia. [32] The project provides emotional support, through the use of mandalas and other art work, for traumatized children who are victims of violence in Comuna 13 (Fig. 7.1). This is the most poverty-stricken and violent neighborhood in Medellín, where young people are murdered daily, houses are burnt down, freedom of movement is curtailed by invisible boundaries, and the danger of being hit by a stray bullet is an ever-present reality. I have seen touching pictures of children creating a "Mandala of Rights," a "Mandala of Inner Strength," and

Figure 7.1: Personal mandalas from the Dreaming High Project, 2011.

beautiful joint mandalas, which foster a sense of community solidarity and strengthened individual identity, which are helping them to cope more effectively with the traumatic realities of their lives (Fig. 7.2).

The local therapist in Columbia, who trains female therapists to tend to women suffering from trauma is convinced of the therapeutic value of mandalas and uses them in the hope of helping the women to overcome their emotional blockages by expressing their fears and anxieties through the creation of pictorial narratives of violence and forced displacement (Fig. 7.3). I saw a group mandala that they drew depicting the wounds of personally experienced violence (Fig. 7.4). In the center was a weapon surrounded by various symbols separated by wavy lines. There were also teardrops painted into the mandala to express humiliation, and small circles of red and purple to represent the experience of sexual abuse and wife battering. Other circles simply represented the abuse of the soul. Finally, the mandala contained figures of people that resembled crosses and a solitary house representing death and forced displacement. The facilitator reported: "I observed at the time they painted these mandalas, that the women grew calmer. They

Figure 7.2: Personal mandalas from boys and girls.

Figure 7.3: Local therapists meditating with mandalas.

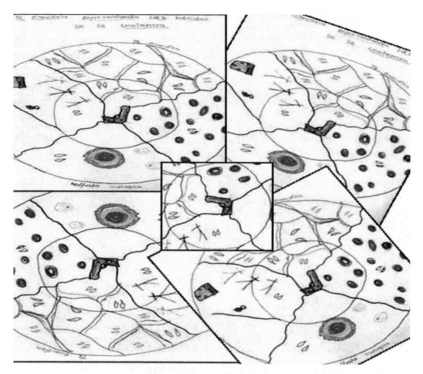

Figure 7.4: Mandala representing the wounds of violence.

were extremely cooperative and willing to engage, even though they
were not familiar with this kind of practice. Some spoke of how long it
had been since they had held a coloring pencil or done a drawing."
Before a final sharing of their inner experiences while creating the
mandalas, they meditated on their mandalas and reached a state of
relaxation and concentration.

   I have included this little example to illustrate how Jung's early
insight into the healing potential of creating mandalas has been
incorporated across cultures into the practice of trauma therapy.

Certainty Lost, Paradox Gained

   Jung's fascination with paradox is apparent throughout the Red
Book. For him, the archetypal world of the collective unconscious cannot
be represented adequately in the language of common sense and our

familiar rational discourse, and is best captured in terms of paradox. He declared: "... [O]nly the paradox comes anywhere near to comprehending the fullness of life. Non-ambiguity and non-contradiction are one-sided and thus unsuited to express the incomprehensible."[33] In the Red Book, he mapped out how to penetrate into the fundamentally paradoxical nature of life. This map represents a paradigm shift from rationality and scientific determinism to a valuing of the irrational and the indeterminate, and incorporates the insight that we cannot get beyond thought by means of thought itself.

Jung's defense of ambiguity reminds me of Søren Kierkegaard's statement: "... [R]evelation is marked by mystery, eternal happiness ... by suffering, the certitude of faith by uncertainty, easiness by difficulty, truth by absurdity ...."[34] Early on in my studies of philosophy I felt drawn to Kierkegaard's diagnosis of (and cure for) the sickness of modern man: the torturous paradox of desperately wanting not to be oneself and yet in despair wanting to be oneself.[35] In dealing with the dynamics of conflict and integration in trauma work, it helps me conceptually to keep in mind Hegel's paradoxical concept of *Aufhebung*, usually rendered "sublation" in English. The German verb *aufheben*, from which the noun *Aufhebung* is derived, is used in three senses: (1) to raise, hold, lift up; (2) to annul, abolish, destroy, cancel, suspend; (3) to keep, save, preserve.[36] This threefold meaning of the word can be applied to trauma therapy, which can be seen as a three-stage process of overcoming, involving: (1) preservation; (2) annulment; and (3) elevation to a higher level. In therapy, the traumatic event is "sublated" (*aufgehoben*), that is, it is: (1) preserved in narratives, active imaginations, and symbolic representations; (2) dissolved so as to annul or cancel its all-dominating power over life; and (3) raised to a higher level of meaning and consciousness, and thereby transcended, superseded, and overcome.

In the Red Book, Jung shows that paradox lies at the core of psychological transformation, since the unconscious is, by its very nature, paradoxical and ambiguous: it is dark and light; animalistic, demonic, and spiritual; numinous, frightening, teleological, and chaotic. Paradox violates our everyday logic and common sense; its contradictions create cognitive dissonance and drive us into the realm of the unthinkable, beyond rationality. Like paradox, trauma creates cognitive dissonance. For the trauma survivor, the pivotal question is whether this dissonance can be made tolerable and acceptable. I recall Jung's words from the Red Book:

> *As day requires night and night requires day, so meaning requires*
> *absurdity and absurdity requires meaning.*
> …
> So meaning is a moment and a transition from absurdity to
> absurdity, and absurdity only a moment and a transition from
> meaning to meaning. (Italics in original.)[37]

My trauma patients have no coherent, linear narrative of their experience; they can express the absurdity of their trauma only through paradoxical behavior or by falling silent, for language is powerless to articulate the inexpressible. In trauma, as in philosophy, Wittgenstein's dictum applies: "Whereof one cannot speak, thereof one must be silent."[38]

Paradox brings together contradictory statements, but unlike mere contradictions, which make conflicting claims to the truth, paradoxes assert that two contradictory notions are true at the same time, challenging us to think no longer in terms of "either-or," but in terms of "both-and." In confronting paradox we are forced to break through the narrow confines of our habitual dualistic ego perspective. Early quantum theorists, after their initial disbelief at what they had discovered, embraced the paradoxical nature of the quantum world.[39] Niels Bohr commented: "How wonderful that we've met with a paradox. Now we have some hope of making progress."[40] However, embracing paradox can bring on mental instability in varying degrees, as the lives of some quantum physicists have attested.[41]

A similar effect might be felt when contemplating the paradoxes of Zen koans. Jung referred to them as "those sublime paradoxes that light up, as with a flash of lightning, the inscrutable interrelations between ego and self."[42] He saw them as spiritual monuments that can be aptly used as analogies for the individuation process. The simple, paradoxical advice, "Become who you are," is an injunction to seek for the self that is concealed in our innermost core. Zen teaches that there is nothing to transcend, that by doing nothing, as in Taoism, nothing is left undone. All we need to do is awaken to what is already given and always there, deepen our insight into our true nature, and act accordingly. Just as we need to refocus our eyes in order to see the image hidden within certain optical illusions, we need to refocus our mind to appreciate the paradoxes of reality. Perhaps, as analysts, we should follow Paul Gauguin's paradoxical example as a painter; he is reported to have said: "I shut my eyes in order to see."[43]

I recall from that the German poet Rahel Varnhagen jotted down a brilliant insight into paradox in her diary. She wrote that paradox is a truth that finds no space in which to expand itself, which is why it appears as a dislocation. Dislocated truth is what I often encounter in trauma therapy. Paradoxes seek to reveal some truth, though this truth may not be immediately apparent. Paradox is the wisdom of the spirit of the depths, which says: "The highest truth is one and the same with the absurd."[44]

Paradox and Transformation

A common paradox encountered in trauma therapy is what John Briere calls "the pain paradox": whenever we attempt to resist pain, the pain paradoxically increases.[45] This is a fundamental reality in trauma therapy and it explains why many trauma survivors engage in a range of numbing, distracting, and avoidant behaviors and, at the same time, experience ongoing posttraumatic stress, anxiety, and depression. We need to learn not to resist the pain of trauma, but to face it and engage with it, instead of sinking into dysfunctional coping mechanisms such as substance abuse or dissociation to survive. Briere claims that research reveals that inviting the pain in ultimately reduces distress. This notion is echoed in the Jungian approach of containing conflicting emotions, holding their tension consciously rather than fleeing from them.

Another approach to paradox is Viktor Frankl's logotherapy, which addresses the paradoxical nature of human behavior. Frankl developed a therapeutic method called "paradoxical intention," in which a patient is brought to the point where he or she gives up fighting his or her symptoms or trying to flee from them. As a consequence, the symptoms diminish. The patient is encouraged to do exactly what he or she fears most. It is the "hyperintention" to avoid something that leads inevitably to precisely what the person wishes to avoid. Paradoxically, hyperintention works, subconsciously, to negate the intention of avoidance; hence, only a paradoxical solution will suffice. Intending *consciously* to negate one's intention of negating the symptom breaks the vicious circle. This recalls Hegel's "negation of the negation," which brings about the *Aufhebung* (or "sublation") spoken of earlier.

The element of unexpectedness and the imperative to change one's existing ontological framework are essential to the clinical efficacy of the paradoxical intention intervention. In trauma therapy, paradoxical interventions push patients to their utmost limit, where they have no choice but to let go. This process is often aided by a sense of humor and a playful attitude, both of which help in breaking free from debilitating hyperreflection and achieving some distance and detachment from the trauma.

It is indeed paradoxical that many patients hold on to their symptoms, no matter how agonizing they are, fearfully avoiding anything that might improve their situation. This is a fundamental paradox in psychoanalytic practice generally. Patients come to therapy with a strong desire for growth and change, but because of their inner conflicts there are also strong, conservative inner forces that undermine their resolve and frequently gain the upper hand. They may be unable to take in and "digest" what analysis has to offer. Healing possibilities can become distorted or "shredded" by the ever-vigilant resistance of defense mechanisms.

Here, to illustrate what the paradox of trauma feels like from the inside, I would like to present the voice of my patient Petra, whose years of analysis were shaped by the necessity of bearing the tension between right and wrong, true and false. Reflecting on her analysis, she wrote:

> *The false feels right, and the right can feel false.*[46]
> *My analysis with you, or better, our analysis, began with a dilemma: I was suffering from something, but it also felt right. I felt false to myself, I negated myself. A dubious kind of self-reflection, a sort of tear, seemed to go through my soul. I was constantly tormented by the great questions: What is my place in the world? Where do I belong? What place is right for me?*
> *I had the feeling I was present in life yet didn't belong to it. Alienation. But isn't alienation only possible where*

a connection existed once (but no more), or at least where you anticipate a connection (that is not yet)? It was also a paradox, being allowed into life and yet simultaneously not belonging there.

At that time, I had—along with a lot of despair— the slight hope that I did not have to stay false forever, that you could help me find a way out of the dilemma. But isn't it the nature of a dilemma that there is no way out, no solution? Looking back, I think the transformation from dilemma to paradox began only later. At some point the first facet of a paradox was revealed: I wished for help in transforming the false into something true. At the same time I wanted you to understand and confirm where I was, to confirm that "falsehood" represented an important part of my inner reality, my self-understanding. Again and again I had the feeling that—for you (too)—I was just faking something. It was just another way of being false, trying to prove myself, and at the same time wishing for the release of having my falsehood disproven.

In the course of my analysis I have noticed that whenever my needs for autonomy come up, and also whenever I try to trust my perceptions, the false turns virulent. Yet in order to be involved with my therapist, it is important that I be in contact with the world and with myself, making concrete, sensory discoveries. For this to happen, sitting on the meditation cushion is a helpful method. Recently it has occurred to me, in this connection, that perceptions occasionally become "really real" to me only through the use of concepts, rather in the way received experiences gain certain intensity and direction only when they are put into words. In this way, familiar constructions are created and established.

The false is oriented to what is outside and in the past.
I have a hard time grasping the false and finding a language for it. And yet, without question, it is there. Amazing that something so enormously important to my

inner life can be so fleeting. Like a ghost.

Being false was like an involuntary movement forwards and backwards. It was like a notorious "yes, but," spoken to a "spirit who always says no,"⁴⁷ making no headway, sliding around on the couch.

My patient experienced her self-negation subjectively, as an active construction, not merely as a passive state of falseness. It was precisely this self-negation that felt right to her and dictated her preferred practices: rumination, self-reproach, and a process she called "shredding." While walking from my office to the train station, after an hour that we both experienced as intense, rich in insights, and full of moving encounters, she promptly started destroying everything good in the experience. She had the image of an electronic machine into which she fed all the contents of the hour to shred them.

For a long time I had the wish and the hope that analysis would make a new, different person out of me, a person who was authentic. For this to happen, my past would have to be rewritten, for I had the feeling that the false had been written into me at an early age. That doesn't work, and yet it works. My perspective on the past has changed in many ways and is still changing. I still clearly remember how, after one of my therapy hours, I became aware that I must live with myself, and that life goes on outside the false system.

At times during meditation I can't really feel my breathing; but I know it's there, it must be there, otherwise I would not be sitting on the cushion. That didn't happen in the same way with the false: it seemed so real and yet was not quite locatable, although I was trying to build evidence for my state of being false.

Destruction is the follower of the false, or maybe even the companion. This showed in the shredding, in rumination, and in tending the grave in a tomb. (The dead mother.) Or it showed in emptiness, a state of being not-really-here, not-really-alive.

In the early stages of analysis with this patient, who was very dear to me and whose ability for reflection I valued, I experienced an unusually powerful and disabling counter-transference reaction. Overcome by leaden fatigue, so that I could hardly keep my eyes open, I experienced a deathly pull into a state of complete emptiness. I could not sustain a thought, had no ideas, and became totally lifeless and incapable of emotion. I tried to fathom what was happening to me during these hours. I also sought supervision in connection with the experience and decided to address it directly with the patient. The "sleeping helmet," as we playfully called the phenomenon at first, became a key and gave us insight into an occurrence that has been described by psychoanalyst André Green, using the metaphor of "the dead mother."[48] Green is not referring to the literal death of the mother (which my patient, however, had also witnessed as a young adult), but to the child's experience of a psychically absent, depressively withdrawn, unavailable mother.

In psychoanalytic terms, the child introjects the mother imago and at the same time splits it off, which means that it cannot be properly buried and mourned. The result is the emergence of a psychic hole, a great emptiness. Not sufficiently mirrored by her absent mother, my client was catapulted into a state of inner emptiness, a terrible inability to feel, which was also painfully constellated in her relational life. This dead-mother complex also had an important structure-providing function for my patient. It promised the illusory security of the familiar, a structure around which she had organized herself for years. Whenever she once again felt unreal and empty, she used the metaphor of the tomb, and grave-tending.

> *"Grave-tending" usually felt right to me. Those were the psychic places I kept searching out, because they gave me—paradoxically—a feeling of security and of being somehow at home. From dilemma to paradox—what's allowed can be transformed. I wanted something to change fundamentally in my life, and at the same time I wanted to keep on being true in my false system, or false in my true system.*

In reviewing the time after her analysis, Petra wrote that, as a counterweight to the static quality of the dilemma, she wanted to comment on transformations:

Transformations through analysis are subtle and vital; they show up even in the way my body feels. Another thing that has changed: I no longer lose myself so much in contact with others. This loss of contact, or the experience of alienation that seemed to come up so suddenly, used to happen for example when I was struggling in conversation, striving to bring a thought somehow to conclusion. I would be present, but only mechanically, as if my strength had suddenly left me or I had become disoriented when I was halfway there, and didn't know any more where I had originally been heading. Also, my fear of the gaps, the pauses in contact, has disappeared, and with it the awful question, "How do I go on from here?" or "What now?" or even the doubt that I could go on at all.

The automatisms of the false haven't disappeared completely; I'm not a new person. And yet in the wake of the automatisms, after the emptiness, something different and new sometimes emerges. Maybe the same power is at work here as in quitting smoking, which continues to amaze me even today. It would be nice if I could trust it even more. These days I'm turning my attention, at least theoretically, to the growth-promoting aspects of the negative—yet another paradox.

Freud took the approach that "the neurotic ego's 'loyalty', so to speak, is primarily to the neurotic status quo (which has, in fact, been ingeniously crafted by that very ego)" and patients seem strongly motivated *not* to know their own mind, since this resistance operates unconsciously, by definition.[49] Traditional psychoanalysts dwell more on the neurotic psychopathology, on the "paradoxical transformation of the opportunity for a cure in treatment into a new version of the 'disease'."[50] A different way of dealing with this paradox has been developed by contemporary interactive psychoanalysts: they embrace the paradox and get lost in it together with their patients in order to find a way out.

Self-contradictory behavior and entanglement in paradoxical knots are part of the human condition, but they often seem magnified in trauma therapy where striving for intimacy with the patient is coupled with striving to establish distance, an interplay of union and separation. Depending on the psychic dynamics of a particular patient, as well as the attachment issues underlying the traumatic configurations, one encounters in analysis either the schizoid fear of intimacy or the depressive fear of abandonment, and the struggle with the paradoxes of love and hate, of boundaries and fusion.

I often feel trapped in the paradoxes of my professional role. Mainstream ideology and insurance companies require a quick fix, creating expectations in patients of wanting to get to the heart of the matter as fast as possible. However, I know from professional experience that we need to move slowly and that the "being with" will be the doing. Furthermore, analysis is the paradoxical assistance towards dying in order to live as learning to live is learning to die and become. I am involved in the paradoxical task of strengthening the ego while simultaneously deconstructing it. It is true that a strong ego is needed to work through trauma and it is also true that, on another level, the ego is a construct that needs to be shed.

The analytical situation, with its analytic dyad and "talking cure," is in itself a paradoxical enterprise. The analytic space must be bounded even as it is open, because there is no safety without boundaries. Furthermore, the process is both gratifying and frustrating; it engenders ambiguity, conflict, and pain as well as growth; it is safe and yet it activates anxiety; it furthers individuation but threatens with severe fragmentation; the setting is extremely structured in terms of time and yet is pervaded by a sense of timelessness. Analysis honors both the conscious self's need for talking and symbolizing, on one hand, and the soul's need for reflection and silence, on the other. One could say, paradoxically, that the soul or the Self speaks to us in silence.

Paradoxical Transference and Countertransference

In *I Hate You—Don't Leave Me*, Kreisman and Straus explore the paradox encountered by analysts working with patients who have experienced trauma and boundary violations.[51] They note that such patients often reenact their experience of the threat of annihilation, of the bottomless pit, of utter helplessness in an unconscious attempt to transfer to the therapist what they felt and are feeling. By pushing the therapist to the very limits of his or her patience, by making him or her feel incompetent, angry, and impotent, these patients make the therapist experience what they have been through. They turn the tables, transforming themselves from victims into victimizers. Within the analytical space, they create the same paradoxical no-win situation of their trauma. Whatever the therapist may say or do—or not say or do— is wrong. There is no way out, and the relational field is highly charged with explosive emotions on both sides. The double-bind dynamics of these no-win situations create a countertransference, over which the analyst often feels guilty.

Didier Anzieu has elaborated this paradoxical interplay of transference and countertransference, and its often unfortunate consequences for both patient and therapist.[52] I have seen this dynamic play itself out often in supervising abuse cases, where the constant pressure on the therapist to be less neutral, less reserved, more caring, more nurturing, more empathic and engaged has led the therapist into a hopeless trap, where all the changes the therapist made pertaining to the setting, the interpretations, the self-revelations concerning authentic personal reactions were doomed to fail from the start and ultimately elicited accusations from the patient and claims of having been abused yet again, this time by the therapist. Paradoxically, the desire on the part of the therapist to gratify the patient's demand for greater spontaneity and personal self-disclosure turns out to be the very means by which the patient-therapist relationship is damaged beyond repair.

It is often difficult for the therapist to witness and endure the degree of devaluation and violence that he or she encounters in trauma therapy. The discovery of mirror neurons has deepened our understanding of the "infectiousness" of the spiritual wasteland that fills the therapeutic space. To witness extreme emotions, to be submerged in the patient's evocative narratives, and at the same time control one's emotional and physiological responses places paradoxical demands on the therapist who is, ideally, expected to maintain a stance of detached engagement.

The severity of emotional disturbance of abused patients can be deeply unsettling and anxiety provoking for the therapist. It can lead to counter-transference reactions, including denial, repression, and a refusal to admit the reality he or she is facing. These reactions can be so intense that the therapist becomes numbed, dissociative, and disengaged from what is being said. Consequently, he or she hears the patient's narrative without listening to it, and the patient once again feels misunderstood, abandoned, and betrayed. The lack of responsiveness from the therapist often leads to bitterness or resignation in the patient, who may experience it as a retraumatizing abuse of trust, or as proof that he or she is truly crazy and hopelessly beyond redemption.

NOTES

[1] "The Red Book as Medicine for Our Times" is the title of a lecture that Nancy Furlotti has given several times in various cities across the United States since the publication of *The Red Book*. See, for example, http://junginla.blogspot.ca/2011_01_01_archive.html.

[2] Jung, *MDR*, pp. 45–107.

[3] For an overview of this therapy, see David Hartman and Diane Zimberoff, "Ego States in Heart-Centered Therapies," *Journal of Heart-Centered Therapies* 6, no. 1 (2003): 47–92.

[4] John G. Watkins and Helen H. Watkins, *Ego States: Theory and Therapy* (New York: W. W. Norton, 1997).

[5] C. G. Jung, *The Psychology of Kundalini Yoga: Notes of the Seminar Given in 1932 by C. G. Jung*, ed. Sonu Shamdasani (Princeton, NJ: Princeton University Press, 1996), p. 27.

[6] Richard Rohr, *The Naked Now: Learning to See as the Mystics See* (New York: Crossroad Publishing, 2009), p. 12.

[7] Steven C. Hayes, Victoria M. Follette, and Marsha M. Linehan, eds., *Mindfulness and Acceptance: Expanding the Cognitive-Behavioral Tradition* (New York: Guilford Press, 2004).

[8] Jon Kabat-Zinn, *Full Catastrophe Living: Using the Wisdom of Your Body and Mind to Face Stress, Pain, and Illness* (New York: Delta Trade Paperbacks, 1990), p. 12.

[9] Polly Young-Eisendrath and Shoji Muramoto, eds., *Awakening and Insight: Zen Buddhism and Psychotherapy* (Hove, UK: Brunner-Routledge, 2002).

[10] See, for example, Tara Brach, *True Refuge: Finding Peace and Freedom in Your Own Awakened Heart* (New York: Bantam Books, 2013).

[11] See, for example, Jack Kornfield, *Meditation for Beginners* (Boulder, CO: Sounds True, 2004).

[12] For more information on John Briere and his work, see his website http://www.johnbriere.com.

[13] John Briere, "Working with Trauma: Mindfulness and Compassion," in *Compassion and Wisdom in Psychotherapy: Deepening Mindfulness in Clinical Practice*, ed. Christopher K. Germer and Ronald D. Siegel (New York: Guilford Press, 2012), pp. 265-279.

[14] Rick Hanson with Richard Mendius, *Buddha's Brain: The Practical Neuroscience of Happiness, Love, and Wisdom* (Oakland, CA: New Harbinger Publications, 2009).

[15] Jung, *CW* 14, § 706.

[16] Jung, *CW* 13, § 20.

[17] Richard Hull, letter to William McGuire, dated March 17, 1961, quoted in Jung, *RB*, p. 221, note 257.

[18] For an English source on Silberberg, see Gideon Grief, *We Wept without Tears: Testimonies of the Jewish Sonderkommando from Auschwitz* (New Haven, CT: Yale University Press, [1995] 2005), pp. 310-334.

[19] Ursula Wirtz, *Seelenmord: Inzest und Therapie* (Stuttgart: Kreuz Verlag, 1989). See also, Glen Hester and Bruce Nygren, *Child of Rage* (Nashville, TN: Thomas Nelson Publishers, 1981).

[20] Donald Kalsched, *The Inner World of Trauma: Archetypal Defenses of the Personal Spirit* (London: Routledge, 1996).

[21] Christian Roesler, "A Narratological Methodology for Identifying Archetypal Story Patterns in Autobiographical Narratives," *Journal of Analytical Psychology* 51, no. 4 (2006): 574-586.

[22] Jung, *CW* 16, § 270.

[23] Jung, *RB*, p. 267.

[24] Jung, *CW* 8, § 800.

[25] Jung, *CW* 8, p. 211.

[26] Jung, *MDR*, p. 177.

[27] Ursula Wirtz, "The Symbolic Dimension in Trauma Therapy," *Spring* 82 (2009): 31–53.

[28] Luise Reddemann, *Psychodynamisch Imaginative Traumatherapie: PITT—Das Manual* (Stuttgart: Klett-Cotta Verlag, 2004).

[29] Michaela Huber, *Der innere Garten: Ein achtsamer Weg zur persönlichen Veränderung* (Paderborn: Junfermannsche Verlagsbuchhandlung, 2005).

[30] Luise Reddemann, *Imagination als heilsame Kraft* (Stuttgart: Klett-Cotta Verlag, 2001).

[31] Jung, *RB*, p. 206.

[32] I wish to thank Ana Sofia Restrepo Saldarriaga, the project coordinator, for sharing her report with me.

[33] Jung, *CW* 12, § 18.

[34] Søren Kierkegaard, *Concluding Unscientific Postscript to Philosophical Fragments, Volume I*, ed. and trans. Howard V. Hong and Edna H. Hong (Princeton, NJ: Princeton University Press, 1992), p. 432 (footnote).

[35] See Søren Kierkegaard, *The Sickness unto Death: A Christian Psychological Exposition for Uplifting and Awakening*, trans. Howard V. Hong and Edna H. Hong (Princeton, NJ: Princeton University Press, 1983), p. 2.

[36] Michael Inwood, *A Hegel Dictionary* (Oxford, UK: Blackwell Publisher, 1992), pp. 283-285.

[37] Jung, *RB*, p. 242.

[38] Ludwig Wittgenstein, *Tractatus Logico-Philosophicus*, trans. C. K. Ogden (New York: Cosimo Classics, [1922] 2010), p. 108.

[39] See Neil Turok, *The Universe Within: From Quantum to Cosmos* (Toronto: House of Anansi Press, 2012).

[40] Ruth Moore, *Niels Bohr: The Man, His Science, and the World They Changed* (New York: Alfred A. Knopf, 1966), pp. 140, 196.

[41] Paul Dirac, Wolfgang Pauli, and Max Born all experienced some form of mental or emotional instability, to a greater or lesser extent, at some time in their adult life.

[42] Jung, *CW* 8, § 431.

[43] Quoted in Julia Cameron, *The Artist's Way: A Spiritual Path to Higher Creativity* (New York: Jeremy P. Tarcher/Putman, 2002), p. 58.

[44] Jung, *RB*, p. 242.

[45] John Briere, *Mindfulness and Trauma: The Pain Paradox* (presentation delivered at the FACES Conferences, La Jolla, California, March 31, 2011). For a video of Briere's presentation, see http://vimeo.com/23342920.

[46] "*Das Falsche fühlt sich richtig an, und das Richtige kann sich falsch anfühlen.*"

[47] In German: "*einem 'Geist der stets verneint.*'" The allusion is to Mephistopheles, who introduces himself to Faust: "*Ich bin der Geist der stets verneint*" (Goethe, *Faust I*).

[48] Gregorio Kohon, ed., *The Dead Mother: The Work of André Green* (London: Brunner-Routledge, 1999).

[49] James H. Hansell, "The Interactive Paradigm and a Psychoanalytic Paradox," *The Psychoanalytic Quarterly* 66, no. 5 (1997): 475.

[50] *Ibid.*, p. 480.

[51] Jerold J. Kreisman and Hal Straus, *I Hate You—Don't Leave Me: Understanding the Borderline Personality* (New York: Penguin Group, 2010).

[52] Didier Anzieu, "Le Transfert Paradoxal: De la Communication Paradoxale à la Réaction Thérapeutique," in *Psychoanalyse des Limites*, ed. Catherine Chabert (Paris: Dunod Editeur, 2007).

CHAPTER EIGHT

CIRCUMAMBULATING
COMPLEMENTARITY

I n the Red Book, as in Jung's later work, complementarity plays as
important a role as paradox; the two are intimately connected to
each other as well as to his concerns as an explorer of the soul. For
him, trauma and spirituality are both governed at a fundamental level
by the principle of complementarity. Ego strengthening goes hand in
hand with ego transcendence, speech with silence, dialogue with
contemplation. In its broadest sense, complementarity implies a "both-
and" approach. It has to do with apprehending things in their totality
from opposed perspectives. Oneness and wholeness are often best
perceived through the use of opposing or contradictory means, the
results of which, when taken together, provide an all-encompassing view
of the phenomenon under investigation.

The concept of complementarity was first articulated by the
psychologist William James in 1890, but it was the Danish physicist
and Nobel laureate Niels Bohr who popularized it by applying it first
to the field of quantum physics in 1927 and then beyond that to
biology, philosophy, psychology, mathematics, politics, religion, and
culture.[1] Bohr's enthusiasm for extending the applicability of the
principle of complementarity was shared by Wolfgang Pauli, from

whom Jung derived much of his understanding of the principle's application in physics.[2]

While some commentators have questioned Bohr's and Pauli's extensions of the principle of complementarity beyond the borders of physics to other fields, I believe their basic insight, namely, that various "incompatible" approaches to observing or studying a given phenomenon can serve to complement each other, is still largely valid and can be applied profitably in the field of trauma therapy.[3]

In trauma therapy, I combine the complementary perspectives of clinical work and spiritual practice, alongside alchemical and archetypal images, so as to create a unitary understanding that supersedes the one-sided concentration on progress and the goal-obsessed overemphasis on efficiency and rationality, which only leads ultimately to stagnation of libido. When this one-dimensionality prevents our psychic capacities from working harmoniously together, some aspects of our psyche become crippled. The lack of balance in the collective psyche is often reflected in the individual psyche. To this one-sidedness also belong the repression of life's shadow aspects and a rejection of the ancient wisdom that sees death and transformation as two sides of the same archetypal reality.

Complementary Modes of Viewing Trauma

I see a mutually complementary relationship in several apparently contradictory conceptualizations of trauma. Trauma may be conceptualized within the framework of the medical model as PTSD, a highly individualistic concept, which is often applied in a stigmatizing and pathologizing manner. This approach disregards the social context in which trauma occurs and embraces the mistaken assumption of a monocausal relationship between the traumatic experience and the symptoms. Trauma is viewed as a predominantly psychobiological event, and research concentrates on memory formation, intrusive thoughts and flashbacks, persistent overstimulation, avoidance, and numbing. A slightly different approach emphasizes primarily the intrapsychic aspect of trauma, focusing on the collapse of psychic structures and the "processual" character of traumatic experience, an idea expressed in Hans Keilson's term, *sequential traumatization*.[4] In sharp contrast to both these approaches, traumatologist David

Becker maintains that traumatization is a psychosocial process. Rather than focusing on the victim's deficits, he views the trauma in its social context. He locates the source of traumatic suffering within the social system, thus implying that society needs to strive for greater security and solidarity.

To these conceptualizations I would like to add a view of trauma as an experience with spiritually transformative potential, which brings about a new orientation and creates meaning through a surrender to the numinous depths of the psyche. I see destruction and growth as complementary and discern a paradoxical unity between abyss and terra firma. In this holistic approach I see a "loving" *coniunctio* of spirituality and depth psychology, in which existing clinical psychological knowledge is expanded on and bound together into a greater whole.

Trauma-related experiences of the abyss are complementary to the process of the expansion of consciousness, which can be understood as the effect of what Jung called the transcendent function, which "arises from the union of conscious and unconscious contents."[5] John P. Wilson, one of the few trauma researchers to make use of Jung, draws upon Jung's notion of the transcendent function and the complementary relationship between consciousness and the unconscious to articulate what he calls the trauma complex.[6] This complex consists of the abyss experience, the inversion experience, and the transcendent experience. The abyss experience is characterized by a disturbance of unconscious contents manifesting as a confrontation with evil, a sense of soul death and nonbeing, and feelings of abandonment, despair, and loss of meaning. The inversion experience is characterized by a disruption of conscious contents manifesting as a reversal of normal, everyday reality with regard to the norms of morality, the political order, the social order, interpersonal relations, or the structural coherence of the self. When these two fundamental traumatic experiences are juxtaposed, the transcendent experience emerges; in the process, the ungrounded self of the abyss experience becomes grounded and the decentered self of the inversion experience becomes re-centered. "The fusion that occurs at conscious and unconscious levels in the Transcendent Experience is subjectively experienced as an acute and immediate sense of organismic strength that emanates from death-in-life versus life-in-death paradigms of self-existence."[7] A path may thus be opened up to a new understanding of self and world and to an affective and motivational restructuring of the personality.

Another approach to trauma therapy is transpersonal psychotherapy, especially the school of integral psychotherapy based on the theories of Ken Wilber, which views growth as inherently incorporative and cumulative.[8] Traumatic memories and injuries do not simply disappear but are outgrown and integrated into another level of consciousness and development and in this way raised to a higher functional plane.

This brief overview of the multiplicity of approaches used in trauma therapy shows that the methods of the behavioral sciences and the psychology of consciousness represent complementary theories of knowledge. In the area of research, too, complementary modes of access are employed—evidence-based as well as postmodern. We have to integrate widely differing epistemologies to arrive at "reality" and "truth." The various theories of knowledge arise from differing assumptions about the world and humanity, and they produce correspondingly divergent therapeutic styles, which often confront each other as adversaries. I am reminded of Jung's statement: "The factors which come together in the *coniunctio* are conceived as opposites, either confronting one another in enmity or attracting one another in love."[9]

In present-day scientific discourse on trauma, the polarized views refuse to "attract one another in love." "Trauma," a clinical concept in psychiatry and neurology, is played off against "trauma" as a cultural, interpretive pattern. At numerous international conferences devoted to trauma and its sequelae, the two modes of access can be clearly discerned. At one set of conferences, trauma is regarded as a disorder with comorbidities—a clinical concept described diagnostically in a way that allows it to be entered into the International Classification of Diseases (ICD) and the Diagnostic and Statistical Manual of Mental Disorders (DSM) and treated accordingly. Along with studies of its effects on the psyche of victims, research is presented on various personality-specific vulnerabilities as preexisting factors predisposing individuals to a diagnosis of PTSD; statistical evidence is cited, along with references to intervention manuals. At other conferences, by contrast, the discussions have a more holistic orientation. Such an orientation regards the effects of trauma not primarily as illness or dysfunction but as a necessary, natural psychic reaction to abnormal conditions in our society. Traumatizing experience is seen as a sociopolitical phenomenon, one that does not take place in a vacuum but is rooted in an interpersonal context, attested to in world literature, myth, music, and art, where it is portrayed in metaphoric language that drives home its reality.

In the two ways of looking at trauma—dealing with the brute fact of trauma objectively versus approaching the traumatized individual subjectively—I see two apparently incompatible approaches that must ultimately be taken together as a complementarity, that is, as a sort of procedural syzygy. The subjective perspective on trauma involves both the symbolic-mythological approach and the attempt to understand the impact of society on victims of violence. To achieve a truly holistic perspective, clinical methods need to be balanced with hermeneutical considerations. Effective trauma therapy demands both a firm grasp of psychological theory as well as maximum openness to the unknown and the unknowable. Finally, because this work takes place in an archetype-laden field, a religious attitude is called for, one that seeks to unite ego and Self (as in the Latin *religare*, "to bind together"—one possible etymological root of the word *religion*) as well as "to pay careful and scrupulous attention" (as in *relegere*, another possible root of the word), that is, to consider everything in the trauma victim that is threatened with annihilation. Complementarity is the only orientation that can avoid an adversarial relationship between what seem to be mutually exclusive procedures.

The question of who decides what should be counted as trauma continues to be explosive. I have done deep and ongoing work on the ways incest and other asymmetrical relationships are placed under taboo, trivialized, and denied. Even in the matter of compensation for victims of war atrocities, there has been a tendency to individualize the consequences of sexual violence and to displace the psychic wounding of raped women onto their supposed preexisting vulnerabilities and personality disorders. Thanks to the feminist discourse on trauma, attention has now been drawn to the structural violence of gender relationships. As a German citizen who grew up in post-war Germany, I recall the discussions of the compensation laws. At one time it was the practice to grant the compensation claims of severely traumatized victims of the Nazi regime only if they could prove they were "not unsubstantially" harmed. The psychiatrist Kurt Eissler attacked this unconscionable practice in an article published in 1963, in whose title he sarcastically asked: "How many of our children do we have to see murdered before our eyes without flinching in order to prove we have a normal constitution?"[10]

Discriminatory laws against trauma victims in Germany were heavily influenced by the work of the German psychiatrist Karl Bonhoeffer, who invoked Freud's notion of trauma neurosis and cast it as a social illness whose real etiology was not the trauma itself but the morbid desire to seek compensation wherever it was available. Thus, claims of long-term consequences of trauma were dismissed and only immediate traumatic reactions were considered legitimate.[11] I am experiencing a new version of this attitude in current claims assessment protocols regarding traumatized refugees, asylum seekers, and victims of political violence.

The notion of resilience in the face of severe stress, especially in Antonovsky's work on salutogenesis, has proved to be a double-edged sword.[12] Those who were able to adapt to the extreme conditions of the concentration camps and do the cognitive restructuring necessary to survive were later accused of collaborating with the victimizers. Conversely, those who lacked adequate coping skills (i.e., resilience) were subsequently labeled as having premorbid personalities. Lindenthal identifies a further problem with focusing on resilience: it puts the emphasis on training individuals in coping strategies, while traumatizing life circumstances remain unaddressed and unchanged and the status quo is reinforced.[13] Individual, social, and scientific defense mechanisms can be clearly discerned in the increasingly inflationary nature of current trauma discourse. Psychologist Klaus Ottomeyer condemns "the routinization (*Veralltäglichung*) and manualization [i.e., the overreliance on treatment handbooks] of trauma," and David Becker criticizes the so-called "invention of trauma."[14] Both theorists are concerned about the recent decontextualization of trauma discourse. Becker is particularly keen on debunking the illusion of harmony in the healing of trauma and insists on confronting the truth of the Erinyes (the Furies of Greek mythology).[15] All of this suggests that a complementary approach is needed if the extremes in trauma discourse and therapy are to be avoided.

The Relational Dimension of Complementarity

In clinical trauma practice, the relational complementarity of mutually completing poles expresses an archetypal principle of the soul. It is not an "either-or" matter but the dynamic interplay of complementary phenomena, a swinging back and forth between the poles of restriction, repetition compulsion, and numbness at one extreme and opening, expansion, and bringing-to-life at the other.[16] Thus, the principle of complementarity is an important heuristic instrument in observing intrapsychic and intersubjective connections. The therapeutic process is influenced not solely by the needs and behavioral patterns of the patient and the therapist but rather by their dynamic, reciprocal interaction. One has to ask: What compensatory reactions occur on the therapist's part in response to the interpersonal orientation of the patient, and what style of relating is constellated on the patient's part by the therapist's manner of communicating? The relational modality between patient and therapist is cocreated. Interpersonal theory maintains that complementary interactions help the patient internalize experiences of relationship by reducing anxiety and permitting a trusting closeness.

Psychoanalytic studies of dyadic psychology now take it for granted that the working through of positive or negative complementarity affects the success of therapy.[17] Freud's old paradigm tacitly espoused Cartesian substance dualism (body versus mind, matter versus spirit) as well as the disjunction of the therapeutic dyad. Even the processes of transference and countertransference were conceived of as primarily intrapsychic. Today, however, the emphasis has shifted toward the fluctuating, rhythmic character of interactions in the relational field and the notion of "inter-bodily resonance."[18] Considerations of "fit" (the matching of therapist and patient) and of complementation between therapist and patient have thus become more prominent as objects of research. The degree of concurrence between the interactive partners is explored with an eye to its relevance for therapeutic success or failure.

I have conducted follow-up therapy with many sexually abused women for whom a previous therapeutic relationship was marred by a destructive mismatch. In many of these cases, gender issues, including

considerations of sexuality and seduction, were responsible for the
misalignment and led to painful experiences involving trust and betrayal.

Relationality plays a vital role in trauma therapy, whether expressed
primarily as a need for control in a power and dominance relationship
or as a need for inclusion in a love and friendship relationship.[19] A
traumatic experience often damages the victim's capacity to engage in
relationships, a direct result of his or her subjectivity going
unacknowledged during the traumatizing event. In the process, victims
may lose their capacity to acknowledge, in a genuine way, the
subjectivity of others. This leads to intense ambivalence in relationships:
they yearn for a connection while simultaneously fearing it.

The interactional strategies of sexually abused women often
fluctuate rapidly between closeness and distance. These victims have
sworn never again to let themselves be dependent and exposed; yet at
the same time their need for closeness, trust, and recognition is
boundless. Both equally true, the resolve and the need press for
reconciliation, yet seem irreconcilable. Fear of death and fear of life go
hand in hand. Moments of intimacy in the session, when the patient
feels secure and protected, must then be immediately discounted.
Consequently, the patient hates herself for her neediness and hates the
therapist for having constellated these feelings in her. In addition to
devaluing herself, she devalues the therapist as well as her own progress
in therapy. The therapist has to summon great patience and empathy
to deal with the manifestations of this process, to tolerate the
controlling form of the relationship and gestures of mistrust, while
carrying on trustfully.

In their work on mirror neurons and vicarious traumatization,
Pearlman and Saakvitne draw attention to the tight interweaving of
subject and object.[20] Today we know that trauma is contagious and
that the danger of being infected by toxic psychic material poses a
professional risk to trauma therapists. Vicarious or secondary
traumatization resulting from countertransference has been described
in a variety of ways: Figley speaks of "compassion fatigue," Wilson and
Lindy of "empathic strain."[21] A particularly expressive term, in my view,
is Wilson's "traumatoid states," by which he means states that resemble
trauma reactions, although those affected have not experienced trauma
themselves but have only come into close contact with severely
traumatized individuals. In such states, individuals exhibit symptoms

that were not present before the exposure to the secondary trauma—
"dysregulated affects, somatic reactions, hyperarousal, and tendencies
to reexperience or avoid the traumatized person's report."[22]

Trauma therapy has a wounding character, and it is often painful
to witness how persistent traumatic introjects, manifested in the
patient's unconscious as archaic, often sadistic, superego authorities
and acted out in self-injuring behavior, are aggressively produced in
the relation with the therapist. It is supremely challenging to deal with
the failed ego boundaries of patients and to tolerate their projected,
traumatogenic fantasies. As therapists, we are embedded in the
complementarity of the wounded and wounding healer archetype.

The Complementarity of Being and Doing in Trauma Therapy

Donald W. Winnicott distinguished between the experiential
modes of being and doing.[23] "Doing" and "letting be" are
complementary concepts not only for the art of psychotherapy but also
for the art of living, an art that requires flexible handling. These modes
mirror each other in trauma therapy. I see in the mode of being the
feminine connotation of motherly containment and in the mode of
doing the masculine connotation of action or active engagement with
the world, a fatherly impulse.[24] In the father-oriented paradigm, a
cognitive approach, with a focus on confrontation and mastery in
conflict, is the primary modality, whereas the mother-oriented analytic
attitude embraces affective fine-tuning and nurturing.

Sándor Ferenczi, whose importance for trauma therapy is
increasingly being recognized, hinted at the complementarity of a
father-oriented (asymmetric) and a mother-oriented (mutualistic)
therapeutic attitude.[25] In his clinical diary, he fostered a loving
presence and "mutuality."[26] In his emphasis on mutuality, Ferenczi
comes close to our present understanding of intersubjectivity. Like
Ferenczi, Jung viewed therapy as a process of mutuality between
patient and therapist:

> The personalities of doctor and patient are often infinitely more
> important for the outcome of the treatment than what the doctor
> says and thinks. . . . For two personalities to meet is like mixing
> two different chemical substances: if there is any combination at
> all, both are transformed.[27]

Holding, containing, and mirroring belong in the being mode, where they facilitate continuity and safety, whereas interpretation and active techniques are employed in the modality of doing. Just as a mother alternates flexibly between these two modes in meeting the infant's needs of the moment, the therapist needs to function flexibly in both modes to achieve the greatest possible attunement and resonance with the patient.

The promotion of well-being after traumatic affliction and the fostering of salutary effects may call for the doing mode, a goal-oriented modality, which repairs damaged need states, restructures dysfunctional thought patterns, develops a differentiated perception of the body to release and discharge energy, and "shakes off" trauma, as Peter A. Levine would say, to integrate split-off body parts and restore a sense of physical boundaries.[28] The being mode requires waiting, pausing, so as to perceive better, to let imaginal states emerge, to play with ideas; it involves making time for the creation of a relationship. Pausing also affords time to formulate questions, to withhold pat answers and glib judgments, to let insights ripen, to digest events, and to lie fallow.[29]

When I adopt the being mode in a session, the patient and I slow down and pause, become conscious of what we are feeling and thinking, and notice how we are breathing. This condition of heightened awareness and alertness, of all-embracing consciousness, helps us to perceive and accept the reality of the present moment. In order to know how to proceed in the therapy, we need an attitude of creative oscillation between limit-setting structure and supportive containing, between ego reinforcement, insight-fostering interventions, focusing, and verbalizing on the one hand and waiting, contemplation, making space, and letting things happen on the other. Which of the two poles I emphasize at any point depends on a differentiated process of diagnostics and indications.

Traumatic experiences disturb the balance between being and doing through loss of openness and receptivity and an attitude of heightened distrust and guardedness. Trauma patients resist quietude for fear of intrusive flashbacks and tend to take defensive flight into a mode of exaggerated action. Thus, both poles of the being-doing complementarity are compromised. In distrustful withdrawal, trauma victims set boundaries compulsively as a defense mechanism. Tunnel vision and distorted perception emerge. Abandoning the flexible dialectic of doing and being, the victim retreats into the deathly freeze of an overconditioned stillness or erupts in a hypervigilant alarm reaction. Creative activity is blocked, the energetic flow inhibited, and the capacity for empathy is often stifled by identification with the introjected victimizer.

It is precisely to deal with this disjunction between being and doing that complementary modes of treatment are called into play, to reintegrate the dissociated, fragmented experience and resolve the multidimensional phenomenon of splitting. The loss of cognitive-affective relationality is often experienced as a loss of the essence of humanity; thus, the dissociation resulting from the broken body-spirit unity is experienced as a loss of soul, a condition that requires a spiritual approach for healing.

The mode of letting be, of non-intentionality, is found in all spiritual traditions. A state of mind in which the controlling, volitional ego retreats into the background, a state of willing submission, of nondeliberative trust, of observant passivity—these are all aspects of the world of mystics and of meditative practice. For Jung, Meister Eckhart's way of letting things happen, of acting by not acting, became the key that unlocked the door to the way. He was convinced that one must become spiritually able to let things go.[30] The relinquishing of ego consciousness, the kenotic self-emptying described by Meister Eckhart and the Zen masters, is a prerequisite in my clinical approach to trauma therapy. The dissolution of subjective boundaries—between self and other, between self and the world—increases our permeability, an essential precondition for an intersubjective therapeutic relationship, for it increases the capacity for resonance and intuitive perception of the other's psyche.

In Jungian therapy, Freud's "evenly hovering attention" is blended with the paradoxical Taoist *wu wei* principle. *Wei wu wei*, the action of nonaction, is a feminine principle that refers to spontaneous action that arises from the center of being, not from the ego but from the creative powers of instinct. *Wu wei* is described as a soft yielding, not resisting the flow, a kind of vigilant passivity. The attitude of letting things be, in which the being is the doing, engenders diverse modes of awareness, including imagination, intuition, and sensory perception, modes that are extremely important for an analyst working with trauma.

The particular focus I choose to adopt with a particular patient—symbolic, archetypal, intrapsychic, interpersonal, social-political-cultural, or spiritual—depends on the nature of his or her trauma and determines the proportion of each of these modalities. For example, when dealing with refugees and victims of persecution or war, I might put greater emphasis on doing and empowerment than on being. I have observed that the dialectical interplay of doing and letting be and the therapeutic handling of this dualism depends not only on the therapist's personality type and personal equation, but also on his or her image of humanity, spiritual attitude, and socialization within a specific therapeutic school.

The interdisciplinary pillars of the therapist's identity and the associated value system put their mark on the way he or she handles this complementarity. Personally, I have learned much from Stoic therapy and gestalt therapy, as well as from my Zen meditation practice: the present-centeredness in the here and now, the emphasis on experience, the mindful perception of all that is without judgment.[31] The trust in organismic self-regulation and the valuing of sensory awareness and bodily experience—these are pivotal in my understanding.

Several doing approaches to trauma treatment have been developed over the years, covering a wide spectrum from psychodynamically based treatments to cognitive behavioral approaches (CBT).[32] Outcome studies identify CBT as the so-called gold standard of effective trauma treatment; but even more helpful, in my view, is a holistic, restorative approach. I see the construction of meaning, the centrality of the body, and the role of emotion as being essential.[33]

Across the range of theoretical approaches there is basic agreement that the primary need in therapy is to establish safety and trust. This must happen before the deeper work of processing severe trauma can occur. To create the *temenos* of a reliable working alliance, the therapist needs to maintain an open, engaged stance. Stabilization and normalization are the first steps in any trauma therapy. These entail explaining to the patient the ways in which trauma affects perception, memory, identity, relations with others, emotions, and the body. Also, on the principle of empowerment in trauma treatment, an overall concern is to help the patient regain control and to bear the emotions that are aroused whenever the trauma complex is activated. At a later stage, when this complex invades with autonomous force, the therapist must assist in making this complex more conscious and putting the traumatic experience into perspective within the larger frame of the person's life.

To do all this, the therapist must help the patient process sensations, images, behaviors, affects, and core beliefs about the traumatic event and thereby correct false attributions. Contemporary attributional therapy has great importance for trauma treatment. Ultimately, the meaning that the victim attributes to a traumatic event, the attitude he or she takes toward it, determines how he or she will process the trauma. This interpretative framework, which arises from what Jung calls the "personal equation," is responsible for the damage *and* the cure.

Traumatic experiences disrupt the brain's information processing mechanisms. My understanding of this phenomenon, and of the differences between explicit and implicit memory, has been enhanced by recent discoveries in neurobiology. I have learned that trauma causes abnormal organic states in which the various types of stimuli (cognitive, discursive, affective, and perceptual) cannot be integrated or processed as a whole, but only in fragments. To see why the potential of a talking cure is limited in trauma treatment, one need only consider the neurobiological finding that the recalling or revisiting of traumatic experiences inhibits activity in the speech center in the brain's left hemisphere (Broca's area) and floods the right hemisphere, thus hindering the ability to verbalize experiences.[34]

The therapist needs to facilitate the restoration of the patient's self-regulation processes, reestablish contact with the unconscious, and initiate structural changes in the psyche, a process that Wilson calls "optimal organismic integration."[35] Wilson has developed highly structured treatment goals for the attachment system that address issues of intimacy, ego defenses (such as avoidance, numbing, and denial), traumatic memory symptoms, and dissociative disorders. By working on dissociation and self-sabotaging defenses, we enable the transformation of psychic energy and make the petrified psychic system more flexible. Ego resources need to be strengthened and mobilized to shore up the patient's coping faculties and boost resilience. Self-soothing and self-nurturing behaviors need to be learned, and boundaries need to be modified. Working with traumatized war survivors, I found it crucial to help them confront their anxieties, but only after they have learned the basic techniques of relaxation and have regained their ability to control affects and reduce the hyperarousal that comes from overstimulation of the brain's right hemisphere.

I have seen how important social support is in the response to trauma. Social support is established through the creation of a supportive network of other individuals, as opposed to Jung's solitary way. A form of social support may also be provided by the therapist. The therapist can support victims of injustice by adopting an unequivocal stance of acknowledgment, partisanship, and solidarity with the victims to help them regain their dignity and their ability to act.[36] Active engagement by the therapist is required to support victims and stand by them, even to advocate on their behalf, until they are ready to stand up for themselves.

Frequently, action-oriented interventions are necessary to help survivors contain their aggressive impulses, establish boundaries, and experiment with new kinds of behavior. The treatment of acute trauma may require behavior modification techniques, which are less often used in analytical psychology, rooted as it is in an ontology of hope and meaning. Traumatic experiences affect more than just the spiritual dimension of *being*. They are biopsychosocial events that injure the individual's ego identity as well as the collective social identity and which therefore require integrative therapeutic *doing*.

In integrating torture survivors' traumatic experiences into their subjective structures of meaning and reestablishing the perspective that has been lost, it may be necessary to take sides. Therapists are sometimes called upon to address structures of political violence and, if necessary, expose torture for the traumatic sociopolitical reality that it is. Failure on the part of the therapist to take a stand can be retraumatizing. What is needed is a judicious blend of empathic engagement, sympathetic holding, and critical reflection.

Trauma destroys psychic structures; consequently, new pathways to healing need to be cocreated. Since the victim's social network is damaged in the trauma process, network therapy takes on special significance as a therapeutic intervention. Having suffered a rupture in their connection to the past and having lost a sense of coherence, survivors need engaged therapeutic assistance and clinical posttraumatic interventions to reestablish a healthy, integrated ego identity. As Wilson has shown, survivors can actualize their innate human potential and transcend the extreme adversity of their lives when support is provided for the "organismic striving" of the individual and the "drive towards intrapsychic unity."[37]

Without a holistic perspective and the complementary application of being and doing, the shattered self cannot be reintegrated and ego identity cannot be restored. Identity is not fixed; it is a fluid, subjective construct of the self, which is constantly being recomposed into an ongoing life narrative to maintain coherence through life's vicissitudes. Following the total dissolution of a coherent sense of self through trauma, the survivor needs support in constructing a meaningful narrative of the traumatic event whereby the broken framework can be reconstructed and "optimal intrapsychic congruence" can be restored.[38]

Presence and Reflection

Presence is the quality of being grounded, centered, and fully there. Shari M. Geller and Leslie S. Greenberg identify it as an essential attribute of the expert therapist, a state that resembles the "empty mind" of the Zen path.[39] It is a way of being with the patient authentically. In his old age, Carl Rogers had intimations about this kind of presence, with roots in the mystical, spiritual realm:

> I find that when I am closest to my inner, intuitive self, when I am somehow in touch with the unknown in me, when perhaps I am in a slightly altered state of consciousness in the relationship, then whatever I do seems to be full of healing. Then simply my presence is releasing and helpful.[40]

He writes that this experience cannot be consciously forced or "made"; it occurs spontaneously:

> When I can relax and be close to the transcendental core of me . . . it seems that my inner spirit has reached out and touched the inner spirit of the other. Our relationship transcends itself and becomes a part of something larger. Profound growth and healing and energy are present.[41]

In such experiences, a healing energy pulses through the therapeutic space that resonates with the Jungian understanding that healing occurs only in relationship with the Self and *Deo concedente*.

Presence implies openness to the emergence of archetypal manifestations. It requires the therapist to be open to whatever the patient is experiencing, while simultaneously remaining open to his or her own inner experience. Then the archetypal energies that emanate from the constellated inner figures can permeate the entire field. Tuning in to the silence and the body language of the patient can lead into a state of analytic reverie rich in metaphors; the therapist listens attentively to his or her own experiences of resonance and uses the reciprocal healing images that arise as part of a joint fantasy and intuitive dialogue. This turning toward the other involves our whole being and touches both the vertical and the horizontal axis. Martin Buber taught that one must be at home with oneself before one can reach out to the other. Openness to the vertical dimension of one's own unconscious enables the horizontal encounter with the Thou of the other. Only then can both therapist and patient experience themselves as part of a single, all-embracing reality.

Presence involves listening for intermediate tones, for what speech does not express, for energy, mood, and movement. Psychoanalyst Josef Dantlgraber's description of "musical listening" as a process of unconscious communication in psychoanalysis strongly resembles my experience in trauma therapy.[42] Starting from the idea that music is a meta-language of feelings, Dantlgraber suggests that analysis can involve a sort of "affective listening." By this he means the complex, affect-laden process in the analytic atmosphere in which the sound of the patient's voice and the melody and rhythm of his or her narrative bring up musical associations in the analyst, which are experienced as intuitive inspirations. Musical listening is a kind of bridge, a way to hearken affectively to the total feeling world of the patient. Through it an affective attunement is created, as in a mother-child relationship. This fine attunement to the feeling state of the patient is naturally impossible without empathy. If this affective harmony is successful, it markedly expands the analyst's capacity for containment. This kind of affective listening is a prerequisite for the reflective process of interpretation. The two processes are complementary.

From the *Tibetan Book of the Dead* we learn that it is a difficult thing to listen rightly to the suffering soul. In such situations, we should not interfere but linger peacefully where we are and listen without passing judgment—a hearkening with the heart that is familiar from spiritual traditions. Only by quieting ourselves can we hear the "still small voice" (1 Kings 19:12, KJV). Essential truth can reveal itself only when noise is silenced.

I find it helpful to maintain a Socratic attitude in trauma therapy, to form a play space in which my patients can take risks, experiment with their essential being, and ask themselves questions about life and transcendence, for questioning, as Heidegger once formulated it, is "the piety of thought."[43] Asking questions involves opening up a potential space for dialogue. I sometimes work with the "miracle question," developed by family therapist Steve de Shazer, a question that opens the space for imagination: Suppose that while you are sleeping a miracle happens and that the problems and symptoms that brought you to therapy are solved and disappear. When you wake up, what changes in thinking, feeling, and behavior would let you know that a miracle has happened during the night?[44]

The technique of Socratic dialogue is especially apt in trauma therapy for discerning the interplay of the possible and the impossible, for investigating dysfunctional cognitive schemata, guilt-laden attributions, and fixations, and for identifying resources that support healing and growth. The reflective posture is essential in doing psychotherapy with wounded souls; particularly within this relationship, where emptiness tends to be constellated, a posture of *wu wei* and letting be is often contraindicated. Where the interpersonal aspects of relationship cannot be internalized and nameless fears mark the interaction, we need a language capable of organizing the inexpressible into a meaningful framework. Through empathic, mirroring presence, but also by offering a framework of understanding, the therapist makes it possible for the patient eventually to reflect on the traumatic experience, to speak about it, and to tolerate the associated affects in measured doses.

Experience in analysis is followed by reflection on what is happening here and now in the analytic encounter and also by reflection on the process of becoming, whether this involves the impact of traumatizing events or of childhood patterns. Jung went so far as to identify reflection as one of four basic human instincts.[45] In his 1936 lecture at Harvard University, entitled "Psychological Factors Determining Human Behavior," Jung characterized the reflective instinct as typically human, a "cultural instinct *par excellence*," which transforms the other instincts into conscious contents in various tangible forms.[46] He also emphasized that reflection

> should be understood not simply as an act of thought, but rather as an *attitude* . . . a spiritual act . . . whereby we stop, call something to mind, form a picture, and take up a relation to and come to terms with what we have seen. It should, therefore, be understood as an act of *becoming conscious*.[47]

In psychotherapy, we need the transformative power of reflection as a "coming to consciousness" to keep us from lingering in the enmeshment of *participation mystique*. If we have encounter without understanding, or experience without recognition, we fall short of the goal. What is needed is the complementarity of perception and reflection, phenomenology and interpretation, differentiation and integration, *separatio* and *coniunctio*; that is, we need to engage in a process that is both analytic and synthetic. When stabilizing a trauma patient's self-organization and treating deficits in his or her ego structure, an approach that combines structure creation, reflection, and interpretation is called for. Trauma therapy requires a combination of boundary-setting reflection and the subtlety of shared presence and a form of after-nourishment, a nurturing of the soul.

In psychoanalysis, reflection is implicit in Freud's recommendations for treatment: "remembering, repeating, working through." This reflective mode of analytic work has been described by Weischede and Zwiebel as a cocreative endeavor between therapist and patient involving processing, working through, and refining yet again, oscillating between complementary modes— "between primary and secondary process, between dream-thought and discursive thought, between activity and passivity, between letting go and holding on."[48]

Analytical reflection is an important tool for uncovering whatever hinders total presence and access to consciousness. Recognition of and insight into the defense mechanisms that promote avoidance, denial, detachment, and emotional constriction are not just treatment goals for my patients. They also help me to deal reflectively with my own tendencies toward disengagement and withdrawal, which I unconsciously activate in attempting to gain control over archetype-laden fields.

Without going into the specifics of depth psychological treatment techniques as modified by psychotraumatology, note that concepts such as "perpetrator introject," "revictimization," "intergenerational transmission of trauma," "cycle of abuse," and "victim-perpetrator reversal" cannot be adequately grasped without reference to the insights of attachment theory and the concept of mentalization, which is closely associated with reflection.

Mentalization

Mentalization, or "reflective functioning," is the process of extending one's perception into the mental states of others in order to understand their goals, wishes, and convictions and, through this process, to understand their behavior.[49] It is "a form of imaginative mental activity, namely perceiving and interpreting human behavior in terms of intentional mental states (e.g., needs, desires, feelings, beliefs, goals, purposes, and reasons)."[50] Mentalization-based treatment (MBT) was developed by Fonagy, Allen, and Bateman and is recommended in clinical discourse and described in detail in various handbooks.[51]

I view the ability to mentalize traumatic experiences in the safe container of a secure attachment relationship as highly relevant for trauma therapy.[52] Here we are working within the intersubjective field through mirroring, after trauma and attachment disturbances have damaged the victim's capacity to assess the interpersonal situation adequately, to manage affects, to recognize projections coming from internalized experiences of abuse, and to avoid reenacting earlier relational injuries.

The concept of deactivation of the mentalizing system in traumatic attachment disorders explains phenomena such as the internalization of the victimizer and helps in understanding how the destructive-sadistic affects of traumatizing attachment figures are internalized. The perpetrator introject, what Fonagy calls "the alien self," is like a foreign body within the self, terrorizing the psyche from within, leading to self-hatred and unbearable emotional states.[53] Victims try to expel this disturbing, torturing interior "foreign body" and transplant it into others, through the familiar phenomenon of projective identification; it is a defense strategy especially characteristic of borderline patients, which serves "to create a terrified alien self in the other—therapist, friend, parent—who becomes the vehicle for what is emotionally unbearable."[54]

When patients are afflicted with flashbacks, they clearly feel that they are once again in the traumatizing situation, that is, they find it impossible to differentiate between past and present. Their perception of both time and space becomes distorted. Their inner world is experienced as coextensive with outer reality, rather than being recognized as an inner representation of a mental state. For this mind-world isomorphism in the very young child and in borderline patients, MBT uses the term *psychic equivalence*, a mode in which internal reality and negative cognitions are experienced as real and as having power over the external world.[55] What is involved is a kind of regression to ideas of omnipotence.

Therapeutic work involves transforming these overwhelming affects of the here and now into an experience of the past, a remembered occurrence whose painful affects can be tolerated. The task is to differentiate fantasy from traumatic reality. Mentalization, in the framework of secure therapeutic containment, stabilizes and helps to create a buffer against stifling raw emotions.

When the capacity for mentalization is curtailed as a result of early traumas, dissociative disorders often develop, in which the victim resorts to fantasy to insulate the self from the real world. This can serve to defend against an exploitative outer reality. Thus, MBT distinguishes the "psychic equivalence" mode from the "pretend" mode, in which the mental world is totally decoupled from reality rather than merged with it.[56] In that case, the therapeutic task is to foster in the patient, through mentalization, a reflective process that facilitates the recognition of the true relationship between past and present and between the inner and outer worlds.

For the therapist, mentalization is more than a technique; it is an inner stance and attitude toward the patient, characterized by the greatest possible openness and a willingness to explore together the complicated inner world of the patient and of others and to investigate with perceptiveness and sensitivity the relational models that are constituted in the therapy process.[57] The basic stance of intuitive openness and becoming attuned in a way that permits the greatest possible resonance is the precondition for preparing an intersubjective space, in whose silence the archetypal limit themes are constellated.

NOTES

¹ William James, *The Principles of Psychology*, vol. 1 (1890; reprinted: New York: Cosimo Classics, 2007), p. 206. See also Arkady Plotnitsky, *Niels Bohr and Complementarity: An Introduction* (New York: Springer, 2013); and Harald Atmanspacher and Hans Primas, "Pauli's Ideas on Mind and Matter in the Context of Contemporary Science," *Journal of Consciousness Studies* 13, no. 3 (2006): 21.

² Atmanspacher and Primas, "Pauli's Ideas on Mind and Matter," pp. 20–23; Beverly Zabriskie, "Jung and Pauli: A Meeting of Rare Minds," in *Atom and Archetype: The Pauli/Jung Letters, 1932–1958*, ed. C. A. Meier (Princeton, NJ: Princeton University Press, 2001), pp. xxviii–xxxii.

³ See for example Plotnitsky, *Niels Bohr and Complementarity*, p. 158ff; Atmanspacher and Primas, "Pauli's Ideas on Mind and Matter," pp. 42–43.

⁴ Hans Keilson and Herman R. Sarphatie, *Sequential Traumatization in Children: A Clinical and Statistical Follow-up Study on the Fate of the Jewish War Orphans in the Netherlands*, trans. Yvonne Bearne, Hilary Coleman, and Deirdre Winter (Jerusalem: Magnes Press, Hebrew University, 1992).

⁵ Jung, *CW* 8, § 131.

⁶ John P. Wilson, ed., *The Posttraumatic Self: Restoring Meaning and Wholeness to Personality* (New York: Routledge, 2006).

⁷ *Ibid.*, pp. 191–192.

⁸ Ken Wilber, *Integral Psychology: Consciousness, Spirit, Psychology, Therapy* (Boston: Shambhala Publications, 2000).

⁹ Jung, *CW* 14, § 1.

¹⁰ Kurt R. Eissler, "Die Ermordung von wie vielen seiner Kinder muss ein Mensch symptomfrei ertragen können, um eine normale Konstitution zu haben?" *Psyche: Zeitschrift für Psychoanalyse und ihre Anwendungen* 17, no. 5 (1963–1964): 241–291.

¹¹ See Nathan Durst, "Emotional Wounds That Never Heal," *Jewish Political Studies Review* 14, no. 3–4 (2002): 119–129.

¹² Aaron Antonovsky, *Health, Stress and Coping: New Perspectives on Mental and Physical Well-Being* (San Francisco: Jossey-Bass Publishers, 1979); German edition: *Salutogenese: Zur Entmystifizierung der Gesundheit* (Tübingen: dgvt-Verlag, 1997).

¹³ Michael J. Lindenthal, "Wie das Normale über das Abnormale zur Frage werden kann: Reflexionen zu Traumatisierungen und ihren Kontexten," *Journal für Psychologie* 9, no. 3 (2011): 1–20, accessed October 4, 2013, http://www.journal-fuer-psychologie.de/index.php/jfp/article/view/88/34.

¹⁴ Klaus Ottomeyer, "Traumatherapie zwischen Widerstand und Anpassung," *Journal für Psychologie* 19, no. 3 (2011): 4, accessed October 4, 2013, http://www.journal-fuer-psychologie.de/index.php/jfp/article/view/89/35; my translation; see also, Klaus Ottomeyer, *Die Behandlung der Opfer: Über unseren Umgang mit dem Trauma der Flüchtlinge und Verfolgten* (Stuttgart: Klett-Cotta Verlag, 2011); and David Becker, *Die Erfindung des Traumas—Verflochtene Geschichten* (Freiburg: Edition Freitag, 2006).

¹⁵ David Becker, "Confronting the Truth of the Erinyes: The Illusion of Harmony in the Healing of Trauma," in *Telling the Truths: Truth Telling and Peace Building in Post-Conflict Societies*, ed. Tristan Anne Borer (Notre Dame, IN: University of Notre Dame Press, 2006), pp. 231–257.

¹⁶ Gerald Weischede and Ralf Zwiebel, *Neurose und Erleuchtung: Anfängergeist in Zen und Psychoanalyse—Ein Dialog* (Stuttgart: Klett-Cotta Verlag, 2009), p. 249.

¹⁷ Andreas Gross and Wolf-Peter Riedel, *Therapieergebnis und Komplementarität in der Therapeut-Patient-Beziehung: Eine Analyse mit Hilfe von SASB (Strukturale Analyse Sozialen Verhaltens)* (Regensburg: S. Roderer Verlag, 1995).

¹⁸ Tom Froese and Thomas Fuchs, "The Extended Body: A Case Study in the Neurophenomenology of Social Interaction," *Phenomenology and the Cognitive Sciences* 11, no. 2 (2012): 205–235.

¹⁹ See Stephen A. Mitchell, *Relationality: From Attachment to Intersubjectivity* (Hillsdale, NJ: Analytic Press, 2003).

²⁰ Laurie Anne Pearlman and Karen W. Saakvitne, *Trauma and the Therapist: Countertransference and Vicarious Traumatization in Psychotherapy with Incest Survivors* (New York: W. W. Norton, 1995).

²¹ Charles R. Figley, ed., *Compassion Fatigue: Coping with Secondary Traumatic Stress Disorder in Those Who Treat the Traumatized* (New York: Routledge, 1995); John P. Wilson, "Empathic Strain, Compassion Fatigue, and Countertransference in the Treatment of Trauma and PTSD," in *Living with Terror, Working with Trauma: A Clinician's Handbook*, ed. Danielle Knafo (Northvale, NJ: Jason Aaronson, 2004), pp. 331–368); John P. Wilson and Jacob D. Lindy, eds., *Countertransference in the Treatment of PTSD* (New York: Guilford Press, 1994).

²² John P. Wilson, *Empathy in the Treatment of Trauma and PTSD* (New York: Brunner-Routledge, 2004), p. 23.

²³ D. W. Winnicott, *Playing and Reality* (London: Tavistock, 1971).

²⁴ It is not my intention to engage here with a possible feminist critique of gender-role stereotypes.

²⁵ Axel Hoffer, "Asymmetry and Mutuality in the Analytic Relationship: Contemporary Lessons from the Freud-Ferenczi Dialogue," in *Ferenczi's Turn in Psychoanalysis*, ed., Peter L. Rudnytsky, Antal Bókay, and Patrizia Giampieri-Deutsch (New York: New York University Press, 1996), pp. 107–119.

²⁶ Sándor Ferenczi, *The Clinical Diary of Sándor Ferenczi*, ed. Judith Dupont, trans. Michael Balint and Nicola Zarday Jackson (Cambridge, MA: Harvard University Press, 1985). See especially p. 68 for an articulation of the complementarity between the father-oriented and mother-oriented approaches to therapy.

²⁷ Jung, *CW* 16, § 163.

²⁸ Peter A. Levine, *Waking the Tiger: Healing Trauma* (Berkeley, CA: North Atlantic Books, 1997).

²⁹ Brigitte Wanzenried, "Über das Verweilen in der Therapie: Gedanken zum therapeutischen Prozess," unpublished lecture given at the University of Basel, May 17, 2004.

³⁰ Jung, *CW* 13, § 20.

³¹ Inspired by the work of Hilarion Petzold on the meaning of soul guidance in the ancient world, I have returned to reading Seneca and Marcus Aurelius and put their wisdom to use in my clinical practice. See Daniel N. Stern, *The Present Moment in Psychotherapy and Everyday Life* (New York: W. W. Norton, 2004).

³² See Bessel A. van der Kolk, ed., *Psychological Trauma* (Arlington, VA: American Psychiatric Publishing, 1987); Frank M. Ochberg, "Post-

Traumatic Therapy," in *Psychotraumatology: Key Papers and Core Concepts in Post-Traumatic Stress*, ed. George S. Everly Jr. and Jeffrey M. Lating (New York: Plenum Press, 1995), pp. 245–264; Edna B. Foa, Terence M. Kean, and Matthew J. Friedman, "Guidelines for the Treatment of PTSD," *Journal of Traumatic Stress* 13, no. 4 (2000): 539–588.

[33] See Colin Wastell, *Understanding Trauma and Emotion: Dealing with Trauma Using an Emotion-Focused Approach* (Crows Nest, Australia: Allen and Unwin, 2005); Mardi J. Horowitz, *States of Mind: Analysis of Change in Psychotherapy* (New York: Plenum Medical Book Company, 1979); Mardi J. Horowitz, *Stress Response Syndromes: PTSD, Grief, Adjustment, and Dissociative Disorders*, 5th ed. (New York: Jason Aronson, 2011).

[34] Bessel van der Kolk, "Posttraumatic Stress Disorder and the Nature of Trauma, *Dialogues in Clinical Neuroscience* 2, no. 1 (2000): 7–22 (see especially pp. 17 and 18). See also Alastair M. Hull, "Neuroimaging Findings in Post-Traumatic Stress Disorder: Systematic Review," *British Journal of Psychiatry* 181 (2002): 102–110.

[35] Wilson, *Posttraumatic Self*, p. 427.

[36] See Hilarion Petzold, Hans-Ulrich Wolf, and Birgitt Landgrebe, *Das Trauma überwinden: Integrative Modelle der Traumatherapie* (Paderborn: Junfermannsche Verlagsbuchhandlung, 2002).

[37] Wilson, *Posttraumatic Self*, pp. 104, 211–212, 447, 103.

[38] *Ibid.*, pp. xxiv, 427.

[39] Shari M. Geller and Leslie S. Greenberg, "Therapeutic Presence: Therapist's Experience of Presence in the Psychotherapeutic Encounter," *Person-Centered and Experiential Psychotherapies* 1, nos. 1–2 (2002): 71–86. See also Shari M. Geller and Leslie S. Greenberg, *Therapeutic Presence: A Mindful Approach to Effective Therapy* (Washington, DC: American Psychological Association, 2012).

[40] Carl R. Rogers, "Client-Centered Therapy," in *Psychotherapist's Casebook: Theory and Techniques in the Practice of Modern Therapies*, ed. Irwin L. Kutasch and Alexander Wolf (San Francisco: Jossey-Bass Publishers, 1986), p. 198.

[41] Carl R. Rogers, *A Way of Being* (Boston: Houghton Mifflin, 1980), p. 129.

[42] Josef Dantlgraber, "Musikalisches Zuhören: Zugangswesen zu den Vorgängen in der unbewussten Kommunikation," *Forum der Psychoanalyse* 24, no. 2 (2008): 161–176.

[43] Martin Heidegger, *The Question Concerning Technology and Other Essays*, trans. William Lovitt (New York: Garland Publishing, 1977), p. 35.

[44] Steve de Shazer, *Clues: Investigating Solutions in Brief Therapy* (New York: W. W. Norton, 1988).

[45] See Peter Amman, "Rock Paintings and the Instinct of Reflection: The Perspective of a Jungian Psychologist," in *Cape Town 2007—Journeys, Encounters: Clinical, Communal, Cultural* (Proceedings of the 17th International IAAP Congress for Analytical Psychology), ed. Pramila Bennett (Einsiedeln, Switzerland: Daimon Verlag, 2009), p. 158.

[46] Jung, *CW* 8, §§ 232–262.

[47] Jung, *CW* 8, § 235, note 9.

[48] Gerald Weischede and Ralf Zwiebel, *Neurose und Erleuchtung: Anfängergeist in Zen und Psychoanalyse—Ein Dialog* (Stuttgart: Klett-Cotta Verlag, 2009), p. 170.

[49] Peter Fonagy, György Gergely, Elliot L. Jurist, and Mary Target, *Affect Regulation, Mentalization, and the Development of the Self* (London: Karnac Books, 2004), p. 23ff.

[50] Antony Bateman and Peter Fonagy, "Psychotherapy for Borderline Personality Disorder: Workshop on Mentalization Based Treatment," accessed October 3, 2013, http://web.archive.org/web/20070812072835/http://www.riksforeningenpsykoterapicentrum.se/pdf-doc/mbt_training_jan06.pdf.

[51] See, for example, Jon G. Allen and Peter Fonagy, eds., *Handbook of Mentalization-Based Treatment* (Chichester, UK: John Wiley and Sons, 2006); Jon G. Allen, Peter Fonagy, and Anthony W. Bateman, *Mentalizing in Clinical Practice* (Arlington, VA: American Psychiatric Publishing, 2008).

[52] See Jon G. Allen, *Mentalizing in the Development and Treatment of Attachment Trauma* (London: Karnac Books, 2013).

[53] Anthony Bateman and Peter Fonagy, *Mentalization-Based Treatment for Borderline Personality Disorder: A Practical Guide* (Oxford, UK: Oxford University Press, 2006), pp. 11–15.

[54] *Ibid.*, p. 14.

[55] Allen, *Mentalizing in the Development and Treatment of Attachment Trauma*, p. 152; Allen and Fonagy, *Handbook of Mentalization-Based Treatment*, p. 17; Allen, Fonagy, and Bateman,

Mentalizing in Clinical Practice, pp. 90–91; Fonagy, Gergely, Jurist, and Target, *Affect Regulation, Mentalization, and the Development of the Self*, pp. 199ff, 258ff.

[56] Allen, *Mentalizing in the Development and Treatment of Attachment Trauma*, p. 152, 257; Allen and Fonagy, *Handbook of Mentalization-Based Treatment*, pp. 17, 39; Allen, Fonagy, and Bateman, *Mentalizing in Clinical Practice*, pp. 90–91, 176ff; Fonagy, Gergely, Jurist, and Target, *Affect Regulation, Mentalization, and the Development of the Self*, pp. 199ff, 261ff.

[57] For modified interventions to promote mentalization, see Allen and Fonagy, *Handbook of Mentalization-Based Treatment*, pp. 141–267; Anthony Bateman and Peter Fonagy, *Handbook of Mentalizing in Mental Health Practice* (Arlington, VA: American Psychiatric Publishing, 2012). See also, Josef Brockmann and Holger Kirsch, "Konzept der Mentalisierung: Relevanz für die psychotherapeutische Behandlung," *Psychotherapeut* 55, no. 4 (2010): 279–290.

CHAPTER NINE

THE CRUCIBLE OF TRANSFORMATION: THE MERCURIAL PSYCHE

From Chaos to New Order

All true things must change, and only that which changes remains true.

—C. G. Jung, *Mysterium Coniunctionis*

Transformation is a central theme in trauma therapy. It is associated with shape-shifting, metamorphosis, movement from disorder to order, changes in psychic structure, and changes in the interaction between therapist and patient. It is based on the belief that even at the darkest point of the *nigredo,* humans experience the perpetual process of becoming and that psychic energies are in a state of constant flux. The plasticity of the human brain and the basic regulatory competence of the mind are responsible for our susceptibility to emergent processes and our capacity for new thinking and new behavior. Our mind and brain have the built-in flexibility to adjust to changes in our external environment, and trauma therapy capitalizes on this innate flexibility to transform trauma-generated behavior patterns into more productive modes of relating to ourselves and the world.

In trauma therapy, transformation lies at the heart of transcendence. To transcend trauma is to rise above it, to go beyond it, to overcome its painful and deleterious effects through a process of internal transformation. Transcendence is characterized by crucial shifts in awareness, by the passage from disintegration to reintegration; it is pregnant with archetypal energies that can expand consciousness and bring about self-extension and self-transformation.

Jung wrote in the Red Book that the "spirit of the depths . . . leads mankind through the river of blood to the mystery."[1] Unfortunately, many do not make it through this river; some drown, unable to transcend the blood-drenched experience and thereby arrive at the mystery. However, in some cases, the passage through the river of blood is followed by a sudden leap in consciousness; everything goes strangely quiet, and a space of living stillness opens up, a state of consciousness beyond ordinary ego identification, in which everything simply is what it is. After being dragged through the river of blood, after everything falls apart and the center no longer holds, some individuals paradoxically experience unexpected spiritual maturation.[2] How does this transformation, this reversal of psychic energy, come about?

In my attempts to comprehend trauma's incomprehensible turning points, I have been helped by quantum physics, complexity theory, and nonlinear dynamic systems theory, all of which shed interesting light on the sudden, unexpected processes of psychic transformation. The transformative power of trauma is best grasped by abandoning linear thought, yielding to intuition, and cultivating openness to the inherent mystery of Being. Albert Einstein expressed this general sentiment when he wrote:

> The fairest thing we can experience is the mysterious. It is the fundamental emotion which stands at the cradle of true art and true science. He who knows it not and can no longer wonder, no longer feel amazement, is as good as dead, a snuffed-out candle.[3]

When transformation involves the emergence of a new order from earlier chaotic states, breakdown and breakup give way to breakthrough. When the old structure falls away or is cast off like an old skin, a new structure emerges, one that is of a higher order, with a greater degree of complexity. The dissolution of old structures and old ways of being and the emergence of new patterns are imaged in the symbolic multistage transmutation process of alchemy. In the *calcination* stage, everything nonessential is burned away, a necessary purification, a prerequisite for the later stages of *solutio, sublimatio*, and *albedo*.

In this sort of metamorphosis, new forms of perception and meaning can emerge spontaneously out of seeming chaos. One might even argue that chaos is a prerequisite for the emergence of a higher level of sophistication and development in an organism or system. According to chaos theory and complexity theory, the seemingly random behavior and instability of nonlinear complex systems (such as the weather, the economy, or the human brain) are in reality surface manifestations of deeper, underlying, nonobvious patterns of interrelationships, which can produce major unexpected outcomes in response to often minor events or changes in the system and thereby give rise to new surface phenomena, in what is known as a "phase transition."[4] Thus, complex dynamic systems live on the edge of chaos.[5]

Current thinking in the biological sciences holds that life itself emerges and thrives on the edge of chaos. Some writers use the neologism "chaord" (*cha*[os] + *ord*[er]) to describe the liminal realm between chaos and order. The term, coined by Dee Hock, refers broadly to any self-organizing, self-governing, adaptive, nonlinear, complex system that incorporates the characteristics of both chaos and order.[6] Hock understands chaord as a fundamental organizing principle of nature in which both chaos and order collaborate and neither dominates. As such, chaord opens the mind to possibilities beyond our natural tendency to think in dualistic terms. The chaordic approach has some bearing on trauma therapy if the latter is conceived of as a mercurial psychic journey that seeks a middle ground between the disordered confusion of the traumatized mind and the overly ordered clarity and certainty of the ego-controlled mind.

Systems theory and catastrophe theory have identified dramatic shifts and changes in the behavior of systems of all sorts.[7] Systems theory posits that living organisms—like other complex adaptive systems and healthy, robust networks—have the innate ability to reorganize themselves during periods of instability such that they are transformed and reconstituted from within and equilibrium is restored to the system. New forms of organization emerge when a system reaches a "bifurcation point," a point of critical instability at which the system is called upon to reorganize itself.[8] This arising of new structure in the phase transition between incoherence and coherence is known as emergence.[9] Emergence occurs in "the movement from low-level rules to higher-level sophistication."[10] That is to say, new laws that govern higher level, more complex behavior appear at higher levels of the system's hierarchy, laws not present or operative at lower levels.[11]

This capacity for self-organization and self-regulation is manifested supremely in the human organism, not just in the physical realm but in the psychic domain as well.[12] Embracing this perspective can provide the basis for creative adaptations to traumatizing situations. It is an approach that resonates with the Jungian conviction that self-healing energy is inherent in the psyche. Analytical psychology, with its drive to connect with what is missing in order to achieve wholeness, believes in the human potential for change and the healing that comes from having wrestled with the devil and seen the face of God. Just as the numinous may present itself to us through our wounds, healing potential is present when a crack appears in the system, a crack through which the light can come in. As Leonard Cohen sings: "There is a crack in everything. / That's how the light gets in."[13]

The theory of complex adaptive systems (CASs) can readily be applied to psychological processes associated with growth, creativity, and goal-directedness, processes that can be understood in terms of emergence.[14] Joseph Cambray has explored the relevance of emergence and the self-organizing nature of CASs for synchronicity and other aspects of analytical psychology.[15] His work corroborates my understanding of transcendent experiences as emergent phenomena. He points out that psychotic, borderline, and severely traumatized individuals (the so-called liminals) are more susceptible to synchronistic, numinous states.[16] This brings to mind a discussion I had with Jerome Bernstein in which we agreed that traumatized individuals are more grounded in the primordial mind and more open to primary process thinking and intuitive hunches.

Jung always marveled at archetypal situations that seemed to create syntheses and generate apparently "miraculous" new developments. He described the process thus:

Its beginning is almost invariably characterized by one's getting stuck in a blind alley or in some impossible situation; and its goal is, broadly speaking, illumination or higher consciousness, by means of which the initial situation is overcome on a higher level.[17]

To discuss this process of transformation in my practice, I use the image of a spiral, which moves around a center point at increasingly higher levels. Jung wrote:

The way to the goal seems chaotic and interminable at first . . . [it] appears to go round in circles . . . to go in spirals . . . . As a matter of fact the whole process revolves about a central point or some arrangement round a center . . . , drawing closer to it [i.e., the center] as the amplifications increase in distinctness and in scope. . . . We might draw a parallel between such spiral courses and the processes of growth in plants.[18]

I often ponder the wisdom of living organisms and the dynamics of order and disorder in the context of the pressing question, Why is it that some traumatized people remain stuck forever in destructive cycles of disorganization and fragmentation while for others trauma functions as a catalyst for growth?[19] I constantly feel that I am faced with "the cloud of unknowing," the mystery of transformation and transcendence. A poem by Erin Martz speaks to my soul in this connection:

Reflections on Healing

How people survive
in a circle of hell
I'll never know.

How they trust
again in the
human family
I'll never know.

How they can
smile once more
after seeing evil
deeply and repeatedly
I'll never know.

How they let the
horrors fade and
live for the future
I'll never know.

How they learn
to trust themselves
again and find their voices—
this I know.[20]

Uncertainty about what patterns of order and complexity will emerge seems to be intrinsic to dynamic systems and thus to our analytic art. In my work with traumatized individuals, I am never sure when and how a leap in consciousness will occur after the traumatic landslide that precipitates disorganization. I can never know in advance when to expect the turning point from being crippled in a state of intolerable suffering and "not being at home in the world any more" to redesigning oneself and "saying yes to life in spite of everything." The achievement of a new level of consciousness, springing from the excruciating struggle with trauma, often expresses itself in a worldly-wise attitude toward life. Survivors of trauma sometimes come upon this *metanoia* as something completely surprising and unexpected. They do not feel they did anything, but rather that something completely unpredictable, something beyond their conscious control, happened to them.

Conversely, it is also impossible to predict when the therapeutic process will take a turn for the worse. Sometimes all it takes is a single wrong word, an inapt formulation, an insensitive comment, a yawn, a raised eyebrow, or a drawing of attention to the time limit of the session to trigger an avalanche of resentment and a release of accumulated feelings of being unseen, undervalued, or misunderstood. I can never be sure in advance which word or look or gesture will cause a systemic collapse, rupture contact, and break trust. As in the physical world, in some situations, the slightest movement, the smallest vibration or tremor, can trigger a landslide or set off an avalanche. With experience, I have learned to be cautious when approaching critical points, when I sense the possibility of this kind of avalanche or a snow bridge that might suddenly give way underfoot with unstoppable speed. However, as a patient once commented to me, even the most experienced mountain climbing guides sometimes die in avalanches, taking their roped-in climbers along with them. She was afraid that her inner chaos would create a fracture in the crust of her psychic earth, allowing unconscious material to well up like lava and transform the landscape of her soul into a Pompeii. She asked at the beginning of her therapy, "Will you be able to bear sitting with me, so close to an erupting geyser?" And later, "Do you think I can survive a landslide if it happens? Will you be able to hold me?"

Here the question of trust becomes especially pressing, for it takes enormous trust simply to allow this chaos to enter into consciousness. Looking back over her psychic landscape, my patient once described the long phase of latency, before this chaos broke in, as a time of apparent deadness. To explain, she offered the image of the nuclear reactor at Chernobyl, entombed in concrete, standing in the middle of territory that is off limits to the living, land the produce of which cannot be eaten. Chaos is like radiation, invisible, a destructive energy unperceivable by the senses that produces only the semblance of life. The path into therapy begins when the sufferer can no longer bear the pain of this façade of life or when this false world undergoes total collapse.

Together we work to transform this phantasmal life into physically embodied, living reality. To depict the therapeutic process of creating trust, I like to use Antoine de Saint-Exupéry's beautifully moving account of the Little Prince's encounter with the fox.[21] The Little Prince learns how one tames a fox and the actual meaning of *tame*. He has to wait for the fox to become accustomed to him. Exercising great patience and keeping his distance at first, he gives the fox an opportunity to watch him out of the corner of his eye. It takes some time before it is all right for him to come closer. He must also be silent, for language is the source of all misunderstandings; and he learns how important rituals are in the process of taming.

For me, analysis involves such trust-building rituals. I must be very careful. I may approach only slowly. I must allow space and time and be able to stay silent. I must be and remain there, quietly and unshakably, in loving, compassionate presence. Only then is it possible for the plea to be expressed, whisperingly: "Please, I beg you, don't leave me alone when this great, torturing, destructive fear comes, this constricting, annihilating fear of being alone; when I fall apart into ever-smaller fragments and see in the mirror all the things that are inside me; when I'm driven here and there to every little ice floe in the frozen sea of life. I fear the chasms that open up and pursue me, and into which I am in danger of falling. I stand at the edge of this volcano and stare into the glowing, bubbling mass. For God's sake, please, don't leave me!"

That is how it sounds when erupting unconscious energies take on the form of a smothering avalanche, or a splintering into a thousand pieces, or a bone-shattering earthquake, or an explosive volcano. Then, if not earlier, it becomes clear how dangerous trauma therapy can be. Inflationary fantasies of healing have no place here; the danger of failure is omnipresent. I have learned through painful experience with my patients that not all traumas can be transcended. Not all of my patients arrive at a sense of the beyond with a renewed and stronger lust for life, capable of tuning into the cycle of destruction and renewal. Order is not always born out of disorder. The phoenix that rises from the ashes is sometimes painfully absent. Not all my patients experience their breakdown as a gateway to breakthrough.

There is no guaranteed way out of liminal states of being. Sometimes a dangerous, permanent liminality sets in, in which one is stuck in a no-man's-land, without hope of reintegration, without a sense of meaning. In some cases, this leads to the ultimate solution, a violent suicide, when the power of trauma overrides the adaptive capacity for recovery and the individual loses his or her faith that every descent is followed by an ascent. The heart may be broken open by trauma, or the spirit may be broken up by it; both are equally possible. Some of my patients hold back from crossing the threshold for fear that a breakthrough would cast them out into limitless space, without a regulating self to intervene and assist. Such individuals never grow out of their conflicts and agony. For them the psyche's self-regulating system of growth and moving on through reorganization has failed.

Though trauma can be a catalyst for posttraumatic growth and the acquiring of wisdom, I maintain respect, perhaps even an appropriate fear, before the archetypal power of the collective unconscious as manifested in trauma. Nature and the self-regulating mechanisms of the psyche do not always work well. As Jung pointed out, "Our prisons and hospitals are full of people with whom nature has been experimenting to unhappy ends."[22] This caution also applies to emergence: there is no guarantee that emergence will occur, and if it does, it may not be beneficial to the system.

Transfiguration and Healing Transitions

Enantiodromia, the healing swing to the opposite pole after "being torn asunder" represents a "catastrophic reorganization" of the personality.[23] In trauma therapy it is important to watch for potential phase shifts and to hold oneself intuitively open to transcendent experiences of *enantiodromia*, which can show up in the spontaneous appearance of healing symbols. Although the tension that arises from engaging with the opposites—the struggle between conscious and unconscious, good and evil, love and hate, life and death—is intense, it is also a liberating force, releasing us from the struggle, and directing us toward the birth of a new attitude. This happens, as a rule, only when we feel we are at the end of our rope.

Spiritual traditions often seek to precipitate such a breakdown. In the Zen tradition, for example, koans employ paradox to thrust the truth seeker into uncertainty and despair: the seeming hopelessness of finding the correct answer to a deeply puzzling question grinds the ego down to the point of disintegration, a point at which a phase transition occurs. The result is a spiritual awakening, a state of maximal clarity and insight, a form of *metanoia*, a new way of being—not just of seeing. Such *enantiodromic* experiences of transcendence are common in situations of extreme stress. The trauma archetype, which lies behind trauma complexes and altered states of consciousness, also opens up the possibility of spiritual transformation and makes healing energy available.[24] Wilson draws a connection between the trauma complex and transcendent experiences.[25]

In the dreams and visualizations of traumatized people who still retain their capacity for symbolization, one finds images of transition and transcendence. One such symbol is the bridge, which, as a symbol, intimates the possibility of finding a way across the gulf between the unconscious and consciousness, a path from traumatic imprisonment in a constricted existence to a new, more open way of being in the world. Crossing a narrow, shaky bridge in a dream creates feelings of anxiety and fear. Sometimes it appears that the bridge does not reach the other side, and the dreamer awakens with the terror of falling into a dark and bottomless abyss. Sometimes helpful beings appear on the bridge, requesting a sacrifice or pointing the way and guiding the dreamer safely to the other side.

The tunnel is another symbol that occurs with striking frequency in the dreams of traumatized individuals. The tunnel can symbolize a yearning for light after a prolonged period of utter darkness, and its appearance in the dreams and visualizations of my patients has often heralded the onset of a new phase in the therapeutic process. My patients see it as a hopeful image, one that presages their desired transition to another life, comparable to the image of the birth canal.

Toward the end of therapy, when the theme of reconciliation is constellated, the rainbow may appear in dreams. It is a particularly moving sign. This archetypal image is usually accompanied by intense numinous feelings. The bodily shiver that accompanies the recounting of such a dream, no matter how slight, is often distinctly detectible in the *temenos* of the analytic encounter. The rainbow's beauty, the overwhelming sight of harmonious contact between heaven and earth, can be deeply stirring. It can evoke an intimation of the union of opposites, of the possible fruits of the painful work of integrating "what has been spoiled."

In the *I Ching*, hexagram 18, *Ku*, refers to the necessary, if dangerous, crossing of the great water, so that the time of "standstill" may be overcome through confrontation with "decay."[26] Trauma therapy is almost always "work on what has been spoiled," on the "worms" breeding in the bowl, as the Chinese character *ku* depicts decay. The worm motif comes up repeatedly in dreams, always accompanied by disgust. The mouths of my sexually abused patients are often filled with worms in their dreams, worms on which they nearly suffocate. They pull at the worms to prevent themselves from choking, and the more they pull, the longer the worms get. They pull and spit to the point of complete exhaustion.

Motifs of change and growth are especially striking when they occur in a series of dreams. I am thinking of the long analysis I did with a woman (I will call her Kathy) who came to me when she was sixty-three. She had a pinched nerve in her back and could neither sit nor stand; she felt dizzy and nauseated. She had started to work with a chiropractor, and this work had triggered a flashback to when she was thirteen, the first time her stepfather approached her sexually. A voice within her said, "How could you have allowed it? It was so humiliating. You should have left home!" A week later she stumbled upon my book *Soul Murder* in a bookstore. She read it and contacted me to start analysis.

Her initial dream frightened me:

> *There is a hospital room with beds arranged along a wall.*
> *There is a woman with babies and a man with a gun. I*
> *am the man, and I'm shooting the babies one by one.*

It was a chilling dream; I felt I had been introduced to the agony of soul alienation. Kathy was extremely cerebral. She had moved efficiently through a male-dominated world, but she was haunted by an overpowering, negative mother imago, an absent father who had committed suicide, and a stepfather who had drawn her into an incestuous relationship. Inside this seemingly functional adult was a child with an overwhelming compulsion to grab someone and not let go of him or her on any account. Her feeling was that as long as she had ahold of someone, she would be in one piece; but if the contact was lost, she would fall apart into little pieces, scattered all over the place. She experienced her need to hold on as imperative and unbounded, and she recalled a frightening inner image of herself as a child, falling down a chute into infinity.

When she entered analysis, she stated that her goal was "to stay out of prisons and hospitals," as she was afraid of "going mad." Her sister, one year younger, had been taken to a mental hospital for the first time when she was fifteen and been in and out of hospitals ever since, diagnosed with a manic-depressive psychosis with a schizophrenic core. Kathy was afraid that her own murderous rage would totally engulf her. She had started to find some relief by hitting, smashing, or throwing things, but she was afraid of losing control over her fits of fury and feared fragmentation. Our long years of working together were a kind of roller coaster ride. But her rich fantasy life, her ability to reflect and to think in images, helped us bridge the abyss and touch the wound that had split open. When she first came to me, she was overwhelmed by an energy overload; she was bordering on fragmentation, having lived for so many years frozen, blocked, emotionally contaminated with the energy of her abuser. She felt as if she was on the *Titanic*, headed straight for an iceberg.

Through creative symbolic expression, we slowly and patiently worked on integrating the psychic energy that had been held captive for so long in the trauma complex. We struggled to recover what was lost in the underworld, that hiding place for her vulnerable soul. Some of her dream motifs illustrate her development in transcending trauma.

> *Two elephant heads, doll-sized, swimming in water in a*
> *basin like a kitchen sink. They must be removed. I start to*
> *pick one up with chopsticks and realize with horror that*
> *it's dead and wake up.*

Extremely painful memories surfaced of her childhood and her relationship with her mother: she meant nothing to her mother; she was superfluous. She sobbed as she told me that she felt as if she should never have been born. She was an unfinished, misshapen product that her mother had never wanted. Over long periods in our work, she expressed the feeling of having something rotten in her, of being garbage. Intellectual achievement and acknowledgment in the world were her only source of compensation for this debilitating feeling.

The notion that there can be a life that is not a living death seemed nice to her, but unreal. She said, "It's as if the ovens in Auschwitz have been turned off, so there is less noise, and the doors are open so one can walk out, but one is not certain that this is for real, that they won't be turned on again, and the people hauled back in, and the doors locked." She found it extremely hard to trust the analytic process. The agony of annihilation was her constant companion. This made for a very rocky transference relationship in the first years. Ultimately, after many years, during which she tested my capacity as a container, we developed a very intimate relationship of mutual trust and respect.

Kathy was Jewish and had had to escape as a child from Nazi Germany, first to England, then to France, and then to the United States. She was forced to leave behind her language, her home, her "all"; she had become a polyglot mongrel, not knowing who or what she was.

A year after she started analysis her inner landscape changed:

> *I try to repot my big Benjamin plant, or at least lift it out*
> *of the pot. In the process, most of its roots fall off. Only a*
> *fraction is left. I pot it in fresh soil. It stands up, but I*
> *don't know whether it can grow or even live.*

She was hoping it would grow and felt bothered that she could not be sure that it would. In her next dream, she was on a boat on an ocean in a grey mist on a grey sea, and some sort of document was circulated in which everyone's role was described, because a war or change of regime was expected. On awakening she wondered how people made the transition from living in their persona to living in their selves, becoming real. One day, she had, for the first time, the fleeting feeling that she had shed a skin. Much later, she thought she had even shed pieces of metal armor. This changed to an image of herself as an iceberg about to melt, which filled her with dread that there would be nothing but a puddle left. She tried to take this image positively, musing that water facilitates life and growth, whereas an iceberg is all wrapped up in its solidity. Once she saw herself as a little animal, frozen in a block of ice. Over rather a long period of time, images of her frozen psyche prevailed, followed by a process of gradual thawing.

For most of her life, Kathy had engaged compulsively in various inconsequential tasks, in an obsession she called "taskomania," to take her mind off what she experienced as a horrible desert beneath the surface. She dedicated herself to her work as a businesswoman to the point of forgetting everything else. She later viewed this mode of being— striving to be a good girl, to overadapt, to become what she believed others wanted her to be—as an ineffective path to salvation. A long series of "cripple" dreams put her in touch with the archetypes of the invalid and the beggar, helping her to embrace split-off parts of herself, of which she had hitherto been oblivious. After she was thrust out of her unconscious state with great force, a transcendent opening up tentatively began taking place:

> *I am in a dim place, outside a church—in Spain? A little blind cripple is sitting under a blanket next to the wall. She says something. I can't understand it. I think she wants money. I try to give her some. In the process, the coins spill. I bend over to pick them up and see that I gave her only two cents. So I look again and find a Swiss franc. I bend down and say to her, "Here is one franc." She says, though I can't hear her distinctly, "Hug me, ma'am." So I get down. I still can't see well and first hug a statue that is a little behind her. The statue is a brown rag "statue," a cross*

*between a rag doll and a rag cross. It's smaller than a
baby. Then I find the child, who is about the size of a
baby, really too small to hug, and I very gently put my
cheek to hers. She shudders and sort of falls back. I think
I hurt her, but she says it's not me, it's a growth spasm.
Her growth is painful because she's a cripple. I never got
to see her face or her body.*

It took many anguish-filled years before she could see and hear
clearly what the unconscious wanted to communicate to her. She
learned to attend to the cripple and her crippling complexes,
searching for the key to her inner self. It was a very challenging and
moving homecoming from exile, finding the door that led to the
secret of transformation and renewal, bearing her own cross and
reconnecting to her Jewish roots, which she had turned her back
on throughout her life.

In enunciating the principle of *enantiodromia*, Jung started from
the understanding that every extreme provokes its opposite and may
thus trigger a sudden swing to the other extreme. He wrote: "The best
is the most threatened with some devilish perversion just because it
has done the most to suppress evil."[27] However, the reverse is also true:
"Only out of disaster can the longing for the saviour arise."[28] When
the horrifying face of evil is exposed, when the human propensity for
brutality and atrocity is revealed to us in all its starkness, we may be
pushed over the brink, either to shatter or to experience an
enantiodromia. Trauma is such an extreme experience for the psyche that
it calls for its own opposite, as one sees in the dialectical relationship
between good and evil. Jung writes: "we can never know what evil may
not be necessary in order to produce good by enantiodromia, and what
good may very possibly lead to evil."[29]

In reading the testimonies of survivors of the Khmer Rouge, I
see two opposite responses to trauma: remaining stuck in feelings
of revenge and transcending the pain by actively transforming it.
On one side are people like Ou Seng Thy, who wants an eye-for-
an-eye style of revenge for atrocities committed by the Pol Pot
soldiers. After recounting his discovery of how they killed his father,
Ou Seng Thy says:

> This was 1983, and I was eighteen years old. I was so angry, I
> became a soldier to take revenge. I want the Khmer Rouge leaders
> who are accused, like Duch, to be judged and tortured. His flesh
> should be cut little piece by little piece until his death. We should
> do to them whatever they did to us. . . . If they cut our ears, we
> cut their ears a little; if they hit us, we hit them a little; if they
> burned us, we burn then a little back. We do that little by little
> until their death.[30]

On the other side is Qouch Sun Lay, a musician and former teacher,
who sings and accompanies himself on the guitar about the losses during
the dark times of the regime and writes poetry about what happened.
His wife and children were killed because his wife was half Vietnamese.
His persecutors told him she was like useless skin on his body that
should be cut off. He feared that they may have raped her before killing
her, like they did the two women he found dead in the forest, naked,
with long bamboo sticks inserted into their vaginas. But his songs and
his wishes are for peace: "More than anything I want peace. Peace is
the most important factor, first inside yourself, then in your family,
then in your country."[31]

The notion of justice is extremely important in transcending
trauma. I was deeply touched by the account of Yun Bin. He relates
that he fainted and felt his soul leaving him when a soldier struck
him on the head with an ax and he fell into a mass grave on a pile
of dead bodies. He regained consciousness, but his soul had already
gone. He continues:

> I tried to kick the bodies off of me and scratch the string off my
> hands. It smelled horrible. The warmth of blood and fat was all
> over my body. I looked up and heard someone yell to kneel, then
> I heard the breaking sound, like someone breaking a coconut,
> and then another body was thrown down. I tried to pile the
> bodies and climb out, but I couldn't. I started to pray to my
> ancestors, to the Buddha, to anyone. I prayed that if the bodies
> could help me to get out, I would seek justice for them. Then
> the bodies started to decay and swell so the level rose.[32]

He finally managed to climb out. About his post-trauma life, he
says: "During important days of the year the souls of the people
visit me. I have to offer food so they will go away. I hope that before

I die I learn who ordered this killing, and that the families of the children and people can find justice."[33]

The Transcultural Psychosocial Organization (TPO Cambodia), which I know and dealt with as a board member of a Swiss foundation dedicated to war trauma, has done impressive work in promoting psychological healing for those who have suffered such atrocities. Its work in providing space for memory and testimony, combining psychological and spiritual support, especially through testimony therapy, plays an important role in transcending the wounds of trauma and initiating healing. Testimony therapy can be a meaningful and healing instrument in processing trauma because it requires remembering and articulating the betrayal and confronting the uncertainty in a supportive environment. Survivors take an important step toward building up their capacity for transcendence by bearing witness against their oppressors and reducing the collective amnesia regarding genocide by preserving memories and making them public.

Working through TPO Cambodia, Zélie Pollon, a journalist from Santa Fe, New Mexico, traveled to Cambodia in 2010 to conduct interviews with survivors as part of her research on storytelling in postconflict societies.[34] She was accompanied by her friend and photographer Alan M. Thornton, who photographed those who testified, placing them in their most natural environment. His images celebrate the dignity of the human spirit and the courage of telling the truth while also revealing the agony. He writes that the subjects of his photographs wanted to teach the younger generation, to serve as role models providing strength. In the work done by TPO Cambodia, testimony therapy is combined with the performing of rituals of various kinds—rites to mourn the dead and rituals of purification and cleansing—bringing survivors together with psychologists, social workers, and Buddhist monks, uniting the profane with the sacred.[35]

Grief and sorrow are creative emotional processes that serve a healing function and thus have great importance in trauma therapy. Without the capacity to grieve, the patient remains dominated by inner deadness and is therefore frozen in his or her personal development. Grief and sorrow imply the realization that our existence is a "Being-towards-death."[36] They help us to confront the wound and the insult that death often represents for human beings. Whether we mourn physical death or the death of the ego our grief makes our distress visible—our distress at the fact that living entails dying.

People who have endured situations that brought them to the gates of death have learned something deep about themselves and about the mystery of life. Sorrow and despair, the void, the muteness and numbness of pain, the tears and rage, the whole spectrum of grief reactions, are part of living and dying. In the process of mourning, as seen in the most diverse cultural manifestations of grief, the whole person says farewell to the lost loved one. That is, we grieve with everything we have and everything we are, with physical movement, with voice and tone and resonance. The whole organism responds to the situation of loss, even when the death is symbolic. Grieving has many facets, and manifestations of grief vary widely across cultures as well as through time. However, a common core persists that associates the lost object with the griever's identity and self-construal. Traumatic losses damage a person's sense of self-worth and destroy life's underlying meaning. Grief work thus involves a search for cognitive understanding, attempting to verify causes, observe consequences, create meaningful connections, or name the absurdities and injustices.

In the camps of the war-ravaged former Yugoslavia, I was told by the refugees, "There's nothing to live for any more." In such cases of collective trauma, grief work may involve a shared groping for values that have been lost, allowing room for feelings of pain, desperation, and rage. It often requires shared grieving: searching for collective rituals and symbols that can provide comfort and constructing modes of social action and solidarity that can reestablish a sense of connectedness and the easing of burdens. Shared grieving may also be facilitated by invoking cultural myths and rituals associated with life and death. In providing images for the archetype of change and renewal of life, myths mediate comfort and hope. They stimulate awareness that one's individual existence is rooted in greater cosmic relationships that link back to the existence of those who came before.

Processing grief is a deeply dynamic process in which all the senses are mobilized. Through the use of every kind of medium (music, painting, modeling with clay, role playing, acting out fairy tales and scenes in psychodramas, letter writing, poetry writing, active imagination, working with dreams and daydreams), grief begins to flow and finds its creative, outward expression. Always a metamorphosis is involved, a transformation from chaos to cosmos, aggression to compassion, the building of a healing structure, and a grounding process, to find a counterweight against the psychic deconstruction that threatens during the overwhelming pain of grief. Rituals and symbolic work provide support in this process of releasing the agony of loss and separation.

Being able to grieve means finding a way back to oneself and mastering things that were once experienced as overwhelming. It involves a thawing of what was frozen. Grief and lamentation have a great potential for transformation, because in naming and identifying his or her losses the patient once again takes ownership of what has been lost, and blocked energies can once again begin to flow. But such a process of grieving can be retraumatizing unless it is accompanied by encouragement and comfort.

My training in integrative gestalt therapy has sensitized me to "comfort work" (*Trostarbeit*), which is found in all cultures, universally, as a program of unburdening and support. In his groundbreaking work on therapeutic handling of grief and consolation, Hilarion Petzold has shown persuasively how resilience can be strengthened and the ground laid for a meaning-oriented way of working, which makes an essential contribution, cognitively and emotionally, to the integration of trauma.[37] This work, which is well attested to by neuroscience, avoids the overexcitation of the amygdala and the toxic hyperregulation of corticosteroids, which tend to occur during cathartic trauma processing. As much as we are accustomed to viewing abreactive grief work as an important phase in the process of working through traumatic experiences, we are unfamiliar with the meaning of comfort and solace as an effective clinical intervention from the heart. Comfort, however, is significant in the therapeutic process, because—as distinct from grief—it does not focus primarily on the past but opens up hopeful perspectives, soothes pain, and buffers emotional shocks.

The comforting relationship is a helpful factor in the mastering of grief, as trauma research has demonstrated. Reliable companionship and shared endurance, in spoken exchanges and the silent dialogue of gazes, bring mutuality to the painful experiences and provide hope in the solitary wasteland of trauma. What is needed here is not the classic analytical detachment but an engaged and shared solidarity in which the therapist is internalized by the patient as an auxiliary ego or inner scaffolding. To recover one's blocked creativity, one needs the presence of an empathic, cocreative other. Comforting support and caring from the therapist enables survivors to face up to existential burdens and concerns. Only if we, as therapists, accept a holding function, if we allow our patients to use us in such a way that through our integrity and solidarity structures become visible to them, reminding them of their own demolished structures—only then will they be able to regain their subjectivity.

I have learned from Heidegger that we cannot heal another person unless we are prepared to restore his or her connection with being. In the case of traumatized individuals, the relationship to being has been ruptured. That is why existential analysis—*Daseinsanalyse*, as Swiss psychoanalytic psychiatrist Medard Boss practiced it—suggests that as analysts we should lend our patients for a certain time our own greater human freedom, until they can exercise their own capacity for relationship freely, on their own.[38] I also hand my patients the torch of hope when they cannot see any hope on the horizon. Sometimes, they are not yet able to accept the torch. Then I will carry it for them until they can detect some glimmer of hope in themselves. Thus I am able to shed light on their dark path, trusting that through my empathic, compassionate presence their hope can be awakened and that it is still possible for them to reconnect with their original, pretrauma image of what it means to be human.

Trauma survivors need to learn new strategies for regulating themselves, finding new horizons of hope, the capacity for emotional resonance, and courage to take new steps in life. The confidence of the therapist, the promise of comfort, and the provision of a protected space in which the patient can experience safety—all of these soothe the pain, awaken the capacity for symbolization, and strengthen the patient's courage for uttering the unspeakable.

Petzold considers grief work to be an intersubjective endeavor, supporting the processes of grieving, working through, and mastery. He elaborates that the healing effect of comfort operates on the physiological level, reducing stress and diminishing hyperarousal. On the psychological level, it counters feelings of self-derogation, indecisiveness, bitterness, and resignation. On the social level, it leads to the resumption of trusting contact and relationship and to the overcoming of isolation and contempt for others. In particular, grief work with survivors of torture and refugees and the recovery of their lost dignity depends largely on the quality of this intersubjective relationship. Solace thus constitutes an expanded resource: it reinforces the patient's resilience, contributes to calming, and opens up a reconciling perspective with self and with fate.

In trauma therapy we must take to heart what is said, because only in this way can we perceive a human being in his or her potential space. Through this kind of related, loving gaze a relational field might be created in which patients will be able to become once again, in their innermost selves, what they truly are and always have been. This form of loving, comforting companioning, through listening, creative form-giving, and the interventions of body therapies, can prevent somatic disorders and bitterness from becoming chronic. As a hermeneutic undertaking, such a therapeutic approach, using clarification, interpretation, grieving, and comforting, can help a person who has become lost find his or her way back into the world and create meaningful connections that will once again allow full scope for action. As a result, the trauma survivor may achieve not only a new way of seeing the world but possibly also a changed way of being in the world.

Grief work, testimony therapy, and purification rituals serve as catalysts in the inducing of *enantiodromia* when it does not occur automatically. But I have also encountered traumas in which *enantiodromia* has failed to set in. I have heard torture survivors lamenting, with a deep sense of resignation, "There is no way to heal it. Nothing could possibly relieve the pain. There is no God to listen; no amount of praying helps. I am condemned to live in this psychic hell forever." Why some individuals experience *enantiodromia* and others do not may be explained by the concept of transcendence competence, that is, the individual's capacity for transcendence.

The Capacity for Transcendence

The capacity for transcendence has been investigated empirically by Cornelius von Mitschke-Collande, who uses the framework of consciousness studies to explore what he calls "transcendence competence."[39] He is interested in identifying what gives some human beings the capacity to remain open and engaged even in the throes of an existential crisis, what is the source of the ability to develop a new, more integrated perspective on life and even take the traumatic content into account in the process. He has demonstrated that transcendence competence is an innate growth dynamic that arises at all levels of consciousness. It can be learned and developed. In his doctoral dissertation on this subject, Mitschke-Collande draws on the gestalt psychology principle that inherent in any gestalt is the tendency to overcome contradictions, disharmonies, and imperfections and to change imbalances into higher forms of organization.[40] He understands the capacity for transcendence as arising from the capacity and the drive to create more comprehensive gestalts.

Wilson provides a complementary conceptualization of how transcendence comes about:

> In the Transcendent Experience that occurs in connection with trauma, the power of the experience is so great that it releases inhibitions, censorship, resistance, and ego-defenses against material that previously had been rendered unconscious. The relevance of old, previously unconscious material is now capable of being reappraised and reconstructed into new cognitive perspectives at a very rapid rate.[41]

This snapping of restraints is experienced as a transcendent opening, in which weakness is transformed into strength. It can bring a sense of liberation from former attachments and encumbrances, a stepping out from darkness into light. I understand this opening up to life following a traumatic shock as an initiation into a deeper insight into human nature. Dimensions of wisdom may become available when traumas are transcended through deep compassion and love and concern for the well-being of humanity.[42]

I am reminded of the concept of peak experience, a term introduced in the 1960s by Abraham Maslow.[43] Peak experiences, which Maslow also refers to as "transcendent experiences," are characterized by clarity of perception and an apprehension of ultimate reality, in which the ego's perspective is transcended, and the meaning of the whole, the relativity of time and space, and the ultimate interconnection of all things are realized.[44] For Maslow, peak experiences are a transient expression of optimal states of self-actualization and the integrated functioning of the personality.[45] He also identified "plateau experience," a special form of peak experience, which is less intense and emotional than the peak experience, has a calming rather than an excitative influence, and is longer lasting than the more transient peak experience. The plateau experience has a "noetic and cognitive" quality to it, is more voluntary than the autonomic peak experience, and, like Mitschke-Collande's transcendence competence, it "can be achieved, learned, earned by long hard work" and is, in fact, "a lifelong effort."[46]

Wilson shows how the resilience of trauma survivors is related both to Maslow's findings on peak experiences and to Peterson and Seligman's work in the area of positive psychology.[47] According to Wilson, resilient trauma survivors (i.e., those with a high degree of transcendence competence) display "high-order personality functioning."[48] He suggests that such high-order functioning requires the character strengths and virtues listed by Peterson and Seligman as essential for the development of a positive personal psychology and the promoting of human potential. Transcendence is one of six core virtues analyzed by Peterson and Seligman.[49] In their classification, transcendence is seen as having five character strengths: appreciation of beauty, gratitude, hope, humor, and spirituality.[50] Peterson and Seligman believe that transcendence and all the other virtues and character strengths associated with them are not fixed, innate, and unchangeable but can be acquired, learned through experience, and developed.[51] In this respect, their position is similar to that of Mitschke-Collande and Maslow.

In Jung's thought, this learning takes the form of becoming increasingly conscious. According to Jung, the sole purpose of human existence is to kindle a light in the darkness of mere being by becoming conscious. Furthermore, he maintained that just as the unconscious affects our conscious behavior, so an increase in consciousness affects the unconscious. The capacity for transcending trauma and experiencing posttraumatic growth involves a shift in consciousness to a higher level of self-awareness and wisdom.

Along similar lines, Viktor Frankl noted that humans are the only creatures able to transcend themselves, to create a new noetic dimension for themselves.[52] Frankl's concept of self-transcendence involves the transcendence of the ego and a broadening of the visual field, which results in an ability to view oneself and life in general more comprehensively.[53] Out of his experiences in Nazi concentration camps,

Frankl developed his concept of the will to meaning, that is, "the striving to find concrete meaning in personal existence," an insight that echoes Nietzsche's dictum, which Frankl renders as: "He who has a *why* to live for can bear almost any *how*."[54] Using language that recalls Maslow, Frankl notes that self-transcendence produces self-actualization as a side effect.[55] The capacity to overcome existential limits, outgrow former boundaries, and invest life with meaning manifests itself in three ways: (1) in creative or deliberate action; (2) in the way we experience the beauty and goodness of life and in the loving encounter with others; and (3) in the attitude we adopt to unavoidable suffering.[56]

As several of the theorists mentioned here have noted, the metamorphosis that is achieved through transcendence—the reinvention of the self, especially the "posttraumatic self"—requires hard work.[57] Repairing the damage to self-processes and reintegrating and transfiguring the ego identity are lifelong endeavors. Wilson writes: "The resynthesis of personality processes . . . includes restoring ego-coherence, identity integration and self-transfiguration."[58]

This process of resynthesis is fraught with great uncertainty, which constricts the capacity for transcendence. Doris Brothers, who works on trauma from a relational systems perspective, starts with the proposition that the betrayal of trust in traumatic experiences shatters the individual's organization of his or her self-experience, precipitating unbearable existential uncertainty and destabilizing his or her relational world. This robs the individual's life of meaning and threatens him or her with annihilation. In the face of this threat, the individual's relational system attempts to restore itself by reducing uncertainty through a reduction in complexity. This is achieved through dissociation and the creation of dualities or dichotomies.[59]

Brothers goes on to comment that the hope offered to trauma patients in therapy may serve only to compound their uncertainty, given that hope implies the possibility of failure. From the patient's perspective, "all certainty is exposed by trauma as a cruel myth," and hope must therefore "be crushed lest it add further uncertainty to a future that is already unbearably precarious."[60] She reflects: "I have wondered if some of the patients who have been characterized as resistant to the therapeutic process are those who demonstrate their need to evade what might be conceptualized as a tyranny of hope."[61] I would add that without hope the capacity for transcendence is crippled.

In my practice I often encounter dissociation and other forms of defense against unbearable uncertainty, as well as resistance to hope as described by Brothers. I find helpful the insights of Barbara Jakel, who maintains that in the face of dissociative splitting, a feeling of ego identity is nevertheless preserved on the transpersonal level, providing the traumatized individual with the assurance that on a deeper level his or her wholeness is still intact, despite the threat of annihilation posed by the trauma.[62] This intact ground, the "inviolable personal spirit," as Donald Kalsched calls it, is where I focus my attention in trauma therapy, an approach that may well be the antidote to the resistance to hope that therapists encounter in dealing with traumatized individuals.[63]

Despite the therapist's best efforts, however, the unbearable uncertainty associated with betrayal of trust and the obliteration of the traumatic experience from the patient's store of conscious memories can confound the task of achieving transcendence, as I have learned from torture victims in Cambodia and from the narratives of Chilean patients, Bosnian prisoners of war, and victims of mass rape in the former Yugoslavia.

Following the massacre of 220 civilians at Tiananmen Square in Beijing, Chinese writer and musician Liao Yiwu was awarded the Peace Prize of the German Publishers and Booksellers Association (*Friedenspreis des Deutschen Buchhandels*). In his acceptance speech at the awards ceremony, he spoke about the importance of refusing simply to go along, to conform to whatever is the order of the day. As I listened to him, I wondered how a nation can collectively transcend such traumas. During the Great Famine in China (1958–1962), an estimated forty-five million people died from starvation, execution, brutality, and hard labor.[64] During the Cultural Revolution (1966–1976), by Liao Yiwu's count, twenty to forty million people were tortured to death. In the killing fields of Cambodia, as in Auschwitz and Dachau, I have felt the question pressing down on me as to whether "moving beyond" and transcendence after such experiences is even possible. I know how enormously difficult it is to outgrow such traumas and reconcile oneself to experiences of injustice and violence.

Only recently, in October 2012, at the Iran tribunal hearings in The Hague, Nargess Eskandari-Grünberg, a politician and psychotherapist who is the Frankfurt City Councilor for Integration, testified about her experience of incarceration during the Khomeini regime at the age of seventeen in the infamous Evin Prison in Tehran. In a newspaper interview given just before appearing at the hearings, she revealed that during her imprisonment she could hear, day and night, the screams of the tortured prison inmates and would count the gunshots from the executions in the back courtyard, never knowing who would be the next to be subjected to a sham trial and then dragged out and executed, anxiously hoping it would not be her.[65] The Iranian method of torture was to suspend prisoners upside-down and whip the soles of their feet until they bled. This practice gave rise to the saying among the prisoners: "Feet are a second memory." Eskandari-Grünberg explained that those who betrayed others under torture say their feet are a constant reminder of their act of betrayal. She describes the horrific experience of being kicked in the abdomen by the prison guards while she was pregnant and having to give birth to her daughter while blindfolded during her incarceration.

It is no wonder that people who have been subjected to such unimaginable violence and horror are unable to remember, that they become emotionally frozen, that their experiences can never be integrated into the ego. Many lose permanently their appreciation of what makes life worth living. Many can never again trust their fellow human beings. After physical and spiritual violation of this magnitude, one common strategy for self-restoration is a retreat into numbness. Self-anesthetization is a means of preserving oneself by turning off one's feelings in order to keep from falling apart. The aim of torture is, in fact, to abuse a person until he or she is no longer a person, no longer has a will or identity of his or her own.

How is it possible, then, for victims not to shatter in the face of such a massive assault on their humanity? Eskandari-Grünberg, who was forced to sign her own death sentence, was not broken by her experiences but was able to transcend them. She went on to become an engaged politician, fighting for human rights, freedom, and democracy. Despite the utter chaos of her imprisonment, she did not lose her ability to trust but managed to transcend her inhuman treatment and retain her sense of solidarity with the human race.

Syrian writer, journalist, and documentary filmmaker Samar Yazbek provides a similar chronicle of terror from the Syrian Revolution of 2011.[66] In words that are disturbing, moving, and courageous, she fights back against oppression, torture, and despair. Her writing testifies both to the human capacity for cruelty and to the humanity of a deeply suffering people as well as to her own capacity for transcendence.

Nargess Eskandari-Grünberg and Samar Yazbek have lived through trauma; they have an intimate acquaintance with brutality and human vulnerability. They know all about the fragility of the constructs we create for and about ourselves. And yet they did not stop believing in the human capacity to change, and they have not stopped risking their lives to help others like them who have suffered extreme forms of trauma. I have a deep respect for traumatized individuals who achieve some form of self-mastery, who are able to step out into the open, find within themselves "the courage to be," overcome pain, helplessness, and despair, and move beyond hatred and the desire for retribution.[67] To free oneself from fixations and self-destructive patterns and, in place of these, to practice compassion and self-love, something must be consciously overcome and left behind. We must cease grasping for what is irrecoverably lost and let go of bitterness and resentment if we are to develop the capacity for transcendence.

NOTES

[1] Jung, *RB*, p. 254.

[2] This imagery comes from Yeats's poem "The Second Coming": "Things fall apart; the centre cannot hold; / Mere anarchy is loosed upon the world, / The blood-dimmed tide is loosed, and everywhere / The ceremony of innocence is drowned." William Butler Yeats, *The Collected Poems of W. B. Yeats*, ed. Richard J. Finneran, rev. 2nd ed. (New York: Scribner Paperback Poetry, 1996), p. 187.

[3] Albert Einstein, *The World as I See It*, trans. Alan Harris (Secaucus, NJ: Citadel Press, 1979), p. 5.

[4] Michael J. Spivey, Sarah E. Anderson, and Rick Dale, "The Phase Transition in Human Cognition," *New Mathematics and Natural Computation* 5, no. 1 (2009): 197–220. See also George Hogenson, "The Self, the Symbolic and Synchronicity: Virtual Realities and the Emergence of the Psyche," *Journal of Analytical Psychology* 50, no. 3 (2005): 271–284.

⁵ Roger Lewin, *Complexity: Life at the Edge of Chaos* (Chicago: University of Chicago Press, 1992).

⁶ Dee Hock, *Birth of the Chaordic Age* (San Francisco: Berrett-Koehler Publishers, 1999).

⁷ J. Scott Jordan, ed., *Systems Theories and A Priori Aspects of Perception* (Amsterdam: North-Holland, Elsevier Science B.V., 1998).

⁸ Spivey, Anderson, and Dale, "The Phase Transition in Human Cognition," p. 199ff.

⁹ *Ibid.*, p. 212ff. See also Hogenson, "The Self, the Symbolic and Synchronicity," p. 277ff.

¹⁰ Steven Johnson, *Emergence: The Connected Lives of Ants, Brains, Cities, and Software* (New York: Scribner, 2001), p. 18.

¹¹ Fulvio Mazzocchi, "Complexity in Biology: Exceeding the Limits of Reductionism and Determinism Using Complexity Theory," *European Molecular Biology Organization Reports* 9, no. 1 (2008): 11.

¹² Erich Jantsch, *The Self-Organizing Universe: Scientific and Human Implications of the Emerging Paradigm of Evolution* (Oxford, UK: Pergamon Press, 1980).

¹³ Leonard Cohen, "Anthem," *The Future*, Columbia Records, 1992.

¹⁴ Intersubjectivists use the term *intersubjective systems theory*. See Robert D. Stolorow, "Intersubjective-Systems Theory: A Phenomenological-Contextualist Psychoanalytic Perspective," *Psychoanalytic Dialogues* 23, no. 4 (2013): 383–389. See also Robert D. Stolorow, George E. Atwood, and Donna M. Orange, *Worlds of Experience: Interweaving Philosophical and Clinical Dimensions in Psychoanalysis* (New York: Basic Books, 2002).

¹⁵ Joseph Cambray, "Towards the Feeling of Emergence," *Journal of Analytical Psychology* 51, no. 1 (2006): 1–20; "Synchronicity and Emergence," *American Imago* 59, no. 4 (2002): 409–434; and *Synchronicity: Nature and Psyche in an Interconnected Universe* (College Station, TX: Texas A&M University Press, 2009).

¹⁶ See James A. Hall, "The Watcher at the Gates of Dawn: The Transformation of Self in Liminality and by the Transcendent Function," in *Liminality and Transitional Phenomena*, ed. Nathan Schwartz-Salant and Murray Stein (Wilmette, IL: Chiron Publications, 1991), pp. 33–51; and Cambray, "Synchronicity and Emergence."

¹⁷ Jung, *CW* 9i, § 82.

¹⁸ Jung, *CW* 12, § 34.

[19] Jungian analysts have made an extensive study of new discoveries in various disciplines, searching for a unified theory that encompasses our concepts of consciousness, *unus mundus*, the Self, synchronicity, archetypes, the psychoid realm, and the transcendent function. A brief overview and bibliography can be found in Hester McFarland Solomon, *The Self in Transformation* (London: Karnac Books, 2007).

[20] Erin Martz, "Reflections on Healing," in *Trauma Rehabilitation after War and Conflict: Community and Individual Perspectives*, ed. Erin Martz (New York: Springer, 2010), p. v.

[21] Antoine de Saint-Exupéry, *The Little Prince*, trans. Richard Howard (1943; reprinted: New York: Harcourt, 2000), p. 56ff.

[22] C. G. Jung, *Analytical Psychology: Notes of the Seminar Given in 1925*, ed. William McGuire (Princeton, NJ: Princeton University Press, 1989), p. 10.

[23] Jung, *CW* 7, § 113.

[24] For a summary, see table 5.1 in "Dimensions of the Trauma Archetype," in John P. Wilson, ed., *The Posttraumatic Self: Restoring Meaning and Wholeness to Personality* (New York: Routledge, 2006), p. 166f. The *trauma complex* is "the unique, individual constellation of the trauma experience in cognitive-affective structures located in the self and intrapsychic processes" (p. 157).

[25] *Ibid.*, p. 188ff.

[26] *Ku*: Work on What Has Been Spoiled [Decay], in *I Ching*, or *The Book of Changes*, trans. Richard Wilhelm, rendered into English by Cary F. Baynes (Princeton, NJ: Princeton University Press, 1977), pp. 75–77.

[27] Jung, *CW* 5, § 581.

[28] Jung, *CW* 9i, § 487.

[29] Jung, *CW* 9i, § 397.

[30] Muny Sothara and Judith Strasser, *IWitness: Testimonies by Survivors of the Khmer Rouge*, trans. K. Tongngy and S. Sokhalay, TPO (Phnom Penh, Cambodia: JSRC Printing House, 2011), n.p.

[31] *Ibid.*

[32] *Ibid.*

[33] *Ibid.*

[34] Zélie Pollon, "Journey to Cambodia: Learning the Power of Trauma and the Healing of Testimony," *Santa Fe Reporter* (online

edition), May 11, 2011, p. 1, accessed October 16, 2013, http://www.sfreporter.com/santafe/article-6060-journey-to-cambodia.html.

[35] *Ibid.*, p. 2.

[36] Martin Heidegger, *Being and Time*, trans. John Macquarrie and Edward Robinson (New York: Harper and Row, 1962).

[37] Hilarion G. Petzold, "Integrative Traumatherapie und 'Trostarbeit'—ein nicht-exponierender, leibtherapeutischer und lebenssinnorientierter Ansatz risikobewusster Behandlung," *Polylogue: Eine Internetzeitschrift für "Integrative Therapie"* 3 (2004), accessed October 8, 2013, http://www.fpi-publikation.de/images/stories/downloads/polyloge/Petzold-Trauma-Trost-Polyloge-03-2004.pdf.

[38] See Medard Boss, *Psychoanalysis and Daseinanalysis*, trans. Ludwig B. Lefebre (New York: Basic Books, 1963).

[39] Cornelius von Mitschke-Collande, "Gestärkt durch die Krise," *Bewusstseinswissenschaften, Transpersonale Psychologie und Psychotherapie* 18, no. 1 (2012): 65–77.

[40] Cornelius von Mitschke-Collande, "Die Kompetenz der Transzendenzfähigkeit: Eine Studie zur Bewusstseinsforschung" (PhD diss., University of Oldenburg, 2010), accessed October 17, 2013, http://oops.uni-oldenburg.de/954/1/mitkom10.pdf.

[41] Wilson, *The Posttraumatic Self*, p. 191.

[42] *Ibid.*, p. 4.

[43] A. H. Maslow, *Religions, Values, and Peak-Experiences* (1964; reprinted: New York: Penguin Books, 1970), p. 33.

[44] *Ibid.*, especially pp. 19–20.

[45] *Ibid.*, p. 80.

[46] *Ibid.*, pp. xiv–xvi.

[47] For a discussion of transcendence in the framework of positive psychology, see Christopher Peterson and Martin E. P. Seligman, *Character Strengths and Virtues: A Handbook and Classification* (New York: Oxford University Press, 2004), pp. 517–622.

[48] Wilson, *The Posttraumatic Self*, p. 4.

[49] Peterson and Seligman, *Character Strengths and Virtues*, pp. vii, 13, 36 (and throughout the book). Peterson and Seligman draw upon the work of Katherine Dahlsgaard, who identified six core virtues that are common to all cultures and traditions: wisdom, courage, humanity, justice, temperance, and transcendence.

[50] *Ibid.*, p. 518ff.

[51] *Ibid.*, p. 5.

[52] Viktor E. Frankl, *Man's Search for Meaning: An Introduction to Logotherapy* (Boston: Beacon Press, 1992).

[53] *Ibid.*, p. 110.

[54] *Ibid.*, pp. 101, 104; italics in the original.

[55] *Ibid.*, p. 111.

[56] *Ibid.*, pp. 111–112.

[57] Wilson, *The Posttraumatic Self*, pp. 70, 82, 421, 438.

[58] *Ibid.*, p. 81.

[59] Doris Brothers, "Trauma-Centered Psychoanalysis: Transforming Experiences of Unbearable Uncertainty," *Annals of the New York Academy of Sciences* 1159 (2009): 51–62.

[60] *Ibid.*, p. 60.

[61] *Ibid.*

[62] Barbara Jakel, "Spirituelle Aspekte des pränatalen Erlebens und ihre künstlerische Verarbeitung," in *Trauma und Kreativität: Therapie mit künstlerischen Medien*, ed. Ruth Hampe et al. (Bremen: Universität Bremen, 2003), pp. 133–143.

[63] Donald Kalsched, *The Inner World of Trauma: Archetypal Defenses of the Personal Spirit* (London: Routledge, 1996), p. 193.

[64] Frank Dikötter, *Mao's Great Famine: The History of China's Most Devastating Catastrophe, 1958–1962* (New York: Walker Publishing, 2010), p. x.

[65] Philip Eppelsheim, Friederike Haupt, and Volker Zastrow, "Ich kenne nur die Stimmen," *Frankfurter Allgemeine Zeitung*, October 27, 2012, accessed October 21, 2013, http://www.faz.net/aktuell/politik/ausland/opfer-des-chomeini-regimes-ich-kenne-nur-die-stimmen-11940962.html.

[66] Samar Yazbek, *A Woman in the Crossfire: Diaries of the Syrian Revolution*, trans. Max Weiss (London: Haus Publishing, 2012).

[67] Paul Tillich, *The Courage to Be* (New Haven, CT: Yale University Press, 2000).

CHAPTER TEN

TRANSCENDENCE, TRAUMA, AND SACRIFICE

T he idea of transcending trauma through sacrifice is a challenging one, perhaps beyond our capacity to grasp fully. Yet, as trauma patients strive to move beyond their emotionally paralyzed state to a higher level of functioning, it seems sacrifice is a necessary step. Violent trauma forces us to sacrifice ideas of invulnerability, control, and ego strength, to let go of the illusion that we can defend ourselves against hopelessness, despair, and loss. Life "demands sacrifices," Jung wrote to Sabina Spielrein in 1911. "Only in the course of . . . self-sacrifice will you gain yourself in a new and more beautiful form."[1] Indeed, there can be no psychological development of consciousness without sacrifice. Jung wrote:

> Human nature has an invincible dread of becoming more conscious of itself. What nevertheless drives us to it is the self, which demands sacrifice by sacrificing itself to us. Conscious realization or the bringing together of the scattered parts is in one sense an act of the ego's will, but in another sense it is a spontaneous manifestation of the self, which was always there.[2]

The archetype of sacrifice has far-reaching implications in the fields of anthropology, sociology, theology, and beyond.[3] The metaphor of sacrifice seems especially helpful in the treatment of traumatized individuals, since it casts light on the dialectic between victim and sacrificer. It contributes greatly to an understanding of why we suffer loss. As an archetypal occurrence, sacrifice is generally not a matter of choice but rather of psychic necessity, to which we are compelled by fate.

Early in his career, Jung developed a preoccupation with the energy and transformative character of sacrifice.[4] However, his writings about sacrifice remain at the symbolic level: the sacrifice of instinctual libido, of one's animal nature, of the ego's sovereign power in order to form a conscious relationship with the Self. In the Red Book, he speaks of the necessity of the sacrifice demanded by the spirit of the depths, adding, "Sacrifice is not destruction, sacrifice is the foundation stone of what is to come."[5] In his analysis of his Siegfried dream, he explains the necessity of sacrificing the hero ideal so that a new adaptation can be made.[6] "Murder of the Hero," as this section in the Red Book is titled, concerns the sacrifice not only of the hero but also of the gods, for "they require renewal."[7] Jung later commented that his Siegfried dream signified the killing of his intellect and the deposing of his dominant function, for only then would there be "a chance for other sides of the personality to be born into life."[8]

Jung understood that the sacrifice of the superior function is a necessary step toward releasing the libido needed to extricate the inferior functions from the unconscious and stimulate their development, and thereby to transcend the limitations they impose upon the personality.[9] This sacrifice brings about an unleashing of unconscious energy, which is central to understanding how trauma might be transcended. Some parts of the self must be sacrificed in order that other parts might be saved. This makes the individual both the sacrificer and the sacrificed. After originally addressing the dialectic of sacrificer and sacrificed in the Red Book, Jung took it up again in 1942: "What I sacrifice is my egotistical claim, and by doing this I give up myself. Every sacrifice is therefore, to a greater or lesser degree, a self-sacrifice."[10]

I have often wondered why the theme of sacrifice has such a central place in Jung's work. I recall his statement that psychological theories are a form of "confession" on the part of the theorist with regard to his (or her) "personal psychology."[11] I believe that such confessions also provide insights into the theorist's personal blind spots, so I find myself reflecting on Jung's possible blind spots in connection with early experiences of trauma and victimization. It seems to me that in bringing about a separation from Freudian psychoanalysis and establishing an independent theory, Jung's giving birth to analytical psychology itself involved a traumatic sacrifice. In his autobiography, Jung describes a two-month period during which he was so tormented by conflict that he could not do any writing, for he knew that by disassociating himself from Freud's phallocentric theory, he had sacrificed his friendship and collaboration with his mentor.[12] With the publication in 1911–1912 of *Wandlungen und Symbole der Libido*, which addresses the theme of sacrifice extensively, Jung sealed his break with Freud, thereby sacrificing his status as Freud's "successor and crown prince" and "heir apparent."[13] Asserting his independence and freedom in this manner also meant the sacrifice of his "solace," a notion Jung explores in the Red Book in the section "The Gift of Magic," where we find a long dialogue between Jung and his soul in which solace is presented as the price one has to pay for undertaking to submit to life, and "severity toward oneself and others takes its place."[14] Jung clearly felt that his path would be one of solitude, for he must follow his inner voice without evasion: "There is only one way and that is your way; there is only one salvation and that is your salvation."[15]

In *Wandlungen und Symbole der Libido*, Jung challenged Freud's dogma regarding the sexual etiology of psychopathology and proposed a completely different understanding of libido a move that had far-reaching implications for his attitude to incest. I see in it, as well, the beginnings of a sacrifice that eventually restricted Jung's access to the wounded parts of his own soul. He grossly underestimated the extent of literal incest and downplayed the severity of its psychological consequences, asserting that it "signified a personal complication only in the rarest of cases."[16] Jung liked to suggest that, as a country child, he naturally took sexuality in stride and thought that no special explanations were needed for incest and sexual perversions. Jung's vehement rejection of childhood sexual trauma as a cause of neurotic development seems to me to serve as a psychological defense. He developed the theory that incestuous fixations should be understood as an infantile, regressive standstill in the deep-rooted human yearning to remain a child. He thought this arrest of libido on the objects of early childhood must be sacrificed for the fulfillment of this regressive yearning.

From Spiritual Emergency to Spiritual Emergence: Traumatic Roots and Self-Transcendence in the Red Book

I regard Jung's descent into the abyss as a borderland experience of spiritual emergency and renewal that brought about an awakening that was growth-promoting and transformative. In the Red Book Jung documents a highly personal search for "the supreme meaning beyond meaning and meaninglessness."[17] I thus consider the book's central message to be a spiritual one, namely, that there is a connection to the Beyond within the human soul, a link to a realm that transcends the ego. The book is a testament to the possibility of self-transcendence following a period of massive destabilization. I see depicted in it a path leading from the chaotically imbalanced condition of torturous psychic flooding to a new, meaningful order and a state of centeredness. Jung's process in the book clearly shows the kind of energetic power that drove him upward and forward. This power, which he tapped into during the crisis that almost cost him his sanity, is the same power that he later conceptualized as the transcendent function.

In the Red Book, Jung, like the shamans of old, conveys the need for an initiatory journey of descent, separation, return, and transformation, stages that are paralleled in the process of working through trauma. Jung's lifelong concern with the spirit of reconciliation, with redemption and forgiveness, with reconnecting all that has been split off, is also a spiritual leitmotif in trauma therapy. I find what transpersonal psychology calls symbolic and spiritual intelligence presaged in the mythopoetic imaginings of the Red Book. Jung gives us a salutogenic, resource-oriented perspective on confronting and mastering terror and fear, healing wounded parts, and reconciling "the spirit of the time" with "the spirit of the depths."[18] The book delivers hope that there is within the psyche a creative potential for growth, which pushes forward relentlessly in search of meaning and purpose, in an often extremely painful process of symbolization.

Jung's strivings resulted in a kind of cosmology of the human soul. He was struggling with the big questions: What is the essence of life, the nature of evil, and the place of humanity in the larger matrix of life? The search for meaning and wholeness in the Red Book has its counterpart in the pressing questions with which trauma survivors struggle in their attempt to integrate and make sense of traumatic suffering. Jung's perspective is an orientation toward the transformative possibilities of the human soul, an orientation that can also be found in recent models of posttraumatic growth such as adversity-activated development (AAD). This is the term that Jungian analyst Renos Papadopoulos uses to designate the emergence of the positive, "growthful" developments that arise as a result of being exposed to adversity or trauma.[19] Without underestimating the devastating sequelae of trauma, it points to the psyche's potential for strengthening resilience and generating renewal. The noetic dimension that shines through the Red Book testifies to the creative faculty of the psyche to heal itself, to generate destruction in the service of creation.

I read the Red Book as a description of the unfolding stages of one man's symbolic healing journey and transformation after a traumatic breakdown, a moving depiction of integration and psychological growth through dialogue between consciousness and the unconscious in a *coniunctio oppositorum*. This most intimate account of Jung's attempt to overcome severe personal crisis constituted a form of "analytical psychology," but I suggest that it can also be read as a foundation for a deep understanding of what trauma work entails: making peace with tormenting inner and outer experiences and learning how to "be patient with the crippledness of the world," arriving ultimately at a worldview that embraces the paradox.[20]

In order to master his traumas, Jung chose a highly individual, creative path—or perhaps one should say he was forced into it. His striving for transcendence and his rethinking of the divine followed an unsettling phase of seeking and wandering that caused him deep insecurity as he confronted "an impotent Christianity that may well have received its death-wound."[21] It seems that Jung had to free himself first from all restrictions, to become a completely empty vessel to receive what wanted to reveal itself through him. This took tremendous courage, for he attributed to his soul a reality "which we cannot grasp with our present means of understanding."[22]

It also shows a specific mode of mastering intense, critical psychic states of affect, such as those that Jung was already acquainted with in his childhood and youth. Murray Stein describes this pattern in terms of Jung's relationship to God:

> The 12-year-old Carl Jung survived the fantasy of destruction, and, in the experience of grace, a soothing inner object (the "good breast") returned. He was strong enough, therefore, to endure the annihilating attack, perhaps because his paranoid defenses were able to depotentiate it, and then to be able to work on integrating the good and bad sides of God into a single image. This pattern would occur repeatedly in Jung's lifetime. A sever inner attack would threaten annihilation; this persecutory inner object would be defended against by the use of paranoid thoughts and fantasies, which would function to place it "out there": the crisis would then be followed by an experience of relief and restoration; and the final step would be an attempt to integrate the good and bad sides of the self, often in a symbolic formulation (paintings of mandalas, concepts of God as *unio oppositorum*, psychological theories).[23]

This model of mastery has little to do with the classical triad of remembering, repeating, and working through, but under certain circumstances, in the context of trauma work, it may be the approach indicated for healing. Not every trauma can or need be remembered and worked through. Some traumas are so destabilizing, they can only be sealed up in order for the victim to go forward in life.

In discussions of trauma, the question often arises as to whether posttraumatic growth is a self-deception whose real purpose is inner stabilization. In the same vein, intersubjectivists such as George E. Atwood and Robert D. Stolorow view Jung's self-transcendence, his idea of the transcendent function, and his whole theory of the reconciliation of opposites as a defensive strategy, a dysfunctional means of living with his schizoid tendencies. For these researchers, his theory is nothing but the expression of an unresolved psychopathology.[24]

I have learned from the testimonies of Holocaust survivors that after they lived through the danger of losing their innermost self, survived the attempted soul murder, and reconciled with their woundedness, many of them did not feel the need to work through past atrocities in a "talking cure." C. Fred Alford, who did research in the Fortunoff Video

Archives for Holocaust Testimonies at Yale University Library, which contain interviews with more than 5,000 survivors, found that "most have managed to partition off that obliterated portion of themselves in order to go on living—not with their souls intact, in most cases, but with a goodly portion of soul remaining."[25]

Not all Holocaust survivors returned from their trauma with a "narrative charge" the way Primo Levi and Viktor Frankl did. I have met many survivors who did not want to talk about their traumatic experiences, even when their children asked them about it. I have also learned in my work across cultures that each individual has his or her own way of coping with trauma and suffering. Some are able to overcome the challenges of traumatization and become self-transcendent survivors, mobilizing their resources, differentiating between what is essential in life and what is not, determining which values should take priority, and identifying where they need to move on with life. Others remain stuck, incapable of balancing affect; they lose their sense of kinship with others, become engulfed by guilt and deprived of cognitive efficacy and positive emotions. Their maladaptive defenses do not allow creative transformations, but instead perpetuate their original trauma.

In order to master his traumas, Jung chose a highly individual, creative path—or perhaps one should say he was forced into it. His striving for transcendence and his rethinking of the Divine followed an unsettling phase of seeking and wandering that caused him deep insecurity as he confronted "an impotent Christianity that may well have received its death-wound."[26] It seems that Jung had to free himself first from all restrictions, to become a completely empty vessel to receive what wanted to reveal itself through him. This took tremendous courage, for he attributed to his soul a reality "which we cannot grasp with our present means of understanding."[27]

Jung undertook to understand "the centralizing processes in the unconscious that go to form the personality," especially when traumatic events have caused a condition of instability.[28] This, he felt, could be accomplished only by finding the dark ground within and then reclaiming oneself. I read the Red Book with the eyes of a psychotraumatologist, because I believe it was born out of a traumatic state, an "anticipated psychosis" (as Jung himself later framed his experience of mental disintegration), which opened the doors of his perception and allowed him to see beyond the limits of his former level of consciousness.[29] Jung likened this confrontation with the unconscious to the mythic hero's quest, in which the hero is challenged to overcome his fears, slay the dragon, and emerge victorious.

The Red Book testifies to the psyche's remarkable ability to rescue itself. In Jung's experience I see a salvific energy at work, which enabled him to transcend the trauma that might otherwise have destroyed him. By engaging his unconscious, he was able to tap into four traumatic sources of his mental breakdown and eventually rise above them.

The Trauma of Being a Replacement Child

The first source of trauma for Jung was that of being a "replacement child." In her paper presented at the Borderlands conference in St. Petersburg, Kristina Schellinski talked about the traumatic consequences of being born in the wake of the death of a family member, when one's birth fills the empty space left by a loved one who has recently died.[30] In the Jewish tradition, children who are born following the death of a sibling are called "memorial candles." I know from working with such children what a heavy burden they carry. Additionally, I know from my own personal experience what it means to be born in the wake of death.

Jung was born after his mother Emilie suffered three stillbirths (two daughters and a son). This meant that his soul contained the imprint of death from the very beginning. He was, thus, a replacement child for the three, who came before him. As an adult, he saw it as his task to carry on the work of his ancestors and complete their unfinished business. He wrote:

> The meaning of my existence is that life has addressed a question to me. Or, conversely, I myself am a question, which is addressed to the world, and I must communicate my answer, for otherwise I am dependent upon the world's answer. That is a suprapersonal life task, which I accomplish only by effort and with difficulty. Perhaps it is a question which preoccupied my ancestors, and which they could not answer.[31]

In his dialogical relationship with the paradoxical nature of death I see an opening to transcendence, a continuous interplay between the "here" and the "hereafter."[32] Kurt R. Eissler discusses Jung's "unconscious suicidal urge"—apparent in his dangerous fall down the stairs, his head injury from falling against the stove, and his near-fatal slip under the railings on the bridge over the Rhine Falls—in the context of the death of his brother: Jung seemingly had to wrestle with the spirit of the deceased and struggle for his own identity.[33] Death and departed souls who cannot find rest were recurring themes for him. These concerns found their fullest expression in the *Septem Sermones ad Mortuos* (1916) and in the Red Book, where he wrote, "Why don't they stay quiet? Because they have not crossed over to the other side."[34]

The Trauma of Abandonment

The second source of trauma was abandonment. Jung ascribed great significance to his childhood memories. In his autobiography, *Memories, Dreams, Reflections*, written at the end of his long life, he recorded in detail his earliest recollections, beginning at the age of two. At the age of eight-three, he wrote that his earliest memories were "like individual shoots of a single underground rhizome, like stations on a road of unconscious development."[35] Painful reenactments of early childhood experiences are often the key to understanding an individual's adult psychology. In an early essay on the contents of psychosis, Jung wrote of a "primarily psychological failure of function whose history can be traced back into early childhood as being responsible for the later illness."[36] I take this as a reference to the etiology of posttraumatic reactions. When he found himself in an unusual psychological state after his break with Freud, "under constant inner pressure," he logically thought first about possible unresolved childhood conflicts and suspected some psychic disturbance in himself. After reviewing his memories, however, he withdrew this hypothesis, as this retrospection led to nothing.[37] This is all the more remarkable, since the dramatic circumstances preceding the episode of the little carved manikin, which Jung held to be an essential experience of his childhood and which he described in great detail, went into total eclipse in his memory until his thirty-fifth year, suggesting that his memory could not be trusted. A better explanation would be that defense mechanisms played a role in this case. As a rule, Jung set his memories in a mythological context, but his early experiences with his mother, at the age of three, constitute a clear exception.

Jung's mother effectively abandoned him when she was hospitalized for depression. It is clear from developmental psychology that such an absence can have a grave impact on a young child, whose environment consequently becomes unattuned. Jung later suggested that his mother's depression was a reaction to her unsatisfactory marriage. Furthermore, with regard to her absence from his early life, he confessed:

> I always felt mistrustful when the word "love" was spoken. The feeling I associated with "woman" was for a long time that of innate unreliability. "Father," on the other hand, meant reliability and—powerlessness. That is the handicap I started off with.[38]

I cannot make a pronouncement here on whether Jung was ever able to overcome his mistrust of the word *love*. Nevertheless, I would not hesitate to say that prolonged maternal absence in early childhood usually elicits shock, fear, and dissociation in a young child; it exposes the child to an early experience of things being out of control. Jung reacted to his mother's abandonment of him with severe eczema, accident proneness, nightmares, and self-destructive fantasies and behavior. The phallus dream, the creation of the manikin, and the terror of the "man eater" can all be traced to this gloomy period of his childhood years.[39] According to Brian Feldman, these symptoms all seem to point to childhood depression in Jung.[40] Jung himself later commented that at that time he suffered from "an unconscious suicidal urge or, it may be, to a fatal resistance to life in this world."[41]

I believe that the suffering Jung experienced as a child led him early on to split off the indigestible contents of his experience from his consciousness. It is known that children who suffer from a relational disconnect tend to shut down and dissociate. What is originally meant as an intrapsychic defense against unbearable psychological pain becomes an obstacle to the integrative processes of consciousness and an inhibition of healthy attachment.

I believe the painful break with Freud in 1913 triggered Jung's early abandonment complex and subsequent difficulty in coping with object loss. In 1912, Jung had already perceived "abandonment" by Freud in what he called Freud's "Kreuzlingen gesture" (referring to Freud's visit to Binswanger in nearby Kreuzlingen without visiting Jung).[42] The rupture in this important relationship, sealed by that chilling sentence (quoting Hamlet's dying words) at the end of Jung's last personal letter to Freud, "The rest is silence," activated Jung's attachment system.[43] My best understanding of this moment in Jung's life is that the usual defensive strategies broke down and dissociative symptoms emerged like "a stream of lava."[44] He felt "as if gigantic blocks of stone were tumbling down upon" him; "one thunderstorm followed another."[45] Freud had originally chosen Jung as his "successor," like a father passing on the family inheritance to his son; but at the same time he feared that Jung would dethrone him and usurp his place. Jung, no doubt, sensed this tension and felt offended.

The issue of closeness and distance played a major role in the relationship between Jung and Freud, as is evident in Freud's final personal letter to Jung, dated January 3, 1913. In it, Freud stated that he wished to free Jung from any oppressive intimacy with him and proposed to end their personal relationship, justifying this decision by referring to Jung's earlier confession that "an intimate relationship with a man inhibited [his] scientific freedom."[46] I think the break with Freud must also be seen against the backdrop of Jung's admission to Freud that his feelings toward him were colored by the fact he (Jung) had been sexually assaulted by a trusted older male as a child. In a letter to Freud dated October 28, 1907, the thirty-two-year-old Jung confessed "with a struggle" that he felt toward Freud a "'religious' crush," which he regarded as "disgusting and ridiculous" because of its unmistakably "erotic undertone." Jung went on to explain: "This abdominal feeling comes from the fact that as a boy I was the victim of a sexual assault by a man I once worshipped."[47] Later on in the same letter, Jung admits to being guarded in his confidences with Freud for fear that such intimacies would eventually render their relationship "sentimental and banal or exhibitionistic." To a large extent, then, Jung's trauma over Freud's "abandonment" of him was a circumstance of his own making, consequent upon his unresolved childhood trauma of sexual abuse and his fear of male intimacy.

The Trauma of Sexual Abuse

Jung's experience of homosexual abuse—a third source of trauma—had far-reaching consequences for his psychosexual development and for the theoretical construction of analytical psychology. In his letters to Freud we see clearly that this homosexual attack had a lasting impact on him, leading to a massive effort of repression. What Jung called his "self-preservation complex" oppressed him like an evil spirit and prevented him from writing.[48] He suffered from feelings of guilt and wrote to Freud concerning his agonies and fears "about the possible consequences" of his "confession."[49]

Many of the somatic symptoms of Jung's "fateful year" can also be seen through the lens of his homosexual assault. They coincide strikingly with the psychological results of sexual abuse: dissociation, a split into two personalities, fainting spells, apparent epileptic fits, obsessive guilt, identification with the aggressor, loss of memory, insomnia, and tortured thoughts. Elsewhere, I have explored more fully how Jung's self-reports can be read in terms of his sexual seduction, and I have outlined the kinds of defensive strategies he used to avoid confronting the trauma and minimize its consequences.[50] In *Memories, Dreams, Reflections* he declared that with regard to sexuality it was his chief aim "to investigate over and above its personal significance and biological function, its spiritual aspect and its numinous meaning," which he believed had eluded Freud.[51] With Marvin Goldwert, perhaps we can see this turn toward the Beyond, toward relocating sexuality in a spiritual dimension, as an attempt to transcend the trauma of childhood seduction.[52] But a deep-seated mistrust of intimacy continued to dog Jung's relationships and color his psychology for the rest of his life.

Jung's Traumatic Visions

The fourth source of trauma, occurring in the fall of 1913, was a twice-recurring vision of a flood covering the land between the North Sea and the Alps, which turned to blood. These violent waking visions Jung later considered to be a prefiguration of the First World War, a kind of prophetic vision—though more subjective interpretations concerning aggression are possible. At the time, Jung concluded that they had to do with himself and decided he was "menaced by a psychosis."[53] In December 1916, he wrote an important comment about the war, and about his attitude toward the transformation of trauma:

> This war has pitilessly revealed to civilized man that he is still a
> barbarian . . . [but] the psychology of the individual is reflected
> in the psychology of the nation. What the nation does is done
> also by each individual, and as long as the individual continues

> to do it, the nation will do likewise. Only the change in the
> attitude of the individual can initiate a change in the psychology
> of the nation.[54]

I find this demand for a shift in consciousness particularly necessary for us as analysts working in the field of trauma. Jung made it very clear that the attitude with which we approach traumatic or other overwhelming fantasies makes all the difference. What counts is how we accommodate traumatic catastrophes in our worldview and frame of reference, how capable we are of stretching our schemata to integrate the experience, to transcend traumatic states, and to remain open to the call from the Beyond. When I view the Red Book in the context of broken systems, dissipative structures, or an emerging expansion of consciousness, I understand Jung's process of mastering traumatic intrusions as an adaptive self-organization. The reorganization of his personality created a new, more complex, more stable state—a cohesive, functional whole.

With the publication of *Wandlungen und Symbole der Libido,* Jung began a process of spiritualizing and mythologizing sexual life and its meaning for psychic development and behavior, perhaps in order to deal with the sexual trauma that he himself had undergone. I see this as a defensive-protective strategy, the purpose of which was to shut out of consciousness experiences that he could not integrate because they were unacceptable to his sense of self. To be sure, in such cases, the memory of the traumatic event does not go away; but the meaning of the trauma for one's psychic development—and also, in Jung's case, for the development of his theoretical position—is excluded from reflection. Jung's concern with sexuality, as he wrote in *Memories, Dreams, Reflections*, was "to investigate its spiritual aspect and numinous meaning."[55] This led him to probe the archetypal, symbolic, and spiritual underpinnings of traumatic phenomena, without conceptualizing the actual traumatic events or the dissociative and often self-destructive defense mechanisms they trigger.

As essential as I find it for understanding psychic phenomena in order to have access to their symbolic and mythological underpinnings, and as much as I prefer Jung's teleological, synthetic approach to reductionism, I nevertheless see a weakness in his discussion of real traumas, and I can only explain this weakness in terms of a structural division in his own psyche. It cannot be denied that Jung made an early and very useful contribution to the discussion by drawing attention to the work of Pierre Janet on dissociation. But he sacrificed children abused in real life and their associated traumas by yielding to his repressive tendencies and his defense system, a dynamic that is also seen in connection with his abandonment complex, which left its mark on his manner of dealing with issues of intimacy. Attachment theory shows clearly that children instinctively develop strategies to deal with the unpredictability or unreliability of their caregivers. As mentioned earlier, Jung experienced his mother as unpredictable, and as a result his relationships with women throughout his life were plagued by ambivalence.

Renate Höfer critiques Jung's approach on the basis of the principle that if sexual abuse and early childhood sexual humiliation are not worked through in a liberating way, the experience remains virulently masochistic or sadistic for a lifetime and establishes itself in compensatory ways in the individual and in the perpetuation of secrets in society.[56] She explores the splitting that occurred in Jung's personal history and the formulation of his ideas and shows—in the light of the phallus dream, the manikin episode, and his experience with the Basel Cathedral—how Jung, in the process of repressing the unassimilated traumatic experiences of his childhood and youth, created a mythological and symbolic system of exoneration, which ultimately sanctioned his "boundary violations," that is, his acting out in relation to Sabina Spielrein and Toni Wolff.[57] She bases her argument on the premise that the phallus dream, which Jung disclosed only at the end of his life, is "the veiled representation of a scene of sexual molestation."[58] She connects that dream with the appearance of the Jesuit, the man hidden in a woman's black dress, who caused Jung the "deadly terror and hellish fear," which Jung identified as his "first conscious trauma."[59]

Here I am concerned not so much with the accuracy of Höfer's interpretation as with the possibility that Jung's unconscious personal defense mechanisms led him to give short shrift to the reality of trauma. Perhaps we should understand his high-flying, symbolic, and religio-mythical interpretations as constructive, imaginative, meaning-making narratives designed to deal with intrusive, heavily affect-laden, anxiety-provoking experiences. Jean Knox has argued that defensive fantasies serve to protect against a humiliating sense of helplessness and deep narcissistic wounds. She also writes that "wishes, desires and fears not only influence and distort the way we experience events but also form part of that experience, and so themselves become incorporated into the memories of those events."[60] This insight might provide a better understanding of the many gaps in Jung's theoretical construction, including aspects of retraumatization, the repetition compulsion, the psychology of victimizers, the psychosexual development of children traumatized at an early age, and devastating, self-destructive defense mechanisms.

Andrew Samuels has argued that it was difficult for Jung "to conceive of the ego as anything other than completely conscious," and he was therefore unable to "say much about ego defences, which are . . . unconscious in operation."[61] Samuels goes on to say: "The main problem is not simply that the idea of *defence* is undeveloped [in Jung's thought] but that insufficient stress is laid on *anxiety* as the reason for defences in the first place."[62] I see a quite credible causal connection between this lacuna in Jung's thought and his unassimilated personal life experiences. It is no wonder that he gave priority to the symbolic-spiritual interpretation over other approaches. To arrive at this position, however, he had to sacrifice the ego's perspective and the objective reality of traumatic experiences.

The Red Book testifies to this fundamental shift in Jung's approach and forms the foundation for his phenomenological, highly subjective psychological theory. In it we see symbols used to represent the capacity of libido to enliven psychological events and launch a process of transformation. From his descent into the depths Jung derived his conviction regarding the transformative power of symbols and his faith that the gods enter through our wounds. The Red Book is a moving documentation of an archetypal, often uncanny sacrificial process, in which the ego lays down its presumption of dominance before that which is experienced as the Self.

In the Red Book, Jung sacrificed his allegiance to the zeitgeist of his day in order to follow the merciless spirit of the depths. But in so doing, he also sacrificed the possibility of publishing the Red Book during his lifetime. The prevailing culture was not ready to receive such a work. In his quest, Jung was therefore compelled to follow a solitary path, an experience he later incorporated into his concept of individuation. He wrote: "The patient must be alone if he is to find out what it is that supports him when he can no longer support himself. Only this experience can give him an indestructible foundation."[63]

Traumatized individuals, however, are robbed by their traumas of their capacity to lay a stable foundation, and the vast majority of them lack the ability to establish or restore it by themselves, as Jung did on his "solitary path." The sacrifice that has been thrust upon them is far beyond their capacity to endure. For many, their only salvation lies in a holding relationship that will carry them through the suffering and facilitate discovery and the integration of what they are unable to integrate on their own. Regardless of how it is dealt with, however, sacrifice appears to be an inescapable aspect of initiation on the path to individuation, and trauma patients have to confront the necessity of "drinking the cup" of sacrifice if there is to be any hope of transcending their trauma. In the Garden of Gethsemane, Jesus prays, "My Father, if it is possible, may this cup be taken from me" (Matt. 26:39, NIV), but he ultimately yields to the will of the Self and drinks from the cup, choosing to confront rather than avoid the trauma, and thereby he achieves transcendence.

Kierkegaard, in *Fear and Trembling*, speaks of the anguish and trauma that the call to sacrifice itself can generate, as dramatized in the biblical story of Abraham being called to sacrifice his son Isaac and the seemingly impossible and paradoxical "leap of faith" required to transcend this trauma.[64] Kierkegaard also focuses on Isaac's trauma in the role of sacrificial victim and the transformation that occurs in both Abraham and Isaac once the leap of faith has been taken.

I want to explore whether trauma patients can, through the transformation wrought by sacrifice, achieve what Steven Levine sees as a Nietzschean sort of "tragic wisdom" along the lines of Greek tragedy, that is, "an affirmation of existence that sees suffering and death as intrinsic to it [i.e., to existence] and nevertheless says 'Yes!' to life."[65] In the trauma literature we read that various possibilities exist for overcoming the seemingly insurmountable and thus achieving a transformation. Even in the Nazi death camps, not everyone became a *Muselman*, a human automaton bereft of hope; there were also acts of compassion and self-sacrifice in defense of basic humanity. Using art therapy, Levine seeks to activate the capacity of traumatized individuals to react positively to their injuries and win back their self-agency. For him, the goal of therapy is "to restore the person to the ground of human existence, to the experience of embodied being in the world with others."[66] Therapy, then, is a "rite of restoration" involving transformation. In the application of the arts to therapy, Levine says, giving form to the source of our suffering is a transformational act, because "it brings something into being by shaping the world in which we live in a new way."[67] The symbols that arise in dreams and fantasies give form to the nameless fears generated by trauma, thereby objectifying them and effectively robbing them of their power to incapacitate us. For this to happen, however, trauma victims must sacrifice their sentimental wallowing in self-pity and victimhood and their yearning for the ideal of "harmonious totality."[68] In keeping with his view of trauma as dramatic tragedy, Levine notes that "the effect of tragic drama . . . is not to expel pity and fear or terror but to transform them into compassion and awe," that is, to "purify them of their sentimental degradation" and thus help us to "face them full on."[69]

The Red Book shows that the way to sacrifice our victimhood in the aftermath of trauma is to respond to the shattering effect of the trauma with imagination and symbolism and to reassemble the fragments into a new whole. As I see it, the Red Book is a product of the "traumatic imagination."[70] According to Levine, who introduced the term, the traumatic imagination reimagines trauma by "find[ing] ways of representation that are true to its [trauma's] chaotic and meaningless character" and refiguring "the concept of beauty . . . within the horizon of terror."[71]

Another sacrifice that trauma victims are called upon to make is the sacrifice of conscious control over their fate. In the Red Book, Jung documented the spontaneous independent emergence of new consciousness in the darkness of the abyss. He also made it clear that the human will has very little say in this process.

> Willing creates blindness, and blindness leads to the way. Should we will error? You should not, but you do will that error which you take for the best truth, as men have always done. . . . He [i.e., "the God"] takes your conflicting will in his hand, in the hand of a child whose will is simple and beyond conflict. You cannot learn this, it can only develop in you. You cannot will this, it takes the will from your hand and wills itself.[72]

During the therapeutic process, this involuntary subjection to archetypal energies is often experienced as menacing. When we are exposed to such dark, overwhelming archetypal powers, personal volition and the ego are no longer involved. We become the victims of something infinitely larger than the ego.

Often in my work with people who have experienced sexual violence, incest, or torture I have encountered extreme forms of self-blame and self-loathing, which are expressed in self-destructive thoughts and behaviors. Drawing on Freudian drive theory, psychoanalysis invokes the notion of the death instinct to explain such behaviors. Often, in such situations, traumatized individuals are willing to sacrifice a portion of themselves so that the rest of their being can go on living.[73] Conversely, there is also in some traumatic experiences an *un*willing sacrifice. This appears in the work of Christopher Bollas as "extractive introjection," in which "one person steals for a certain period of time . . . an element of another individual's psychic life."[74] Bollas conceives of traumas (whether mild or severe) in terms of intersubjective violence, in which a part of the victim's soul, that is, some element of his or her psychic life, is stolen by the victimizer, and the victim is "temporarily anaesthetized and unable to 'gain back' the stolen part of the self."[75] What Bollas calls theft is, in fact, a form of sacrifice: the victimizer sacrifices the victim's psychic integrity for the sake of his or her own needs or desires. It may take many years of therapy to recover the stolen (or sacrificed) parts of the self.

A particularly difficult form of traumatic sacrifice is that which springs from feelings of utter powerlessness and despair. Some of my patients feel they have lost their innocence irrecoverably, and those who have been tortured may even feel they have lost their humanity.[76] It seems to them that their only option is to sacrifice themselves to the power that holds them in thrall. Self-sacrifice that springs from despair and desperation reminds me of the sacrifice of Jesus, with which many traumatized individuals identify. Grotstein presents a case in which he implies that reenacting the sacrifice of Christ (the innocent victim) seems to be an attempt on the part of the trauma victim to recover his or her lost innocence.[77] The case Grotstein discusses is that of a male patient who had been abused by his father as a child. This patient talked about a "dead child within," which Grotstein says, "is universally ensconced in these abused and traumatized patients and is transformed into the 'undead child,' the one who relentlessly haunts them for their having made a 'Faustian bargain' with an internal dark force in order to survive."[78] In fact, Grotstein's patient specifically expressed a "belief that he had unconsciously signed what he called a 'Faustian bargain with the devil' in order to be safe from anxiety and terror."[79]

I find the idea of the Faustian bargain (a recurrent motif in fairy tales) helpful in understanding what is happening to patients who seem numb and physically shut-down.[80] This defense mechanism can be regarded, from a relational point of view, as a creative way of addressing a problem that demands an immediate solution. The abused child has no choice but to depend on his or her caregivers. So in order to ensure that they will continue to be present and available, he or she takes their guilt upon himself or herself—much as Christ archetypally took upon himself the sins of the world and died in its stead. Abused children willingly take on the role of scapegoat and sacrifice themselves and their developmental potential in the interests of survival. The sacrifice of one's sense of wholeness seems preferable to the immediate threat of alienation and annihilation. The essence of this principle is enunciated by Caiaphas, the high priest, in the story of the plot to kill Jesus, as recorded in the Gospel of John: "It is better for you that one man die for the people than that the whole nation perish" (John 11:50, NIV).

Yet this is a Faustian bargain in the sense that it achieves short-term gain for the price of long-term loss, although on the surface, as Caiaphas frames it, the reverse seems to be true. One is reminded of the words of Christ: "For whoever would save his life will lose it . . . . For what does it profit a man to gain the whole world and forfeit his soul? For what can a man give in return for his soul?" (Mark 8:35–37). Relinquishing one's soul for the sake of survival may seem like a necessary sacrifice, but only from the perspective of the immediate situation. In such a Faustian bargain, to borrow Kathleen Nader's words, "the *survival self* replaces the *individuating self*."[81] For Nader, this self-sacrifice represents "the survival self's *misguided* efforts to preserve the personal spirit."[82] I have seen trauma victims blame themselves needlessly and persecute themselves internally without mercy in a desperate—and perverse—attempt to hold on to the illusion of not being utterly powerless. In their situation, it seems better to be falsely guilty and in control than innocent and totally helpless. Trauma often calls for the sacrifice of innocence and psychic autonomy on the altar of mere survival.

In the psychoanalytic literature, sacrifice is generally discussed in terms of primitive defense mechanisms, object relations, and attachment theory. Dissociation, splitting, and identification with the aggressor are interpreted as strategies for ensuring survival in the face of anxiety and highly unstable self-object relationships. Employing these defense mechanisms, however, involves the sacrifice of the reflective function, which brings with it a cascade of negative consequences. Traumatized individuals are unable to adopt the metaperspective necessary for them to understand and empathize with themselves and others. Furthermore, the inability of trauma victims to reflect on the significance of their traumatic experiences and subsequent actions contributes to a dramatic diminishment in their capacity for growth, development, and transformation.

An understanding of the extent to which the individual's autonomy and vitality are damaged by dissociative, pathological self-organization helps us to appreciate more fully the way trauma-related sacrifice impinges over time on the patient's intimate interpersonal relationships as well as on the relationship with the therapist. It is nevertheless true, especially in the context of catastrophic trauma, that a person may owe his or her immediate survival precisely to psychic numbing and the sacrifice of emotional and spiritual vitality.[83] Sacrifice always involves a trade-off, no matter what form it takes, and in the context of trauma, as in other contexts, the psyche is predisposed to make the sacrifice that incurs the least cost to the individual.

The Trauma Membrane

Trauma-related sacrifice can be understood as part of the "trauma membrane," a concept elaborated on by Martz and Lindy. They conceive of it as "a temporary psychosocial structure, a buffer zone or covering that protects traumatized people as part of the healing process in the aftermath of catastrophic stress."[84] This biological metaphor suggests that a thin protective layer forms over psychic wounds. The dual purpose of this membrane is to facilitate psychic healing by keeping curative materials in and toxic, contaminating, or aggravating materials out, but because the membrane is fragile, especially in the initial stages, it can be ruptured quite easily.[85] As with the healing of physical wounds, there is a trade-off, and something is inevitably sacrificed. When a scab forms over a physical surface wound, the healing process is actually slowed down, the formation of new surface skin over the wound is retarded, and there is a risk that the wound may fester under the scab. Similar sacrifices are involved in the formation of the trauma membrane, especially if psychic wounds are not properly tended to.[86]

As an intrapsychic mechanism, the trauma membrane works partially by sealing off traumatic memories and thus permitting the individual to go on functioning despite the traumatic event. By sealing off traumatic memories, it protects the individual from toxic affects and painful memories that he or she is not yet ready to integrate. This understanding helps me to avoid initiating a premature confrontation with dissociative processes and repressions or diagnosing these as signs of resistance and defenses. Such symptoms may signify natural or hard-won functional patterns of mastery, which represent an important intrapsychic and interpsychic protective shield that should not be stripped away prematurely, much as a physical scab should not be picked but allowed to fall off of its own accord. By acting as an ego-defense against retraumatization, the trauma membrane facilitates adaptation and healing. As Lindy observes, "The psychic organism is capable in its own time of breaking down the impact of traumatic stressors and their associated states into manageable amounts that permit gradual intrapsychic processing."[87]

In order to be processed, the trauma must first be broken down into more digestible bits. Timing and pacing are thus of utmost importance in this process, so as not to further enlarge the tear in the psychic fabric or overtax the individual's capacity for working through the trauma. Our current understanding is that trauma constitutes an information overload and that information processing following a traumatic experience requires its own time. A well-functioning, semipermeable trauma membrane is needed, so that treatment can go forward in the *temenos* of the therapeutic relationship, digesting overwhelming affects and memories in small doses. In addition to the intrapsychic function, then, the trauma membrane also performs an interpersonal function, often serving to insulate the victim from contact with the outside world. Most importantly, it controls how far the therapist is permitted to enter into the victim's inner sanctum. If the patient's interpersonal membrane is thick and rigid through fear of contact, it serves as an impenetrable wall between patient and therapist.

Many trauma patients sacrifice relatedness and the possibility of healing for fear that someone will penetrate their armor and they will once again lose control. To be able to relinquish the rigidity of this armorlike interpersonal trauma membrane, the patient needs to be in a truly nurturing therapeutic relationship with a therapist who has a lot of patience and trustworthiness. The therapist must not respond to the patient's life-preserving defenses with "analytic aggression."[88] What is called for is an empathic holding environment, so that with time, as healing takes its natural course, this membrane can gradually dissolve and the patient can let others in and arrive at insight into his or her situation.

Beyond its operation in trauma therapy at the intrapsychic and interpersonal levels, the trauma membrane also operates at the community or social level.[89] The concept of the trauma membrane has proved instrumental in my work with nongovernmental organizations (NGOs) and the War Trauma Foundation, where I have also seen the way rehabilitation, reconciliation, and peacemaking efforts form trauma membranes around displaced, wounded, and war-torn communities.

The Dialectic of Victim and Victimizer

The formation of trauma membranes around individuals and communities often conceals a peculiar dialectical tension that is generated by trauma, namely, the tension between the survivor's simultaneous identity as victim and as victimizer. The trauma membrane model focuses almost exclusively on the trauma survivor's role as *victim* and systematically neglects his or her manifestation as *victimizer*. Gustav Dreifuss draws attention to this widespread neglect in his analysis of the archetype of sacrifice and its manifestation in modern consciousness.[90] He speaks of the "eternal victim" in his discussion of the Jewish people's identification with the victim aspect of the archetype as a result of their long history of suffering. He points out, however, that the repressed victimizer aspect also needs to be integrated into consciousness.

A complementary relationship exists between these two modes of being. Victim and victimizer represent two opposing aspects of the same archetype: sacrificing and being sacrificed, wounding and being wounded, overwhelming and being overwhelmed. The paradox of both sacrifice and trauma is that these contrary aspects of the archetype may manifest themselves in the same individual. The traumatized often becomes a traumatizer. As a feminist therapist, I am all too aware that discussions of victims and victimization can activate defense mechanisms that create a powerful blowback. Feminists are often accused by their detractors of perpetuating a "victim culture," that is, of attempting to raise the moral status of women by portraying them as victims of a patriarchal society.

Tragically, the constant focus on the role as victim often develops into an addiction, a compulsive attachment to suffering, because only suffering provides them with a sense of identity. With their thinking fixated on the victim archetype, others perceive them unsympathetically as "professional victims" and may feel manipulated by them.

I have worked for many years on commissions devoted to helping victims of crimes. I have been particularly struck by the widespread tendency to blame the victim. In my capacity as a consulting supervisor I have noticed that my colleagues are not always in sympathy with the victims. They have difficulty with what they frequently see as the manipulative behavior of female survivors of violence, and they often criticize these women for their reluctance to let go of their victim identity.

It is not easy to grant that victims need to defend themselves in the crucible of transformation by holding steadfastly to what is familiar and what gives them their identity. They adapt, often reluctantly at first, to their role as victims and then find a degree of security there. With sexually exploited women especially, this dialectic between victim and victimizer is a painful reality. When working with such women, often victims of unimaginable violence, we must recognize that they unconsciously inflict violence on their own psyches and act out the dialectic of victim and victimizer, in destructive and self-destructive behavior of all kinds.

Both individually and collectively, the victim archetype is tied to the archetype of the shadow. To deal with it, we need to give up projection and scapegoating and come to terms with our own share of the responsibility for the presence of victimization in our society. In our time, the ancient Hebrew ritual of the scapegoat has returned in the form of terrorism, genocide, and mass shootings. Perhaps the silenced gods are forcing themselves into our awareness through these atrocities. Where once the gods spoke to our ancestors through animal sacrifices, today, in the absence of sacrificial rituals, they are forced to speak to us through "man's inhumanity to man."[91]

Lyn Cowan takes up this theme when she writes that "the experience of victimization makes aspects of the victim visible to herself or himself . . . with the shocking emotional immediacy characteristic of genuine trauma." She goes on to say:

> Contained within the figure of the victim is a lesson concerning the nature of the god to whom sacrifice is being offered, for the victim bears the likeness of the god. . . . In Jewish tradition, the justice of God required a sacrificial animal to be innocent and well-formed; hence the lamb without blemish. . . . In that region of the soul where we are victimized, through whatever circumstance, we must look for the likeness of a god, and there build an interior altar to ensure that our sacrifice is made holy. The wisdom to be discovered is not that "you brought it on yourself," but that it brought you to your Self.[92]

In a similar vein, Jerome Bernstein, speaking from his clinical experience with "borderlanders" (individuals who have transrational experiences and for whom the experience is "nothing short of sacred"), expands on the relationship between sacrifice and the sacred.[93] He argues that Homo sapiens as a species bears collective guilt for exploiting the planet and not treating it with respect. In raping the earth, our species has compromised its sense of sacredness and is in need of atonement for this violation. He writes: "Borderlanders unconsciously may carry this guilt on behalf of all of us. That is their sacrifice—and also their offering—in the interest of healing our collective deep wound."[94] In sacrificing themselves as an "offering," they are simultaneously the sacrificer and the sacrificed, living embodiments of one aspect of the victim-victimizer dialectic.

NOTES

[1] C. G. Jung, letter to Sabina Spielrein dated (probably) September 21–22, 1911, "The Letters of C. G. Jung to Sabina Spielrein," trans. Barbara Wharton, *Journal of Analytical Psychology* 46, no. 1 (2001): 180–181.

[2] Jung, *CW* 11, § 400.

[3] See Judith Fulton Lamp, "Like Smoke to the Gods: Toward a Theory of Sacrifice in Depth Psychological Process" (PhD diss., Pacifica Graduate Institute, Carpinteria, CA., 2004), ProQuest/UMI 3264666.

[4] See especially chapter 8, "The Sacrifice," in Jung's *Wandlungen und Symbole der Libido*, first published in 1911–1912 and translated into English in 1916 under the title *Psychology of the Unconscious: A Study of the Transformations and Symbolisms of the Libido—A Contribution to the History of the Evolution of Thought*. (A greatly revised edition of this early work was published in 1956 as *Symbols of Transformation*, now found in *CW* 5.) Following the original publication of *Wandlungen*, Jung returned to keeping a journal, which took the form of the Red Book, where he once again took up the theme of sacrifice.

[5] Jung, *RB*, p. 230.

[6] It is worth noting here that Siegfried was the name that Sabina Spielrein wanted to give the son she fantasized having with Jung and that Jung's life demanded the sacrifice of this fantasy.

[7] Jung, *RB*, pp. 241–242.

[8] Jung, *RB*, p. 242, n.115.

[9] Jung, *CW* 6, §§ 763, 764.

[10] Jung, *CW* 11, § 397.

[11] Jung, *CW* 4, § 772.

[12] Jung, *MDR*, p. 167.

[13] Sigmund Freud and C. G. Jung, *The Freud/Jung Letters*, ed. William McGuire, trans. Ralph Manheim and R. F. C. Hull (Princeton, NJ: Princeton University Press, 1979), pp. 104, 224. See also Gary Brown, "*Symbols of Transformation*, Phenomenology, and Magic Mountain," *Journal of Jungian Scholarly Studies* 7, no. 3 (2011), accessed October 24, 2013, http://www.thejungiansociety.org/Jung%20Society/e-journal/Volume-7/Brown-2011.pdf.

[14] Jung, *RB*, p. 307.

[15] Jung, *RB*, p. 308.

[16] Jung, *MDR*, p. 167.

[17] Jung, *RB*, p. 235.

[18] Jung, *RB*, p. 207.

[19] Renos K. Papadopoulos, "Refugees, Trauma and Adversity-Activated Development," *European Journal of Psychotherapy and Counseling* 9, no. 3 (2007): 301–312.

[20] Jung, *RB*, p. 231.

[21] Jung, *CW* 12, § 559.

[22] Jung, *CW* 12, § 564.

[23] Murray Stein, *Jung's Treatment of Christianity: The Psychotherapy of a Religious Tradition* (Wilmette, IL: Chiron Publications, 1985), p. 75.

[24] George E. Atwood and Robert D. Stolorow, *Faces in a Cloud: Intersubjectivity in Personality Theory* (New York: Jason Aronson, 1979).

[25] C. Fred Alford, *After the Holocaust: The Book of Job, Primo Levi, and the Path to Affliction* (Cambridge, UK: Cambridge University Press, 2009), p. 5.

[26] Jung, CW 12, § 559.

[27] Jung, CW 12, § 564.

[28] Jung, CW 12, § 564.

[29] Aniela Jaffé, *The Myth of Meaning in the Work of C. G. Jung* (Zürich: Daimon Verlag, 1984), p. 58.

[30] Kristina Schellinski, "Dreams and Existential Questions of Clients Whose Family Members Have Died or Disappeared," paper presented at the Second European Conference on Analytical Psychology, St. Petersburg, August 30–September 2, 2012.

[31] Jung, *MDR*, p. 381.

[32] Jung, *MDR*, p. 299.

[33] Kurt R. Eissler, *Psychologische Aspekte des Briefwechsels zwischen Freud und Jung* (Stuttgart-Bad Cannstatt: *Frommann-Holzboog* Verlag, 1982), p. 125; Jung, *MDR*, p. 9.

[34] Jung, *RB*, p. 342.

[35] Jung, *MDR*, p. 27.

[36] Jung, *CW* 3, § 318.

[37] Jung, *MDR*, p. 173.

[38] Jung, *MDR*, p. 8.

[39] Jung, *MDR*, pp. 12, 14.

[40] Brian Feldman, "Jung's Infancy and Childhood and Its Influence upon the Development of Analytical Psychology," *Journal of Analytical Psychology* 37, no. 3 (1992): 255–274.

[41] Jung, *MDR*, p. 9.

[42] C. G. Jung, letters to Freud dated July 18, 1912, and November 11, 1912, *The Freud/Jung Letters: A Correspondence between Sigmund Freud and C. G. Jung*, ed. William McGuire, trans. Ralph Manheim and R. F. C. Hull, abridged edition (Princeton, NJ: Princeton University Press, 1974), pp. 235 and 238 respectively.

[43] C. G. Jung, letter to Freud dated January 6, 1913, *ibid.*, p. 257.

[44] Jung, *MDR*, p. 199.

[45] Jung, *MDR*, p. 177.

[46] Sigmund Freud, letter to Jung dated January 3, 1913, in *The Freud/Jung Letters*, p. 255.

[47] C. G. Jung, letter to Freud dated October 28, 1907, *ibid.*, p. 44.

[48] *Ibid.*

[49] C. G. Jung, letter to Freud dated November 2, 1907, *ibid.*, p. 45.

[50] Ursula Wirtz, *Seelenmord: Inzest und Therapie* (Stuttgart: Kreuz Verlag, 1989), pp. 31–46.

[51] Jung, *MDR*, p. 168.

[52] Marvin Goldwert, "Childhood Seduction and the Spiritualization of Psychology: The Case of Jung and Rank," *Child Abuse and Neglect* 10, no. 4 (1986): 555–557.

[53] Jung, *MDR*, p. 176.

[54] Jung, *CW* 7, "Preface to the First Edition," p. 4.

[55] Jung, *MDR*, p. 168.

[56] Renate Höfer, *Die Hiobsbotschaft C. G. Jungs: Folgen sexuellen Mißbrauchs* (Lüneburg: zu Klampen Verlag, 1993), p. 13.

[57] *Ibid.*, p. 77.

[58] *Ibid.*, p. 52.

[59] Jung, *MDR*, p. 10.

[60] Jean Knox, "Trauma and Defenses: Their Roots in Relationship—An Overview," *Journal of Analytical Psychology* 48, no. 2 (2003): 219.

[61] Andrew Samuels, *Jung and the Post-Jungians* (London: Routledge, 1985), p. 48.

[62] *Ibid.*, p. 54; italics in the original.

⁶³ Jung, *CW* 12, § 32.

⁶⁴ Søren Kierkegaard, *Fear and Trembling*, trans. Alastair Hannay (London: Penguin Books, 2003).

⁶⁵ Stephen K. Levine, *Trauma, Tragedy, Therapy: The Arts and Human Suffering* (London: Jessica Kingsley Publishers, 2009), p. 53 (see also, pp. 63, 80).

⁶⁶ *Ibid.*, p. 44.

⁶⁷ *Ibid.*

⁶⁸ *Ibid.*, p. 18.

⁶⁹ *Ibid.*, pp. 49, 18.

⁷⁰ *Ibid.*, pp. 18–19.

⁷¹ *Ibid.*, p. 18.

⁷² Jung, *RB*, p. 254.

⁷³ James S. Grotstein, "'The Sins of the Fathers . . .': Human Sacrifice and the Inter- and Trans-generational Neurosis/Psychosis," *International Journal of Psychotherapy* 2, no. 1 (1997): 13.

⁷⁴ Christopher Bollas, *The Shadow of the Object: Psychoanalysis of the Unthought Known* (New York: Columbia University Press, 1987), pp. 157–167.

⁷⁵ *Ibid.*, p. 158.

⁷⁶ See James S. Grotstein, "Why Oedipus and Not Christ? A Psychoanalytic Inquiry into Innocence, Human Sacrifice, and the Sacred—Part I: Innocence, Spirituality, and Human Sacrifice," *American Journal of Psychoanalysis* 57, no. 3 (1997): 197–200.

⁷⁷ *Ibid.*, pp. 202ff.

⁷⁸ *Ibid.*, p. 198.

⁷⁹ *Ibid.*, p. 195.

⁸⁰ See also O. H. D. Blomfield, "Parasitism, Projective Identification, and the Faustian Bargain," *International Review of Psycho-Analysis* 12 (1985): 299–310.

⁸¹ Kathleen O. Nader, "Childhood Trauma: The Deeper Wound," in *The Posttraumatic Self: Restoring Meaning and Wholeness to Personality*, ed. John P. Wilson (New York: Routledge, 2006), p. 138; italics in original.

⁸² *Ibid.*; emphasis added.

⁸³ Jacob D. Lindy and Robert Jay Lifton, eds., *Beyond Invisible Walls: The Psychological Legacy of Soviet Trauma, East European Therapists and Their Patients* (New York: Brunner-Routledge, 2001).

⁸⁴ Erin Martz and Jacob Lindy, "Exploring the Trauma Membrane Concept," in *Trauma Rehabilitation after War and Conflict: Community and Individual Perspectives*, ed. Erin Martz (New York: Springer, 2010), p. 27.

⁸⁵ *Ibid.*, p. 30.

⁸⁶ *Ibid.*, p. 28.

⁸⁷ Lindy, quoted in Martz and Lindy, "Exploring the Trauma Membrane Concept," p. 34.

⁸⁸ Richard Kradin, "The Roots of Empathy and Aggression in Analysis," *Journal of Analytical Psychology* 50, no. 4 (2005): 432ff.

⁸⁹ Martz and Lindy, "Exploring the Trauma Membrane Concept," pp. 28, 31–33.

⁹⁰ Gustav Dreifuss, *Studies in Jungian Psychology: Work and Reflections Life Long* (Haifa: Author, 2003), pp. 87–142.

⁹¹ From Robert Burns, "Man Was Made to Mourn: A Dirge," *Robert Burns: Selected Poems*, ed. Carol McGuirk (London: Penguin Books, 1993), pp. 54–55.

⁹² Lyn Cowan, *Tracking the White Rabbit: A Subversive View of Modern Culture* (Hove, UK: Brunner-Routledge, 2002), p. 90.

⁹³ Jerome S. Bernstein, *Living in the Borderland: The Evolution of Consciousness and the Challenge of Healing Trauma* (Hove, UK: Routledge, 2005), p. xvi.

⁹⁴ Jerome S. Bernstein, "The Borderland Patient: Reintroducing Nature as the Missing Dimension in Clinical Treatment—What I've Learned from Navaho Medicine Men," in *Montreal 2010—Facing Multiplicity: Psyche, Nature, Culture, Proceedings of the Eighteenth Congress of the International Association for Analytical Psychology*, ed. Pramila Bennett (Einsiedeln, Switzerland: Daimon Verlag, 2012), p. 290 on the accompanying CD.

CHAPTER ELEVEN

SACRIFICE
OF THE SELF

T he goal of sacrifice as it is commonly understood is to support and preserve life. However, in the context of trauma therapy, the call to sacrifice is often experienced as implying the very opposite because it is a call to sacrifice some aspects of the self, and it is therefore experienced as a threat and is consequently resisted. Kalsched notes that psychic splitting and dismemberment are matters of life and death, necessities for survival; yet splitting is a "violent affair."[1] He says that one of the "most disturbing findings" about trauma is that *the traumatized psyche is self-traumatizing.*[2]

Under such conditions, when the trauma survivor is called upon in therapy to give up self-stabilizing, psychosis-avoiding behaviors and rituals, he or she experiences the call as a mortal threat. It is difficult for the traumatized psyche, which is already traumatizing itself in order to survive, to let go of dysfunctional, self-sabotaging patterns. The libido clings to "reliable" processes, which apparently guarantee survival, even if only on a very basic level. The forgoing of defense mechanisms in the interests of growth and development often happens against great inner resistance, for these mechanisms take on the aspect of a trusted ally whom the survivor is loath to betray. A woman who has, over the years following a traumatic experience, painstakingly forged a "survivor identity" through hyper-controlling, obsessive-compulsive behavior and rigid or hyper-vigilant modes of being will be unwilling—or even unable—to sacrifice this hard-won identity.

Sexually traumatized women often sacrifice all connection to their bodies and desires in order to avoid being reminded of the sexual violation they experienced, as well as to suppress awareness of their ambivalent feelings toward sex. They are disgusted at themselves for visualizing scenes of rape in masturbation fantasies; they loathe themselves for having possibly provoked the attack with suggestive behavior. Splitting is the only reliable way to keep these excruciating feelings at bay. The sacrifice of sexual desire, however, also entails a banishment of the lust for life.

Children who cannot escape physically from their sexual abusers resort to psychic escape. They render both their physical bodies and their immediate surroundings unreal in their imagination. They escape in fantasy to some other happier, more innocent place, with the result that what is left behind operates robotically and without feelings, in a state of torpor, internally and externally petrified. My patient said:

> *I lie on my bed, stiff as a board, as if rooted there. All my limbs are heavy. I drag myself with incredible fatigue through the day. It seems as if my body just wants to stop. Then I'm overcome by this need for sleep. I cannot take anything in any more. I'm like a stone.*

Often the split occurs between an observing part of the self and the rest of the personality, including affects, so that perception of overwhelming physical sensations, such as that of extreme pain, shuts down, and flooding with the emotions of fear and rage does not occur. The price that trauma victims pay for this adaptive mechanism is that they lose touch with reality and experience depersonalization, or loss of soul. Thus, dissociation, depersonalization, and psychic numbing are highly paradoxical defense mechanisms. In serving to protect the self, they have a saving function, but they are also destructive in that they block the flow of vital energy to where it is needed, thereby making it impossible for the victim to transcend the trauma. Therapeutic work is then essentially the task of helping the trauma victim recalibrate his or her understanding of the sacrifice that is required of him or her. In this process, the therapist replaces the defense mechanisms as the trustworthy and trusted ally in the battle against the trauma. As Jung wrote: "No longer does he [i.e., the patient] stand alone in his battle with these elemental powers, but some one whom he trusts reaches out a hand, lending him moral strength to combat the tyranny of uncontrolled emotion."[3]

Elsewhere, Jung noted that traumatic influences cause parts of the psyche to split off and fall into the unconscious, where they form autonomous complexes, which may lie dormant and undetected by consciousness but nevertheless interfere with normal functioning.[4] A trauma-generated complex can lie dormant in the unconscious for years but spring to life suddenly when awakened by seemingly innocuous stimuli. Closely associated with traumatic influences or "emotional shocks" as creators of autonomous complexes is the presence of a "moral conflict, which ultimately derives from the apparent impossibility of affirming the whole of one's nature," a problem often faced by trauma victims, who then sacrifice those parts of themselves that they cannot— or *will* not—affirm and are therefore forced to deny.[5] Jung says that the autonomy of the complex "consists in its power to manifest itself independently of the will and even in direct opposition to conscious tendencies: it forces itself tyrannically upon the conscious mind."[6]

According to Jung, "the existence of complexes throws serious doubt on the naïve assumption of the unity of consciousness . . . and on the supremacy of the will."[7] This is so because the unconscious nature of the complex enables it "to assimilate even the ego, the result being a momentary and unconscious alteration of personality known as identification with the complex."[8] Thus, the strength of the complex is such that it can even, on occasion, exceed the strength of the ego.[9] In that case, dissociation occurs, for when the complex establishes itself on the surface of consciousness, "it can no longer be circumvented," and it "proceeds to assimilate the ego-consciousness step by step."[10] As Jung puts it: "Where the realm of complexes begins the freedom of the ego comes to an end."[11]

Then the task of therapy is to strengthen the fragile ego and develop the patient's ego-agency to the point where he or she can look the inner daemon of his or her complex in the eye. The aggressive powers of the split produced by the trauma patient's complex have to be countered with the eros powers of connection and compassion. In the therapeutic relationship, something must grow and develop that was stifled and stunted by the trauma. The raw, archetypal affects of love and hate must be humanized. Only then can patients develop affect tolerance and take up a conscious relationship to their inner, repressed parts.

Trauma victims, in the desperate effort to reestablish their ego after it has disintegrated under the influence of the trauma, often employ the paradoxical strategy of causing themselves physical pain in order to deaden their emotional pain. This may include rituals of self-mutilation, such as scratching, cutting, or hitting themselves or stubbing out cigarettes on their skin. These rituals are kept secret and are treasured because they are very effective in a perverse sort of way. Part of their value to the victim lies in their ability to make the victim feel his or her physical reality and counteract feelings of emptiness and deadness.

However, self-mutilation—the sacrifice of the integrity of the physical body—is not the kind of sacrifice that the trauma survivor is called upon to make in therapy. The sacrifice of the self that is required of trauma survivors is the sacrifice of their clinging to mere survival, their desire for security and for assurances that life is going on and will go on. This sacrifice is equally as paradoxical as that of self-mutilation, for in making it, the trauma survivor will paradoxically find himself or herself anew and be "born again" as a new person with a new, posttraumatic identity (John 3:3).

Transcending Trauma through Sacrifice of the False Self

In his psychoanalytic practice, Winnicott found it useful to make a distinction between the True Self and the False Self, a scheme in which the False Self serves a defensive function, namely, "to hide and protect the True Self" from "insult."[12] Winnicott saw the development of the False Self as a pathological condition, which nevertheless has the positive aim to preserve the individual's spirit when faced with traumatic conditions.[13] The main concern of the False Self is to hide the True Self, or to search for ways of enabling the True Self to start to live. If, however, suitable conditions cannot be found, the False Self organizes a literal suicide. This extreme measure is ironic, given that Winnicott conceived of the False Self as "a defence against that which is unthinkable, the exploitation of the True Self, which would result in its annihilation.[14]

While Winnicott saw the False Self as originating in irregularities in the mother-infant relationship, much of what he says about it also applies to trauma victims.[15] For example, he mentions feelings of being unreal, the sense of futility and the growth preventing rigid defenses.[16] When the False Self is extremely rigid, there is also a big split between the True Self and the False Self and this splitting is coupled with an impaired capacity of symbol formation.[17] Winnicott asserts that the False Self lacks "the essential central element of creative originality."[18] He further notes that if the False Self adopts the mind as its locus, as it often does in highly intellectual individuals, with the result of a dissociation between intellectual activity and embodiment.[19] These statements could also be made of individuals who experience traumatic events—and at any age, not just in infancy. Thus, it is quite legitimate to use the notion of the False Self in the context of trauma, even if only as a heuristic device.[20]

Winnicott's notion of the False Self corresponds roughly to Jung's concept of the persona. In fact, Jung explicitly equated the false self with the persona when he wrote:

> Toju [a seventeenth-century Japanese philosopher] distinguishes a true self from a false self. This false self is an acquired personality compounded of perverted beliefs. We might define this false self as the *persona*, that general idea of ourselves which we have built up from experiencing our effect upon the world around us and its effect upon us.[21]

Jung defined the persona as "the individual's system of adaptation to, or . . . dealing with, the world."[22] Jung went on to note that the danger arises when a person becomes too rigidly identified with his or her persona. He likened this rigid persona to a shirt that sticks to the skin, the poisoned Nessus shirt of Hercules, which needs to be stripped away before the individual can become what he or she really is (Winnicott's True Self). We hear echoes of Winnicott's description of the False Self in Jung's claim that "the dissolution of the persona is an indispensable condition for individuation."[23] This dissolution of the persona might be spoken of as a sacrifice of the False Self. However, both Winnicott and Jung recognized that the False Self or persona can become so deeply entrenched that in therapy, when the patient is called upon to make this sacrifice,

> there will be resistance to change in the persona, because through
> identification it has become the basis for the patient's interpersonal
> interactions. The relationships which the patient has formed, no
> matter how superficial, are his only relationships and to modify
> the persona is to threaten his entire interpersonal field.[24]

Trauma victims, especially, often latch onto a victim persona, which
they find very difficult to give up, especially when they are confronted
with the fact that they have become identified with it.

Trauma is not transcended by sublimating the libido and the affect
associated with traumatic events through spiritual practice in a process
of "spiritual bypassing" (a defensive maneuver deployed to avoid the
pain of working through trauma).[25] Yearning for spiritual transcendence
can become a flight from reality, a false sacrifice of the libido.

In particular, I recall a young woman, whom I will call Elizabeth,
who had been sexually exploited by her father in childhood. Attempting
to distance herself from this shaming and crippling experience, she
renounced the world, chose asceticism, and retreated to a cloister in
search of refuge. She became a member of the contemplative order that
ran the cloister, took the required vow of silence, and began a regimen
of spiritual development in the hope of transcending her history of
abuse. She forced herself to forgive her father and believed she had
succeeded in doing so; but she could find neither peace of mind nor
balance of psychic energy. Her spiritual suffering was intensified by a
confessor's retraumatizing assaults and guilt projections. Elizabeth
developed striking psychosomatic symptoms: she experienced frequent
fainting spells, dizziness, and anxiety states and struggled with an eating
disorder that reflected her emotional starvation. Finally, she fell apart,
and her abbess allowed her to begin therapy with me.

Elizabeth was haunted by feelings of being evil, sinful, and punished
by God. Priests attempted to "cleanse" her through repeated exorcisms,
which only caused even greater fragmentation and distress and
reinforced these feelings of worthlessness and self-condemnation. She
said, "I am tired of living," and "a rope is tied around my neck. I am
only waiting to be hanged." Even as a child, she had constantly wished
that she had leukemia and could die. Given her suffering from early
relational trauma and subsequent sexual abuse, it took time for her to
build trust in the nurturing potential of a safe human relationship.
Her dreams often began: "*It is very dark, pitch dark. I am standing on*

the brink of an abyss. All around me is blackness," or, *"It is night. A great darkness is everywhere. I don't want any light to come."*

In such dreams, she would often get lost in a dark forest, wander through constricted, barren landscapes, or climb over rubble that looked like the ruins of war, lacking any directional orientation. The image of a tunnel often came up: she had to go through it but was afraid. In one such dream, at the other end of the tunnel there was a river, but she could not see the far bank and feared she would drown. In other dreams, she would be in a desert or locked up in prison. She would try to escape but was unable to call for help and would find herself paralyzed and mute. Her process of becoming conscious guided her to all the inner places that she had systematically tried to avoid in life. Everything that she wanted to be untrue forced itself on her and challenged her. She was compelled to reconsider even her relationship to spirituality. In one dream, she was in a cloister with many columns, where sculptures and paintings were on display. She recounted: "One image was in the form of a circle, completely dark, in a black frame. There was nothing visible, only the darkness. I grew frightened, so I went away." Her relationship with the divine was tinged with fear, and the threatening, dark aspect of the Self overshadowed her entire existence. Her dreams were rich in symbolism and archetypal material; the transference relationship was ambivalent at first, marked by the fear that I would abandon her if I saw her true self.

Not only was Elizabeth abused by her father, but her mother was not a reliable, resonant, relational object with whom she could develop a secure attachment. This woman was what Winnicott would have described as a not good-enough mother, for she could not provide the holding environment that facilitates the process of in-dwelling, nor was she able to nurture the formation of Elizabeth's True Self by adapting effectively to the infant Elizabeth's spontaneous impulses and facilitating the development of her capacity for symbol-usage, a failure that opened the door to the formation of a compliant False Self.[26] Elizabeth's nameless anxieties originated with an emotionally absent mother. Sexual exploitation by her father added to her frozenness and the feeling that there was a black hole inside her, so that whoever came close to her would have to turn away in disgust.

It took a long time for Elizabeth to be able to trust me and believe that I would stand firm by her side, that I would not recoil at seeing her True Self revealed, and that she herself would also be able to face those disowned, disavowed parts of herself hidden behind the iron gates of her False Self. By meeting her relational needs with respect and providing a space for her to take some tentative steps toward self-agency, she was able to summon up the courage to go to the unbearably shameful places of her wounding, to search for who she really was and what she truly wanted.

Elizabeth had sacrificed her instinctual nature and libido for a perfectionist, high-achieving, overly controlling attitude, always wanting to do things right, an attitude that Winnicott noted often characterizes the False Self.[27] To her, this sacrifice seemed necessary for survival. She felt that she owed this to God, that her achievement of external excellence would somehow pacify the wrath of his all-seeing eye. Her dreams, which she recorded religiously, brought home to her a richness of instinctual life that she could ignore no longer. Wounded, smelly, ragged dogs emerged. Violent wolves appeared. So did lions, bears, tigers, and filthy pigs. There was a development from her original anxiety responses of flight, fight, freeze, or fragment to healthier ways of mastering these instinctual challenges— appeasing, tending, befriending.

Again and again she would find herself sitting on a filthy, nearly overflowing toilet. In one such dream, she tried to clean the toilet and spotted in the bowl a huge, ugly-looking crab, which suddenly leaped up and slid its legs into her shirt, causing her to wake up in a panic. In another dream, she found herself trying to clear out a stopped-up sink by scouring the pipes. We were long occupied with the theme of cleaning and trying to get the blocked stream of life to flow again.

The gradual growth in her consciousness of her inner conflicts enlivened her, as if she were passing through a series of deaths, and she burned intensely in the fire of her erupting affects. Jung gives a very vivid description of this coming to consciousness through the awakening of emotions:

> Conflict engenders fire, the fire of affects and emotions, and like every other fire it has two aspects, that of combustion and that of creating light. On the one hand, emotion is the alchemical fire whose warmth brings everything into existence and whose heat burns all superfluities to ashes . . . . But on the other hand, emotion is the moment when steel meets flint and a spark is struck

forth, *for emotion is the chief source of consciousness.* There is no change from darkness to light or from inertia to movement without emotion.[28]

Elizabeth sacrificed her emotions when she entered the cloister. In order to endure the contemplative life of absolute silence as well as to make a break with her traumatic past, she shut out of awareness all the memories and affects that were associated with her sexual abuse. This set in motion a painful underground search for her abandoned emotions, a journey of dying and becoming. She dreamed:

> *In the cellar of a castle a young woman is held prisoner. At first I am an observer, but feel that part of me is in her, too. A female guard gives her a dress, saying it is her wedding dress. The woman is frightened, for she knows she must die, and her death will be by fire. When she puts on the dress, she is panic-stricken. She then goes to a place strewn thickly with ashes and realizes there's been a fire there. Then I am standing outside her cell. I see her coming out of the fireplace in a shining white dress, and I know that she had been purified by the fire. In front of the fireplace, waiting for her, is her favorite pet, a parrot, which had died earlier. She calls out its name joyfully, and they both run away. I am glad she makes it, and I envy her for putting the past behind her.*

In Elizabeth's therapy, with the cocreation of an emotionally safe intersubjective field, the transcendent function was evoked; transformational themes emerged not only in her dreams but also in the way she began relating to me. She brought to her sessions pieces of music that she wanted me to listen to. She was extremely shy and spoke very little, using a subdued voice that I could barely hear. It was more like a whisper, as if breaking the vow of silence had to be done gently, but also as if speaking softly would somehow render her invisible. The pieces of music she chose gave her a voice through which to speak of her inner landscape, her turmoil and terror, her loneliness and yearning. Within the structured framework of a musical composition, she was able to experience emotions without being overwhelmed. A kind of embodiment took place.

As Elizabeth developed a more intimate relationship with her core (or true) self, she found the courage to question her longing for spiritual transcendence: Would the path she had chosen lead her forward to an awakening or backward to a state of unconsciousness? Was it merely a defense against her fear of living an embodied life in the world? This challenge to what she considered her essential identity (her False Self) precipitated a spiritual crisis. She felt lost, unmoored, exposed, having lived nearly half of her life in the secure seclusion of the cloister. She had dreams of collapsing churches, of the cross falling down from the cathedral, of Jesus falling off the cross. She had a sense of having lost her only refuge and now found herself in some kind of wasteland, without meaning or hope for the future. In this journey downward, she experienced deep grief at the loss of her identity and a profound sadness at coming face to face with the abused child she once was.

I felt particularly called to communicate to her my compassion for her affliction. She needed to feel that she was not alone, that there was a witness to her struggles and an anchor to hold her in place when fears threatened to sweep her away. As I have stated before, I believe that an empathic, attuned therapeutic attitude is crucial for the integration of painful material. The curative force of the belief that one is being seen and understood was especially relevant for Elizabeth as an antidote to the trauma caused by the threatening, all-seeing eye of God. God's constant glare had a menacing quality for her, not at all the soothing comfort of being held in the loving gaze of a compassionate Other. Jung observed that when we encounter raw, archaic expressions of psychic energy in our descent into the unconscious, they are so highly charged with affects that they elicit fear. With her religious background, Elizabeth felt in her descent as if she had been captured and imprisoned by demonic forces, which prevented her from becoming whole.

In this *nigredo* state of utter blackness she met her own truth, first in dreams of horrifying dismemberments, then in reflecting on and making sense of what was revealed to her. Gradually, a shift took place in which she no longer had to view herself as a helpless victim of fate, and she awoke to the realization of the possibility of shaping her own destiny. Jung might have called this the dissolution of her victim persona. In the wake of this dissolution, there emerged glimmers of a more compassionate attitude toward herself, and she took the first

tentative steps toward relinquishing those negative self-beliefs that had
caused her entire being to shrivel. It was only after she had sacrificed
her allegiance to her False Self that she was able to surrender consciously
to the beckoning of the True Self from the unconscious.

Elizabeth's painful self-searching led to fundamental changes in
her beliefs and desires. The breakdown of her former identity and the
bewildering insight that she had cultivated a False Self and sacrificed
her true nature led to intense mourning and despair. This agonizing
awareness of her self-alienation was extremely difficult for her to bear;
it was an initiation through desperation and disillusionment. In this
process of growth, she peeled off layer upon layer of defensive armor,
until she was as naked as Inanna in her descent into the underworld.
Down there she discovered those sacrificed parts of her personality that
had not been allowed to live; the buried rage and hate that had been
given no space to breathe; the wild, raw emotions that burned her from
the inside; the forbidden, despised, rejected sexuality; the doubts about
her sterile faith. She discovered in this chaotic realm a rather opposite
view of life from the one she had become accustomed to, and a different
kind of suffering began. Now she no longer suffered because she beat
on and mutilated her body. She suffered on the deeper level of her soul,
a suffering that seemed to serve a larger purpose and gave meaning to
her agony, paving the way for a transformation of her God-image.

Getting in touch with all this shadow material, being cooked in a
relentless fire, and feeling torn apart, she reemerged from her descent
more open to those archetypal forces, both awesome and terrifying,
that she had formerly tried to shut out of her life. A real transformation
and reconfiguration of her identity set in, a process of dying and
becoming. Archetypal images of the death-rebirth cycle pointed to the
activation of the transcendent function. She dreamed:

> My Mother Superior asks me if I want to die. I tell her
> that it is not a matter of wanting to. I simply feel and
> sense a foreshadowing—I will die soon.

In another dream, she found herself in her hometown. On the
street was a coffin. She lay down in it to sleep, but she could not fall
asleep. In a subsequent dream, she dreamed that it would not be long
until her death. She had a premonition in a dream that she would soon
die of heart disease. A long series of death dreams frightened her to

such an extent that she went for a cardiac examination. Only after she was assured that she had no health problem was she able to appreciate the symbolic significance of her death dreams.

After dealing with her previously ignored and disallowed feelings of rage and hate toward her father, and toward herself and her body, her God-image was transformed. She felt called in her dreams to be who she is (her True Self) and no longer to try to be what she thought she was expected to be (the False Self). The viselike grip of her complexes eased, and a long series of birth dreams indicated the start of healing the split between body and mind, heaven and earth, spirit and matter. In this dream series, first she witnessed births, then she herself was giving birth. Then she bore a son, whom she at first did not want to accept but later lovingly cared for. The labor pains of the birthing process signified the hard work and suffering involved in coming to terms with the unconscious. Elizabeth's transformation through the sacrifice of the False Self is reflected in Jung's statement that the meaning and purpose of the transcendent function "is the realization, in all its aspects, of the personality originally hidden away in the embryonic germ-plasm; the production and unfolding of the original, potential wholeness."[29]

More and more, Elizabeth tapped into her inner resources, used creative imagination, dialogued with the symbols in her dreams, and gave them form in clay. Through our therapeutic work she discovered her original voice, and we jointly reframed and reattributed her experiences in a process of meaning making. Her unconscious gave her all the necessary help and encouragement to follow her path. One of her most reliable and helpful inner guides was a dolphin, who, like a mercurial messenger, visited her in dreams and waking visions. Its highly charged presence seemed to release her blocked energy. Numinous moments in which we both felt a shiver were part of this transformational process. Slowly, Elizabeth grew into a new relationship to that which transcends the ego. Her process confirms Corbett's conviction that "numinous experience results from the interaction of soul and spirit, and, if successful, allows for more of the Self to embody as soul."[30]

Elizabeth's gradual psychological and spiritual maturing enabled her to come to terms with her father's betrayal of her trust, to integrate the sexual abuse into her life, to reestablish trust in the world, and to rediscover a sense of purpose, all of which led her to a mature engagement with life. She was able to take up a profession and gradually discovered the power of eros. She found on her journey a new relationship to the spiritual, one that helped her live in closer harmony with the Self and establish a connection with the transpersonal dimension. Her consciousness continually expanded as she integrated the unconscious contents that were revealed in her dreams and were manifested in our analytic field. The sacrifice of the ego, initiated by the Self and experienced as a death, ultimately brought the gift of consciousness and regeneration and a renewed relationship between ego and Self.

She left the religious order and began living a more embodied existence, eventually getting married, wearing a white bridal gown at her wedding, as in her dream. She was able to exchange her punishing God-image for the nonpersecutory, transpersonal reality that she encountered in her dreams, an otherness that invited her into dialogue, without the crippling fear of causing displeasure, and with the possibility of being held by loving forces larger than herself. She was able to adapt to both the demands of her life in the outer world and the call of the inner world.

Those children traumatized in early childhood who sacrifice their soul or parts of themselves in an overadaptation to parental demands in hopes of seeing the gleam in mother's or father's eye face an especially long and difficult road in reclaiming what they have sacrificed. Even as adults, they feel driven by loyalty to the False Self and by the need to hide their shame at having lost their True Self; thus the sacrifice of the False Self does not come easily.

I remember a patient who had been sexually abused for many years at an orphanage. She recounted the day when she symbolically buried what she thought of as her deepest core, her heart, in order to protect it. This burial of a living part of her was a sacrifice to a greater power. As the years passed, she became so identified with her False Self that she lost all memory of having buried her True Self. It was only in the course of analysis that she remembered this act, and it was only then that she embarked on the agonizing quest to unearth her buried heart and become a living, feeling, creative person. She said:

*I want to be able to live in my body. Maybe it's too late
to try, but the split has become as decisive as my
determination to get rid of it. Somehow I'm facing the
question: Where is the rest of me? Digging it up is a
somewhat archaeological undertaking.*

Trauma therapy is like a joint expedition, searching for the
sacrificed and lost True Self, in order to reclaim it and integrate it into
life. The False Self usually becomes identified with to such an extent
that giving it up takes on the quality of a death experience much more
so than the original sacrifice of the True Self, which never had a chance
to take hold. The False Self is, in fact, part of what Kalsched calls the
"archetypal self-care system," which engineers the sacrifice of the True
Self, paradoxically, as a life-saving, death-preventing measure.[31] Kalsched
notes how difficult it is, therefore, for trauma patients to relinquish
this hard-won "self-care protection."[32]

I think of my patient Kathy, who shared her insights about sacrifice
after she had the following dream:

*K. is a young girl under the Nazis. She meets Hitler. He
knows she is a Jew. He talks to K., who is scared, though
he didn't do or say anything threatening. She knows that
he can "get her" anytime he wants. He lets her go. She
knows she must hide.*

When she was discussing the dream with me later, she suddenly exclaimed:

*Hitler was my abusive stepfather. This was the scene in
his study when I was fourteen. I knew that what she
[i.e., K. in the dream] must hide is her feelings of love!
She must on no account let him know or even suspect
what she loves because he would soil it, desecrate it, and
grind it into the ground. That was his game, whether
the love was for a teacher, a friend, an activity, or
whatever. To hide what I loved was equally imperative
with my mother, but for a different reason: she despised
all feelings. She wanted to be admired and feared, not
loved. My feelings, positive or negative, were a kind of
dirt that had to be wiped off things.*

Kathy had great difficulty acting naturally and being herself in relationships. After reflecting on her dream, she was shocked to discover that her trouble in relating to others was that she would not allow herself to show them how much she loved them. This sudden awareness turned her world upside-down. She sobbed:

> *My tar, my scar, my curse, my bane has been the feeling that I was not lovable, that I was poisonous. That everyone would be better off if I didn't exist. Now my dream tells me that what I sacrificed, buried, and denied, and concealed even from myself, were my own outgoing feelings of love—not anything nasty and awful!*

Kathy spoke with agony about her past, about her sense of being a nobody, about having no identity, no sense of who she was—a stateless Jew but not allowed to admit it, German-born but not allowed to mention this, and officially her stepfather's daughter, though that was not true. We worked for hours on end on her unrequited love for her mother, who had no use for a daughter's love. In the "Fuck House" of her childhood, as she called it, love was banned, "systematically crushed, like in a concentration camp." Kathy felt stupid and guilty for wanting to be loved, and worthless and defective for not having been loved. When she sacrificed her loving feelings, all sorts of other feelings and values took control: the desire for approval, the desire to fit in, the desire to perform according to expectations and meet external standards—what Winnicott called "compliance," which he saw as characteristic of the False Self.[33]

Kathy managed to survive, but the severe wounding that comes from chronic abuse and emotional deprivation can lead to sequential traumas, causing the ultimate fragmentation of an already fragile self. I worked for a long time with a repeatedly traumatized twenty-nine-year-old woman, whom I will call Christiane, who suffered from dissociative identity disorder. I had been getting a great many phone calls from other women as well, who would say almost inaudibly, "I am a multiple. Can you work with me?" In the beginning, I had little experience or training in working with patients of this type. In the 1980s, dissociative identity disorder was an extremely controversial diagnosis, although it had found its way into the *DSM-III* as multiple personality disorder. Experienced psychiatrists laughed at me and questioned the connection between dissociative identity disorder and early sexual violation and other early childhood traumas, maintaining instead that the symptoms were merely hysterical enactments. Today the professional literature includes frequent descriptions of the connection between multiplicity and severe physical, sexual, and emotional abuse in early childhood. In those early days, I was helped greatly by Jung's writings and his references to the work of Pierre Janet.

Working in Paris around the turn of the twentieth century, Janet uncovered past traumatic experiences as the cause of splits in consciousness, which he called dissociation. Jung built on Janet's discoveries in his formulations of the autonomous complex, fragmented consciousness, and splinter psyches. Jung saw no fundamental difference between a split-off personality and a complex, and he stressed that the dissociative phenomena—splitting, depersonalization, and multiplicity—are not necessarily pathological.[34] Undoubtedly, he had in mind his own split into two personalities. The crucial factor for Jung is the capacity to integrate these split-off parts, to change the inner *disiunctio*—the state of "being torn apart into many people and things"—into a *coniunctio*.[35]

My patient Christiane described in very simple language who it was that protected her soul, what inner struggles she had to undergo, what she had to sacrifice. There was little C., as she called her inner child, about three years old, who wanted to be weightless and featherlight and to hide under the "wing" of her therapist, whom she imaged as a "great stork." Little C. wanted to remain silent, to stay a child forever, and be held tightly and carried around. She was the perfect embodiment of the child archetype. As Christiane described her, "C. is soft, frightened, and quiet. She has no words, is often sad, feels helpless, and hides behind the protective Jo." Jo was the personality under whose control Christiane started therapy on the recommendation of her doctor. She was referred to me for chronic posttraumatic stress disorder, with a severe somatization disorder and anorexia. She presented as not fully embodied, as if part of her soul was split off.[36] She had this to say about Jo:

> *Jo always wants to be strong. She feels responsible for C.*
> *She is aggressive, highly functional, and can manage the*

daily world. She has, however, "gotten rid" of her emotions,
so she cannot always understand little C. very well.

In our sessions, the one who talked was usually the strong Jo, who split off her feelings and protected C. She was able to meet the world in a hyper-adapted way, and no one who had contact with her could see what her inner life was really like. She was not kind to her body. She had been anorexic for years and pricked herself with needles as a form of self-torture. She embodied the shadow, which included aspects of her victimizer as well as her struggles with suicidal impulses. We worked together for a long time, and I found I had to communicate with C. and Jo on very different levels. Not until the later stages of the therapy was I permitted to meet Ares, the evil, destructive personality who threatened C. and Jo and held them both in check: "Ares is like an evil demon. Jo protects C. from him and tries to blunt the evil. She must always bring offerings to Ares, so he will spare C." Ares was a ruthless internalized victimizer modeled on Christiane's abusive father and the men who violated her. Over several years of her childhood, she had been sexually enslaved and abused by her father and other men, and her psychic integrity and her sense of self-agency were consequently severely damaged—her resilience was crippled, her trust had been betrayed. In her psyche and her dreams she felt dominated and persecuted by a dangerous, overwhelming, malignant power that sucked all her energy into a big, black hole: "C. often suspects that Jo might become like Ares. This makes her very afraid."

I felt acutely the enormity of the extent to which Christiane's deep soul injury was reenacted in her relationship to herself and to others and the degree to which power and control became her governing patterns of behavior and her inner life had become dominated by her identification with her aggressors. She never directed her aggression against her victimizers, only against herself, in the form of a violent yearning for death. In our work together, we often visited the realm of Hades. However, she did not experience this underworld as a sacred realm with redemptive, transformative power but rather as a state of demonic possession. Christiane characterized her inner deadness as soul murder. Her forced entry into the underworld and her forced submission to masculine power robbed her at an early age of her innocence, and her only hope of survival lay in dissociating on a massive scale. She lacked a holding environment, in which she could develop a healthy attachment to her mother. The only way she could cope with the intense overstimulation of her affective system was through self-medication and self-mutilation. The price for this survival was severely arrested psychic development and an internalization of a murderous, malignant force, which drove her to internal and sometimes external destruction.

Often her frustration at the futility of her Sisyphean task would break through in her exhaustion at falling and getting up, and falling once again and having to get up yet again. She was repeatedly tempted to lie where she had fallen, to give up the fight and flee into a world of fantasies. But then once again there came, from deep within, the impulse to stand up, and I could see the spark of hope in the ashes of resignation. This appears to have been the work of Jo. In Jo I met the controlling "Caretaker Self" described by Winnicott, the progressive part of Christiane's personality, which tried to protect C., the regressive, timid part.[37] But the price of this division of labor was high: complexities could not be tolerated, feelings were numbed, and creative thinking was blocked. I often felt that the splitting had robbed Christiane of the energy needed for further ego development.

Severely traumatized people do not make their sacrifice to a kind and compassionate god; they make their offerings on the altar of the Self in its dark, evil aspect. In Christiane I saw how powerless the ego is in the face of archetypal, self-traumatizing forces, how exposed to tormenting symptoms: the compulsion to wash or count or ritualized self-mutilation. Having to deal constantly with disintegration anxiety, those traumatized in early life often cannot fathom the kind of fate that marked them for victimhood. They describe themselves as the prisoners of a daimon, by whom they are possessed to the point of complete loss of will. Kalsched notes:

> In many respects it is not they, the patients, who resist the process at an ego level. Rather, their psyches are battlegrounds on which the titanic forces of dissociation and integration are at war over the traumatized personal spirit. The patient must, of course, become more conscious and responsible for a relationship to his or her tyrannical defenses, but this consciousness must include the humble realization that archetypal forces are much more powerful than the ego.[38]

On the surface, avoidance, minimization, distancing, splitting, and attempting to place a positive value on painful experiences may look like dreadful self-deception. In reality, however, this self-regulation of negative affect performs a life-saving function. For precisely that reason, trauma patients find it dangerous, even impossible, to give up these survival strategies and self-healing measures, even though they block creativity and growth and lead eventually to stagnation and decay. Even healthy people struggle with "the specific inertia of the libido, which will relinquish no object of the past, but would like to hold it fast forever."[39] How much more difficult is it, then, for traumatized individuals to let go of that around which they have painstakingly built a secure identity? Even their morbid attachment to their victimizer, their identification with his or her aggression, is difficult to give up, for it has become part of their capacity for self-direction and has afforded them sufficient protection for survival. I often think about Jung's fundamental reflection:

> Man is constantly inclined to forget that what was once good does not remain good eternally. He follows the old ways that once were good long after they have become bad, and only with the greatest sacrifices and untold suffering can he rid himself of this delusion and see that what was once good is now perhaps grown old and is good no longer. This is so in great things as in small.[40]

The sacrifice of one's self-protection strategies and the loosening of one's rigid defense mechanisms are dreadfully painful and threatening processes, for they uncover old wounds associated with safety, trust, power, esteem, and intimacy.

In the course of working with trauma patients, I became painfully aware of the limitations of the psyche's automatic self-regulatory processes, especially when a sadistic part of the psyche violently attacks the developing ego and destroys its capacity for seeing creative links between events and their interpretation.[41] The damage to the linking faculties interferes with the dynamics of meaning making and renders it impossible for the trauma victim to integrate experiences, with the result that affects, images, perceptions, thoughts, and bodily sensations remain disconnected.

The BASK model sees dissociation as occurring among the domains of behavior, affect, sensation, and knowledge (thought). The unconscious sacrifice of any of these dimensions—the severing of any one domain from the others—creates a disorder of association. According to this model, therapy involves the restoration and reestablishment of the psyche in all four dimensions, a reclaiming of whatever was once sacrificed in the name of survival. The goal is to integrate traumatic experiences into the victim's experiential schema. However, even this ideal of integration may have to be sacrificed in some cases, since there are certain experiences that defy integration and the only option is to seal them off in order that the patient can get on with his or her life. In some instances, the core of the complex cannot be accessed and assimilated; no dismantling of the defenses is possible or even indicated; no release or abreaction of the emotional charge of the traumatic complex can occur since no healing energies are released to mend the split.

I am reminded that not every soul who is forced to make the painful journey to the underworld will be able to return, and the therapist may wait in vain for reemergence and renewal. In trauma therapy, there is no guarantee that the sacrifice of the False Self will bring about the desired transcendence.

NOTES

[1] Donald Kalsched, *The Inner World of Trauma: Archetypal Defenses of the Personal Spirit* (London: Routledge, 1996), p. 13.

[2] *Ibid.*, p. 5; italics in original.

[3] Jung, *CW* 16, § 270.

[4] Jung, *CW* 8, § 253.

[5] Jung, *CW* 8, § 204.

[6] Jung, *CW* 16, § 267.

[7] Jung, *CW* 8, § 200.

[8] Jung, *CW* 8, § 204.

[9] Jung, *CW* 8, § 208.

[10] Jung, *CW* 8, § 207.

[11] Jung, *CW* 8, § 216.

[12] D. W. Winnicott, "Ego Distortions in Terms of True and False Self" (1960), in *The Maturational Process and the Facilitating Environment: Studies in the Theory of Emotional Development*, ed. M. Masud R. Khan (London: Hogarth Press and the Institute of Psycho-Analysis, 1965), p. 142–143.

[13] *Ibid.*, pp. 143, 147.

[14] *Ibid.*, pp. 143, 147–148.

[15] Kalsched uses the term *false self* in the context of trauma when he writes of Ferenczi's notion of the Orpha, a sort of guardian angel, or "an inner, all-knowing, precociously intellectual part of the self" that descends to "help the shattered [sexually abused, traumatized] child assemble some kind of minimally functioning *false self* with which to go on existing." Donald Kalsched, "Trauma and Daimonic Reality in Ferenczi's Later Work," *Journal of Analytical Psychology* 48, no. 4 (2003): 480; emphasis added.

[16] Winnicott, "Ego Distortions," p. 148.

[17] *Ibid.*, p. 150.

[18] *Ibid.*, p. 152.

[19] *Ibid.*, p. 144.

[20] Jean Knox suggests that False Self (as articulated by Winnicott) should be understood as a psychic process rather than as a psychic structure. See Jean Knox, "The Fear of Love: The Denial of Self in Relationship," *Journal of Analytical Psychology* 52, no. 5 (2007): 546.

[21] Jung, *CW* 6, § 370 (p. 218). See also Wayne C. Hudson, "Persona and Defence Mechanisms," *Journal of Analytical Psychology* 23, no. 1 (1978): 59.

[22] Jung, *CW* 9i, § 221.

[23] Jung, *CW* 7, § 505.

[24] Hudson, "Persona and Defence Mechanisms," p. 59.

[25] John Welwood, *Perfect Love, Imperfect Relationships: Healing the Wound of the Heart* (Boston: Trumpeter Books, 2006), p. 197. See also Jerome S. Bernstein, *Living in the Borderland: The Evolution of Consciousness and the Challenge of Healing Trauma* (Hove, UK: Routledge, 2005), p. 168.

[26] Winnicott defined in-dwelling as "the achievement of a close and easy relationship between the psyche and the body, and body functioning." D. W. Winnicott, "Providing for the Child in Health and Crisis" (1962), in *The Maturational Process and the Facilitating*

Environment: Studies in the Theory of Emotional Development, ed. M. Masud R. Khan (London: Hogarth Press and the Institute of Psycho-Analysis, 1965), p. 68. See also Winnicott, "Ego Distortions," pp. 145–146.

²⁷ Winnicott, "Ego Distortions," p. 144.

²⁸ Jung, *CW* 9i, § 179; emphasis added.

²⁹ Jung, *CW* 7, § 186.

³⁰ Lionel Corbett, *The Religious Function of the Psyche* (London: Routledge, 1996), pp. 16–17.

³¹ Kalsched, *Inner World of Trauma*, p. 4.

³² *Ibid.*, p. 12.

³³ Winnicott, "Ego Distortion," pp. 145–146.

³⁴ For an in-depth analysis of these themes, see Christian Vincent, *Viewing Dissociative Identity Disorder through a Jungian Lens* (M.A. thesis, Pacifica Graduate Institute, Carpinteria, CA., 2010), ProQuest/UMI 1489804.

³⁵ Jung, *CW* 16, § 397.

³⁶ See Corbett, *Religious Function of the Psyche*, p. 144.

³⁷ Winnicott, "Ego Distortion," p. 142.

³⁸ Kalsched, *Inner World of Trauma*, p. 26.

³⁹ Jung, *CW* 5, § 253.

⁴⁰ Jung, *CW* 6, § 313.

⁴¹ W. R. Bion, "Attacks on Linking," *International Journal of Psycho-Analysis* 40, nos. 5–6 (1959): 308–315.

CHAPTER TWELVE

THE TRAUMATIC DIMENSIONS
OF SACRIFICE

J ung was interested in sacrifice primarily from a psychological point
of view; however, for him the concept also had a religious
significance. The English word *sacrifice* is derived from the Latin
sacer, meaning "sacred, dedicated, holy, accursed." Similarly, the
English *victim* is derived from the Latin, *victima*, which was originally
used to refer to the animals that were offered up in sacrifices to the
gods. There is, indeed, an intimate association between victimhood
and sacrifice. More specifically, the trauma associated with being a
victim is inherent in the offering of sacrifice, whether in the religious
or the psychological sense.

Early humans believed that blood sacrifices were needed to appease
the anger of vengeful gods. However, as Corbett points out, with the
development of consciousness, a new understanding of the relationship
between the human and the divine has emerged. Vicarious blood
sacrifices are no longer necessary; rather, as the apostle Paul writes, "I
urge you . . . to offer your bodies as a living sacrifice . . . [for] this is
your true and proper worship. . . . be transformed by the renewing of
your mind" (Rom. 12:1–2, NIV). According to Corbett, "each
individual must make his or her own sacrifice as demanded by the

Self."[1] Nevertheless, the Self can be as vengeful and traumatizing as any primitive, bloodthirsty god. Victims of trauma often experience themselves as inescapably cursed, predestined by fate or a higher power to be a sacrificial lamb. Perhaps it is this numinous aspect of the sacrifice archetype that makes it so traumatizing for them to renounce their victimhood and let go of their victim persona.

Every sacrifice, whether religious or psychological, has a meaning to the sacrificer, a meaning that makes the sacrifice necessary. However, in the context of trauma, victims are often sacrificed needlessly, meaninglessly, to the madness of a religious or political ideology, unnatural passions, or an overwhelming hunger for power and dominance. The trauma victim spontaneously struggles to invest his or her experience with some meaning in the face of this meaninglessness. Paradoxically, meaning is to be found in yielding oneself up as a sacrificial victim, as Isaac does to Abraham in the biblical story. Cowan observes that

> it is precisely within one's capacity to offer sacrifice that one finds meaning: the victim who is able to make a sacrifice becomes psychologically active in her or his affliction, a participant in the holy work of making meaning out of incomprehensible chaos. Whether the sacrifice consists of one's naivety, innocence, cherished ideal, or self-image, one's capacity to yield to a deeper necessity is tested in victimization.[2]

Despite the etymological connections, victim and sacrifice are usually not associated with each other in our everyday thinking. A victim is understood as a person who is oppressed, hurt, exploited, tortured, or killed by some other person in some situation of power inequality. Sacrifice is understood as the giving up of something cherished or desirable for the sake of some greater good. While sacrifice is valued positively, victimization is assigned a negative value, and the two are placed at opposite ends of the spectrum. As Cowan suggests, however, trauma victims will not achieve transcendence of their trauma unless the lost connection between sacrifice and victim is restored.

Sacrifice mediates between the profane and the sacred, providing a point of access to the transpersonal dimension. In intrapsychic terms, its function is to create a relationship between the ego and the Self. In depth psychology, sacrifice is understood as a transformational process, an initiation, which is inherently traumatizing. It is part of the numinous archetypal cycle of life and death. The myth of Inanna, the goddess with the extraordinary ability to transcend boundaries, bespeaks a self-chosen initiation. Hers is a voluntary descent into the underworld—in contrast to that of Persephone—and she returns from that realm with an intimate acquaintance with death. The descent of the Dark Goddess involves a letting go, a giving up of everything, until she is completely naked, stripped of every shred of her persona. She must leave behind her old ego structures if she is to rediscover, in the underworld, her long-repressed values and feminine wisdom. This voluntary sacrifice is offered, as Sylvia Brinton Perera writes, with "the purpose of retrieving values long repressed, and of uniting above and below into a new pattern," thus forging an integrated consciousness.[3]

Unlike Inanna's sacrifice, however, traumatic victimization at the hands of another is completely involuntary, and the resulting demolition of ego structures is followed neither by regeneration nor by re-creation, but by a sense of drowning in chaos. This involuntary sacrifice does not usually lead to a deeper relationship with the Self. When the wound of betrayal and dehumanization is unable to heal, when faith and self-worth, dignity and self-respect are lost, many victims sacrifice their relationship to their instincts and their body, as well as their relationship to a transpersonal dimension, in order to stay afloat. The kind of death that is associated with this sacrifice is a vehement denial of life, a categorical rejection that precludes regeneration. In this soulless state, the victim experiences the diabolical side of the numinous, the negative pole of the sacrifice archetype, which becomes enacted in the therapeutic relationship when the victim enters therapy. The basic trust in the rhythm of growth, decay, and regrowth is put severely to the test. The trauma therapist does not always have the same certainty as Jung, who wrote:

> When we think of the unending growth and decay of life and civilizations, we cannot escape the impression of absolute nullity. Yet I have never lost a sense of something that lives and endures underneath the eternal flux. What we see is the blossom, which passes. The rhizome remains.[4]

In the context of trauma, the ego's death is experienced as an annihilation, an overwhelming experience of nothingness without any redemptive qualities. And yet, as Stanton Marlan insists, "the Self can be discovered and recollected through the nothingness of the mortificatio process."[5] Extreme suffering often serves as a catalyst for change and for the emergence of new insight. It brings a person to the end of his or her rope, so that he or she has no other recourse but to surrender to its power. This sacrifice of control can bring about the transformation of fate into destiny, through a newly gained attitude toward unchangeable reality.[6]

At the psychic level, the power of sacrifice consists in the transformation of energy. And yet, in my work with my patients, I have encountered the painful experience of failure. Sometimes, despite the sacrifice and surrender, the descent into the unconscious does not lead to a reintegration into consciousness of what was split off and lost. Sometimes it is too late to bring order out of the chaos and no energic transformation is possible. I have become aware that there are in the soul powers that do not promote individuation, psychological "counterpowers." I have observed that even the smallest first steps toward openness and positive change can be experienced as life threatening and traumatizing since they point to a dissolution of the structures that formerly provided security (the False Self). A metamorphosis of psychological structure is not achieved without the traumatic sacrificial act of destroying old, ossified patterns of thinking, schemas, and behaviors. This sacrifice is often experienced as a kind of crucifixion, in which one feels torn between holding on to the familiar on one hand and heeding the inner urgings to reach out to the unknown on the other.

Traumatic though the process may be, the sacrifice of ego control and ego dominance must take place in order for the psychic system to become flexible again. As Jung pointed out, "creation is as much destruction as construction," a concept echoed in the shamanic motif of dismemberment and re-memberment as well as in the alchemical process, which requires that base metals be burned, dissolved, and broken down before the sought-after gold can be attained.[7] The images that arise from the unconscious during this process indicate that the transformation of consciousness that results from the sacrifice of the False Self is both archetypal and traumatic. The dreams of my trauma patients are filled with acts of self-annihilation and dismemberment, dream motifs of hacked-off hands, chopped-up babies' corpses, human and animal torsos, and images of decapitation, ritual excision of flesh with a sharp knife, and over and over the image of the cut-out heart, the empty shell.

In trauma therapy—as in the practice of homeopathy—it would appear that the principle of "like cures like" is fundamental.[8] It takes trauma to heal trauma. Voluntary sacrifice is the antidote to involuntary sacrifice. The trauma of the sacrifice of the False Self, experienced in the safety and security of the therapeutic relationship, can bring about the healing of the trauma of physical and psychic violation.

The Sacrifice Motif in Myths and Fairy Tales

The realization that sacrifice, traumatic though it is, can heal the wounds inflicted on us by what Shakespeare called the "slings and arrows of outrageous fortune" is as old as the ancient myths, legends, and fairy tales told by people around the world.[9] In them we find sacrifices for love, sacrifices for a higher principle, sacrifices that enable the sacrificer to take the next step, cross a threshold, or ward off danger. We read of sacrifices made to mollify a dragon or to lull Cerberus to sleep in the underworld so that the hero may slip past him.[10]

In myths and fairy tales, the sacrifice of a daughter—whether for fortune in war, as in the biblical story of Jephthah (Judges 11), or for the father's sexual pleasure—is an archaic motif that portrays the painful launching of the victim's individuation process. The daimonic aspect of the father imago is often split off and projected onto the devil, as in the story "Der Teufel als Lehrer" ("The Devil as Teacher").[11] In this tale, a mother takes her three daughters to school every day, where the devil has taken possession of the male teacher. He promptly falls in love with the youngest daughter. As she grows older, he becomes more and more infatuated with her, but he cannot find an easy way to abduct her. So he makes a glass coffin and a magic ring. Then, while she is playing, he grabs her and puts the magic ring on her finger. The ring causes her to fall immediately into a deep sleep, and when she has fallen asleep he puts her into the glass coffin and throws the coffin into the sea. The young girl asleep in the glass coffin is a striking representation of the spiritual condition of girls who have been sacrificed, whose libido has sunk into the unconscious. All their instinctive energies are split off, and their emotions have become vitrified. In the dreams of such girls I have often encountered the motif of living inside a bell jar, where everything is experienced as unreal, for the bell jar serves to insulate the dreamer against harsh reality, but at the same time isolates her from it as well.

In the Brothers Grimm tale "Allerleirauh," a king's daughter can save herself from her father's determination to take her as his wife after the death of her mother, the queen, only by sacrificing her status as princess and queen-to-be, separating herself from the royal household, disguising herself, and withdrawing into a Cinderella-like existence.[12] A similar tale is that of the daughter in "Des Reussenkoenigs Tochter" ("The Russian King's Daughter"). When she hears that she must marry her father, she cuts off her hair, throws away her bridal gown, dresses in ordinary clothes, and scratches her face until it bleeds. She must sacrifice her relationship to her father, which is about to become dysfunctional, in order to develop a healthy relationship with the masculine.

An important fairy tale that speaks of the kind of sacrifice that ultimately leads the victim closer to the Self is the Brothers Grimm tale "Das Mädchen ohne Hände" ("The Maiden without Hands" or "The Handless Maiden").[13] In the tale, a down-and-out miller is tricked into sacrificing his daughter when he makes a bargain with the devil for personal material gain. The devil forces him to cut off his daughter's hands in order to keep his end of the bargain. For her part, the maiden willingly sacrifices her hands out of compliance with her father's values (echoing Winnicott's observation that compliance is the hallmark of the False Self).

There are many possible ways to understand the theme of the sacrificed hands. In a practical sense we might think about the loss of the ability to act, about helplessness, dependence, and vulnerability, about the inability to take hold of the wheel of fate. Sexually traumatized young women experience themselves as similarly mutilated and deprived. Loath to abandon the illusion of the loving father (a stand-in for all men), they would rather sacrifice themselves instead, giving up their identity and relinquishing their desires. Only as maidens without hands, without any volition of their own, can they hope to please the father. Only at the price of their own souls, by blocking their own drives and denying their own needs, can they remain their father's daughter. Von Franz sees the sacrifice of the maiden's hands as revealing the inner devil in the form of a negative animus, and her subsequent wandering as a quest for the true Self, leading to her liberation from a crippling father complex.[14] Especially persuasive, I find, is the work of Sonoko Toyoda, who interprets the hands in the tale as a symbol of feminine creativity and spirituality. She describes how the motif of hands comes up in the dreams of her women patients—often cut, injured, decaying, or amputated. Her main point is that the heroine's loss of her hands can be interpreted as a loss of her feminine spirituality, "a *sacrifice* on her part in order to evade an internal devil . . . and it thus indicates the heroine's passiveness."[15]

In the tale, the maiden knows that once her hands are cut off she cannot stay with her father any longer. She can individuate only by detaching herself from her father's world. But the question remains: How can this young woman free herself from her past? How is she to reach out for a loving encounter with another human being, when she has no hands? The dependency patterns of such women are not easy to change. To be sure, in the tale the king who falls in love with and marries the handless maiden gives her silver hands; but these prostheses do not help her achieve independence and autonomy. Rather they bind her to the king through gratitude and the feeling that she owes him something in return.

Communication between the couple while the king is away is disrupted when their letters to each other are intercepted and changed by the devil. Here the daimonic aspect of the father is revealed when he intrudes destructively in the loving companionship of the couple. Once again the maiden rises up, sacrifices what is dear to her, and sets off to save herself and Sorrowful, her newborn child. In the solitude of the forest, she turns to her wounded inner child, just as in the therapeutic process we must find access to this inner child. The path of self-discovery, and the new growth of her hands, is possible only through the sacrifice of everything that originally promised to make her secure. The insight that no one else can bring about emancipation from dependency, that healing is possible only from within after a prolonged process of attending faithfully to grief and dreams—this realization liberates the violated woman from the rape of her soul. In the fairy tale this process is portrayed as a religious experience of grace, in which only God can restore what human beings have destroyed. It is this spiritual dimension, this experience of the Self, that helps many patients make the painful sacrifices necessary to transcend their trauma and create themselves anew.

The Transcendent Function:
Transformation in the Relational Field

Jung's concept of the transcendent function is intimately associated with his understanding of how change occurs in the psyche. He conceived of the idea just prior to 1916, in the wake of his great emotional crisis. Through his confrontation with the dark reaches of his own psyche, in what amounted to an initiatory crisis, he experienced a renewing power, which he later formulated as the transcendent function. Though this crisis took him to the brink of madness, it was precisely there, at the edges of his familiar way of thinking about himself and the world, that the transcendent function was activated, and he experienced it as a force that put him in touch with the Beyond. This is why the concept, despite all its contradictions and the critiques it has received in recent Jungian scholarship, is still meaningful to me, especially in the context of trauma therapy.[16]

Over the span of his career, Jung wrote about the transcendent function in many different ways, but he always insisted that it is in no way a metaphysical concept. Rather, he saw it as functioning organically, even though its numinous aspect is continually in evidence. He wrote: "There is nothing mysterious or metaphysical about the term 'transcendent function.' . . . The psychological 'transcendent function' arises from the union of conscious and unconscious contents."[17] This self-regulating function operates through processes of differentiation and integration, through dialectical and dialogical communication with the contents of the unconscious, but also through the resonance of the therapeutic relationship.

Jung made it clear that the creative power of the psyche pushes us toward transformation and transcendence, but only in the sense of "ordinary transcendence," as Polly Young-Eisendrath once phrased it.[18] For her psychotherapy is a practice of ordinary transcendence, a process in which self-protectiveness, isolationism, and the desire for omnipotence are overcome and the patient comes to the insight that human beings are interdependent. In my view, this process of transcendence is the surmounting of a boundary, a change of perspective to a higher level. When a person feels bogged down, traumatically cornered, and stuck, then the process-oriented energy of the transcendent function brings movement back to the psyche, and life energy can be turned to new goals. This energy has effects that are intrapsychic and interpsychic, but also transpersonal, flowing back and forth between these different perspectives. It provides room for reflection and thus bears a similarity to Winnicott's concept of a potential space for play in the therapeutic relationship.[19] It enables the overcoming of the opposites and the development of a new inner attitude, one that rises above either-or to embrace the paradoxical both-and.

Through the transcendent function, we become receptive to what is attempting to reveal itself to us. It becomes possible to experiment with new insights and viewpoints, and to accept gracefully the uncertainty of the direction of emerging processes and the apparent randomness of the flows of psychic energy. Therein lies the distinctive character of Jungian analysis, which has little in common with current solution-focused brief therapy with its emphasis on efficiency, symptom relief, and "instant cure." What marks the soul-focused analytic attitude is the greatest possible openness to the possibility of profound psychological renewal.

The transcendent function is, as Jeffrey Miller puts it, "a phenomenon ubiquitous to human experience that implicates opposition/duality, liminality, descent, initiation, and transformation."[20] The process often begins with a descent into dangerous, bottomless depths after containing structures of meaning and elements of order have collapsed. Associated with this descent is the enormous fear that, after one falls into the yawning abyss, no bottom will be found, and no return will be possible.

The transcendent function is a driving, goal-directed power, a self-actualizing tendency of the living system, transforming the structures of the soul, bringing order and manageability to affects that had previously been fragmented and overwhelming. At the same time, one needs to be aware that the processes of transformation are dialectical; nothing is ever completely worked through. The trauma is often reenacted anew in later phases or other areas of life. The process of disintegration and reintegration is continually repeated on the path of individuation, for the psyche independently remains in a lively dialogue with the things that threaten us, that are unknown to us and unconscious. The transcendent function can nurture awareness through an ongoing dialogical process, so that we are, hopefully, freed gradually from acting out. In the context of trauma especially, the healing process has no clear beginning and no clear end. Chhim Sotheara, executive director of the Transcultural Psychosocial Organization Cambodia (TPO Cambodia), who has been working for several years with survivors of the Khmer Rouge, asserts: "The work of healing is ongoing. There is no time limit to the work on the effects of genocide. . . . Healing will never be too late, and healing can still be achieved."[21]

In writing about the sacred dimension of the healing *temenos*, von Franz invokes the concept of the *unio mystica*, "a fated togetherness in eternity," where there is no longer any division between inner and outer, subject and object.[22] Here we feel ourselves contained within an energy-charged field, which embraces therapist and patient and may be perceived in subtle-body experiences. This sense of the sacred, when it is constellated by the transcendent function, can lead to an altered state of consciousness in the analytic dyad and the shared relational field.

Early on, Jung recognized the energetic charge of the unconscious contents that emerge into consciousness, seizing patient and analyst and changing them both. Archetypal transference can be seen as an energetic individuating force, provided that it is not reductively devalued as a mere replay of childhood patterns. In trauma therapy, transference has an underlying energy, which drives the process of bringing the scattered pieces together, thus satisfying the yearning for some greater inner unity. From an archetypal perspective, the healing potential is not located primarily in that which is mutually projected in the transference; rather, it is found in whatever is activated by the relational field, constellated between patient and therapist. Indeed, this field has its own *telos*, as Schwartz-Salant has shown; it works quite autonomously toward its goal, which is the union of order and disorder.[23]

I understand the analytic space as a *temenos*, a "sacred cauldron," in which the transcendent function operates.[24] This larger presence within which therapist and patient are held reminds me of Rumi's invitation:

Out beyond ideas of wrongdoing and rightdoing,
there is a field. I'll meet you there.[25]

The concept of a relational field has been applied profitably in quantum physics and features prominently in Rupert Sheldrake's work on morphic resonance, but it is also central to complementary medicine and the modern practice of homeopathy.[26] More recently the concept has been applied to the practice of psychotherapy based on the oscillations of energy exchange, the dynamic interchange of psychic energy that is generated in the relationship between therapist and patient.

In Jungian psychology, as early as 1980, Marie-Louise von Franz drew attention to "the archetypal idea of the field."[27] There are numerous articles in Jungian literature concerning the clinical relevance of this concept, for example the work of Nathan Schwartz-Salant, Michael Conforti, Murray Stein, Victor Mansfield and Marvin Spiegelman, and two creative dissertations from Pacifica Graduate Institute.[28] Robert Stolorow and his coauthors speak of the "intersubjective field."[29] Schwartz-Salant calls it the "interactive field" and considers it to be autonomous, that is, not dependent on the subjectivity of patient and therapist.[30] Winnicott describes operating in the realm of possibilities as working in "transitional" or "potential space."[31] Thomas Ogden speaks of the "analytic third," referring to the "subject of the analysis," which emerges from the intersubjective interaction of the analyst and the patient, but nevertheless has its own subjectivity.[32] This "third" is cocreated, yet, at the same time, it contains and influences analyst and patient. It is in this area of cocreation of meaning that transformation occurs, and a new level of reflection and mentalization—a broadened consciousness—can emerge.

The reciprocal energy that pulses through patient and therapist as a vital force is an energy potential that generates resonance and brings about change and healing. This concept of the relational field and the notion of the subtle body (drawn from the wisdom traditions) greatly enhance the understanding of transference and the archetypal undercurrents of psychotherapeutic work. Consequently, promoting awareness of the relational field, internal somatic states, and energy flows is an essential aspect of my work.

Although the analytic relationship is recognized as a strong bond of mutual influence, as the "*mixtum compositum*" of two different substances as Jung described it, I remain conscious that the relationship with the other, as Levinas has said, is ultimately a relationship to mystery.[33]

With Levinas, I consider love to be the matrix for this transformation, which calls new being into existence. Love has the power to reawaken and bring to the fore what has been entombed or distorted by traumatic forces or has retreated out of defensiveness and self-protection. Without love and compassion for the fragility of human identity in the face of death and the reality of evil, the madness found in these barren spaces of the soul might not be meaningfully encountered. For the stripping away of the constricting cocoon of traumatic fixations and the untangling of what has become distorted and convoluted during painful traumatization, love is needed. Love is also instrumental in purifying the "doors of perception," to borrow a phrase from William Blake, and resetting the energy field, which has been co-opted by the introjected victimizer.[34] Survivors who have mastered their trauma often exhibit a special capacity for love, an embodied concern for others, a deep kindness and caring for humanity as a whole.

Relational psychotherapy and the findings of research in the literature covering psychotherapeutic outcomes have shown that an attuned therapist and the quality of the therapeutic relationship are the major components of successful treatment. Ferenczi was the first to emphasize the importance of the analyst's loving attitude for the healing process. He introduced the concepts of empathy, emotional aliveness, and availability in the analytic space and made the point that the presence of the analyst is the healing agent, facilitating the reassembling of the personality. Ferenczi's *Clinical Diary* and his early works on trauma as a "confusion of tongues" are still very poignant in the context of abuse. I can also subscribe to his dictum: "Understanding is necessary, in order to employ sympathy in the right place (analysis), in the right way. Without sympathy there is no healing."[35] In today's clinical context, Ferenczi's notion of sympathy has been replaced by compassion, particularly under the influence of Buddhist psychology, combined with a focus on mindfulness.

I would now like to sketch out how the transcendent function operates within the relational field, enabling the transition out of the fossilized structures of earlier thinking and into a new attitude, whereby the opposites are united and a "living third thing" is created, "a living birth that leads to a new level of being, a new situation."[36] I would like to illustrate the processes of transcendence and transformation in terms of the relationship between my patients and me, but also in terms of the numinous dimension of the ego's relationship to the Self and the archetypal principle of dismemberment and re-memberment, destruction and re-creation. The following vignette demonstrates how spiritual transformation can occur at the level of the imagination, and it highlights the importance of being related and open to the unknown and the other if this transformation is to be accomplished effectively.

My patient, whom I will call Vera, had been the victim of incestuous sexual assaults as a child. Early disturbances in maternal affective mirroring led to an attachment disorder and a reduced capacity for mentalization. The frequent devaluing messages of those directly related to her were represented within her personality as an "alien self," so that mockery and self-hatred came to constitute essential parts of her inner world.[37] Her early traumas had deeply damaged both her self-perception and her perception of the world, and she felt anxiously inhibited in the presence of others. She could not evaluate interpersonal situations accurately nor set healthy personal boundaries. When she came to me for therapy, she was suffering from suicidal impulses and increasingly frequent panic and anxiety attacks. She felt developmentally blocked and wanted to escape from the states of paralysis that she had earlier dealt with by drinking, with the purpose of "sending herself away." (When she came for therapy, she had been dry for ten years.)

To her first session Vera brought a small red suitcase. She spoke very little and could not maintain eye contact, but she presented herself through an image that she took out of this little suitcase (figure 12.1). "That's me," she said, handing me a small wooden manikin. It was naked except for a wire structure covered with parchment that was wrapped around the body in the region of the torso (figure 12.2). The naked wooden figure was paired with an empty eggshell-like structure made of papier-mâché, a representation of her shell-like existence (figure 12.3).

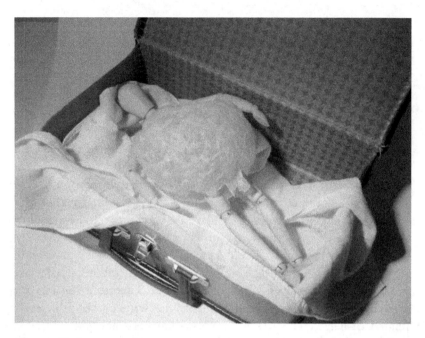

Figure 12.1

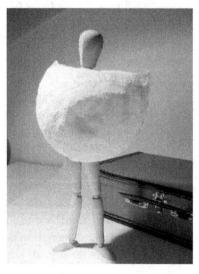

Figure 12.2

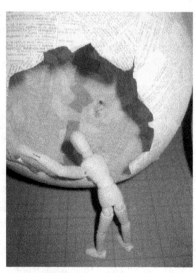

Figure 12.3

Figure 12.4

Our work began with a circumambulation of this shell-like existence, her state of emptiness, of not knowing what was inside the shell, which, for her, was often filled with blackness. We embarked on a search for her identity, her heart space, for who she could be beyond the empty shell, for an answer to the question of whether her existence mattered. During the crucial years of her early development, she was unable to secure a sense of herself as a subject; her abuse had reduced her to being permanently an object. She constructed the empty shell in an attempt to explore her inner life, an endeavor that, of course, put her at considerable risk. To protect herself, she created another figure, of Maria-Sophia, who stood on top of the shell and oversaw her activities like a guardian angel (figure 12.4).[38] I felt that the sacred made itself present in her sculptures and also in the transference, connecting the realms of the divine and the human, the sacred and the profane.

At the next session, she had a fresh batch of objects in her suitcase: a robot, a warrior with a sword, a clown's nose, and a brimstone butterfly in a box, with no indication of their symbolic meaning. She gradually disclosed to me the things of her private world, her "flotsam of life," as she called them. She invented and formed figures and slipped into them as if into clothes, perhaps in hopes of finding herself in them. Each of her objects had its own life. Collectively, they served as guardians of her memories, protecting them from being lost in the world of thoughts. For her, these objects were not simply there—they looked at her, communicated with her through their materiality, provided a reassuring grounding, a connection to reality, albeit a split reality.

I have often wondered whether trauma patients compensate for the lack of introjected good objects, the insufficient internalization of positive relationships, by engaging with material objects, by developing an especially ensouled relationship to matter and to the collective unconscious. For Vera, with her passion for collecting things, this was

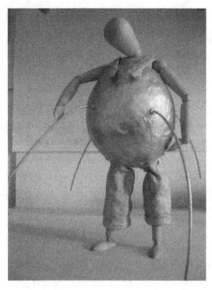

quite obvious. But I remember other trauma patients who developed a striking relationship to things accompanied by a subtle psychic transparency, with no clear separation between subject and object.

Sometimes I got the impression that Vera was a shadow being, floating through a twilight zone, a human *Sputnik* (as she once represented herself) lost in liminal space (figure 12.5). Working with her, I often thought of Bernstein's description of borderland individuals as "thrust into reconnection with transrational reality."[39] Vera was suspended between two apparently irreconcilable opposites and was thus often in a state of extreme tension and uncertainty. She described her condition as being in the midst of a breakdown. She felt as if she were being pulled from both ends, by heaven and hell simultaneously, and was in great fear of being torn apart. Her abysmally deep despair left her no choice but to surrender to whatever was emerging from the unconscious. I was astonished, again and again, by how deeply anchored in her was the knowledge of *enantiodromia*.

Figure 12.5

> When this absolute lostness and abandonment attacks me so deeply, the pain becomes unbearable, and I let myself fall into this unknowability; but then I'm taken up by a decisiveness, an energy that comes from a deep, unfathomable, inscrutable source and gives me back to myself, naked, pure, incorruptible, unassailable, deeply convinced, and aligned.

Her description suggests the presence of a guide, and in my imagination I see Hermes, the guardian of crossroads, who provides compensation by taking care of inner balance and eases the traveler's bewilderment. Vera is a borderland traveler. Liminality is inherent in her way of being, and mythopoetic imagination is her medium. Her conundrum in life has been finding words to express her experiences. Having nobody to share these experiences with had made her question her sanity. Though she functioned normally in her daily activities, she felt an irresistible inner drive to create sculptures to represent her threshold state, betwixt and between. It was as if a creative force had taken over that did not originate in the ego.

Analysis became vitally important to her. We worked intensely with the symbolic realm, probing the unknown. Her healing depended crucially on giving the symbolic its space, tending to it, inviting it in. Only when her internal images were allowed to take concrete shape in external three-dimensional space was she able to access the full emotional range of her traumatic experiences, which until then had been merely faint, fleeting memories. When she was working on her sculptures and her tears began to flow, she sometimes could not understand what was going on inside her. She could not reflect on her symbolic creations until she had brought them into our therapy sessions. As we considered them together, thinking and feeling came together for the first time, and she could feel herself as "whole" again. She said: "By your acceptance of the objects I bring in, your trusting reception of these objects, it seems as if I were led right away to the true parts of myself, so that I can see these parts and name them." She not only gained insights into her own complex landscape and the interconnectedness of her diverse emotions, thought patterns, and affective eruptions, but she also experienced a new kind of mutuality and connection with the people in her environment.

In the course of therapy, Vera's empty shell was gradually laid aside as a place no longer needed. With a hint of surprise, she remarked: "Hard shells soften into an elastic membrane, a thin layer of skin." Nevertheless, the process of letting go of her old persona and becoming something new was deeply traumatic. She felt herself suddenly defenseless and lost without her familiar protective shell: "What if this unknown interiority is just emptiness, after all—a nothing?" Then hope came back, and Vera talked about a fluid "faith" that saved her from floating in ungrounded lostness. She dared to desire again and began to talk, with great excitement, about the possibility of the impossible: "With a grand gesture to wipe away all doubt from the sky of questions; in this moment I was both 'me' and 'everything.'"

Mutuality and resonance were important factors in the process of bringing eros into the therapeutic process and nurturing Vera's growing capacity for opening her heart. In one of our sessions, Vera, who had started shivering and fretting, looked at me wide-eyed when I handed her a blanket. She experienced my gesture as an act of protection that saved the fragments of her soul from getting lost. I grieved with her as she spoke of her longing to become a "real person" and wept from the darkest depths of her soul. After this quantum leap in trust and relatedness, after summoning up the courage to live and to venture out on the still-frozen lake of life, after experiencing being seen and accepted at the deepest level, Vera began the descent, the destruction of all the structures that were holding her together up to that point, a *nigredo* state of *putrefactio.*

She dreamed that she had a baby's bloody corpse in her pocket, that she was the baby's murderer, and that she had secretly written a confession but was afraid of being found out. As the dream progressed, she began to have serious doubts about whether the corpse was that of a baby or a man. After such death dreams, she would wake up with an uncanny feeling, as if someone—a threatening presence—were in the room, and she would have to make sure that no one was hiding in the closet or under the bed. She began an intense confrontation with her shadow world. She would watch her physical shadow as it silently accompanied her. She invested it with a physical reality: she saw it as a life-sized figure that

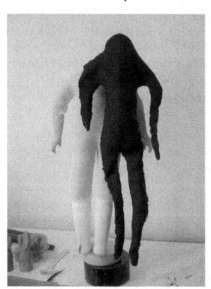

Figure 12.6

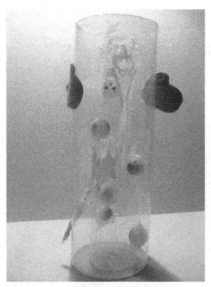

Figure 12.7

"crouched" behind her, persecuting her (figure 12.6).

Vera's entry into the shadowland drew painful memories out of the dark forgotten past: basement scenes of abuse, being caught in the lecherous gaze of her abuser, grasping hands reaching for her. She commented to me: "The flesh was taken away. The bones were left to me and still carry me through my life. I am still only a fleshless shell, a skeleton that tries desperately to claw its way out of the constricting shell" (figure 12.7).

During this dark period in the therapy, impelled by an inner force, she went into the basement, tore off a doll's arms and legs, cut them into pieces, and shattered its head with a hammer (figure 12.8). To destroy and tear apart—that was her revenge, and her liberation. And when she saw the desolation of the fragments, which once constituted a whole, she wept. She remembered her impotent rage at her own desolation, and how she hit herself until her arms were numb from the pain. And then it occurred to her that by tearing apart and cutting into pieces she was releasing her body from the pain, giving it the ability to move again, freeing it from its long captivity. Then she got a thread and, with care and tenderness, hardly believing what she was doing, she strung the dismembered parts together. In doing so, she heard the unloved parts crying out that they wanted to be held together once more.

Vera explained that she had to descend into this reenactment of cruelty and become a destroyer herself in order to grasp the reality of the destruction by establishing contact with it, observing it, feeling it, experiencing it as real. She needed first to be certain about how it happened through participating in the falling apart of these fragments. Then, by looking and touching lovingly, and by caringly stringing the pieces together, she would be able to nurture them into wholeness again.

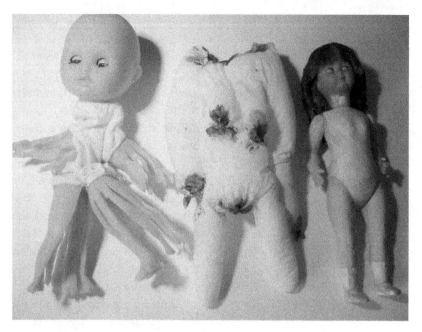

Figure 12.8

She brought the little crippled, mended doll to the next session in the red suitcase and laid it in my lap, very gently, so that I could look at it and accept it. This intimacy with objects, this manner of bringing and showing herself to me, this intentional way of preserving and presenting past events, constituted healing for her broken, devalued soul. After this session, she composed the following statement:

> The interplay of terror and comfort is the only way my suffering-howling-empty animal can calm itself. In a horrible birth, in mortal combat, in being helplessly, abysmally beaten up, it is freed, released into existence.

Now, for the first time, she could transform her self-destructive impulse of hate into empathic self-care and rescue her wounded, frightened, lonely inner child from the terrifying scenes in the basement and the attic—lift her up, warm her, speak to her, and assure her of protection. A great energy emanated from the inner images produced by her soul's imaginal faculty. These images enabled her to see what her psyche needed in order to overcome her state of dissociation. They not only reflected her original traumas but also showed her what she could become.

Later, a set of numinous images emerged from her psyche with such emotional intensity that words could not convey her inner experience. Again, she needed to translate her sensuous experiences into matter and form. She created the "Fur Madonna" with its blue velvet Mary cloak.[40] She sewed a rosary around the cloak and laid the mended doll, now swaddled, in the Madonna's arms like a wounded Baby Jesus.[41] In her archetypal transference, I became her Fur Madonna, lovingly embracing and protecting her. When she thus projected the archetype of the Self onto me, the relational field became charged with numinosity. The emerging archetype of the Madonna became a transpersonal container that restored her wounded sense of self. I agree with Hogenson that "transformation and symbol are intimately connected" and that a reductive interpretation of symbol formation along the lines of object relations theory (as compensatory to maternal deprivation) is inadequate and unable to explain how the emergence of an archetypal symbol such as that of the Blessed Virgin Mary "is able to transform the psyche and the behavior of the analysand."[42]

In our work together on the themes of suffering, sacrifice, abandonment, cruelty, redemption, and transcendence, Vera went through a profound experience. In the process, the symbol of the cross emerged, and she developed the notion of taking Christ off the cross, because she could not bear to see him stretched out in rigid suspension. His transfixed pose mirrored her own unbearable rigidity. From the time she was old enough to attend church with her mother as a child, she had found the practice of crucifixion incomprehensible and was still tormented by it. She bought a large crucifix at a thrift store, detached the Christ figure, sawed it into many small pieces, then bored a hole through each piece, and strung the pieces together to form a movable whole (figures 12.9 to 12.12).

She told me that before she cut up the Christ figure, as it lay on the sheet of white paper in front of her, she felt an indescribable moment of intimate identification with the dead Jesus, almost like déjà vu. She said softly:

> Yet we were very afraid of what had to happen. I gazed on him
> and cried, full of pain. With trembling trust and deep awe, and

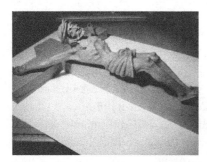

Figure 12.9

Figure 12.10

Figure 12.11

Figure 12.12

> in complete solitude, I sawed him in pieces and bound him
> together again. For two long nights, far from other people,
> devoted, contemplative, and confident, I worked away at this
> handicraft. What consternation overwhelms me, finally, when
> the movable wooden parts, full of life, are lying in my hands!
> (figure 12.13)

Then, referring to this other, "living" Jesus, she said, "Now at last
he's saved. Now he can finally embrace; he has overcome the cross."
This was Vera's way of wrestling with the archetypal energies that were
released by her encounter with the shadow. I felt that the deep work
she engaged in was a kind of active imagination, bringing her directly
into contact with the spiritual powers of her psyche and showing that
wholeness, self-knowledge, and the expansion of consciousness are
conditional upon prior discrimination.

I experienced the heart of our work as an archetypal energy in the
relational field that seized us both and opened a potential space richly
filled with images, metaphors, and symbols. This space felt very dense,

Figure 12.13

sometimes even vibrating. In the shared imaginal realm, similar images erupted spontaneously in both of us. As we processed these images together, they assisted us in developing a reflective attitude. I remember one session in which she tried to explain why, in states of great emotional abandonment, she sometimes felt an uncontrollable need to call and hear my voice. Then, I had only to speak a single sentence, and she could calm herself. As she spoke, I found myself remembering the words of the Roman Catholic liturgy: "Lord, I am not worthy, . . . but only say the word, and my soul shall be healed." Before I could complete the thought, she quoted these very words, though not without some embarrassment at transferring this numinous healing faith onto me.

In my work with her, I experienced the transcendent function as a "*transitus* to the Self."[43] I felt that a strong kinship libido connected us. We shared many moments of synchronistic, intense, empathic attunement originating in the resonant field.[44] Of course, I also experienced vicarious trauma in my work with Vera, when I came into contact with what Schwartz-Salant has called the "mad parts of sane people," sharing her despair, and worrying about her suicidal fantasies.[45] Jung expanded on this phenomenon when he wrote:

> The doctor, by voluntarily and consciously taking over the psychic sufferings of the patient, exposes himself to the overpowering contents of the unconscious and hence also to their inductive action. . . . Doctor and patient thus find themselves in a relationship founded on mutual unconsciousness.[46]

Jung went on to say: "the psychotherapist . . . should clearly understand that psychic infections . . . are . . . the predestined concomitants of his work, . . . and this provides the most favourable basis for treatment."[47]

In keeping with Jung's observation, an emotional contagion nurtured my work with Vera, enabling her previously closed system to open up to the archetypal world in a wholesome way.

It was evident that the transformative process by which the personality fragmented by trauma becomes gradually integrated is both relational and numinous. Aside from her relationship with me as her analyst, Vera experienced a growing relationship to her spirit, the part not damaged by trauma. From this true core, by means of the transcendent function, there emerged a wealth of transformative archetypal symbols that facilitated healing.

The transcendent function was similarly operative in my work with Kathy, whom I mentioned in chapter 11. My encounter with Kathy was marked from the beginning with themes of traumatic attachment (abandonment, abuse, war, persecution, loss of home and country). She insisted that without me as her analyst she would get nowhere, that if any healing was to take place, it had to occur in the presence of another person. It was as if the transcendent function was activated by this intense dependency, and some kind of interpenetration was fostered between her and me. Jung likened the patient's "desperate clinging" to the therapist to "the tentacles of an octopus."[48] For Kathy, this clinging was necessary for her survival. I had to bear it so that she could feel that she was being carried by me.

In my work with Kathy, I often thought about Jung's statement that "the analyst has the character of an indispensable figure absolutely necessary for life."[49] Jung explained that in this idealizing transference is contained an extremely valid and important demand that we need to respect, not disappoint. This insight guided me as we worked through Kathy's idealization phase. This was followed by an extremely aggressive, raging, negative transference, which often pushed me to the limit. Kathy's tendency to alternate between idealizing and demonizing me—part of the dynamics of the transcendent function—was made more bearable by my conviction that the passion of violent contrary emotions in the intersubjective field is fundamental to transference and an essential condition for transformation. The process of building trust and the rocky journey through rage—Kali's cremation grounds were always present when she talked about dwelling in a land of garbage—were terrifically long and painful for us both. But the transcendent function set in motion a maturation process that gave a whole new dimension of depth to Kathy's relationship to herself and the world.

Often, we both got stuck in a *nigredo* state, in which nothing seemed to move; but we persisted in our work, knowing that if we did, the blockage would eventually open up. As Schwartz-Salant observes:

> When partners know and experience each other through chaos and destructiveness as well as through beauty and growth, they create a container which encourages and supports the process of individuation and which becomes each person's most sacred possession.[50]

A reliable container emerged for Kathy over the many years of our work together, as a result of my ongoing, unconditional, trustworthy presence coupled with my firmness in confronting her. Psychic containers are expandable, thus allowing for more than just corrective emotional experiences. Kathy and I both consciously made ourselves available to the so-called third area, and we were markedly affected by it. I found it helpful to direct my attention closely not only to verbally expressed content but also to the constellated field and to my own emerging fantasies and bodily reactions, which I made fruitful for our therapeutic work through symbolization and mirroring. It was not always easy to find and maintain the right balance between healthy engagement and nonintrusive observation. Over long stretches in my work with Kathy I was not allowed to say anything, but I had to remain fully aware and present, a silent, attentive witness, while she sat on the floor and enacted rituals using the objects in my office or engaged in imaginary dialogues with disowned parts of herself.

I learned a great deal from working with Kathy, helped in my understanding especially by the work of Nathan Field.[51] Although Kathy and I walked through the darkness of "mutual unconsciousness," as Jung called it, I also performed a holding function, which gave her a sense of security such as she had never experienced before on account of her sequential traumas. The work was extremely demanding, because the relational field was populated by split-off affects, overwhelming rage, devaluations, hatred, and all the aspects of herself that she had disowned, all of which I had to carry. My task was to detoxify this toxic material within my own system and give it back to her in a purified form for reintegration. During this period, I was thankful for supervisory guidance. I appreciated the wisdom of Judith Herman's advice that a therapist should never work alone with trauma patients but seek ongoing support in understanding and containing countertransference reactions. Through this mutual labor of love, it became possible for Kathy to relinquish old patterns and ways of being, form a living relationship to the unconscious, achieve greater authenticity, and acquire the capacity to let others in.

My work with Vera, Kathy, and my other trauma patients supports Miller's assertion (based on Corbett's work) that "the transcendent function operates as much through the analytic relationship as it does intrapsychically."[52] As Miller notes, the transference that occurs within the therapeutic relationship is the means by which the transcendent function is activated, and I believe love operates at the core of this transference. The process of transcendence as love's labor of transformation within the container of the therapeutic relationship is amplified vividly in the following summation written by Paula, another patient of mine, after seven years of arduous therapeutic work:

> I think love turns up the ground, pulls out the weeds, and prepares the bed for planting, so that the transformation can happen. It is a labor that unites, as we work together to turn and loosen the Alma Mater, or Mother Earth, the ground on which the soul grows. Love in this sense also has an aspect of being side-by-side in a protective pairing. Someone does the labor with me, someone who cares about, about my innermost being, who gives me courage when the shit wells up to the surface, who gets her hands dirty along with me and stays with me, even when the whole place is full of thorn bushes and crawling with vermin.
>
> But this love needs a special setting, for it is decisively important how and where we do our shared farming . . . . It is crucial that these activities take place on a kind of island, a time-island in daily life. The therapeutic setting can become the "Promised Land" when things get tough. You don't need a whole archipelago of such islands, but only as many as are necessary to let you carry on with the rest of life and let your soul breathe. The owner of the soul has complete authority on this island; she owns the prepared cultivated land. Hers is the dung that fertilizes the young plants. . . .
>
> A time will come when the owner of the soul begins to wander around this island, and to cultivate her other properties on the

mainland, which she begins to bring into relationship and connection with the island. She will ponder what is different about this love, why it transforms so much. She will try to make the island last eternally, because she is so happy to have found, and to possess, an easily surveyable island for two. She will be moved by the realization that she has succeeded in sharing the island, while yet having it for herself. At some point she will try to dig out the first seedlings from the island and put them in her handbag, to transplant them somewhere else. If they flourish, she will be able to leave the island, expressing her thanks, and go her own way with a pocket full of seeds and plants and the certainty that, there on the island, in secrecy, a small, enormous miracle has occurred, which she herself caused to grow.

Working through trauma in the loving presence of a therapist gives patients the courage to surrender unfruitful ground, win back lost territories, and achieve greater freedom in shaping their existence, mastering their destiny, and accepting life as it is.

NOTES

[1] Lionel Corbett, *The Religious Function of the Psyche* (London: Routledge, 1996), p. 111.

[2] Lyn Cowan, *Tracking the White Rabbit: A Subversive View of Modern Culture* (Hove, UK: Brunner-Routledge, 2002), p. 89.

[3] Sylvia Brinton Perera, *Descent to the Goddess: A Way of Initiation for Women* (Toronto: Inner City Books, 1981), p. 15.

[4] Jung, *MDR*, p. 4.

[5] Stanton Marlan, *The Black Sun: The Alchemy and Art of Darkness* (College Station, TX: Texas A&M University Press, 2005), p. 76.

[6] Robert Ohotto, *Transforming Fate into Destiny: A New Dialogue with Your Soul* (Carlsbad, CA: Hay House, 2008).

[7] Jung, *CW* 8, § 245.

[8] See Greg Mogenson, *A Most Accursed Religion: When a Trauma Becomes God* (Putnam, CT: Spring Publications, 2005), pp. 141–168, especially pp. 160–161.

[9] Shakespeare, *Hamlet*, act 3, scene 1, line 58.

[10] See Marie-Louise von Franz, *The Problem of the* Puer Aeternus, 3rd ed. (Toronto: Inner City Books, 2000), p. 100.

[11] See Verena Kast, *Mann und Frau im Märchen: Eine psychologische Deutung* (Olten and Frieburg: Walter Verlag, 1983), p. 36.

[12] The Brothers Grimm, "Thousandfurs," in *Grimm's Complete Fairy Tales* (San Diego, CA: Canterbury Classics, 2011), pp. 251–255. This tale appears under other titles, such as "The Princess in Disguise" and "Cat-skin."

[13] *Ibid.*, pp. 112–116.

[14] Marie-Louise von Franz, *The Feminine in Fairy Tales*, rev. ed. (Boston: Shambhala Publications, 1993), pp. 81–107.

[15] Sonoko Toyoda, *Memories of Our Lost Hands: Searching for Feminine Spirituality and Creativity* (College Station, TX: Texas A&M University Press, 2006), p. 30; emphasis added.

[16] See Jef Dehing, "The Transcendent Function: A Critical Re-evaluation," *Journal of Analytical Psychology* 38, no. 3 (1993): 221–235. For an example of recent critique of the concept of transcendent function, see Alison Clark, "'Fascination,' 'Contagion,' and Naming What We Do: Rethinking the Transcendent Function," *Journal of Analytical Psychology* 55, no. 5 (2010): 636–649.

[17] Jung, *CW* 8, § 131.

[18] Polly Young-Eisendrath, "Psychotherapy as Ordinary Transcendence: The Unspeakable and the Unspoken," in *The Psychology of Mature Spirituality: Integrity, Wisdom, Transcendence*, ed. Polly Young-Eisendrath and Melvin E. Miller (London: Routledge, 2000), pp. 105–114.

[19] D. W. Winnicott, *Playing and Reality* (1971; reprinted: London: Routledge Classics, 2005), p. 55ff.

[20] Jeffrey C. Miller, *The Transcendent Function: Jung's Model of Psychological Growth through Dialogue with the Unconscious* (Albany: State University of New York Press, 2004), p. 99.

[21] Muny Sothara and Judith Strasser, *I Witness: Testimonies by Survivors of the Khmer Rouge*, trans. K. Tongngy and S. Sokhalay, TPO (Phnom Penh, Cambodia: JSRC Printing House, 2011), n.p.

[22] Marie-Louise von Franz, *Projection and Re-collection in Jungian Psychology: Reflections of the Soul*, trans. William H. Kennedy (Chicago: Open Court Publishing, 1980), p. 58; *Psychotherapy* (Boston: Shambhala Publications, 1993), p. 245.

[23] Nathan Schwartz-Salant, *The Borderline Personality: Vision and Healing* (Wilmette, IL: Chiron Publications, 1989), p. 43.

[24] Lionel Corbett, *The Sacred Cauldron: Psychotherapy as a Spiritual Practice* (Wilmette, IL: Chiron Publications, 2011).

[25] Jalal al-Din Rumi, *The Essential Rumi,* trans. Coleman Barks with John Moyne, A. J. Arberry, and Reynold Nicholson (New York: HarperCollins, 2004), p. 36.

[26] See Rupert Sheldrake, *Morphic Resonance: The Nature of Formative Causation* (Rochester, VT: Park Street Press, 2009; and L. R. Milgrom, "Conspicuous by Its Absence: The Memory of Water, Macro-Entanglement, and the Possibility of Homeopathy," *Homeopathy* 96, no. 3 (2007): 209–219; and "Towards a New Model of the Homeopathic Process Based on Quantum Field Theory," *Forschende Komplementärmedizin (Research in Complementary Medicine)* 13, no. 3 (2006): 174–183.

[27] Marie-Louise von Franz, *On Divination and Synchronicity: The Psychology of Meaningful Chance* (Toronto: Inner City Books, 1980), p. 61; see also, pp. 8, 63–66, 72, 74–76, 96, 109.

[28] See Schwartz-Salant, *Borderline Personality*, and also Nathan Schwartz-Salant, *The Mystery of Human Relationship: Alchemy and the Transformation of the Self* (London: Routledge, 1998); Michael Conforti, *Field, Form, and Fate: Patterns in Mind, Nature, and Psyche* (New Orleans: Spring Journal Books, 1999); Murray Stein, ed., *The Interactive Field in Analysis,* vol. 1 (Wilmette, IL: Chiron Publications, 1995); Victor Mansfield and J. Marvin Spiegelman, "On the Physics and Psychology of the Transference as an Interactive Field," *Journal of Analytical Psychology* 41, no. 2 (1996): 179–202; A. David Hill, "Souls' Body: An Imaginal Re-viewing of Morphic Fields and Morphic Resonance" (PhD diss., Pacifica Graduate Institute, Carpinteria, CA., 1996); and Valerie Hinard, "Hidden Dilemmas in the Interactive Field" (Master's thesis, Pacifica Graduate Institute, Carpinteria, CA., 1996).

[29] Robert D. Stolorow, Bernard Brandchaft, and George E. Atwood, *Psychoanalytic Treatment: An Intersubjective Approach* (Hillsdale, NJ: Analytic Press, 1987).

[30] Nathan Schwartz-Salant, "On the Interactive Field as the Analytic Object," in *The Interactive Field in Analysis*, vol. 1, ed. Murray Stein (Wilmette, IL: Chiron Publications, 1995), pp. 1–36.

[31] D. W. Winnicott, *Playing and Reality* (London: Tavistock, 1971), p. 55ff.

[32] Thomas H. Ogden, *Subjects of Analysis* (Lanham, MD: Rowman and Littlefield, 1994).

[33] Jung, *CW* 16, §§ 163 and 358; Emmanuel Levinas, *Outside the Subject*, trans. Michael B. Smith (1987; reprinted: Stanford, CA: Stanford University Press, 1993), pp. 25–32.

[34] "If the doors of perception were cleansed every thing would appear to man as it is, infinite."—William Blake, *The Marriage of Heaven and Hell: A Facsimile in Full Color* (1794), plate 14 (New York: Dover Publications, 1994), p. 36.

[35] Sándor Ferenczi, *The Clinical Diary of Sándor Ferenczi*, ed. J. Dupont, trans. Michael Balint and Nicola Zarday Jackson (Cambridge, MA: Harvard University Press, 1995), p. 200.

[36] Jung, *CW* 8, § 189.

[37] See Anthony Bateman and Peter Fonagy, *Psychotherapy for Borderline Personality Disorder: Mentalization-Based Treatment* (Oxford, UK: Oxford University Press, 2004), pp. 97–103.

[38] For the guardian angel motif in relation to trauma, see Donald Kalsched, "Trauma and Daimonic Reality in Ferenczi's Later Work," *Journal of Analytical Psychology* 48, no. 4 (2003): 479–480, 482, 485. See also Ferenczi, *Clinical Diary*, pp. 9, 105.

[39] Jerome S. Bernstein, *Living in the Borderland: The Evolution of Consciousness and the Challenge of Healing Trauma* (Hove, UK: Routledge, 2005), p. 84; see also pp. 94, 97, 168.

[40] Vera's figure of the Fur Madonna bears a remarkable resemblance to the figure of the Blessed Mother described by Kalsched in discussing the case of one of his patients, a young female incest survivor who was molested by her father every Sunday in the basement of their home. This patient said that while she was being sexually assaulted, she "was in the arms of the Blessed Mother" (Kalsched, "Trauma and Daimonic Reality," p. 479). Kalsched notes that the archetypal Blessed Mother figure parallels Ferenczi's concept of Orpha, a notion Ferenczi conceived of in analyzing the case of one of his female patients, whom he called R. N., who suffered sexual abuse from a very early age (p. 480). For details of the case and a discussion of Orpha, see Ferenczi, *Clinical Diary*, pp. 8–10, 121, and elsewhere.

[41] The German word that Vera used for "Baby Jesus" is *Fatschenkind*, a word denoting a devotional image, common in South Bavaria and

Austria, of the Baby Jesus wrapped tightly in swaddling bands, in the manner of a Native American papoose.

⁴² George Hogenson, "Archetypes: Emergence and the Psyche's Deep Structure," in *Analytical Psychology: Contemporary Perspectives in Jungian Analysis*, ed. Joseph Cambray and Linda Carter (Hove, UK: Brunner-Routledge, 2004), pp. 50–51, 53.

⁴³ C. G. Jung, letter to Victor White dated April 10, 1954, *C. G. Jung Letters, Vol. 2: 1951–1961*, ed. Gerhard Adler and Aniela Jaffé, trans. R. F. C. Hull (Princeton, NJ: Princeton University Press, 1976), p. 168.

⁴⁴ See Joseph Cambray, *Synchronicity: Nature and Psyche in an Interconnected Universe* (College Station, TX: Texas A&M University Press, 2009), p. 88.

⁴⁵ Schwartz-Salant, *Mystery of Human Relationship*, p. vii (and throughout).

⁴⁶ Jung, *CW* 16, § 364.

⁴⁷ Jung, *CW* 16, § 365.

⁴⁸ Jung, *CW* 16, § 371.

⁴⁹ Jung, *CW* 8, § 146.

⁵⁰ Schwartz-Salant, *Mystery of Human Relationship*, p. 212.

⁵¹ Nathan Field, "Projective Identification: Mechanism or Mystery?" *Journal of Analytical Psychology* 36, no. 1 (1991): 93–109. See also Nathan Field, "The Therapeutic Function of Altered States," *Journal of Analytical Psychology* 37, no. 2 (1992): 211–234.

⁵² Miller, *The Transcendent Function*, p. 195.

CHAPTER THIRTEEN

TRAUMA AND THE BODY: PORTAL TO THE SOURCE

T raumatic experiences affect the body as much as they affect the mind and the soul.[1] Since the body is the portal to the source and the existential ground of the self, trauma cannot be transcended without restoring the body and reestablishing the connection to the instinctual life.[2] As Jung wrote, "the source is underground and therefore the way leads underneath . . . . These depths constitute the natural history of man, his causal link with the world of instinct."[3]

Since trauma ruptures the relationship between matter and consciousness, treatment of trauma requires a holistic approach. The essential work of therapy starts with the body. Consciousness is often unable to process the energy overload precipitated by trauma. And yet, paradoxically, the mind has the capacity to reverse the effects of trauma on the body. Likewise, the physiological processes in the body, and especially in the brain, can control affective states.[4]

Current research in neuroscience is beginning to uncover the brain processes involved in affective states and thinking. Neurobiological findings increasingly call into question the mind-body dualism of Descartes and support the view that thinking and feeling are inextricably bound up with the body. For example, the work of Antonio Damasio and Joseph LeDoux deals with the "emotional brain," which operates independently of and prior to consciousness.[5] Damasio's findings confirm the claim of attachment theory that the development of structures in the brain associated with affect regulation and the capacity to relate emotionally to others is dependent on the kinds of attachments an individual forms in infancy with its caregivers. In trauma therapy, the therapist provides the caring figure to whom the patient can form an attachment in the process of developing the brain structures needed for regulating his or her overwhelming affects.

The work of other researchers, such as Gerald Hüther, focuses on providing a neurobiological explanation for embodiment as well as on the neurological impact of anxiety and stress on the body.[6] Along similar lines, Daniel Siegel conceives of the human mind as "a relational and embodied process that regulates the flow of energy and information."[7] He places great emphasis on the various steps that create secure attachment in therapy, especially in the context of trauma: resonant communication; reflection on thoughts, beliefs, and feelings; the rupture-and-repair cycle; soothing comfort and compassion; and developing a coherent narrative.

Other writers, too, have explored the broad implications of neurobiological findings for clinical work with trauma. They propose the idea of a body-based bridge to the unconscious and of the unconscious itself as being rooted in the body. For example, Allan Schore's studies elucidate the body's connection to the brain processes that are involved in moving the traumatized person out of systemic deadlock by regulating bodily and emotional states.[8] Schore notes in particular that the right hemisphere of the brain is particularly susceptible to attachment transactions in early infancy and is of paramount importance in the early development of the "emotional and corporeal self" or what he elsewhere calls "the implicit self."[9] Similarly, van der Kolk focuses on the impact of trauma on thinking, feeling, and bodily sensations.[10] His work confirms my long-standing experience that the talking cure alone is insufficient when working with severely traumatized patients. His clinical approach represents a paradigm shift in the treatment of trauma, but it has also come under criticism from mainstream theorists for its use of bottom-up, somatic methods such as eye movement desensitization and reprocessing (EMDR) and yoga.[11]

In fact, body-oriented therapeutic practices use both bottom-up (body to mind) and top-down (mind to body) methods, based on a neurobiological understanding of trauma physiology, to modulate hyperstress, to avoid "kindling," and to quench hyperarousal.[12] Siegel explains top-down processing as "the way that our memories, beliefs, and emotions shape our 'bottom-up' direct sensation of experience."[13] Top-down approaches use cognition to manage disruptive emotions; they are involved in high-level executive functioning and are mostly used in talk therapy. However, top-down processing does not reveal the inner states of the body. The sensorimotor approach of practitioners such as Pat Ogden and colleagues works from the bottom up and focuses directly on the primitive, involuntary functions of the brain, which underlie traumatic and posttraumatic responses such as hyperarousal and movement inhibition.[14] For trauma therapy to be effective, top-down and bottom-up approaches need to be integrated in order to balance arousal, sensations, and emotions with insight and understanding.

Analytical psychology, and in particular Jungian analysts in Britain such as Margaret Wilkinson and Jean Knox, have incorporated the findings of recent neuroscientific research into their understanding of psychic dynamics and have begun to explore the clinical implications of the mind-brain relationship.[15] Body-oriented psychotherapy is now being used increasingly in treating and rehabilitating torture survivors.[16] Treatment primarily consists of attempts to reduce pain, manage anxiety, process emotions, and improve body feeling by encouraging in the patient a more differentiated perception of the body. Various techniques are used to integrate split-off body parts and establish clear body boundaries. Safety, stabilization, and anchoring of body resources are fundamental therapeutic goals.

The work of Peter Levine has shown that traumatic symptoms do not arise primarily from the triggering event itself but "from the frozen residue of energy that has not been resolved and discharged; this residue remains trapped in the nervous system where it can wreak havoc on our bodies."[17] His healing technique—somatic experiencing—seeks to reconnect soul and body by reintegrating split-off or fragmented parts of the essential self through a gradual process of thawing, which releases frozen energy from its trauma-serving tasks.[18]

Embodiment is central to who we are, for body and psyche are, according to Jung, very probably "two different aspects of one and the same thing."[19] He wrote: "The mysterious truth is that the spirit is the life of the body seen from within, and the body the outward manifestation of spirit—the two being really one."[20] Thus, being fully embodied becomes a fundamental goal of trauma therapy; it means being truly at one with our inner nature, alive and grounded in reality.

Body and Consciousness

Neuroscientific research reveals that the brain and its neural pathways can actually be structured and reorganized by focused attention. This discovery confirms the insight of the ancient Eastern traditions that by paying attention to our thoughts (in effect differentiating primary sensory experiences from secondary cognitive processing) we can purify our mind and detach ourselves from overwhelming emotions.

Eastern spiritual traditions have long emphasized that bodily well-being is of the utmost importance for the development of consciousness and for body-centered mindfulness. Just as there can be no ascent without a descent, so also being grounded in the body is a prerequisite for spiritual attainment. Michael von Brück emphasizes in his Zen *sesshins* that Zen is body. For him, yoga exercises, with their focus on breath control, are an integral part of zazen, because breathing is the cornerstone of meditation, which in turn centers the practitioner both physically and spiritually.[21]

Conscious breathing is the key to deeper self-knowledge and self-healing.[22] Biologically, measured inhaling arouses the sympathetic nervous system and calm exhaling activates the parasympathetic nervous system. Measured breathing can bring balance to a chaotic, traumatized physiological system by allowing negative energies to flow out and positive energies to flow in. Breathing awareness is extremely important in working with traumatized states, for breath is a life force—like *prana,* the life energy that links psyche and soma. Practices such as qigong (or chi kung) and tai chi involve focusing attention on breathing and movement through an exchange of energy. Practitioners observe their breath coming and going and thereby become mindful of subtle changes in the patterns of their breathing. This awareness has a calming effect on both body and mind.

My Jungian colleague Bruno Rhyner, who works with trauma patients, uses mindful breathing routinely in his work. He says: "Mindful breathing is a must when working with patients who have feelings of anxiety or panic. It can cut depressive circles and is a preparatory step to introducing any method of relaxation and EMDR in trauma therapy" (personal communication, January 23, 2013). Controlled breathing helps the patient to become anchored in the here and now instead of being stuck in the then and there of the trauma. It reestablishes a sense of present time. Body awareness furthers an anchoring in the here and now, thereby distancing the patient from the painful, traumatic past and equipping him or her to embrace life in the present moment.

Conscious breathing is a powerful tool of transformation through which we can assess our present emotional state, bring it under conscious control, and possibly trigger early body memories that were previously inaccessible. According to Diana Zimberoff and David Hartman, the benefits of breath work include:

> managing pain and physical healing; balancing the left and right hemispheres of the brain; retraining your nervous system to tolerate higher charges of energy; balancing the sympathetic and parasympathetic nervous systems of the body; getting past resistance; accessing deeply unconscious psychical material . . . ; resolving early trauma; and enhancing the experience of deep spiritual connection.[23]

These benefits notwithstanding, a word of warning is in order: breath work can disarm psychological defenses, so it is important, when using it in trauma therapy, to monitor closely the changes that are taking place in the patient and to guide him or her proactively in the process of soul retrieval.

Mindful awareness of the body brings nonjudgmental conscious attention to the now. It promotes spaciousness of mind, bypassing habitual conditioned responses and creating a more stable container for painful encroaching emotions. For clarity of mind and expanded

awareness, one must be unreservedly receptive to whatever sensations
might arise. This involves registering whether the sensations are pleasant
or unpleasant, sensing even the slightest tension in any parts of the
body, and letting go of everything that distracts one's attention from
just being there.

Reconnecting with the traumatized body can open the way to a
different level of consciousness and spiritual awareness. In process
therapy, which is based on Arnold Mindell's process-oriented
psychology, working with trauma involves focusing primarily on bodily
symptoms and their symbolic meaning through body-based
amplification. Mindell works symbolically with the symptoms of
trauma in the same way that he does with dreams, using his notion of
the "dreambody."[24] Somatization is a predominant feature of
traumatized individuals. Accordingly, reading bodily symptoms as a
symbolic expression of a rupture in the psyche-body unity can assist
in rebuilding the bridge between the ego and the Self. In gestalt therapy
workshops with Erving and Miriam Polster, I learned to sharpen my
awareness of and sensitivity to the language of the body in order to
help my trauma patients reestablish contact with the alienated parts
of their body.[25] I have learned to pay close attention to what the body
reveals about the depth of the affliction, the abode of nothingness, and
the terror of groundlessness.

It is important to keep in mind that our senses are the carriers of
consciousness and that physical sensation is the basis of consciousness
arising from the body. The primacy of the senses makes touch
indispensable to healthy attachment in infancy. Absence of touch and
inadequate nurturing body contact in childhood can have a detrimental
effect on ego formation and the emergence of a sense of self. Indeed,
without touch there can be no sense of self, for touch demarcates where
self ends and other begins, thereby grounding the individual in the
human world of relatedness.

One of my patients was a fifty-five-year-old man who felt like a
nobody, in both the literal and the symbolic sense of the word. Feeling
like a nobody reflects the agony of a deep psychic and physical
estrangement from the body and the loss of the sense of self-worth.
This man's lack of embodiment was the result of deprivation of his
mother's touch during infancy. His mother had read that touching the

infant might cause premature sexualization of the child and should be avoided. Consequently, she had withheld the soothing, nurturing maternal touch along with the loving maternal gaze. This was the unfortunate fallout of her own unprocessed experience of boundary violation in the form of sexual abuse by her father.

This man developed core anxieties and dysfunctional attachment patterns growing out of a very unstable sense of self. He could never truly inhabit his body and often suffered from feelings of derealization. "I am not incarnated," he would say years later, with an agonizing sense of alienation from his vital life source. His many years of psychoanalysis had only intensified the split between body and soul. A growing awareness of his instinctual side and a yearning to reconnect with it, a yearning he attempted to satisfy through compulsive masturbation and sexual acting out, led him ultimately to yoga. This embodied practice tended to the needs of his split-off body and gave him access to his life energy, which had been dormant and inaccessible throughout his life.

The belief in the healing power of touch has a long tradition, from the Bible in the West (Jesus is said to have performed many of his miracles of healing through touch) to the Eastern practice of *shaktipat*, the transmission of energy from one person to another, to the contemporary therapeutic use of healing touch. Jungian analyst Anita Greene argues for integrating the reading of the symbolic language of the body and the use of touch as a therapeutic tool into analytic practice, although touching of any sort in analysis is still highly controversial and is strongly discouraged.[26] Touch can be either beneficial or harmful, as is well known from the number of abuse cases associated with psychotherapy; nevertheless, I consider touch, when used ethically, to be an important healing force for trauma survivors. In some cases, when a patient of mine is ready to engage with the body, I refer him or her to Nel Houtman, a body therapist I respect highly, who is also a teacher of Vipassana meditation.

She told me:

> *I remember, as if it happened yesterday, the first encounter with Professor Graf Dürckheim. I was fifteen years old and severely traumatized from several accidents and suffering from a puberty crisis.*

*As I met him, Count Dürckheim took my hand in his
hand and covered it with his other hand. He kept my hand
for a while in his hands while looking quietly into my eyes.
I could not say a word, so overcome with strong feelings.
Then he said: "I can see that you have a lot of pain," still
keeping my hand in his hands. I felt like a bird finally
coming home to its nest, after having fallen out a long time
ago. This encounter changed my life from the roots. It was
only much later that I consciously realized that the sacred
encounter that had taken place, had taken me home to a
place beyond pain.*

*When I became a body therapist later on and studied
finally a few years with Count Dürckheim, I realized also
that the way we touch, the way we look and listen and
speak, this mindful approach, is the key to the door of the
soul. That it needs a spiritual attitude to be able to enable
the realm of the sacred to spread into a therapeutic setting.
(Personal communication, January 27, 2013)*

Pierre Janet was one of the first to appreciate the centrality of the
body in psychotherapy. According to David Boadella, Janet is a seminal
figure in the development of body psychotherapy. Boadella quotes Janet
as saying: "It is in becoming aware of your body that you discover your
personality. . . . The characteristics of the personality, unity, identity,
distinction, derive from the characteristics of the body."[27] Janet believed
it was impossible to make a clear distinction between the physical and
the mental. He considered movement and consciousness to be
inseparably related, noting that "there is nothing in consciousness but
action and the derivatives of action."[28]

The body speaks its mind, and it is the therapist's task to decipher
its language using both imaginal and corporeal approaches.[29] These
include body reading, which explores body schemas and body images.
I invite my patients to find symbolic representations for their pain and
suffering, to open their minds to receive the images hidden in the
emotions, to draw boundaries around their body for protection, or to
imagine sending energy and healing light into those body parts that
are aching and wounded. Exercises that promote a sense of grounding
and rootedness in the earth are helpful, such as visualizing oneself as

tree, which connects above and below and evokes a sense of being nurtured by the earth and the sky.

Information encoded in the body can be transmitted to consciousness by means of the imagination. Knox writes:

> The imaginative world, in all its richness, is the thread that links psyche and soma and that weaves archetypes, attachment and analysis together into a synthesis of the developmental, emergent and introjective aspects of the human mind.[30]

Working on a differentiated perception of the body-self is part of the healing process of survivors of childhood trauma. In exploring body images, in dialoguing with wounded body parts, and in inviting the vagina, or the anorexia, or the whole silenced body to speak, new body narratives emerge.[31] There can be no healing from trauma without a rebuilding of the fragmented body-self. Attuned body work assists in breaking defensive holding patterns, and the resulting release of blocked energy can manifest itself in spasms, twitches, shaking, tingling, and weeping or laughing.

I view the body as a medium through which to connect the inner and outer realms. I work with the patient to access the transformational energy needed for a renewal of the wounded soul as it knits together and rebalances the fragmented mind-body-spirit relationship. Although the exact relationship between energy and matter is not yet clear, the trauma therapist needs to be aware of the relationship in order to identify where in the body energy is stuck or the flow of energy is blocked. Some knowledge of the chakra system, of Kundalini energy as *"embodied* spirituality," can be helpful in understanding the dynamics of a traumatized psyche.[32]

Jung declared that "individuation can only take place if you first return to the body, to your earth, only then does it become true."[33] He had long been interested in body-based affective experiences, as evidenced by his creation of the word association experiment, his psychophysical research, and his conceptualization of the complex, which "with its given tension or energy has the tendency to form a little personality of itself. It has a sort of body, a certain amount of its own physiology. It can upset the stomach. It upsets the breathing, it disturbs the heart."[34] Although Jung does not offer concrete advice on how to work with the body, it is clear that he viewed symbols as arising from the depths of the body, and he held that "the symbol [itself] is . . . a living body, *corpus et anima*."[35] But for Jung, the body also has a shadow aspect.[36] He wrote: "There are too many things about the body which cannot be mentioned. The body is very often the personification of this shadow of the ego. Sometimes it forms the skeleton in the cupboard."[37] In the individuation process, this shadow aspect must be embraced and integrated, not repressed or excluded. However, for trauma survivors, it is often extremely painful, even shameful, to acknowledge the body, for it has been the repository of their grief and pain.

Many mystical and esoteric traditions recognize the existence of what is known as the subtle body—a psycho-spiritual entity that corresponds to (and can be mapped onto) the physical body. The concept of the subtle body has always attracted Jungians. Jung himself was deeply interested in the subtle body, as is evidenced in his seminars on Kundalini yoga in 1932 and in his studies of Patanjali's yoga sutras, the chakra system, and Buddhist meditation practices. He wrote: "I have often felt tempted to advise my patients to think of the psyche as a subtle body in which subtle tumours can grow."[38] He incorporated the subtle body into psychic dynamics through the psychoid archetype, which has its locus not within the individual but in the field between self and other.

Contemporary Jungians have explored in some detail the implications of the subtle body for clinical practice. Marvin Spiegelman, for example, understands the subtle body as "a union of unconscious with consciousness" and "calls attention to the subtle-body energies awakened in deep analytic work."[39] Likewise, Schwartz-Salant conceives of the subtle body as "the somatic unconscious," the place where mind-body splitting is healed.[40] Extending the concept beyond clinical boundaries, the BodySoul Intensives and workshops conducted by the Marion Woodman Foundation operate at the level of the somatic unconscious to redeem matter, to bring consciousness to the subtle body, and to evoke bodily images via creative imagination. Woodman has written:

> The density of matter is infiltrated by Light so that the individual, instead of lugging around a heap of dark flesh, experiences both the calm, rich wisdom of the conscious ego

in the conscious body and the authenticity of the
transpersonal love that impregnates Being.[41]

Notwithstanding the work of these Jungians, and despite Jung's
assertions about the role of the body in psychic dynamics, there has
been and continues to be in the Jungian world a certain "theoretical
ambivalence towards the body" and a general failure to integrate it into
clinical practice.[42]

Perhaps this ambivalence can be traced to the concerns and cautions
that Jung expressed in his 1936 essay, "Yoga and the West," in which
he sounded a pessimistic note about the usefulness of body-related
practices such as yoga for people in the West.[43] Early on in his
experience, however, he had himself resorted to yoga exercises during
his breakdown, as he records in his autobiography, where he relates
that he did "certain yoga exercises . . . to hold my emotions in check,"
but "only until I had calmed myself enough to resume my work with
the unconscious."[44] Perhaps Jung knew intuitively that the yoga exercises
would help him feel more grounded and centered. Unfortunately, he
later warned against the practice of yoga in the West, noting that he
was "critically averse" to it because the West had developed along lines
that presented "the most unfavourable soil one can think of for the
application of yoga."[45]

Recently, Leon Schlamm has revisited Jung's "dialogue with
yoga," pointing out what he considers to be Jung's
misunderstanding of Indian spiritual practice and Jung's
exaggeration of the differences between the individuation process
and the Indian mystical tradition.[46] The most balanced Jungian view
of yoga and psychic dynamics, in my opinion, is that of Judith Harris,
who suggests that the energy accessed through yoga "brings psyche
and body together, uniting them in the sacred union that gives birth
to new consciousness, and the gift of a life fully lived."[47]

The Transformative Power of Chi and Yoga

The energy that flows through the body—variously named chi or
ki, *prana*, libido, or psychic energy—shapes identity and personality.
In Chinese culture, chi is understood to be the creative, interconnecting
life energy that circulates through the universe, animates it, and unites

the opposites of existence. It is "the mediator between body and mind, the transformative agent that brings consciousness to unconscious content, and the creator of psychic images."[48] It is this transformative function of chi (or its equivalent) that is central in processing trauma effectively. Medicine pays considerable attention to the meridians and pathways along which energy flows through the body. In trauma therapy, we understand that traumatic events can cause blockages in these pathways and thus inhibit the proper flow of energy through the body, causing an imbalance in both body and mind. Removing the blockages and restoring the flow of chi can reestablish the balance and bring healing to both body and mind.

In my experience, two Eastern body practices in particular are highly effective in restoring this balance: tai chi and yoga. Tai chi chuan (or tai chi, as it is commonly known) is an ancient Chinese movement practice that relieves stress on both body and mind and helps one regain and maintain homeostasis. This makes it an excellent complementary tool in working with trauma patients. The calming effect of tai chi comes from the spiraling energy that emerges out of the nameless ultimate source and manifests itself in the dynamic movement of the complementary yin and yang energies through the body. In trauma therapy, viewing the traumatic event in the context of this bipolar dynamic allows survivors to reestablish the broken connection between the mind and the body.

Yoga also works with chi energies, bridging mind and matter, uniting dualities, and creating a new narrative, which leads ultimately to a new attitude to oneself and the world, that is, to a transformation of consciousness. Yoga exercises first quiet the body, thereby heightening perception of subtle somatic states. This opens the way for chi energy to arise in stillness. Yoga practice thus builds a bridge to the unconscious and expands consciousness through a heightened awareness of the body, a better attunement to internal bodily sensations, an activation of energy, and an enhancement of the ability to relate to and regulate emotions. Yoga exercises and body scans are helpful in working toward a more embodied presence. They awaken the senses to the ever-changing, intermingling flow of sensations, emotions, and thoughts; this allows one to witness nonjudgmentally whatever emerges. Research has shown that yoga has a positive impact on the core regulatory centers in the brain and empowers trauma survivors to engage actively in their healing process.

Integrating yoga into trauma therapy facilitates the binding together of what has been severed through traumatic shock, which is a key element in initiating healing.[49] Interestingly, even the US military has begun using trauma-sensitive yoga therapy for war veterans who suffer from posttraumatic stress disorder (PTSD).[50] Bessel van der Kolk, director of the Trauma Center in Boston, is a pioneer in the implementation of yoga for patients working through trauma. The center provides ongoing yoga classes to survivors of all kinds of trauma. Two of its yoga teachers, David Emerson and Elizabeth Hopper, have published a systematic presentation of mindfulness, breathing, and trauma-sensitive yoga exercises for trauma survivors that can be used both by individuals and in clinical practice.[51]

Several studies have been published that outline a specifically trauma-sensitive yoga practice. Evidence suggests that yoga can be a helpful practice for patients with PTSD. The findings show that yoga heightens body awareness and facilitates greater tolerance of distressing emotional states while enhancing the survivor's ability to stay in the present moment rather than repeatedly replay the traumatic past.

It is important to note that trauma-sensitive yoga is a *modified* yoga practice, since the heightened awareness of what is going on in the body that is triggered by certain yoga poses may also trigger body memories that are too difficult for the trauma survivor to cope with. Trauma-sensitive yoga is attuned to the survivor's capacity to contain this new awareness. It is directed at building resilience to stress, evoking a sense of gradually increasing strength under conditions of greater relaxation, and creating a feeling of being at ease. As healing chi energies begin to flow again and balance is restored in body and mind, a gradual transformation takes place and the trauma is left behind.

NOTES

[1] See Bessel A. van der Kolk, "The Body Keeps the Score: Memory and the Evolving Psychobiology of Posttraumatic Stress," *Harvard Review of Psychiatry* 1, no. 5 (1994): 253–265.

[2] For a discussion of the importance of the body as revealed in dreams, see Edward C. Whitmont and Sylvia Brinton Perera, *Dreams, A Portal to the Source* (London: Routledge, 1989).

[3] Jung, *CW* 12, § 157.

[4] See Babette Rothschild, *The Body Remembers: The Psychophysiology of Trauma and Trauma Treatment* (New York: W. W. Norton, 2000).

[5] Antonio R. Damasio, *Descartes' Error: Emotion, Reason, and the Human Brain* (New York: G. P. Putnam's Sons, 1994); Joseph LeDoux, *The Emotional Brain: The Mysterious Underpinnings of Emotional Life* (New York: Simon and Schuster, 1996); and *Synaptic Self: How Our Brains Become Who We Are* (New York: Penguin Group, 2002).

[6] Gerald Hüther, "Wie Embodiment neurobiologisch erklärt werden kann," in Maja Storch et al., *Embodiment: Die Wechselwirkung von Körper und Psyche verstehen und nutzen* (Bern: Verlag Hans Huber, 2006), pp. 73–98.

[7] Daniel J. Siegel, *Mindsight: The New Science of Personal Transformation* (New York: Bantam, 2010), p. 52. See also Daniel J. Siegel, "An Interpersonal Neurobiology of Psychotherapy: The Developing Mind and the Resolution of Trauma," in *Healing Trauma: Attachment, Mind, Body, and Brain*, ed. Marion. F. Solomon and Daniel J. Siegel (New York: W.W. Norton, 2003), pp. 1–56; and *The Mindful Brain: Reflection and Attunement in the Cultivation of Well-Being* (New York: W. W. Norton, 2007).

[8] Allan N. Schore, *Affect Regulation and the Origin of the Self: The Neurobiology of Emotional Development* (Hillsdale, NJ: Lawrence Erlbaum Associates, 1994).

[9] Allan N. Schore, "Attachment, Affect Regulation, and the Developing Right Brain: Linking Developmental Neuroscience to Pediatrics," *Pediatrics in Review* 26, no. 6 (2005): 205;

Allan N. Schore, "The Right Brain Implicit Self Lies at the Core of Psychoanalysis," *Psychoanalytic Dialogues* 21 (2011): 1, 75–100. See also: Judith R. Shore and Allan N. Schore, "Modern Attachment Theory: The Central Role of Affect Regulation in Development and Treatment," *Clinical Social Work Journal* 36, no. 1 (2008): 9–20.

[10] More information about van der Kolk's work can be found at www.traumacenter.org.

¹¹ For details, see Mary Sykes Wylie, "The Limits of Talk: Bessel van der Kolk Wants to Transform the Treatment of Trauma," *Psychotherapy Networker* 28, no. 1 (2004): 30–41.

¹² Kindling is the "capacity of triggers with diminishing strength to produce the same response over time"; Bessel A. van der Kolk, "Posttraumatic Stress Disorder and the Nature of Trauma," in *Healing Trauma: Attachment, Mind, Body, and Brain*, ed. Marion. F. Solomon and Daniel J. Siegel (New York: W. W. Norton, 2003), p. 181. For a detailed discussion of IDR and IDR-T, an integrative and differentiated method of regulation and relaxation, and the relevant literature, see Hilarion G. Petzold, "Trauma und Beunruhigung, Trauer und Trostarbeit: Über Katastrophen, kollektive Gedächtnisdynamik, heftige und sanfte Gefühle— Kulturtheoretische und neuropsychologische Überlegungen der Integrativen Therapie," *Polyloge: Eine Internetzeitschrift für "Integrative Therapie"* 29 (2008), accessed December 9, 2013, http://www.fpi-publikation.de/images/stories/downloads/polyloge/hg_petzold-polyloge-29-2008.pdf.

¹³ Siegel, *Mindful Brain*, p. 16.

¹⁴ Pat Ogden, Kekuni Minton, and Clare Pain, *Trauma and the Body: A Sensorimotor Approach to Psychotherapy* (New York: W. W. Norton, 2006). See also Pat Ogden and Kekuni Minton, "Sensorimotor Psychotherapy: One Method for Processing Traumatic Memory," *Traumatology* 6, no. 3 (2000): 149–173.

¹⁵ Margaret Wilkinson, *Coming into Mind: The Mind Brain Relationship—A Jungian Clinical Perspective* (Hove, UK: Routledge, 2006); Jean Knox, *Archetype, Attachment, Analysis: Jungian Psychology and the Emergent Mind* (Hove, UK: Brunner-Routledge, 2003).

¹⁶ Sylvia Karcher, "Body Psychotherapy with Survivors of Torture," in *Broken Spirits: The Treatment of Traumatized Asylum Seekers, Refugees, and War and Torture Victims*, ed. John P. Wilson and Boris Droˇdek (New York: Brunner-Routledge, 2004), pp. 403–418.

¹⁷ Peter A. Levine, *Waking the Tiger: Healing Trauma* (Berkeley, CA: North Atlantic Books, 1997), p. 19.

¹⁸ *Ibid.*, pp. 61–62.

¹⁹ Jung, *CW* 8, § 418.

²⁰ Jung, *CW* 10, § 195.

[21] See Whalen Lai and Michael von Brück, *Christianity and Buddhism: A Multicultural History of Their Dialogue*, trans. Phyllis Jestice (Maryknoll, NJ: Orbis Books, 2001).

[22] See Gay Hendricks, *Conscious Breathing: Breathwork for Health, Stress Release, and Personal Mastery* (New York: Bantam Books, 1995).

[23] Diane Zimberoff and David Hartman, "Breathwork: Exploring the Frontier of 'Being' and 'Doing,'" *Journal of Heart-Centered Therapies* 2, no. 2 (1999): 42.

[24] Arnold Mindell, *Dreambody: The Body's Role in Revealing the Self*, 2nd ed. (Portland, OR: Lao Tse Press, 1998).

[25] See Erving Polster and Miriam Polster, *Gestalt Therapy Integrated: Contours of Theory and Practice* (New York: Vintage Books, 1973).

[26] Anita U. Greene, "Conscious Mind—Conscious Body," *Journal of Analytical Psychology* 46, no. 4 (2001): 565–590.

[27] David Boadella, "Awakening Sensibility, Recovering Motility—Psycho-physical Synthesis at the Foundations of Body-Psychotherapy: The 100-Year Legacy of Pierre Janet (1859–1947)," *International Journal of Psychotherapy* 2, no. 1 (1997): 48.

[28] Pierre Janet, *Principles of Psychotherapy*, trans. Helen Macdonald Guthrie and Edwin Ray Guthrie (New York: The Macmillan Company, 1924), pp. 242–243.

[29] Stanley Keleman, *Your Body Speaks Its Mind* (Berkeley, CA: Center Press, 1981).

[30] Knox, *Archetype, Attachment, Analysis*, p. 204.

[31] I attended a moving rendition of Eve Ensler's *The Vagina Monologues*, which reminded me of the Bosnian women who had been gang-raped. The play is based on Ensler's interviews with women from around the world.

[32] Judith Harris, *Jung and Yoga: The Psyche-Body Connection* (Toronto: Inner City Books, 2001), p. 120.

[33] C. G. Jung, *The Visions Seminars*, vol. 2 (Zurich: Spring Publications, 1976), p. 473.

[34] Jung, *CW* 18, § 149.

[35] Jung, *CW* 9i, § 291.

[36] See John P. Conger, *Jung and Reich: The Body as Shadow* (Berkeley, CA: North Atlantic Books, 2005).

[37] Jung, *CW* 18, § 40.

[38] Jung, *CW* 11, § 36.

[39] Victor Mansfield and J. Marvin Spiegelman, "On the Physics and Psychology of the Transference as an Interactive Field," *Journal of Analytical Psychology* 41, no. 2 (1996): 186.

[40] Nathan Schwartz-Salant, *The Mystery of Human Relationship: Alchemy and the Transformation of the Self* (London: Routledge, 1998), p. 154.

[41] Marion Woodman, *The Pregnant Virgin: A Process of Psychological Transformation* (Toronto: Inner City Books, 1985), p. 70.

[42] Gottfried Heuer, "'In My Flesh I Shall See God': Jungian Body Psychotherapy," in *New Dimensions in Body Psychotherapy*, ed. Nick Totton (Maidenhead, UK: Open University Press, 2005), p. 106.

[43] Jung, *CW* 11, §§ 859–876.

[44] Jung, *MDR*, p. 177.

[45] Jung, *CW* 11, § 876.

[46] Leon Schlamm, "Revisiting Jung's Dialogue with Yoga: Observations from Transpersonal Psychology," *International Journal of Jungian Studies* 2, no. 1 (2010): 32–44.

[47] Harris, *Jung and Yoga*, p. 9.

[48] Diana Sau-Hing Chee, "The Gold Elixir: The Circular Path of *Tao*" (PhD diss., Pacifica Graduate Institute, Carpinteria, CA, 2001), p. iv, ProQuest/UMI 3029753, accessed December 11, 2013, http://www.scribd.com/doc/144303574/D-S-Cee-the-Gold-Elixir-The-Circular-Path-of-the-Tao.

[49] Regina Weiser and Angela Dunemann, *Yoga in der Traumatherapie* (Stuttgart: Klett-Cotta Verlag, 2010).

[50] David Wood, "Military Battle PTSD with Yoga," *Huffington Post*, December 12, 2012, accessed December 12, 2013, http://www.huffingtonpost.com/2012/12/12/military-ptsd-yoga_n_2273524.html.

[51] David Emerson and Elizabeth Hopper, *Overcoming Trauma through Yoga: Reclaiming Your Body* (Berkeley, CA: North Atlantic Books, 2011).

CONCLUSION

Dunkel ist das Leben, ist der Tod.
[Dark is life, dark is death.]
> —Gustav Mahler, "The Drinking Song of the
> Earth's Sorrow," from *The Song of the Earth*,
> based on a Chinese poem, "Bei Ge Xing"

This book has been written from a spiritual frame of reference in the widest possible sense. I have attempted to present an emerging paradigm shift in trauma therapy, one that focuses on potential psycho-spiritual growth following trauma in the belief that the dark realm of the *prima materia* can be a source of creative liberation. Moving beyond the stigmatization associated with the structural dissociation of the personality that often accompanies trauma, I submit that traumatic experiences can serve as an initiation into an expansion of consciousness and that traumatic wounding opens the individual up to the possibility of seeing things differently and adopting a new way of being.

I turned to the paradoxical nature of the unconscious, as both dangerous and yet beneficent, containing "the wisdom and experience of untold ages," a wisdom that guided Jung in his time of terror and gave birth to the Red Book.[1] Without trusting in the alchemical wisdom that truth, goodness, and beauty are often found in filth, and without believing in the transforming power of life and the fundamental possibility of becoming, I would not have been able to wander through the death landscapes of the soul. I have been guided in my work by a piece of wisdom passed on by Ramakrishna: "The winds of grace are always blowing; it is for us to raise our sails."

The scope of this book has been broad: from the shattered value system of dehumanized man and experiences "at the mind's limits," which challenge all notions of human dignity and destroy the illusion of posttraumatic growth ("we didn't leave Auschwitz wiser and deeper"), to the recreation of meaning, integrity, and wholeness of the posttraumatic Self.[2] My sphere of thought is a humanistic one, acknowledging human vulnerability as well as human dignity in the face of trauma and the precariousness of life as much as its beauty and preciousness. For me, abysmal evil and darkness are part of our *conditio humana*, of the "drama of human freedom."[3] It is the risk we take, and the price we pay, for freedom.

I have worked almost half my life with trauma survivors, and it remains a mystery to me why people under the most extreme conditions and despite their freedom to choose evil have opted again and again for goodness. I perceive it as the path of wisdom to choose to adopt, even in full knowledge of destruction and evil, a nonviolent and loving attitude to oneself and the world at large. How to give expression to the wordlessness of violence has been the koan I have struggled with endlessly, searching for the *metanoia* that will open our hearts and help us to adapt creatively to what cannot be changed and strive courageously to change what can.[4] I have learned that the paradoxes encountered in dealing with trauma are as incomprehensible as the paradoxes of love, which Jung referred to when he wrote:

> In my medical experience as well as in my own life I have again and again been faced with the mystery of love, and have never been able to explain what it is. . . . Here is the greatest and smallest, the remotest and nearest, the highest and lowest, and we cannot discuss one side of it without also discussing the other. No language is adequate to this paradox. Whatever one can say, no words express the whole. To speak of partial aspects is always too much or too little, for only the whole is meaningful.[5]

"Being is a mystery," wrote the French philosopher André Comte-Sponville.[6] This book is about that mystery. That is why I chose a painting entitled *Abstract Head: Mysterium* by the Russian painter Alexi Jawlensky for the book cover. For me it is a symbol of wholeness in brokenness; it points to the wisdom that the whole is more than the sum of its parts; it speaks to the balance of light and shadow, of fragmentation and integration. The painting captures for me the numinous beauty of the *mysterium fascinans* and the simultaneous *mysterium tremendum*, the mystery of the wounded soul's silent suffering, the inward glance—a different, meditative way of seeing from the threshold, from liminal space.

I have no answer to the mystery of transformation, the fundamental mystery of life's vicissitudes, and throughout the process of writing I maintained the beginner's mind and endeavored to "let no day pass without humbly remembering that everything has still to be learned" and that we "are apt to forget that in psychic matters we are dealing with processes of experience, that is, with transformations which should never be given hard and fast names if their living movement is not to petrify into something static."[7] I am aware of the ambivalence of the *numen*, the captivating, numinous quality of the trauma archetype, which may either shatter psychic structure or transform it and thereby initiate healing.

When delving into the complexity of the transformation of ego identity and moving beyond the threatening darkness of the chthonic realm of trauma, wisdom is needed—a critical consciousness and a synthesis of head, heart, and body—to move beyond embitterment and hate. I am thinking of a wisdom that is more than cognitive adeptness and affective and behavioral maturity: it is the acceptance of the transient nature of life and the impermanence of all that is, the ability to deal with the complexity of the world, the capacity for balance and insight into the nature of reality. Through wisdom we touch what is best within us. Wisdom is as much a process as it is a possible outcome of trauma.[8] It is what gives us the capacity to accommodate evil and traumatic catastrophes in our worldview, to embrace paradox, and to live with uncertainty and incomprehensibility. We need wisdom to acknowledge the violence in ourselves and to commit ourselves to working to transform it, to nurture the courage to strive for justice, peace, reconciliation, and forgiveness.

Unlike Jung, I had no Philemon walking beside me through my garden when I was contemplating this book. Instead, I appealed to Sophia's wisdom, which contains and sustains all of creation, and to the Avalokitesvara Guanyin, the bodhisattva of compassion, the one who hears the cries of suffering of the world; I invited them to accompany me through my search and my writing. Both of these archetypal personifications represent the feminine principle, a relational mode of being that, when confronted with the dragon, endeavors not to slay it but to tame it. I understand this mode of being as assisting in the unfolding of our intrinsic capacities for love and wisdom and as enabling us to become more creative, more compassionate, and more aware of the primary connectedness of all beings.

It is my hope that all of us, those who have struggled through their own dark night of the soul and those who have wrestled with the trauma of their patients, might resurface from their desert wanderings and night sea journeys with the hard-won treasure, the pearl of wisdom, and "the energy of the light that makes the stone break into music."[9]

NOTES

[1] Jung, *RB*, p. 210.

[2] Jean Améry, *At the Mind's Limits: Contemplation by a Survivor on Auschwitz and Its Realities*, trans. Sidney Rosenfeld and Stella P. Rosenfeld (Bloomington: Indiana University Press, 1980), p. 20; John P. Wilson, ed., *The Posttraumatic Self: Restoring Meaning and Wholeness to Personality* (New York: Routledge, 2006).

[3] Rüdiger Safranski, *Das Böse oder das Drama der Freiheit* (München: Hanser Verlag, 1997) [my translation].

[4] "Das spezifisch Böse der Gewalt ist ihre Stummheit" ("The specific evil of violence is its wordlessness"); Hannah Arendt, *Denktagebuch, Vol. 1: 1950–1973* (Munich: Piper Verlag, 2002), p. 345.

[5] Jung, *MDR*, pp. 353–354.

[6] André Comte-Sponville, *The Little Book of Atheist Spirituality*, trans. Nancy Huston (New York: Penguin Books, 2007), p. 83.

⁷ Jung, *CW* 16, § 464; Jung, *CW* 13, § 199.

⁸ P. Alex Linley, "Positive Adaption to Trauma: Wisdom as Both Process and Outcome," *Journal of Traumatic Stress,* 16, no. 6 (2003): 601–610.

⁹ Nelly Sachs, letter to Paul Celan dated September 1, 1958, in Paul Celan and Nelly Sachs, *Correspondence,* ed. Barbara Wiedemann, trans. Christopher Clark (Riverdale-on-Hudson, NY: Sheep Meadow Press, 1995), p. 6.

INDEX

Note: Page numbers followed by "f" refer to figures.

posttraumatic growth (PTG), 76–78
posttraumatic stress disorder (PTSD),
 yoga therapy for, 331
potential space, concept of, 295
presence, 193–194
 listening and, 194–195
process-oriented psychology, 324
protective illusions, as coping
 strategy, 79
psychic equivalence, 198
Psychodynamic Imaginative Trauma
 Therapy (PITT), 159
psychoeducation, 148
psychotherapy. *See also* therapy;
 trauma therapy
 body-oriented, 321
 centrality of body in, 326
 integral, 182
 reflective posture in, 195–196
 transpersonal, 183
PTG (posttraumatic growth), 76–78
PTSD (posttraumatic stress disorder),
 yoga therapy for, 331
putrefactio (rotting), 68, 69, 304

Q

Qouch Sun Lay, 219
quantum philosophy, 49
quantum physics, 49

R

radical evil, 27
reconciliation, forgiveness and,
 103–106
Red Book, The (Jung), 5, 146–149.
 See also Jung, Carl Gustav
 active imagination and, 157
 complementarity and, 179
 dissociation and, 146
 as documentation of sacrificial
 process, 249–253

Jung's fascination with paradox in,
 164–167
 as Jung's healing journey and
 transformation after traumatic
 breakdown, 239–240
 Jung's mystical sayings in, 38
 Jung's view of evil in, 27
 mandalas in, 161–164
 as reflection on nature of soul,
 20–21
 self-transcendence in, 238
 theme of death in, 157
Reddemann, Luise, 159
reflection, in trauma therapy, 195–197
reflective functioning. *See*
 mentalization
reflective posture, psychotherapy,
 195–196
relational field
 concept of, 297
 transcendent function and, 299
relationality, role of, in trauma therapy,
 185–187
repression, 106–107
resilience, 184
resynthesis, process of, 227
Rhyner, Bruno, 323
Roesler, Christian, 155
Rogers, Carl, 193
Rose, Juan Gonzalo, 69

S

Saakvitne, Karen W., 186
Sachs, Nelly, 66–67, 81, 92, 94,
 95–98
sacrifice
 of control, 290
 of ego control/dominance, 290–291
 function of, 288–289
 goal of, 265
 Jung on, 235–238
 Jung's interest in, 288

CPSIA information can be obtained
at www.ICGtesting.com
Printed in the USA
LVHW080323090819
627059LV00021B/307/P

9 781935 528593